CROUCHING DRAGON, HIDDEN TIGER

CROUCHING DRAGON, HIDDEN TIGER

Can China and India Dominate the West?

PREM SHANKAR JHA

Soft Skull Press
New York

Library of Congress Cataloging-in-Publication Data is available.

ISBN: 13: 978-1-59376-248-3

Cover design by Adrian Kinloch
Interior design by Elyse Strongin, Neuwirth & Associates, Inc.
Printed in the United States of America

Soft Skull Press
An Imprint of Counterpoint LLC
2117 Fourth Street
Suite D
Berkeley, CA 94710

www.softskull.com
www.counterpointpress.com

Distributed by Publishers Group West

10 9 8 7 6 5 4 3 2 1

CONTENTS

PREFACE

I BEGAN RESEARCH on this book three years ago. Since then, the world has changed almost beyond recognition. These years have seen a worldwide breakdown of the financial system, and an industrial recession of a severity not known in eighty years. These have ripped the mask of sanctity from the face of the Market and revealed its true nature to millions upon millions of people who have lost their money, their jobs and, in too many cases, their future. A neo-liberal ideology that claimed that free markets were not only efficient but just now lies in tatters, and the world is once again grappling with the problem that societies have faced ever since the dawn of capitalism, of finding the right balance between the two. This epic struggle was the subject of the book I set out to write. My focus was limited to China and India, which were in the middle stages of market-led (if not governed) development and had still to resolve the conflict between growth and equity. But this struggle has now engulfed the entire industrialized world. What had therefore looked like a battle left over from the past, being waged in two late starters in capitalist development, has become a battle to be fought in the future. I believe that this has greatly increased the relevance of the issues that I have raised in this book, in particular my scepticism about the inevitability of China's and India's rise to global dominance in the twenty-first century, for it is not just they who have to find an answer, but the entire globalized world.

These three years have also completed the loss of the West's confidence in itself, which is the starting point of this book. Evidence of this is to be found in former US Secretary of State Zbigniew Brzezinski's January 13, 2009 proposal, made in Beijing, of the need to forge an informal consulting group—a G-2—of the US and China, to manage the affairs of the world. The interest that has been aroused by author Zachary Karabell's notion of a "Superfusion" of the economies of China and the US shows that the idea is gaining traction. Both ideas reflect the US's tacit abandonment of its dream of regaining unchallenged hegemony in the post-cold war world, and its growing flirtation with the idea of replacing the EU with China as a potential partner in hegemony in the twenty-first century. One consequence of this is a sudden cessation of the comparisons between China and India that were fashionable until as recently as 2008. Today, a world that has pinned its hopes on China to pull it out of recession has all but ignored India's nearly as rapid recovery from the downturn in 2008.

A third important change during these years has been the rapid deterioration in the relations between China and India. In September 2006 the two countries were still busily building bridges between themselves. Trade had grown from less than a billion dollars in 1994 to over 40 billion dollars in 2006. Indian companies were investing in China, and Chinese companies were winning bids for infrastructure projects in India. Chinese Prime Minister Wen Jiabao had visited India in 2005, and President Hu Jintao was scheduled to visit Delhi in December 2006. In 2003 and 2005, the two countries had taken giant strides towards resolving their differences over the demarcation of their common border in the Himalayas. Since then, relations between the two countries have gone into a tailspin, and both are quietly preparing themselves for a possible conflict in the region.

It would be surprising indeed if the shadow of these changes did not fall across this book and make readers wonder whether the scepticism that I have expressed about China's future in the final chapters of the book does not reflect a bias, however small, in my perceptions. Since I cannot change my nationality, I cannot prevent readers from coming to this conclusion if they so wish. What I can do is to remind them that I have expressed similar doubts about India's capacity to reconcile growth with equity. I submitted the text of this book to publishers in March 2008, when the deterioration in Sino-Indian relations had barely begun. Other than the inclusion of more recent data to take account of the onset of the recession that I had predicted (for both countries) nothing has been either added to, or subtracted from, that text. The model of China's and India's political economy, upon which I rely to explain the difficulties that the two countries are experiencing, was first developed by me in the late 1970s for India, and is similar to those developed by several other reputable authors who are referred to in Chapter 4.

However, I would be remiss if I did not mention a small but significant change that the two countries' reactions to the recession have made in my perceptions of their respective futures. China's response to it has been a truly spectacular increase in investment. But it has been financed by drawing on the peoples' savings without any thought of ensuring an adequate return on investment. This is likely to result in a further rise in discontent, especially in the rural areas. Recession has therefore made the goal of reconciling growth with equity more difficult to achieve. In India, by contrast, the government has fought the recession by single-mindedly focussing on increasing peoples' incomes. The resulting rise in consumption is ending the recession almost as fast as in China, but without adding to social or political discontent. Indeed the results of the general elections in May 2009, and of state assembly elections in three states in October, all of which were won by the ruling Congress party of India and close allies, suggest that the opposite may be taking place.

This strategy is not without its pitfalls either. India already has the worst infrastructure for development of any country with a comparable level of industrialisation. Its failure to take advantage of the recession to launch a blitzkrieg of investment in power, roads and ports will make it more difficult for it to maintain a high rate of growth in the near future. But it will not face the problems of increasing social discontent and declining legitimacy that Beijing may have to deal with. Beijing's time horizon for reconciling growth with equity has probably grown shorter, but India's has almost certainly grown longer.

October, 2009

A Study in Contrasts

1 HEGEMONY IN DECLINE

AT THE WORLD Economic Forum's 2009 summer conference in Dalian, China, Klaus Schwab, its president, declared it would be China that would lead the world out of the global economic recession. This was not a pro forma obeisance to the host country. On the contrary, Schwab was being utterly sincere. The reason for his implicit faith lay buried in one piece of economic data released by the National Bureau of Statistics a few days earlier: In the first eight months of 2009, domestic lending by China's banks had risen by $1.65 *trillion*. This was a number that far outstripped anything the US or the EU, either separately or together, had been able to achieve till then. Since nine-tenths of the money was going into investment, it had already begun to firm up global commodity prices and fill out order books.

In recent years several projections have indicated that if China and India maintain their present rate of growth, they will soon dominate the world. Underlying the almost obsessive interest in the future of these countries is the fear that the West is losing its economic ascendancy and therefore its capacity to shape the post-cold war international order. The loss of confidence began in the 1970s when, after more than a quarter century of rapid, and harmonious, economic growth, the industrialized nations received the first of a succession of rude shocks that left them with an uneasy feeling that something had changed irreversibly and changed for the worse.

It reached its nadir when the excesses of the free market plunged the world into the worst recession it had known in eighty years and destroyed the neoliberal ideology upon which the West had pinned its hopes for continued economic ascendancy.

THE FIRST SHOCK was a twelvefold increase in the price of crude oil between September 1973 and July 1980.[1] The increase was brought about not by a change in market conditions, nor by political crisis (e.g., the Yom Kippur War of October 1973, which led to a short-lived attempt by the Arab members of OPEC—the Organization of Petroleum Exporting Countries—to impose an oil embargo on the West), but by the deliberate decision of a cartel of oil producers, the OPEC, which had been long in the making. The price rise was therefore perceived as the first successful challenge to the economic power of the industrialized nations and was deeply resented by the West.

The West received its second, more unsettling shock when it failed to deal with the two industrial recessions, in the mid-seventies and early eighties, that followed. The first, which was triggered by a fourfold increase in oil prices between September 1973 and March 1974, was relatively mild. But the second, which followed another trebling of oil prices to $35.63 a barrel in July 1980, was much steeper. When the industrialized countries tried to fight the 1970s recession by increasing public spending, they found that this remedy, which had worked for four decades since the great depression of the thirties, had suddenly ceased to do so. Instead of reviving industrial production at home, the fiscal stimuli they administered increased imports of cheap consumer goods from newly industrialized countries. A new word entered the lexicon of economics. It was "stagflation."

The need for a new term highlighted the permanence of the change that had taken place. This was the onset of globalization. Attempts to promote recovery in order to boost demand by increasing public expenditure had ceased to work because markets had ceased to be national and become global. Quiet revolutions in transport and information technology had made it cheaper to manufacture consumer goods in newly industrialized countries with cheap, skilled labor and ship them back for sale at home. The progressive freeing of trade in the fifties and sixties had removed most of the protection that domestic industry had enjoyed during the era of national capitalist development. As a result, attempts to boost production at home by this means only succeeded in increasing imports and boosting production abroad.

As globalization gained momentum in the eighties, the industrialized countries had to come to terms with something that they had never experienced before and for which, therefore, they had no theoretical explanation.[2] This was deindustrialization—the steady loss of jobs in manufacturing, a simultaneous halving of the growth of labor productivity in the economy, and the emergence of chronic, as opposed to temporary, unemployment.

The blow to the confidence of the industrialized countries cannot be understated. After the Second World War the dominance of the industrial democracies of the West had looked unshakable. In the 1950s and 1960s the West dominated the world: The US economy alone accounted for half the GDP of the world and approximately the same proportion of international trade. Europe was initially exhausted but, with the help of the Marshall Plan, got back on its feet within a decade. Then began a quarter century of the most rapid growth that these countries had ever experienced. Dubbed the "golden age of capitalism" by Anglo-Saxon writers and *les trente glorieuses* (the thirty glorious years) by the French, this period took the US, Europe, and Japan to hitherto unimaginable levels of affluence.

All this occurred in societies singularly free from serious conflict. The philosophical contract that underpinned the welfare state—that the gainers from social change had an obligation to look after the losers had by then been accepted by all industrialized nations.

For the postwar generation in the industrialized countries, this was the best of times in the best of worlds. Generous social security benefits, an abundance of educational opportunities, a constant reinforcement of the middle class, better working conditions on the factory floor as manual labor gave way to automation, but above all the certitude that when one left school or college there would be a job waiting made the future full of promise. It became possible for school and college graduates to plan their lives: to decide when to get married, when and what type of house to buy, how many children to have, and when to have them. For perhaps the first time in human history, insecurity disappeared from young people's psyches across a substantial part of the globe.

The wholesomeness of industrial society during this epoch was captured by the American economist and Nobel laureate Paul Krugman in his memorable image of a picket fence. In a now famous book, *The Age of Diminished Expectations*, he showed that a column graph depicting the annual rise of family incomes in the US between 1951 and 1971 looked like a picket fence because each of its "planks" (each plank in his graph represented the annual rate of growth of income of that particular fifth of society) was of approximately the same height. This was even truer of Europe, where middle-class incomes expanded more rapidly than the national average. The "picket fence" therefore had a decided upward bulge in the middle. Throughout the golden age, therefore, incomes grew but income inequality declined or, at worst, stayed unchanged. Robert D. Putnam, in his pathbreaking book *Bowling Alone*, and Francis Fukuyama, in *The Great Disruption*, have charted how virtually every indicator of social trust rose steadily in American and European societies from the end of the war till the beginning of the seventies and only began to decline thereafter.

The young celebrated the end of anxiety by pushing at the envelope of their social and political freedoms with a vigor never seen before. The sixties and seventies were the era of hippies, cannabis, and flower power, of the pill and free love, of the Beatles, Woodstock, and Ravi Shankar. It was also the era of the campaign for nuclear disarmament, of the civil rights movement in the US, of student power in France, and of the Red Brigades in Italy, Germany, and Japan. What distinguished the golden age from others was the relative benevolence that society, on the whole, felt toward those who were bent upon challenging its anchored beliefs. The young were able to experiment, because they knew that society could afford to let them make mistakes and still forgive and nurture them. It was a time of tolerance and of generosity. Both stemmed from the security and predictability of human life that had bloomed during the golden age. Today we look back on even the worst of those excesses with more than a hint of nostalgia.

No one had the faintest inkling that the golden age would last for such a short time. In the industrialized world, affluence proved its own undoing. As globalization gathered momentum and deindustrialization became more pronounced, jobs became harder to get, paid less, and became less secure. Lifetime employment, and the fervent loyalties it had built, disappeared. "Downsizing" became the order of the day. Young people suffered the most because most companies, especially in the more heavily unionized Europe, followed the "last in, first out" principle of retrenchment. More and more of the jobs they were able to get became temporary, denying them the health and pension benefits their parents' generation had taken for granted. Quite suddenly the secure world of the fifties, sixties, and early seventies disappeared. Anxiety reentered the lives of the young and soon became a permanent feature. They responded by staying longer at university, by staying longer at home, and by postponing whatever plans they might have had to buy homes and get married. Huge numbers simply put life on hold. But the added burden they represented for parents who had retired or were themselves feeling more and more insecure in their jobs began, gradually, to squeeze the life out of the middle class. Income differentials widened dramatically. Paul Krugman's picket fence turned into a stepladder: real declines in income at the bottom, stagnation in the middle-income groups, and an accelerating increase for the top 6 to 10 percent of society.[3]

The industrialized nations were still adjusting to the deindustrialization of the seventies and eighties when they found themselves having to cope with the rise of China. In the early nineties, China joined the ranks of cheap offshore producers of consumer goods and began to flood the markets of the industrialized world. This marked a qualitative change in the restructuring that was being brought about by globalization. The East and Southeast Asian nations, to whom industry and capital migrated first, were small, and their pool of cheap labor was soon exhausted. China's supply of extremely cheap labor seemed virtually limitless. The "tunnel of adjustment" through which the inhabitants of the high-wage countries were told they were passing as they shifted from being manufacturers of products to manufacturers of knowledge (and en route, therefore, to the higher incomes earnable by the latter) suddenly seemed to have no end.

It was when the West was entering this tunnel that China broke the shackles of its rigid command economy and began to grow at a pace never witnessed before. Coming as it did, right at the end of the cold war, China's rise brought into focus an issue that had been in the back of people's minds ever since Paul Kennedy wrote *The Rise and Fall of the Great Powers*: How long could a shift in the balance of economic power remain divorced from a shift in the balance of military power? This issue had not arisen so long as the deindustrialization of the West had benefited only the East and Southeast nations and parts of South America. All the countries that benefited were securely anchored to the West by their common fear of China,

Russia, and Communism. The economic rise of South Korea, Taiwan, and even Japan, not to mention Malaysia, Thailand, Indonesia, Mexico, and Brazil, did not therefore make it necessary to restructure international relations. But China had been an adversary all through the cold war, had an ongoing claim to Taiwan, and possessed a huge pool of surplus "sovereign" capital that it could invest to extend its military and diplomatic reach. Beginning in 2005, it had begun to invest this capital aggressively in Africa and was bidding hard to corner some of the dwindling underground reserves of oil. Its rise therefore threatened to upset the comfortable ascendancy of Europe and the US in the international order.

India, by contrast, aroused few such misgivings. India had fascinated Western scholars and policymakers alike in the 1950s. Its sheer size, and the fact that it was trying to combine democracy and quasi-socialist economic planning, made it a magnet for students of development economics. Its more than 4 percent growth rate in the fifties; its democracy; its charismatic leader, Jawaharlal Nehru; and its relatively open and investor-friendly policies till the end of the 1950s made it the natural counterpoise to China. But the interest faded away in the sixties as Indira Gandhi's government turned inward and adopted more and more draconian restrictions on private enterprise and foreign investment. The resurgence of interest in India during the current decade, after a lapse of more than four decades, is a mirror image of the West's growing uneasiness toward China. China houses a fifth of the world's population, India one-sixth. Its GDP per capita may be only half that of China, but that still makes it the seventh largest economy in the world. Its growth rate of 8.8 percent, since 2003, is not far short of China's and is free from the controversy that surrounds China's GDP estimates. Best of all, it has a younger, faster-growing population and is therefore likely to retain its present high growth rate for longer than China.

But while strategic thinkers have welcomed India's rise, some economists are far less sanguine about it. For one thing, whereas globalization has caused a shift of manufacturing industries to East Asia and China, it is causing a shift of high-end service industries to India. These include software development, accounting, back office business processing, telemarketing, and other computer-enabled services. This shift can pose a more serious threat to well-being and social stability in the high-wage countries because service industries are far more labor intensive than manufacturing. Thus every million dollars worth of back office work that migrates from, say, Chicago to Bangalore causes more people to lose their jobs than the displacement of a million dollars worth of manufacturing to Southeast Asia or China did in the eighties and nineties. What made the migration of service industries even more threatening than that of manufacturing is that those who had lost, or could no longer find, jobs in manufacturing had been flocking to service industries. As more and more service industries disappeared overseas, people in search of employment were left with fewer and fewer places to go.

All through the late seventies and eighties, the governments of the rich nations kept reassuring their people that the problems they were facing were transitory. Globalization was turning rich nations into "knowledge" societies, while the low-wage countries were emerging as "service societies." When they experienced a long, technology-driven boom in the nineties, rich nations began to believe that the worst was over. But the boom of the "Roaring Nineties" turned out to be an Indian summer. It was built upon unsound investments made possible by unprecedented low interest rates that turned investment bankers and fund managers into gamblers. In retrospect, the financial crash of 2008 was an accident waiting to happen. The global recession that followed stripped the West of its last vestiges of self-confidence and lent a sharp new edge to the speculation that was already rampant about the place that China and India would occupy in this new world.

Goldman Sachs' projections—the BRICs report

The most widely discussed projection of the impact that the rise of China and India would have on the world economy has been Goldman Sachs' *Dreaming with BRICs: The Path to 2050*.[4] And the most authoritative assessment of their impact on the global balance of power has come in a report of the US National Intelligence Council's 2020 Project, *Rising Powers: The Changing Geopolitical Landscape*.

The BRICs study, published in October 2003, predicted that well before 2050—in fact, by 2039, if its predictions came true—the combined gross domestic products of Brazil, Russia, India, and China (the "BRICs") would exceed that of the US, Britain, France, Germany, Italy, and Japan, whom it dubbed collectively the G6. In 2050, the study predicted, China's GDP would be $44.5 trillion and India's $28 trillion—125 percent and 80 percent of the US's projected GDP of $35.4 trillion. China would be the world's largest economy, and India the third largest, with the US sandwiched in between. Germany, France, Italy, the UK, and Japan would be left behind. In terms of absolute GDP, China would forge ahead of Japan, the second richest economy, by 2015. India would do so by 2032.

Goldman Sachs' projections were not the first of their kind. But what made them significant was that they measured China's and India's GDP at the actual market rates of exchange for US dollars and not at a rate that reflected the purchasing power of their currencies.[5] While GDP calculated at purchasing power parity (PPP), rates of exchange allow us to measure the standard of living in different countries; their GDP at market rates is a measure of their countries' economic power in the world market. The report reinforced its message by pointing out that the annual increase in demand in the BRICs countries would exceed the annual increase in the G6 as early as 2009. The report was therefore an early warning to transnational firms to start reorienting their production, recruitment, and marketing strategies to a very different world.

Since market power is a prelude to political power, the report also strengthened the long-held belief in the US that in the future China would be its main rival for world dominance. The National Intelligence Council predicted in 2005 that

> China's desire to gain "great power" status on the world stage will be reflected in its greater economic leverage over countries in the region and elsewhere as well as its steps to strengthen its military. East Asian states are adapting to the advent of a more powerful China by forging closer economic and political ties with Beijing, potentially accommodating themselves to its preferences, particularly on sensitive issues like Taiwan. . . . China will continue to strengthen its military through developing and acquiring modern weapons, including advanced fighter aircraft, sophisticated submarines, and increasing numbers of ballistic missiles. China will overtake Russia and others as the second largest defense spender after the United States over the next two decades and will be, by any measure, a first-rate military power.[6]

The BRICs report and the National Intelligence Council's assessment have further polarized opinion in the Western world on whether it would be better to "manage" the relationship with China or to confront and "contain" it. The liberal view, exemplified by the Clinton administration's policy of "constructive engagement," is based upon the assumption that as it grows richer China will develop a stronger and stronger interest in preserving the status quo, and become less and less inclined to enter into confrontations with its neighbors, and with the West. From this perspective, the challenge that China's rise poses to the international order can therefore best be met by promoting this process and easing its entry into the international system.[7]

But the Right brushes this approach aside with impatience. "The history of rising powers, . . . and their attempted "management" by established powers, provides little reason for confidence or comfort," wrote Robert Kagan, the most articulate exponent of its position, in 2005. "Rarely have rising powers risen without sparking a major war that reshaped the international system to reflect new realities of power." Kagan gave the examples of rising Germany's conflict with Britain and France, and Japan's conflict with America. The first clash sparked World War I; the second ensured America's participation in World War II. Kagan extended this logic to China, which, he said, was bound to try to shape relations in Asia to suit its needs, as its economy expanded and its capacity to impose its will on its neighbors grew. Conflict between it and the current hegemon in eastern Asia, the US, was therefore inevitable.

"The majority of today's policymakers and thinkers," he concluded,

hold much the same general view of global affairs as their forebears: namely, that commercial ties between China and the other powers, especially with Japan and the United States, and also with Taiwan, will act as a buffer against aggressive impulses and ultimately ease China's "integration" into the international system without war. Once again we see an Asian power modernizing and believe this should be a force for peace. And we add to this the conviction, also common throughout history, that if we do nothing to provoke China, then it will be peaceful, without realizing that *it may be the existing international system that the Chinese find provocative*.[8] (emphasis added)

Kagan's attempt to argue from history is seductive, but flawed. The crucial difference between the rise of Germany and Japan, in the nineteenth and early twentieth centuries, and the rise of China today, is that the former took place when the "container" of capitalism was the nation-state.[9] During the heyday of the nation-state there were several competing containers—Britain, France, Germany, and the US—each growing larger under the spur of technological change. It was inevitable that these containers would eventually collide. There were economic brakes on conflict even then. As the "hundred years" peace in Europe from 1815 to 1914 showed, the growing interlinkage of the European industrializing countries through trade and the network of international bankers, who bankrolled the governments of Europe and therefore had a common interest in avoiding war (what economist Karl Polanyi called *haute finance*), did contain conflict between the industrial powers for a long time.[10] But the First World War showed that interdependence in trade and finance alone was not sufficient to prevent nations from going to war.

Today's world is almost unrecognizably different. Beginning in the mid-1960s, capitalism broke the container of the nation-state and began to build a new, global container. In much the same way as Dutch finance capital migrated to London in the middle of the eighteenth century when London began to emerge as the new hub of the capitalist system, beginning in the late sixties first industrial, and then finance, capital began to migrate from its home in the highly industrialized countries to low-wage, industrializing countries and began to knit their manufacturing and financial systems into those of the rich nations to form a single global network. By the end of the century two-fifths of what we still call international trade consisted of transfers of components and materials within the same parent company, but across international boundaries. Another 30 percent consisted of sales to and purchases from nominally independent companies that were bound to the transnationals by long-term buying and selling arrangements.

Both China's and India's rapid development is being driven by this change. China exports more than a quarter of all that it manufactures; three-fifths of these exports consist of goods that originate in Japan, Taiwan, South Korea, and the Association of Southeast Asian Nations (ASEAN) countries and are destined for Europe and the US but are assembled and packaged in China to take advantage of its cheap labor. China's economic development is therefore locked into the fate of its main trading partners in a way that was inconceivable in the first half of the twentieth century. As the two world wars showed, countries could survive, and even conduct, prolonged wars without trading with each other. Germany fought the Second World War on synthetic oil produced from coal. But today a vehicle assembly plant in one country can come to a complete standstill if the supply of a single vital component manufactured in another country is disrupted because of war, revolution, or a natural calamity. For China, therefore, the cost of going to war with one of its main trading partners has become prohibitive.

Kagan was aware of this profound transformation. His reliance upon historical parallels from a previous epoch was therefore designed to serve a different purpose: to make a case for preemptive action against China to make sure that it never becomes strong enough to challenge the United States.

THE OBVIOUS CHOICES would seem to lie between ceding American predominance in the region and taking steps to contain China's understandable ambitions. Not many Americans favor the former course, and for sound political, moral, and strategic reasons. But let's not kid ourselves. It will be hard to pursue the latter course without treating China as at least a prospective enemy, and not just 20 years from now, but now.[11]

Two years later, as China's growth kept roaring on, Kagan's views had hardened. He still did not advocate a military containment of China. But he did advocate exploiting and exacerbating internal fissures in China in order to weaken or break up the country. All this, he believed, could be justified as a championship of democracy.[12]

China and India

The global recession has rendered Kagan's views unfashionable, to say the least. By underlining how deeply globalization has interlinked the fates of trading nations, it has tilted the balance in the US sharply away from confrontation toward cooperation. On June 1, 2009, Timothy Geithner, President Barack Obama's new secretary for the treasury, became the second member of Obama's cabinet to visit China within the first hundred days of his administration. He had been preceded by Secretary of State Hillary Clinton who had made Beijing her first port of call on February 21, barely a month after being sworn in. Clinton came to ask for China's help in curbing North Korea's nuclear ambitions. Geithner also came seeking cooperation, but virtually as a supplicant. Unlike Henry Paulson, his predecessor, who had used the *US-China Strategic Economic Dialogue* that he had initiated in 2006 to harangue the Chinese about their need to let the yuan appreciate against the dollar, Geithner came virtually as a supplicant. Obama had announced a fiscal stimulus package that had alarmed the European countries because it promised, among other things, to enlarge the US' three-quarter trillion balance of payments deficit further. Its success hinged on the rest of the world being prepared to fund this deficit by holding dollar securities. China was already the US' largest creditor. Geithner was in Beijing to reassure the Chinese that their money would remain safe.[13]

These are only two of a growing number of recent American

initiatives that add up to a profound shift in its policy toward China, from one of containment to one of partnership in hegemony. Former US Secretary of State Henry Kissinger flagged the change by suggesting that the US-China relationship needed to be taken to "a new level," and his democratic counterpart, Zbigniew Brzezinski, formalized it by suggesting the formation of a G-2 for tackling the international economic crisis, tackling climate change, and limiting the proliferation of nuclear weapons. Today very few people in the US share Kagan's desire to undermine China by any means whatsoever. But many still share Kagan's worries about China's capacity to harm US interests. Differences exist only about how best to neutralize the threat it might one day pose.

The need to manage or contain China helps to explain at least a part of the sudden intense interest in India. The BRICs report's prediction that India's growth rate is likely to forge ahead of China's around 2013 and stay ahead till well beyond the midpoint of the century is virtually a tailpiece to its main conclusions. But the interest it has evoked has been out of all proportion to its importance. While Indians behave as if overtaking China is not only possible but inevitable, interest in the US, and to a lesser extent in Europe, has centered on whether India can become a counterpoise to China in Asia. The National Intelligence Council gave a cautious endorsement to this prospect when it concluded that

> [a]s India's economy grows, governments in Southeast Asia—Malaysia, Singapore, Thailand, and other countries—may move closer to India to help build a potential geopolitical counterweight to China. At the same time, India will seek to strengthen its ties with countries in the region without excluding China.[14]

This assessment has played a not insignificant part in shaping US policy not only toward China but also increasingly toward India.

Notwithstanding strong denials that it was doing so, the Bush administration's policy moved quietly to enlist India in the attempt to contain China's rise. Its strategy was summarized by an Australian scholar, Aurelia George Mulgan, as follows:

> China's emergence as a regional great power is triggering the old Cold War reflex of containment. . . . The Americans prefer the rather more euphemistic terminology of "ensuring that China does not become a negative force in the region." They have, however, see-sawed between military containment and economic engagement for more than a decade with the military containment end of the see-saw now swinging higher. Containment explains the gradual net of encirclement being put into place by the Bush administration around China—the strengthening of the US-Japan alliance in both declaratory policy and military-to-military relations, the overtures to Mongolia, and President Bush's visit to India with the offer of civilian nuclear technology transfers. The US geo-strategic approach exploits the distinct deterioration in relations between China and Japan, and India's long-standing rivalry with China.[15]

When the US Congress gave its approval to the Indo-US nuclear deal, which would in effect make India the sixth recognized nuclear power in the world, governments and think tanks around the world concluded that this was one more step in the US government's master plan for India. Xenia Dormandy, executive director of the Belfer Center at the Kennedy School of Government in Harvard University, summed up the new relationship as follows: "[The US wants to bolster] a country, economically powerful and growing with a large population, [one] that's a democracy in Asia and continues to develop in the way that it is doing [so it] will act as a counterbalance, a second axis within Asia."[16]

THE PURPOSE OF this book is to examine whether China and India can indeed wrest hegemony from the West by the middle of the current century and to sound a warning against framing foreign and military policy on the basis of what are, at present, only a set of economic projections lest these turn its fears into self-fulfilling prophecies. It sets out to show why it is unlikely that either country will enjoy a smooth, friction-free ascent to greatness. The reason is that the capitalist transformation involves not a profound change in economic relationships but a total remaking of society. As the violent history of every major capitalist country from the UK to Japan has shown, this transition has not been easy. The reason is the profound change that capitalism has brought about in the relationship of society to the market. In all preindustrial societies, the market served society. But the harnessing of science to technology and fossil fuels to production for the market gave birth to a new form of organization, the market economy, which converted human beings into commodities—labor—that could be bought and sold. Since people are not commodities, they banded together to resist it. Their efforts gave birth to trade unionism, social democracy, and the welfare state.[17] But it also gave birth to Fascism and Communism and to two world wars that killed an estimated ninety million persons either directly or through war-related famine and disease.

Both China and India are still in the early stages of transformation from precapitalist to capitalist societies and have yet to reconcile rapid market-led development with peace and stability. The proliferation of violent protests in China and of localized insurgencies in India, in particular the resurgence of a purely class-based insurgency that Indians call "Naxalism," shows that they have yet to do so. Any attempt to "contain" China's rise through preemptive action may therefore not only prove unnecessary but also runs the risk of triggering precisely the conflict that both countries want to avoid.

By the same token, India needs a period free from external pressures and demands in which to strengthen existing democratic institutions and develop new ones capable of resolving the new forms of conflict that rapid development is generating. Pitting this weakened Indian state against China could create one more hurdle to its smooth development. It could prove to be one hurdle too many.

THIS DOES NOT mean that globalization has made war obsolete. A prediction on these lines by Norman Angell in 1910, at the tail end of Europe's hundred-year peace, was rendered spectacularly wrong four years later. But it does suggest that China's future conflicts, if any, will be over regional and local issues and will be with its neighbors, not with the established industrial powers. One potent source of conflict could be commitments made during a past era that China or its adversaries feel unable to back out of.[18] Two obvious ones are a declaration of independence by Taiwan and the outbreak of a general uprising in greater Tibet, encouraged and supported by a Tibetan government-in-exile from Dharamsala, in India. The roots of these conflicts lie buried sixty and a hundred years in the past, during the heyday of the nation-state, and none of the countries that could become involved would consider an outbreak of hostilities desirable. But other countries have used small, winnable wars to divert attention from domestic problems, and a China faced with domestic recession and rising social discontent could succumb to the temptation.

But the challenge this poses to the international community is of a very different kind from the one posed by the need to contain China's assumed hegemonic aspirations. It is essentially one of *management*, not *containment*. The first is temporary. It will diminish not only if China fails to maintain political stability and starts to break up, but also if it succeeds. The second is an endless task that can only be conclusively achieved through war.

2 DAVID AND GOLIATH

WESTERN HOPES AND anxieties apart, could India ever in fact possibly pose an economic challenge to China? Four out of five economists outside India would dismiss the very idea, and the number would not be much lower in India. In March 2005 the *Economist* summed it up by stating, "If this is a race, then India has been lapped."[19] Two years later, at a China-India conference in Delhi, Mohan Guruswamy, economic adviser to a former Indian finance minister, echoed this view: "In the 1990s China grew at the rate of 9.7 percent while India grew at 5.9 percent. Quite clearly, far from beginning to catch up, we fell well behind."

Tourists and businesspeople who have visited China and India over the last two decades find the idea that India may catch up with China laughable. In 1985 half the men and women in Beijing still wore the closed-collar jackets and baggy pantaloons of the Mao era. Three-quarters of them rode bicycles to work. To cater to the foreigners who had begun to visit China in increasing numbers, the government had allowed a limited import of Japanese cars to serve as taxis. The lucky taxi drivers earned four times as much in a month as the directors of the state-owned enterprises (SOEs), and male drivers became the prime catch for parents in search of spouses for their daughters.

The first modern hotels were just going up in Beijing, and were prohibitively expensive. Participants in an international conference organized by the World Bank and the Chinese Academy of Social Sciences were put up in SOE guesthouses where power for the air conditioning was switched on only at night. Underemployment was all-pervasive. A popular Szechuan restaurant employed two waiters for each table, and had a separate table where the unoccupied workers could sit together to while away the time.

There were almost no buses, and few traffic lights. But the mortality rate on the roads was high because of frequent collisions between the new taxis, the few official vehicles on the road, and cyclists. Neither the drivers nor the cyclists knew what to do at crossings. The work ethic was poor to nonexistent. The owners of Beijing's Great Wall Sheraton Hotel, the first foreign hotel to be completed, made it clear to the government that they would not employ workers who had previously worked for a state-owned enterprise.

No one who knew the China of those days would recognize the country today. Its highways rival those of Europe and the US; in the eastern coastal provinces the countryside has almost disappeared under endless ribbons of bustling modern small and medium-sized industry. Its cities are sprinkled with skyscrapers that challenge, in elegance and design, the best that Singapore, Kuala Lumpur, Hong Kong, Sydney, and Melbourne have to offer. "Returning to visit Beijing or Shanghai after a few years' gap is a bewildering experience," the *Economist* noted. "After negotiating slick new airports, new expressways whisk you into town. Occasionally, through the new skyscrapers, a familiar building appears, lost in the concrete jungle."

Parts of China have seen perhaps history's biggest construction boom.[20] Shanghai no longer boasts of its forest of cranes. A forest of skyscrapers has taken its place. It has the world's third tallest building and would for a while have had the tallest, had not two others that were even taller been started after work on it was temporarily suspended in 1998.

In 1995 Shanghai's eastern adjunct, Pudong, was a bas-relief map in the foyer of the Pudong development authority, a grid of empty roads demarcating sectors and three brave new office buildings put up by early bird foreign investors. Today it is a futuristic city linked to the airport by the world's only commercial magnetic levitation train. Its container port could be better described as a container city, with giant cargo containers piled six and eight stories high. The bridge linking Pudong to Shanghai is modern engineering at its graceful best.

Shanghai epitomizes everything that modern China aspires to be, but Beijing, Tianjin, Guangzhou, and a dozen other provincial capitals are not far behind. These cities are the centers of a new consumer culture. They have some of the best-dressed men and women in the world, their streets boast the latest luxury cars, and they inevitably have attracted all the most famous international brand-name boutiques in the world. Shanghai in particular has emerged as the alternative to Hong Kong and Singapore as a regional hub of transnational trade and investment. More and more transnational corporations have shifted their regional headquarters to the city.

This economic transformation has been an object of envy all over the world. By the estimates of China's National Bureau of Statistics, its GDP has grown by 9.5 percent a year since 1978. By 2006 its per capita income had risen nearly fourteenfold from $151 to $2010.[21] The percentage of its population living in urban areas had risen from 18 percent to 39 percent, and a prosperous middle class had come into being. Whereas there had been one phone line for every two thousand persons in 1978, there were ninety-eight fixed or mobile phone lines for every one hundred persons in 2006. In 1978 only three out of every thousand families owned a television set. In 2006, 960 out of every thousand families owned one.[22]

According to World Bank yardsticks, China had lifted four hundred million people out of poverty by the beginning of this century. This extraordinary growth has made China the fourth largest economy in the world. No other country, not even Japan, has been able to sustain such a mind-boggling rate of growth for such a long time.

The contrast between the stellar performance described above and India's slow jog after it opened up its economy in 1991 could not be greater. India's economic renaissance drew almost no attention till 2003. In June 1991, when then-finance minister Manmohan Singh announced economic reforms in his budget speech that heralded the end of the "socialist" command economy in India, the *New York Times* gave the changes a grudging twelve column inches of space in a report that mainly highlighted the reforms that he had *not* enacted, and was openly skeptical about India's future. Its subsequent growth, which averaged 6.2 percent between 1991–'02 and 2002–'03, might have attracted attention in an earlier time, but by the mid-nineties the world had grown used to the 7 and 8 percent rates of growth achieved by Japan, and East and Southeast Asia, for thirty years, and the 9.5 percent that China had recorded between 1978 and 1995.

The world first realized that something had changed when, in mid-2003, the Indian stock market, which had been dormant for the previous seven years, suddenly caught fire and yielded returns to investors of up to 350 percent in a single year. Since then India's growth has averaged a shade under 9 percent a year. But in spite of the last five years' spurt, India remains far behind China in almost every parameter of growth. The following tables, abstracted from country profiles published by the World Bank, show India is beginning to catch up with China in some parameters of successful globalization. But they also highlight the wide gap in overall performance that persists, and seems even to be expanding, between the two countries.

Table 2.1

China's Economic Profile

	2000	2005	2006
ECONOMY			
GDP (current US$)	1.2 trillion	2.2 trillion	2.7 trillion
GDP growth (annual %)	8.4	10.2	10.7
Industry, value added (% of GDP)	45.9	47.3	47.0
Exports of goods and services (% of GDP)	23.3	37.3	36.8
Imports of goods and services (% of GDP)	20.9	31.7	32.9
Gross capital formation (% of GDP)	35.1	43.3	40.7
STATES AND MARKETS			
Time required to start a business (days)	..	48.0	35.0
Market capitalization of listed companies (% of GDP)	48.5	34.8	90.9
Fixed line and mobile phone subscribers (per 1,000 people)	182.2	570.2	..
Internet users (per 1,000 people)	17.8	85.1	..
GLOBAL LINKS			
Merchandise trade (% of GDP)	39.6	63.4	66.0
Foreign direct investment, net inflows (BoP, current US$)	38.4 billion	79.1 billion	..

Source: World Development Indicators database, April 2007.

India's Economic Profile

	2000	2005	2006
ECONOMY			
GDP (current US$)	460.2 billion	805.7 billion	906.3 billion
GDP growth (annual %)	4.0	9.2	9.2
Exports of goods and services (% of GDP)	13.2	20.3	..
Imports of goods and services (% of GDP)	14.2	23.3	..
Gross capital formation (% of GDP)	24.8	33.4	..

India's Economic Profile *(cont.)*

	2000	2005	2006
STATES AND MARKETS			
Time required to start a business (days)	..	71.0	35.0
Market capitalization of listed companies (% of GDP)	32.2	68.6	90.4
Fixed line and mobile phone subscribers (per 1,000 people)	35.4	127.7	..
Internet users (per 1,000 people)	5.4	54.8	..
GLOBAL LINKS			
Merchandise trade (% of GDP)	20.4	29.6	32.5
direct investment, net inflows			
Foreign direct investment, net inflows (BoP, current US$)	3.6 billion	6.6 billion	..

Source: World Development Indicators database, April 2007.

What a fifteen-year head start can mean

Appearances can be deceptive. The gap between the two countries is not as great as the official figures informing the above tables make it out to be. China and India employ different methods of calculating many of these indicators. There is, for instance, a fairly widespread belief among economists (discussed later) that the official estimates of China's long-term growth are too high, and that its real growth rate has been somewhere between 8 and 9 percent.

There are even greater differences in the two countries' ways of estimating foreign direct investment. Nirupam Bajpai of Columbia University has adjusted the data for 2000 and concluded that after subtracting Chinese savings that are regularly "round-tripped" through Hong Kong, and making some other adjustments to permit comparability, China's incoming foreign direct investment (FDI) was not $40.7 billion, but $20.3 billion, while India's was not $3.2 billion but $8.1 billion.[23] If one makes an equivalent correction to the data for 2005 given above, FDI into China would be of the order of $40 billion in 2005 against $16.5 billion into India. In 2005 India belatedly changed its method of calculating FDI to bring it in line with international practice. As a result, the official estimate for 2006 is $23.3 billion, against China's $69 billion.

But even this gap is deceptive, for it masks the different function that FDI is playing in the two countries. As the MIT scholar Yasheng Huang has pointed out, in China a large part of the FDI is a substitute for domestic resources. Provincial and township-level enterprises have often had to raise money abroad because the bulk of the resources of their almost entirely state-owned domestic banks have been preempted by the state-owned enterprises and the Chinese central government departments to finance their gigantic infrastructure development schemes. As a result, a dollar of FDI has on an average enabled a little more than two dollars of total investment. In India, by contrast, FDI has acted mainly as a vehicle for modern technology and management practices, and enables five to six dollars of total investment. The rest of the capital is raised in the Indian equity and money markets.

China continues to invest a much higher proportion of its GDP (42.5 percent) than India (32.7 percent). But Indian investment is more productive. This is shown by the country's lower incremental capital to output ratio (ICOR)—the amount of capital it needs to produce an extra dollar of income. If one adjusts for this, then China's effective level of investment is not 30 but only 18 percent higher.

Finally, as the table below shows, although China's reserves of foreign exchange dwarf those of India in absolute terms, when measured by the yardstick of the number of months of imports they can finance they are not much larger. China's reserves in 2006 were sufficient to finance twenty-six months worth of imports; India's were sufficient to finance twenty-three months.

While the above adjustments give a more nuanced picture of the economies of the two countries, they also highlight the considerable difference in the size of the two economies that still remains. However, nearly all of it can be ascribed to the fifteen-year head start that China had over India in its transition to a market economy. During that period China's growth rate was close to 10 percent per annum, while India's was 5.4 percent. The difference of 4.6 percent over sixteen years is sufficient to explain nine-tenths of China's higher GDP.

The interest in India as a possible counterpoise to China becomes comprehensible when one filters out the effect of China's fifteen-year head start on their current positions, and compares only their current performance. In this India compares favorably with China on several counts: First, although India's growth rate after 2003 has still remained about 1 percent below China's official growth rate, it is not a subject of controversy. Second, India's lower incremental capital to output ratio, even when compared to China's official estimates, suggests that it is likely to use domestic and foreign investable funds more efficiently than China, at least in the near future. Third, in the longer run India is likely to sustain a high growth rate for a longer time than China because it is using raw materials and energy far more efficiently than China, and because, thanks to China's one-child policy, it has a larger pool of young people joining the workforce in the coming years. As the table below shows, India uses less than half as much energy and a third as much raw materials per capita as China does to obtain every dollar of additional income.

Two other features of India's economy help to sustain interest in its future growth. These are its higher birth rate and its impressive pool of entrepreneurial talent. India's workforce will grow more rapidly than China's for several decades. People aged fifteen to sixty-four accounted for 71 percent of China's population in 2005. But this has begun to fall and is expected to be 69 percent in 2020 and 62 percent in 2040. The corresponding percentages for India are 63 percent in 2005, and 67 percent in 2020.[24] Based on this demographic data, the Goldman Sachs BRICs report predicted that India's growth rate might actually surpass China's by 2013 or 2014.[25]

And while China has built an impressive physical infrastructure, India has built a less tangible but more important infrastructure of first-class managers and companies. As far back as July 2003, two MIT and Harvard scholars, Yasheng Huang and Tarun Khanna, respectively had noted that *Fortune*'s list of the two hundred best-managed smaller companies in the world contained thirteen Indian firms against four from China.[26]

India, they also pointed out, had much more transparent financial institutions and a much better developed and regulated stock market. This meant not only that savings parked in Indian assets would on balance be safer, but that foreign investors could retain control of a company in India while putting in as little as a twelfth of the total investment against having to furnish roughly half the total capital for an investment in China.[27]

The following table lays out some of the above adjustments in an easily comparable form. The data is for 2006.

Table 2.2

Some China-India Comparisons

Indicator	China	India	Ratio
GDP	$2.7 trillion	$906 billion	2.98 :1*
Per capita GDP	$2010	$800	2.5 : 1*
Investment/GDP ratio	42.5%	32.7%	1.3 : 1
Incremental capital to output ratio (ICOR)	4 : 1**	3.6 : 1	10 : 9
Per capita consumption of energy (China-India ratio)	—	—	2.2 : 1
Per capita consumption of raw materials (China-India ratio)	—	—	3 : 1
Balance of payments	+$160.8 billion (2005)	+$7 billion	—
Foreign exchange reserves	$1.6 trillion (3/08)	$312 billion (6/08)	—
Foreign exchange reserves in months of imports	26	23	—
FDI	$69 billion	$23 billion	3 : 1
FDI-enabled investment	Approximately $150 billion	Approximately $125 billion	6 : 5
Value added in globalized sector	$189 billion (processing trade)	$40 billion (IT-enabled trade)	4.7 : 1

Sources: National Bureau of Statistics of China, China Statistical Yearbook 2007, and the Government of India's Economic Survey 2007–2008.

*These ratios will be smaller if one assumes that the official figures of growth are inflated by 1 to 1.5 percent.

**This will be higher if one concludes that China's growth rate is overestimated.

3 ON PARALLEL TRACKS

THE PREVIOUS CHAPTER gives a more nuanced picture of the way the two countries have actually performed than the one obtained from just comparing economic indices. But it tells us very little about the way they are likely to perform in the future, because comparing China's and India's development is a good deal like comparing apples with oranges. Not only did the two countries start their transition to a market economy from different starting points and at different times, but they are following parallel and, by and large, noncompeting tracks of globalization. Whereas China has become the manufactory of the world, India is rapidly acquiring a comparable position in the emerging global services industry.

Workshop of the world

China's international trade has grown over fifty-five-fold from $20.6 billion in 1978 to $1.15 trillion in 2004. One author has described it in the following terms: "China has administered a bigger shock to the global economy than that created by the UK and US over the eighteenth and nineteenth centuries ... [In 1979] China started with 2.9 percent of world income and grew on an average 6.6 percentage points faster than the world economy for 26 years. The nearest parallel to China was the growth of the United States over the period

1820–'70 during which time the differential compared to the global economy was 3.3 percentage points (with a lower starting share.)"[28] During the ten-year period ending 2004, China accounted for 9 percent of the increase in the world's exports of goods and services. This was second only to the 10.7 percent share of the US. It also accounted for nearly 8 percent of the growth in imports during the same period, a share also second only to the US. In a short period of time, therefore, China has become close to becoming the second biggest growth pole of the world after the US.[29]

The shock has been a benevolent one. China has smoothly filled the slot created by globalization for a platform for the manufacture of labor-intensive goods for the world market. The East Asian countries were the first to fill this slot, and China is going down the same path. In the last two decades it has emerged as the fastest-growing exporter of manufactured goods and has exerted a downward pressure on manufactured goods prices in relation to those of other products and services. It has also become the undisputed global center for the manufacture of consumer goods. Factories located in China make 70 percent of the world's toys, three-fifths of its bicycles, half of its shoes, and one-third of its luggage.[30]

What is more, its dominance is no longer confined to these basic consumer goods, for, as author and professor Oded Shankar explains, it also now manufactures "half of the world's microwave ovens, one-third of its television sets . . . a quarter of its [dish] washers, and one-fifth of its refrigerators; these products represent the fastest-growing segment of its exports. Manufacturers in other countries increasingly rely on Chinese components or subassemblies to stay competitive."[31]

In the nineties, China graduated from solely producing labor-intensive goods to becoming an integral part of the global production system for a larger and larger variety of sophisticated consumer goods. This is especially evident in electronic and information technology products. Exports of these products soared from $16 billion in 1995 to $268 billion in 2005. As a share of China's total exports, electronic and information technology products rose from 11 percent in 1995 to 35 percent in 2005. Electronic and information technology products are produced in China predominantly by foreign-owned firms and predominantly using the processing form of trade—that is, the parts and components required to produce the export goods are imported duty-free. This has become an important aspect of China's trade with Southeast Asian countries."[32]

The role that China now plays in the global production and marketing system is evident in the pattern of its exports and imports. In 2004, for example, China's exports were valued at $593.3 billion, while its imports amounted to $561.2 billion. It thus enjoyed a trade surplus of $32.1 billion. But while it had a trade surplus with the US of $80.3 billion and with Europe of $39.4 billion, it had a trade deficit with Japan of $20.4 billion, with Taiwan of $70.6 billion, with South Korea of $34.4 billion, and with Hong Kong of $17.8 billion. In sum, while it had a trade surplus of $119.7 billion with the high-wage, first-generation industrialized countries of the West, this was more than offset by a trade deficit of $145.2 billion with that relative newcomer Japan, and the "East Asian tigers" (South Korea, Taiwan, Hong Kong, and Singapore).[33] What has happened is not hard to deduce: The basic pattern of transpacific trade established in the sixties and seventies under the initial impact of globalization has not altered. All that has happened is that, faced with rising labor costs at home, Japan and the East Asian tigers have disaggregated the manufacturing process itself. They continue to manufacture components that can be mass-produced, or require high levels of technical expertise, but they have moved the most labor-intensive portions of the manufacturing process to China. These typically include the subassembly and final assembly of components, and packaging for shipment to consumers.

The fortuitous role that timing and location have played in en-suring the success of China's economic reform and triggering its dazzling growth cannot be overestimated. Had exactly the same reforms been carried out in the sixties, they would have had only a limited impact on China's growth. Global tariff barriers were still relatively high, quantitative restrictions and other nontariff barri-ers were in common use even in the industrialized countries, and, most important of all, capital flows between nations were closely regulated. But China opened its economy to foreign investment at just the time when capital flows got deregulated and the search for cheap labor production platforms gathered momentum (the late eighties). What is more, by 1992, when Deng Xiaoping's southern tour ended China's ambivalence about the virtues of growth, Japan seemed to have reached the end of its three-decade-long export-led growth, and wages had begun to rise sharply in Southeast Asia, causing the region to lose its appeal as a destination for investment in search of low-wage production platforms and threatening the Southeast Asian stranglehold on the consumer goods markets of the high-wage economies of Europe and the US. The countries of the region had therefore also begun to look for ways to reduce their costs and retain their competitiveness in developed country markets. The rush of foreign direct investment to China that began in the nineties therefore owed less to any sudden change of policy in China than to the conjunction of circumstances created by the globalization of capitalism.

Liberal economists in India maintain that India too could have become a global center for manufacturing if only it had liberalized its domestic controls on investment more wholeheartedly. They place most of the blame upon the government's stubborn refusal, for political reasons, to dismantle a section of its industrial licens-ing laws that had reserved more than eight hundred products for manufacture solely in the small-scale sector. These included toys, garments, linen, crockery, cutlery, and home electrical appliances of every kind, from steam irons to pop-up toasters—precisely the labor-intensive, low-value, but mass-consumption items whose manufacture had become uneconomical in the high-wage industrialized countries[34] and was taken over by Southeast Asia, and then China. Indeed, almost half of these restrictions were still in place in 2007.

India was also hamstrung by a crippling shortage of infrastructure—notably reliable power, cargo-handling capacity, and highways—and by labor laws that all but prevented any retrenchment of workers, even when a company was making losses and manifestly falling sick. (These hurdles were still in place at the time of writing.) The two constraints ensured that global retailers like Wal-Mart and wholesalers of toys, garments, and the like avoided India. Retailers found that there was little quality control in the small-scale sector, and that even when price and quality were satisfactory the enterprises simply could not meet the size of the orders that the retailers wanted to place, within an acceptable time frame. The wholesalers were scared away by the poor quality of infrastructure and the rigidity of the labor laws. Those laws also effectively foreclosed the manufacture of consumer goods for export, like garments, where demand was seasonal. Manufacturers need to be able to hire workers to meet this demand and then lay them off when the orders have been fulfilled, but Indian labor laws continue to ban such short-term contracting of labor.

But even if India had liberalized far more aggressively in the nineties, it would not have attracted more than a small part of the outsourced manufacturing that went to China. The reformers' argument ignores the impact of established trade patterns on the choice of destinations for outsourcing labor-intensive manufacture. Ever since the late fifties cheap consumer goods had flowed in a rising torrent across the Pacific from East Asia to the seemingly bottomless US market. Thus when wages in the East Asian tigers peaked in the late eighties, American retailers looked for other suppliers in the same region. This trend strengthened in the nineties when not only the Americans but also the ASEAN countries began to look for a cheap, last-stage manufacturing platform for their exports to the US and Europe. Here, in addition to its linguistic and cultural affinity with Taiwan, Hong Kong, and the Chinese communities that dominated trade and manufacturing in the ASEAN countries, the proximity of China to the exporters proved a deciding factor, for the shipping routes across the Pacific were already established. The cost of altering these to include China was marginal. In 2007 and 2008, as labor shortages became acute in coastal China and pushed up the cost of labor at the rate of 25 percent a year, this same geographical principle made many firms that were outsourcing goods from China turn to nearby Vietnam.[35]

A hub for global service industries

India might never have developed into the main hub for the globalizing service industries had Prime Minister Indira Gandhi not been assassinated on October 31, 1984. That traumatic event led to the accession of her son Rajiv Gandhi to the prime ministership, and to his landslide victory in the national elections that followed, five months later. Rajiv was just forty-one when he became the prime minister, and had been a commercial pilot flying jet aircraft. He understood better than anyone in Indian politics how the computer sciences were changing the world. One of his first acts, therefore, was to jettison his mother's two-decade-old policy of self-reliance in the development of informatics, a policy that had all but blocked the import of computers for two decades. Instead, this was the first sector in which import bans were removed; tariffs were brought down to virtually nothing during his five-year tenure.

To appreciate the farsightedness of what Rajiv Gandhi and his advisers did it is necessary to remember that at that time India was a closed economy with a hugely overvalued exchange rate, and that the average duty on imports was 125 percent, and peak duties were over 300 percent.

The new prime minister's early realization of the potential of the information technology (IT) industry created the "Indian miracle." Beginning from next to nothing at the end of the eighties, this industry grew by leaps and bounds to become the main employer of educated young Indians, and the largest single foreign exchange earner for the country. In 1990, the sales revenue of the IT and related service industries was barely half a billion dollars. By March 31, 2008, it had grown over 120 times and crossed sixty-three billion dollars. Its annual growth rate, which was 50 to 60 percent in the nineties, has stabilized at 30 to 40 percent in the current decade. This is twice the 17 percent rate of growth achieved by the IT industry in the US.

India's IT industry growth has been driven by exports from the very beginning. Exports grew from $150 million in 1990 to $40 billion by March 2008.[36] This amounted to 15 percent of the country's total foreign exchange receipts in 2003–'04 and 20 percent of its exports. India's domestic industry was slow to accept computerization of its services, but by 2003, after half a dozen years of recession, it had also become fully aware of computerization's advantages. The demand for software and IT-enabled services (IT-ES) grew from $2.8 billion in 2002–'03 to $23 billion in 2007–'08.[37]

The growth of employment is equally impressive. The industry employed 522,000 IT professionals in March 2002. The number doubled in just six years, an annual growth rate of almost 12 percent.[38] The indirect employment it has generated was estimated to be another two million.[39] What is even more impressive is the quality of employment. Seventy-six percent of the IT professionals are university graduates. Of these, 62 percent hold bachelor of technology degrees. The remainder hold master's degrees in technology or business administration.

The entrepreneurs in the IT industry are a new breed, with backgrounds in science and engineering, and an entirely different view of the relationship of industry to society. For instance, Infosys, one of the most successful of the new companies, has housed its production facilities in a new campus that surely ranks among the most beautiful in the world. To meet the shortage of personnel that it foresees a few years from now, it has set up a technical university where it trains thousands of software engineers. Several companies, including Intel, Microsoft, and the emerging Indian giant Wipro, have taken up the responsibility of providing computers and Internet access to primary schools in the state of Karnataka. Perhaps the most ambitious venture is that of Satyam, another of the IT companies listed on the New York Stock Exchange. Satyam has set up an emergency ambulance service in the state of Andhra Pradesh, with an estimated seven hundred vans, that can respond to calls for help with the goal of taking advanced medicine to the remotest villages. To do this it has been equipped with state-of-the-art equipment, capable of responding to a phone call on a single statewide emergency number within minutes. Titan, India's largest digital watch manufacturer, is fighting the scourge of female infanticide by specifically reserving watch assembly for young unmarried female employees. To its delight, it has found that in this case, at least, philanthropy is proving highly profitable.[40]

No account of the phenomenal growth of this industry would be complete without a reference to its impact on society and politics. Until 1991, thanks to slow growth and an emphasis on heavy industry, the number of new jobs created every year in industry and the services sector fell far short of the number of educated young people who entered the job market. This caused acute frustration among college graduates and spurred, in many, frantic efforts to migrate to the West. The IT industry came as a boon to them. For almost two decades, it has absorbed the surplus. India produces 1.5 million graduates and 167,000 engineering graduates every year. Despite that, in 2005 NASSCOM, the trade association of the Indian software industry, predicted a shortage of 235,000 software engineers by 2008.

But more important than the numbers employed has been the impact of the IT industry upon the work ethic in most other branches of industry and trade. The software industry, which was the first of the IT-enabled industries in the country, came into being almost by accident, in an environment totally free from the protection and spoon-feeding, in the form of tax breaks and subsidies, that other industries routinely expected. Its success showed others that it was possible for Indian industries to dispense with protection and stand up to international competition on their own. The work environment in the IT-enabled services industry also came as a revelation to those who worked in it. The modern, clean office environment, and especially the emphasis on providing a host of amenities, from cafeterias to recreation rooms and gyms, was new to Indian industry. Other firms began to copy them.

Bangalore emerged as the first hub of the IT industry because it had several natural advantages. The first was its location at a height of almost five thousand feet in the center of the Deccan Plateau, where it enjoyed cool winters and mild summers. The atmosphere was also relatively dust-free, as the area received two spells of rain, stretching, intermittently, from June till December. But Bangalore was also an important center of higher technical and scientific education, perhaps unrivaled in the rest of India. It was the home of the prestigious Indian Institute of Science, and of one of the three best Indian Institutes of Management. In addition there were eight state and privately funded institutes of technology, and ninety-three private engineering and technology colleges set up by a private trust under the umbrella of the Visveswaraya Technology University.[41]

It was therefore no surprise when the first transnationals that came looking for outsourcing opportunities to India picked Bangalore as their base. Three in particular deserve mention: Hewlett-Packard (HP), Texas Instruments, and Motorola. All of them established in-house software centers in Bangalore to which they could outsource parts of their software development. HP also established a center for the repair of their laser printer motherboards, which would be airlifted from the US to Bangalore to be repaired. They did this because they found that they were able to get (in 1992–'93) equally good technicians for $5 an hour in Bangalore, while they paid $60 an hour in the US. But the rapid development of the Internet increased the scope for IT-ES outsourcing by leaps and bounds. HP also transferred key accounting functions to Bangalore, because it could do them there at one-sixth of the US cost without sacrificing quality.

Large transnational companies soon found that they could move entire administrative functions like accounting, airline ticketing, and inter-airline fare reconciliation to India. A host of other business processes also began to be outsourced to India. One that attracted a great deal of media attention was the call center business. Call center operators found that educated Indians were not only fluent in English, but could mimic accents easily. The pioneer in this was another American company, GE Capital, which opened a call center with ten thousand employees near Delhi.

The IT industry developed in three waves. The first consisted of transnationals moving some of their software development and back office functions to wholly owned subsidiaries in India. But soon a new, second-wave generation of Indian companies developed, often set up by former employees of the transnational corporations who went out and solicited back office and software development work abroad. The third wave developed when business process out-sourcing, particularly call centers, began to move out of the highly industrialized countries. This last wave came in 1999–2000, when the IT bubble exploded in the US and the nine-year boom in the US economy ended. In 2002–'03, while the software part of India's IT industry continued to expand at 30 percent per annum (twice the American rate of growth), the business processing outsourcing part of the industry grew by 107 percent. In 2005 there were over 1,250 Indian companies in information technology-related indus-tries, and 266 out of *Fortune*'s thousand largest companies were doing substantial parts of their IT-related work in India.

4 EXPLAINING CHINA'S AND INDIA'S RISE

TRACKING CHINA AND India's rapid growth is easy; explaining it is not. Most analysts ascribe the countries' success to the smoothness with which they made their transition from command to market economies. Credit is usually given to them for rejecting "shock therapy," the enactment of all reforms in one go, and adopting a gradual, step-by-step approach to the reform of product markets and the market for labor and capital. But, despite the havoc that shock therapy wreaked on Russia, many authors still believe that most of China's political, and not a few of its economic, problems stem from its decision, in the words of Deng Xiaoping, to "ford the river by feeling the stones." In a recent book titled *China's Trapped Transition*,[42] Minxin Pei holds gradual reform responsible for preventing the political reforms that are needed to end the Communist Party's abuse of its political and economic power. In a comparative assessment of the two economies, the World Bank evaded this issue altogether and simply ascribed their success to their abandonment of centralized planning and controls and decision to embrace a market economy.[43] Implicit in this assessment is the assumption that the space left by the retreat of the state has been filled smoothly by private enterprise. Implicit in it also is the belief that private enterprise is invariably more efficient than the state.

James A. Dorn, vice president of the Washington DC-based

Cato Institute, summed up China's achievements and unfinished tasks at a roundtable discussion in 2003:

> The great success of private and cooperative enterprises over the past 25 years—they now account for more than two-thirds of the value of industrial output—has resulted in official recognition of the importance of the non-state sector as an engine of economic growth. . . . The growth of private enterprise has occurred despite the lack of transparent legal title and restrictions on access to state bank credit. Informal private capital markets have evolved to fund the private sector, and overseas Chinese have been an important source of investment funds. The strong performance of provinces with greater economic freedom, such as Fujian, Guangdong, and Zhejiang, has created a new middle class and a demand for better government and more secure property rights.
>
> Capitalists are now free to join the Chinese Communist Party, and several well-known private entrepreneurs are already members of the National People's Congress. As more entrepreneurs join the party, there will be mounting pressure to change the status quo. At the 16th National Congress of the CCP in November 2002, President Jiang Zemin gave a clear signal that the private sector is an important part of China's future. He said, "We need to respect and protect all work that is good for the people and society and improve the legal system for protecting private property." The party charter now includes "The Three Represents," a doctrine that commits the party to embrace the fundamental interests of the majority of the people, not just the proletariat.[44]

The significant feature of the above description is Dorn's ready identification of "non-state" with "private." It is this that enables him to equate China's success with privatization. India's success is equated even more unequivocally with economic reforms, notably embrace of a market economy and the withdrawal of the state from production and distribution. In their influential book *India in the Era of Economic Reforms,* Jeffrey Sachs, Ashutosh Varshney, and Nirupam Bajpai assert without any qualifying statement that "India's economic reforms have played a critical role in the performance of the economy since 1991."[45]

The equation of economic reforms with growth does look pretty solid if we choose 1978 as the starting point for China and 1991 for India. It is particularly plausible for China because in 1978 China had none of the institutions that market economies take for granted. There was no free market for foodstuffs, and only a rudimentary market for manufactures in the form of complex, many-sided barter deals that were struck at semiannual buyers' conferences between public enterprises. If these resembled anything in the European experience of the transition to capitalism, it was the Piacenza fairs of northern Italy, the first trans-European markets, in the sixteenth century.

Private enterprise all but did not exist. State-owned enterprises and commune-based agriculture produced 97.2 percent of China's output.[46] Centralized planning covered five hundred broadly defined products that accounted for more than nine-tenths of total economic output.[47] There was virtually no market. Food and other basic products were rationed, there was a rudimentary market for products,[48] and the state had total control over the markets for the factors of production—land, labor, and capital. The acceleration of China's growth[49] began only after the first economic reforms in 1978–'80[50] and therefore came to be regarded as a consequence of the reforms.

But a closer inspection shows little correlation between the progress of the reforms and the stepping up of growth. China's GDP growth began to average 11 percent per year in 1981, at a time when the dismantling of planning and price controls had barely started and markets were still in their infancy. Private industry did not exist and was discouraged. Until 1997 the privatization of erstwhile state- or local government-owned enterprises had proceeded at a snail's pace. Even as recently as 2006, grassroots private companies, started, owned, and operated by Chinese entrepreneurs, accounted for only 20 percent and foreign funded enterprises for only another third of industrial production—only half of the industrial output could be considered as driven by market forces alone. The rest was guided by, or susceptible to, pressures and inducements from the state.[51] Thus, if the creation of markets has been gradual and privatization remains incomplete, one needs more than the withdrawal of the state from economic activity to explain China's explosive development from the very start of the reform era.

INDIA PRESENTS THE opposite paradox. If a fully fledged market economy and ubiquitous private enterprise are preconditions for rapid economic growth, then why was India's growth so painfully slow between 1951 and 1991? For in 1947, when it attained its independence, India not only had a well-integrated national market but a well-developed financial system and a robust private sector. *What is more, India had had all of these for up to four centuries.* A subcontinent-wide market for raw materials like cotton, tobacco, indigo, and spices, the finer qualities of wheat and rice, fine textiles, brocades, and jewelry had come about during the heyday of Mughal rule, in the sixteenth century.[52] Mughal India had also developed an efficient, nationwide trading and financial system. In the seventeenth and eighteenth centuries traders-cum-financiers like Virji Vora of Surat, Shantidas of Ahmedabad, and the House of Jagat Seth in Bengal built nationwide banking systems and accumulated capital on a scale that far surpassed the accumulation of wealth by the merchants of Venice and the bankers of Genoa. It made them richer than the kings and nawabs to whom they owed allegiance and, in a manner similar to their European counterparts, made them bankers to the local princes and to the later Mughal rulers in Delhi.[53]

Some idea of Virji Vora's wealth may be had from the fact that when Shivaji, the Maratha guerrilla leader who broke away from the Mughal empire and founded the Maratha empire in western India, invaded and sacked Surat in 1664 and looted Vora's home and warehouses, he carried away, according to a contemporary Dutch source, six barrels of gold, money, pearls, gems, and other precious commodities. Virji Vora lost an estimated fifty thousand pounds sterling (approximately 650,000 silver rupees) worth of gold and other loot. But since his personal wealth was estimated to be around eight *million* rupees at the time, he soon recovered.[54]

But a better idea of the power of these finance houses can be had by comparing their wealth to that of their European counterparts. In 1420, with 1.5 million inhabitants, the city-state of Venice, created and ruled by merchant princes, had a budget of 1.65 million ducats, while with fifteen million inhabitants the kingdom of France, which was a territorial state of the normal mold, had a budget of one million ducats.[55] At an approximate exchange value of six Indian silver rupees for one Venetian gold ducat, Virji Vora's personal wealth in the mid-seventeenth century amounted to 1.3 million ducats, while the capital owned by the House of Jagat Seth in the beginning of the eighteenth century amounted to twelve million ducats.[56]

These trader-financiers financed an equally vast manufacturing system, a large part of which had reached the "putting-out" stage of manufacture in artisanal sheds of the kind found in Europe in the seventeenth and eighteenth centuries. In 1750, on the eve of Britain's colonization of the Mughal province of Bengal, India accounted for approximately a quarter of the manufactured output of the world. Manufacturing also accounted for more than a fifth, and quite possibly more than a quarter, of employment. As late as 1807, half a century after the colonial dismantling of eastern India's industry began, British administrators recorded that 21 percent of the population of Bengal was engaged in industry.[57]

India, moreover, started with an equally strong tradition of private enterprise that four decades of centralized planning and a "mixed" economy, from 1951 to 1991, had barely dented. Colonial rule after 1757 had destroyed its artisan industry, but in the nineteenth and twentieth centuries the British tightened the integration of the Indian market by linking the four corners of the country with forty-five thousand miles of railway tracks. Despite Britain's benign neglect of industrialization in its colonies, India had a small but well-diversified industrial sector when it became independent. The First Census of Manufactures, held in 1946, identified twenty-nine sectors in which industrialization had taken place. These included cotton and jute textiles, steel, sugar, vegetable oils, tea, coal, paper and paper pulp, tobacco and matches, and general engineering that produced consumer goods for mass consumption such as bicycles and lamp bulbs. Cotton textiles, jute manufactures, steel, sugar, and coal accounted for 82.7 percent of the total.[58]

Although India adopted a centrally planned model of economic development in 1951, even during the most extreme years of economic autarchy, state-owned enterprises contributed less than 20 percent of the GDP. All agriculture, the bulk of industrial production, and all service industries except external trade and banking remained entirely in private hands. So, how did India come to record one of the *slowest* growth rates in the world for forty-four years after it gained its independence?

The answer to both this India question and my previous China question is to be found not in economics but politics. The development of both countries has been shaped by a political struggle for power between two groups of investors that has been fostered by state-promoted but market-led economic growth. This has had opposite effects in the two countries. In India it choked economic growth for four decades till the economic crisis of 1991. In China it has caused an explosion of chaotic investment, carried out by investors who have paid scant heed to signals from the market. This has needlessly aggravated social stress, to the point where relieving it has become the main preoccupation of the Hu Jintao government.

In China the two strata of investment decision-makers who competed for control of the investable resources of the nation were the party cadres of the central government on one hand, and those of five tiers of "local" government, ranging from the provincial and city governments to the township and village administrations, on the other. The latter acquired command over investable resources, and the authority to determine where they would be invested, when a host of administrative reforms between 1981 and 1983 rolled back central planning, and devolved the authority to collect taxes, take loans from the banking system, and plan investment upon the local governments. The cadres who manned them took little time to find out that the power this gave them commanded a "price" in the market.

In India the two strata consist of two classes of entrepreneurs. The first, dubbed the "large industrial houses," were already in place at the time of independence. The second, dubbed "small and medium industry" came into being in the era of planned development. The first stratum was a product of the open economy that had existed during British rule, and persisted, with some attenuation, for the first ten years after India became independent in 1947. The large industrial houses were therefore, with rare exceptions, a highly efficient lot, for they had survived and grown in the teeth of competition from British products on which very little duty was ever imposed. The second stratum of investors surfaced suddenly, about a decade after independence, to fill the market space that was created when the Indian government, facing a foreign exchange crisis, suddenly banned consumer goods imports to conserve foreign exchange.

The competition between the two strata had diametrically opposite effects on the two economies. In India it choked investment in industry and therefore slowed economic growth to a crawl. In China it led to more and more investment, with virtually no checks and few guidelines on where it should go. Therefore, while the Indian state had to struggle for four decades with the familiar problem of how to increase the pace of growth, China became the first country in the world in which the state had to struggle to bring the rate of investment and, consequently, the rate of GDP growth *down*. These diametrically opposite outcomes can be traced to the very different starting points of the two countries' respective voyages to capitalism.

Politics and economics of intermediate regimes

Why should economic development within the framework of a market economy have set off such an acute and long-drawn-out struggle between two elements of the same class—the bourgeoisie—in India, and between two strata of the Communist Party itself in China? Second, why should two such utterly different economies have experienced so similar a struggle? And last, but most importantly, why did the conflict between two groups of investors result in explosive growth in China and near-stagnation in India? An attempt to answer these questions takes us to one of the core issues of political economy, the nature of class formation in early capitalist societies.

Conventional growth theory makes a token bow toward this issue when it acknowledges that all classes in a society do not benefit equally from development. The empirical work of Simon Kuznets and others has shown that income differentials increase during the early stages of industrial development, but tend to narrow when capitalism matures, incomes rise, and a middle class comes into being.

Exactly the same thing had happened in Europe during the previous phase of capitalism's expansion in the seventeenth and eighteenth centuries, when Amsterdam had been its hub.[59] But conventional analysis did not ask the next, all-important question: Why did income differentials narrow when capitalism matured? Did this happen automatically, or did it have to be brought about by conscious human— i.e., political—action? Still less did it ask the corollary to this question: If political action was needed, and people had to band together to take it, did their exercise of power affect the course of economic development, and if so, how?

It was left to Marx and Engels to raise these questions. Marx pointed out that while social classes, divided by conflicts of interest, had existed in all earlier societies, capitalism had the negative virtue of overwhelming all previous divisions and replacing them with a single central line of conflict, drawn between those who owned property, the bourgeoisie, and those who did not, the proletariat:

> The history of all hitherto existing society is the history of class struggles. . . . In the earlier epochs of history, we find almost everywhere a complicated arrangement of society into various orders, a manifold gradation of social rank. . . . Our epoch, the epoch of the bourgeoisie, possesses, however, this distinct feature: it has simplified class antagonisms. Society as a whole is more and more splitting up into two great hostile camps, into two great classes directly facing each other—bourgeoisie and proletariat.

Marx did see that in the early stages of the development of industrial capitalism there would be conflicts within the bourgeoisie:

> The bourgeoisie finds itself involved in a constant battle. At first with the aristocracy; later on, with those portions of the bourgeoisie

itself whose interests have become antagonistic to the progress of industry; at all times with the bourgeoisie of foreign countries.

He also saw that the main opposition would come from small proprietors of all kinds:

> The lower middle class, the small manufacturer, the shopkeeper, the artisan, the peasant, all these fight against the bourgeoisie, to save from extinction their existence as fractions of the middle class. They are therefore not revolutionary, but conservative. Nay more, they are reactionary, for they try to roll back the wheel of history.

But he was convinced that this opposition would be swept away by the relentless march of technology and the constantly increasing scale of production:

> The lower strata of the middle class . . . [will] sink gradually into the proletariat, partly because their diminutive capital does not suffice for the scale on which Modern Industry is carried on, and is swamped in the competition with the large capitalists.[60]

What neither he nor Engels could foresee was the exact form that the struggle of the "lower strata" to survive would take, or how successful they would be. Nor could they foresee that conditions could arise in which the "lower strata" might achieve dominance and indeed succeed in "holding back the wheel of history" for a considerable length of time.

The intermediate regime in market economies

This possibility was raised by a Polish economist, Michal Kalecki, in 1964. Kalecki was trying to understand class formation in countries that were in transition to mature capitalism, in which the majority of income earners were not wage earners but rather self-employed. In these circumstances small farmers and the self-employed could constitute an "intermediate class" that could in certain circumstances form an "intermediate regime."[61] The conditions in which this could happen were

1. if at the time of achieving independence the lower middle class was very numerous, while big business was predominantly foreign-controlled, with rather minimal participation of native capitalists;
2. if state intervention in the economy was all-pervasive, thereby restricting the space in which indigenous big business could expand;
3. if the government had access to foreign capital from socialist countries;
4. if there had been land reforms but these had remained incomplete, resulting in the transfer of land not to the actual cultivator but to an intermediate stratum of rentiers.

The first condition was in many ways crucial because it helped the intermediate class to mobilize nationalist sentiment against big business in general. The second and third followed from this first. In the absence of active foreign participation the task of developing infrastrusture falls necessarily upon the state, which cannot carry it out without access to substantial foreign exchange to finance imports.

Kalecki went on to describe the intermediate class as being composed of self-employed groups stretching from farmers to traders, artisans, and manufacturers, in alliance with the state bureaucracy. But his definition of the class remained incomplete—he was unable to define what they had in common, and therefore what put them in opposition to the "large" bourgeoisie. He simply asserted that "representatives of the lower middle rise in a way naturally to power."[62]

That failure has been addressed to varying degrees by several later writers.[63] The common interest that binds all these disparate groups into an "intermediate class" is the need to perpetuate an "economy of shortages" from which they can draw "supernormal" profits on goods in short supply, black market margins on goods under price control, and bribes and kickbacks for the grant of licenses and permits.

But what begins as a means of self-protection rapidly turns into a means of capital accumulation. For shortages breed inflation, and inflation divides society into "price-makers" and "price-takers," swelling the income of the first and eroding that of the second. All of the members of the intermediate class fall into the former category, for the single feature that they all share is being able to adjust their nominal prices and fees (and therefore incomes) to counteract the rise in prices (civil servants who accept bribes and kickbacks for granting permissions become members of this class). By safeguarding their own real incomes, and even increasing them, the members of this class are able to pass on the entire burden of the shortages that underlie inflation onto the shoulders of the "price-takers." Inflation therefore defines and constantly sharpens the central line of conflict between the gainers and the losers in an intermediate regime.

The identification of this central line makes it possible to define the intermediate class more precisely than was done either by Kalecki or by writers after him. For example, not all "big" manufacturers fall outside the pale of the intermediate class.[64] The dividing line runs not necessarily between big and small, but between closely held and widely held firms. The former are run by owner–manufacturers who profit directly from the higher profits accruing to their firms as a result of shortages, while the latter are run by salaried professional managers who gain only indirectly, through salary hikes and bonuses. Professionally managed enterprises therefore view profit itself differently from owner-managed ones. Faced with a sudden shortage of their product in the market, they are more likely to try and increase their share of the market by keeping prices down and increasing output. Owner-managed firms are somewhat more likely to raise prices and cash in the windfall conferred upon them by the shortage.

Similarly, the vast majority of landowning farmers in any economy are likely to fall outside the intermediate class despite being self-employed landowners. The dividing line here runs between farmers who have large enough holdings and investments in their land to be "net sellers-out" of foodgrains or cash crops, and who therefore benefit inordinately when there are shortages, and the majority who own so little, or such poor, land that they not only need to eat what they produce but need to seek employment on other people's land and in nonagricultural enterprises to meet the balance of their needs. The dividing line among state employees is ethics—some take bribes and are "price-makers," but there are also a large number of honest civil servants who would fall among the price-takers, whose real incomes fall in times of inflation.

The intermediate regime in China

What Kalecki found to be true of Indonesia and Egypt, and Raj, Jha, and others of India, is also true, albeit in a very different way, of China. Chinese party cadres were salary earners so long as the holding of private property was banned. Corruption was not entirely absent in the country. Enterprise managers, local party secretaries, and trade union leaders frequently connived with each other to withhold a part of the surpluses of an enterprise and use it to increase their own and their workers' perquisites. Surpluses earned on above-plan output were often used to set up subsidiary enterprises, and nepotism flourished in the selection of workers and managers to run them. But this did not change the fundamental nature of the cadres, whose main road to advancement was the fulfillment of the tasks assigned to them by the party, not the accumulation of wealth.

That changed when the ban on holding private property was lifted. Party cadres began to convert their control over property into ownership of property. They thus became the bourgeoisie in the making. The conflict between the local cadres of the Communist Party and the central cadres for control over the deployment of savings therefore began to mirror, ever more closely, the conflict between the big bourgeoisie and the intermediate class in traditional market economies.

But the resemblance stops there, for in China it led to explosive, albeit uncontrolled growth, while in India it strangled growth. The starkly different outcomes arose from the presence of entrepreneurial risk in India and its absence in China. In India the intermediate class was investing its own money. It therefore sought political influence in order to pass legislation that would check the uncontrolled growth of professionally managed, and therefore, as a rule, more efficient, firms, perpetuate an economy of shortages, and thus create the space in the market for the immediate class to survive.

In China, by contrast, the cadres-turned-investors did not invest their own money, but that of the public and the state. If an enterprise failed it was the public that lost its savings, and it did so in ways it could not easily identify. But by the same token if it made profits these did not accrue directly to the cadres. So the easiest way for them to reward themselves was by increasing the perquisites of their office and by employing relatives to further augment their family incomes. But another route, which soon proved irresistible, was to take commissions and kickbacks, enter into covert partnerships with private investors, and use their positions to buy scarce goods at controlled prices and sell them in the open market at much higher ones. The amount they accumulated depended directly upon the number of investment projects they were able to push through. What undermined the hold of the immediate class was its essentially parasitical nature. The perpetuation of shortages entailed the sacrifice of growth. Thus, for the intermediate class to fatten the economy had to sicken to the point of death. This is a very different conclusion from the one that Kalecki arrived at after his study of Indonesia. Kalecki believed that an intermediate regime could stay in power for a long time if it was able to ensure continued growth. He did not see that the conditions it had to create in order to consolidate its power precluded stable long-term growth. As Barbara Harriss-White put it, "The intermediate classes are enabled to go on feeding off the conditions created by scarcity . . . but in constantly aggravating scarcity they bring about an eventual crisis in the economy. Scarcity becomes a luxury no one else can finally afford."[65]

It certainly became a luxury that no democratically elected government could afford. The crisis of scarcity manifested itself in not one but a succession of foreign exchange crises. While the intermediate class was able to use an economic crisis in 1965–'66 to increase its stranglehold on the economy via tighter exchange controls that would prevent larger companies, or retailers, from importing, its claim that tighter exchange controls were needed to promote self-reliance was destroyed when another crisis occurred only eight years later and yet another only seven years after that. These crises progressively undermined the legitimacy of such controls until, from the late seventies onward, the primary concern of the leaders of successive governments became how far they could push liberalization without provoking the wrath of the leftists (who remained the sole champions of India's petty bourgeoisie), and being accused of betraying Nehruvianism and socialism and selling the nation out to the capitalists. These were populist slogans that would force leaders on the defensive because they could not give a sufficiently convincing reply.[66]

Successive governments therefore resorted to setting up expert committees to examine these highly emotive economic reforms, in order to take shelter behind their dispassionate recommendations. For instance, the progressive liberalization of imports throughout the eighties was based upon the recommendations of a committee that the government appointed in 1978 under a highly respected civil servant, P. C. Alexander. Another committee appointed to study the constraints on exports in the early eighties, under a highly respected technocrat from the public sector, D. V. Kapur, recommended a drastic reduction of protection and a devaluation of the rupee on the grounds that these had made the profit margin on domestic sales twice, and on some products up to four times, as high as that on exports. But in the end these reforms sufficed to give the continuously ailing economy only a small additional lease of life. This piecemeal reform continued until a combination of accelerated growth after 1985 and the foreign exchange crisis caused by Iraq's invasion of Kuwait finally forced the government to dismantle the dirigiste economy. Even then, it was able to do so only in stages. It was not till 2002 that enough of the command economy had been dismantled to end the bias toward the creation of shortages that the intermediate regime had been able to create.

Rent-seeking behavior by the intermediate class did not, in the end, threaten the stability of the state. By cloaking itself in the rhetoric of socialism, egalitarianism, and nationalism, and securing the blessings of the left, which anointed it as the "national" as distinct from the "comprador" bourgeoisie, the intermediate class was able to acquire a high degree of political legitimacy. In the sixties and early seventies, most Indians believed the excuses that were trotted out by the left to justify the controls upon which the class thrived. When Indira Gandhi coined the slogan "*Garibi Hatao*"— Quit Poverty—before the parliamentary elections in 1971, she won a landslide victory and buried her rivals, the "old" Congress Party, in the dust. With that she finally broke the half-century-old connection between the Congress Party and the indigenous entrepreneurial class, now described collectively as the "large industrial houses," that had come up under British rule. By the time the public began to see through the charade, the rulers were themselves looking for a way to end the regime of controls. The rent-seekers therefore corrupted the Indian state, but did not become the state.

In China, by contrast, the cadre-capitalists were members of the Communist Party and therefore a part of the state. Thus, every corrupt, predatory action that came to light threatened the stability of the state. The outbreak of corruption that occurred during the first decade of reform in the 1980s did not provoke a severe reaction from the public, partly because the corruption itself was on a relatively small scale compared to what it became in the 1990s and the 2000s, but mostly because initially nearly everyone in the country was benefiting hugely from the transition to a market economy. Between 1978 and 1984 most of the improvement in living standards took place in the countryside, where the benefits of reform were widespread. There was a free market for food. Peasants were therefore no longer chained to their communes by their ration cards, and became free to move to towns in search of work, and to take up nonagricultural employment. If development can be measured in the widening of options, this was a huge increase in well-being. There were, as yet, very few losers.

This began to change after reforms spread to industry and measures like the lifting of price controls began to cut deeply into the incomes of the still almost entirely salary-earning urban population. The student unrest in 1986 and 1988 was precipitated by a combination of rising prices and the sudden appearance of wealth in the hands of party cadres. This culminated in the Tiananmen uprising. The renewed explosion of growth from 1991 again allayed discontent, but the five-year-long recession that followed, from 1997 to 2001, stoked it again. The number of incidents of mass protest rose tenfold, from 8,700 in 1993 to 87,000 in 2005. With China in another downturn in 2008, the number of losers will once again multiply.

China

5 CHINA: THE MANAGEMENT OF DISORDER

UNTIL VERY RECENTLY there was a near-universal consensus that China owed its phenomenal success to a cautious but determined bid to turn itself into a market economy, guided by a singularly focused and pragmatic central party leadership in Beijing.[67] The reformers began in 1978 by introducing the household responsibility system, which privatized agriculture in all but name, then gradually reduced centralized planning and price controls, removing these first from nonessentials and then, in the nineties, from most essential goods as well. They then turned their attention to reforming the taxation system, freeing the banks from party control, and creating a regulatory and legal framework for private enterprise, a task that is still far from complete.

A succession of reports by the World Bank have reinforced this view. China, the Bank has steadfastly maintained, has succeeded in making a gradual change from a highly centralized command economy to a market-guided one because the control of Beijing over the process never slackened over the entire two-decade period during which the change was made. Beijing, the Bank observed, introduced reforms incrementally, and pragmatically, sector by sector, changing one policy parameter at a time in each sector. It further hedged its bets by allowing some of the advanced provinces to experiment with new ideas and systems first. If these were successful, other provinces copied them and Beijing eventually endorsed them on a national level.[68] China did not make the mistake, therefore, that Russia made, of believing the American liberal dogma that a market economy could be created overnight by simply dismantling controls.

Most students of China's transformation have assumed that the central government's eventual goal is to wind up all but a handful of state-owned enterprises in order to complete its conversion into a market economy. This belief has been nurtured by the statements and actions of China's leaders throughout the nineties. In 1992 Deng Xiaoping spelled out his goal as the creation of "a socialist market economy with Chinese characteristics." In the decade that followed, President Jiang Zemin turned China into what could be called "a socialist market economy with capitalist characteristics." He formalized this conversion in 1999 in a groundbreaking speech on the "Three Represents" that opened membership of the Communist Party to private businessmen. Privatization began hesitantly in the early nineties but accelerated rapidly in the middle of the decade. It attained a breakneck pace after Jiang Zemin and Premier Zhu Rongji announced a three-year "restructuring" program in 1998. This privatization, it is widely believed abroad, is releasing the entrepreneurial energy that is propelling China's growth ever upward.

Nothing could be further from the truth. China owes its prodigious growth not to Beijing's steely and farsighted control over the development process but its progressive loss of control over it. And the entrepreneurial energy that is driving its growth springs not from privatization, whether in letter or spirit, but its exact opposite—from state enterprise run amok. Both are direct results of the struggle for control over investable resources between the central and local levels of government that erupted in the eighties and continues today. The explosion of investment that occurred between

1980 and 1988, and again between 1991 and 1995, was not a product of central planning but of its exact opposite, a lack of planning in an economy with no market-generated control on investment. It was therefore the product of a particular form of chaos—born of exuberance and inexperience—that is associated with the earliest beginnings of industrial capitalism in Europe. That too had been a time when every market was new; when competition was fierce, the risks of investment were enormous, but the fortunes to be made staggering. It was a time when capital markets were in their infancy; when banking was little more than an extension of money lending; when the signals emanating from them were weak and confusing, and when investors and financiers lacked the experience to decipher them. It was therefore a time of huge, uncontrolled surges in investment followed by deep recessions. It was also a time when unfathomable wealth coexisted with unspeakable poverty.[69]

Despite the very different starting point from which China embarked on the road to capitalism, several of these features can be found in its development. Till the end of the nineties China had very little enterprise that could truly be called private in the Western sense of the term. The huge spurt in investment that took place after 1984 occurred almost entirely under state auspices. Township and county administrations did it by setting up rural and urban collectives, and smaller state-owned enterprises. Provincial and city governments set up new SOEs, as well as a variety of trust and holding companies that in turn set up enterprises owned by them. The common feature of both was the absence of true privatization, because that would have meant the loss of control over the enterprises and their funds by the concerned cadres. In all these cases, therefore, the ultimate owner was the state. The expansion was made fatally easy by the continued state monopoly of the banking system, and the subordination of the local managers of the People's Bank of China and the four state-owned commercial banks to the local party committee.[70] The Bank managers were in no position therefore to refuse the demand for loans made by the latter or by its all-powerful party secretary.

The explosion of investment that began in 1979–80 occurred under the auspices of local governments. Between 1978 and 1995, while the central government was dismantling the command economy, and reducing the number of state-owned enterprises by merging them with others or turning them into shareholding companies, the provincial, city, and township governments were *adding* pell-mell to the number of state-owned enterprises. In 1978 there were 83,700 state-owned industrial enterprises in the country, employing 31.39 million workers. By 1996, on the eve of the great privatization drive, the number had grown to 113,800 industrial SOEs employing 42.77 million workers.[71] In 1996, after eighteen years of reform, there were thirty thousand *more* state-owned industrial enterprises than in 1978. These employed nearly one and a half times as many workers as the state sector had employed at the beginning.

The number of "non-state" industrial enterprises, most of which were promoted by the townships, and by the existing SOEs as subsidiary ventures, grew from 244,700 to 7.87 *million.*[72] The whirlwind growth of China's "non-state" sector has been has been praised by scholars in the West and international agencies as an intermediate step in the shift from a centrally planned, state-owned economy to a market-driven, privately owned economy. Indeed, in an even more loose but increasingly frequent use of the term, the "non-state" sector has been equated with the private sector, and the creation of enterprises that do not enjoy the legislated safety net of the Communist era, as "privatization." This description is profoundly misleading and deliberately slurs over the moral and political issues that this type of growth has raised within China itself.

Was the decentralization planned or did Beijing lose control?

Minxin Pei attributes the investment spree by the local governments to Beijing's premeditated decision to loosen the control it had previously exercised over adoption of "a unique form of fiscal decentralization."[73] This made local governments responsible for collecting taxes from the enterprises in their jurisdiction. The tax contracting system that developed between 1980 and 1983 allowed the local governments to tax the enterprises not only on their own account, but on behalf of the central government as well. Since the local governments and the enterprises shared a common desire to retain as much of the surpluses generated by the latter for themselves, they were able to find a dozen ways of minimizing the amount that they had to hand over to Beijing. As the economy opened up, party cadres, township, city and provincial administrators, and enterprise managers all became entrepreneurs. Deng Xiaoping's "retirement" to Shanghai during the conservative backlash that followed the Tiananmen crisis, his southern tour, and his endorsement of the "socialist market economy" in 1992 took all remaining restraints off local administrations and party cadres who had been straining at the leash to run away with investment.

The monolithic and hierarchical structure of the Communist Party made this very easy. All local bank managers were members of the party and subordinate to the secretary of the local party committee. The latter had only to order the managers to provide the loans for his projects in order to be instantly obeyed. The local cadres therefore became a unique type of entrepreneur—they had unlimited funds at their disposal, but had to bear virtually no risk from the funds' deployment. The result was a huge burst of investment, first in the eighties and then from 1991 till 1995. On both occasions most of the new enterprises were created at various levels of local government. By the time it was over, there was massive industrial duplication and severe excess capacity in 80 percent of the products of Chinese industry. An estimated 70 percent of the office and residential space created during the boom years also failed to find any buyers, despite several reductions in prices and rents in 1997 and 1998.[74]

But why did the central government hand over so much power to the local authorities? A number of authors have suggested that the central government did not cede powers voluntarily, but that power was wrested from them by the local governments. What is more, this happened not after the reforms formally began in 1979 but somewhat earlier, at the tail end of the Cultural Revolution. The local cadres began to disobey central diktats in order to cope with pressing local problems that Beijing was either unaware of or unable to address. But behind the local cadres' readiness to "interpret" the directives from the center lay a decline of faith in the central government's sagacity and respect for its authority. The reforms, therefore, emerged not from the center's strength but from its growing weakness in relation to the local cadres.[75]

Dali Yang, who is currently professor in the Department of Political Sciences and Director of the Center for East Asian studies at the University of Chicago, traced the economic assertiveness of peasants and rural cadres even further back, to the catastrophic failure of the Great Leap Forward campaign in the late 1950s. The famine and deaths led to a return to family farming in some areas in the early sixties. But this was nipped in the bud by a fresh bout of radicalism during the Cultural Revolution and a spate of new hardships on the peasants. This left both peasants and local officials disillusioned with and distrustful of central directives. When the political climate changed after Mao's death, peasants and local cadres took the lead in restructuring their economic relations with the state. This created a groundswell that compelled the central leadership to decollectivize agriculture in the early 1980s.

According to Lynn T. White, professor of politics and international affairs at Princeton University, the move toward decentralization of industry started in the early 1970s, when the violence of the Cultural Revolution had abated. Local networks—coalitions of local officials and managers—began to promote the development of rural industry. This proved a blessing in disguise because it relieved local shortages that were a regular byproduct of the miscalculations of centralized planning. The center therefore tolerated it and may even have tacitly encouraged it. But over time rural industry undermined the rationale for centralized planning by showing that decentralized production could meet changing consumption needs much better than production dictated by the cumbersome process of centralized planning. It also initiated the competition for resources and control of output between the central and local cadres in government. The diversion of an increasing share of economic activity from central to local control began to erode the revenues and increase the financial burdens on the central government, forcing central leaders to accept and attempt to streamline the changes that had already begun and were gathering momentum during the mid- to late 1970s.

The earliest reforms—that is, decollectivization, commercialization, and the rise of a private economy in agriculture—were all initiated by peasants rather than the state. Motivated by the desire to escape their economic plight, they went beyond the limits set by central leaders to change the commune system. But although the rural cadres took the initiative, they were able to continue experimenting with reforms because they had, or soon acquired, the tacit consent of the state. The economic alternatives they pursued, such as family farming, led to such sharp increases in output that they also had the unforeseen effect of meeting the grain delivery quotas and other policy imperatives of the state better than the communes had done before. As a consequence, central leaders gave a somewhat grudging recognition to what peasants innovated.[76]

Beijing, therefore, lost a good deal of its hegemony over the local cadres as a reaction to the succession of ill-conceived experiments that Mao launched as he faced the progressive failure of central planning to meet the needs and aspirations of the people. The hardships these inflicted on the people, and the waste of lives that ensued, sapped people's unquestioning faith in the central leaders. This emboldened peasants and local cadres to experiment with better ways of meeting their needs and obligations. But even then, the local cadres might not have mustered the courage to break the rules had provinces like Anhui and Szechuan, later hailed as "pioneer provinces" in agricultural reform, not been hit by a succession of natural disasters in 1977–'79 that forced their village cadres to choose between innovation and famine.[77]

Another reform that also occurred in spite of rather than because of directives from Beijing was the relaxation of controls on migration by villagers to the towns. This too was initiated by local authorities who set up township industries well before 1978. It too was initially opposed by the central leadership, who lifted the ban on rural-urban migration only in 1988, after the migrant workers had already become an indispensable part of the booming industrial economy.[78]

The desire to make a break with the policies of the past depended not only on the assertiveness of local cadres; it was also strong in party cadres at higher levels, because many of them had suffered during the Cultural Revolution. It was also supported by hundreds of thousands of young people who had been sent into the countryside and seen the miserable conditions in which the peasants lived. Inducted into the universities in large numbers in the late 1970s upon their return from the countryside, these youth graduated imbued with a desire for change. Thus when the central government allowed enterprises to retain their post-tax surpluses, decentralized the fiscal system, and legitimized the family farming system, thereby formalizing the dissolution of the communes, it took the lid off a pressure cooker that had been coming to a boil for some time.

The race to monopolize investment

The formal devolution to the local governments of the power to tax, raise loans, and invest set off a race between provinces—and, within them, between prefectures, counties, and townships—to outdo each other in finding new ways of meeting and exceeding targets.[79] Greater autonomy also increased local governments' temptation to use their control of the supply of labor, land, and key raw materials to make money, personally, out of their deployment. These motives, personal and institutional, fused to create a powerful urge in the local and provincial administrations to appropriate the development and liberalization agenda. This touched off an unacknowledged struggle between the central and local cadres to control the deployment of the productive resources of the state—land, capital, and labor. Since the mid-eighties power has swung back and forth between them like a seesaw—into the hands of local government in the eighties, wrested back savagely after Tiananmen in 1989 and 1990, back to the provinces and local governments in 1991, seized again by Beijing through its 1994 tax reforms and yet again by the 1998 centralization of control over bank credit. Somewhat inexplicably, it has been lost once more to the local and provincial authorities since 2002.

The local cadres used four instruments in their battle to control investment. These were their control over provincial markets, over taxation, and over bank credit through the subservience of local bank officials to the secretary of the party committee; and their power to provide the land needed for new industrial ventures to sprout upon.

The struggle to control markets

The struggle to control markets did not surface till the first head-long rush of development began to subside. That happened in 1995. Burdened with excess capacity, and squeezed by recession after 1995, the provincial administrations resorted to the only other means at hand to keep their enterprises running profitably. This was to keep rival products made in other provinces out of their provincial markets. Several scholars believe that local protectionism did not exist before 1978.[80] If this is indeed so, then its rapid rise during the reform era provides additional proof that that reform drastically weakened the authority of Beijing over the provincial governments.

Local protectionism took the form of a variety of administrative and fiscal barriers to trade with other provinces. Some of these were legal; others were not. These included quantitative restrictions; a variety of regulatory hurdles, such as health and trademark inspections; and various "fees" that enterprises wanting to "export" their products to another province had to pay, which were nothing but a novel form of import duty. In 1998 the fees levied by various provinces on automobile sales amounted to 160 billion yuan, of which half was estimated to be illegal, in a year when the total net profit of the automobile industry was only four billion yuan. In 2001 eighteen provinces had passed laws that either banned or imposed a ceiling on the sale of liquor made in other provinces. A survey of 3,539 enterprise managers all over the country, by the Development Research Center of the central government in 2002, showed that all provinces practiced local protectionism, and that it was as prevalent in the less developed central provinces as in the industrially advanced coastal provinces.[81]

Indirect but compelling evidence of this comes from the fact that between 1985 and 1992 China's exports grew by 17 percent,

its imports grew by 10 percent a year, and its annual domestic retail sales grew by 9 percent, yet its interprovince trade grew by
only 4.2 percent a year.[82] The entire economy was therefore turning outward, with the coastal provinces leading the way. And as
their income and wealth became less and less dependent upon their
economic ties with the rest of the country, their ability to ignore
or deflect Beijing's directives, and set up competing economic systems, increased.

The struggle to control tax revenues

Nothing reveals the competition between the central government
and the local administrations in China as unequivocally as the tug-
of-war the two have waged to capture the financial resources of
the state. The struggle began soon after Beijing adopted a series
of tax reforms between 1980 and 1983, as it began the transition
to a market-guided economy. The purpose of the reforms was to
stimulate entrepreneurship in the state-owned enterprises by shifting from a soviet style to a modern taxation system that left control
of post-tax profits in the hands of those who earned them. Under
the new system the enterprises had to pay a tax on their operating
surpluses that was fixed by the center but collected by the city and
provincial governments. The latter then bargained with the center
to determine how much of the tax they would pass on to it.

This "fiscal contracting" system created a powerful incentive for
the enterprises to conceal as much as possible of their surpluses
from the city and provincial authorities, and for the latter to do the
same with respect to the central government. This had two adverse
effects on central revenues. It reduced the buoyancy of tax revenues in response to growth and reduced the central government's
share of the revenues collected by it and the local governments in
the provinces. Whereas a 1 percent increase in output used to yield

a 0.78 percent increase in revenues before 1978, by 1985 the yield had declined to 0.53 percent.[83] This resulted in a steep decline in central revenues, from 35 percent of GDP in 1978 to 10.7 percent of GDP in 1993, and severely curtailed its capacity to take over the welfare obligations of the state-owned enterprises and give them a chance to compete successfully against the newly set up "non-state" sector in the increasingly competitive market for products. In 1990, central expenditures were running 10 percent ahead of revenue. This rose to 23 percent on average between 1995 and 2000. In 2000, the fiscal deficit amounted to 4.55 percent of the GDP. A growing part was being used to finance current consumption.[84]

As the ratio of central taxes to GDP declined, there was a parallel accumulation of funds in the hands of the enterprises and the provincial and city authorities amounting, according to one IMF estimate, to 14.5 percent of the GDP in 1992.[85] The overall effect of the fiscal contracting system was not so much to reduce total government revenue as to divert a large part of it from the central government to the provincial authorities. In 1985, the revenue and expenditure of both the central and the local governments were more or less balanced. But by 1993 the center's share of total revenues had fallen from 38.4 percent to a mere 22 percent, while that of the provinces and municipalities had increased from 61.6 percent to 78 percent. The central government plunged into deficit.

In 1994 the central government passed a tax reform law that replaced fiscal contracting with a "tax sharing" system that sharply wrested control of finances back from the local authorities. Its purpose was to raise the share of central revenues in the total to 60 percent, a goal that it came close to achieving as its share of tax revenues rose to 55.7 percent in 1994, the first year after the reform,[86] and as the local authorities' share of revenues fell from 78 percent to 44.3 percent. However, while the center reduced the share of the provinces' tax it did not reduce their expenditure commitments. As a result in 1994 while Beijing had a revenue surplus amounting to 25.4 percent of total tax revenues, the provinces went into deficit to the same extent. This gap was never filled. After a small recovery to 50.5 percent in 1998, another round of tax reforms caused the share of provincial revenues to fall back again to 45.1 percent in 2004. Their expenditure commitments, however, rose to 72.3 percent. So the budgetary gap increased once more to 27.3 percent in 2004, roughly two percent higher than after the tax reforms of 1994.

Table 5.1

Central and Local Shares of Revenue and Expenditure, 1985–2004

YEAR CENTRAL LOCAL				
	Revenue	Expenditure	Revenue	Expenditure
1985	38.4%	39.7%	61.6%	60.3%
1993	22%	28.3%	78%	71.7%
1994	55.7%	30.3%	44.3%	69.7%
1998	49.5%	28.9%	50.5%	71.1%
2004	54.9%	27.7%	45.1%	72.3%

Source: Wang Qingyi, China Security: Energy Conservation as Security (Washington DC: World Security Institute, China Program, 2006).

The expenditure gap that opened was to be filled by transfers of money from the central government and by cuts in the local governments' administrative and other expenditures. The cuts never occurred, so although the "tax transfers" met 17 percent of the local authorities' expenses in 1994, they did not suffice to close the gap between expenditure and revenue. The mismatch of revenues and expenditure was particularly stark at the county and township levels, where the local authorities were expected to meet both health and education expenses. That the central government's purpose was not to allocate resources better but to wrest back financial power from the provinces was apparent from the fact that while it reduced their revenue it actually increased their expenditure obligations, by making them financially responsible for the full nine years of schooling for children.

The struggle over savings

There was a similar struggle over access to bank lending. Until 1998, local authorities had taken advantage of the subordination of the officials of the state-owned commercial banks' local branches to the local party committee to virtually dictate the loans the local authorites wanted. To access the loans, they had set up a large network of trusts and holding companies and quasi-banking institutions. In October 1997, the Central Committee of the Communist Party of China and the State Council of the People's Republic of China jointly issued a "notice concerning deepening financial reform, rectifying financial order, and preventing financial risk." With one stroke of the pen, local branches of the state banks and of the People's Bank of China were removed from the local party committees' jurisdiction and placed under the newly formed Central Finance Work Committee. The notice also closed down hundreds of locally controlled trust and investment companies and underground banks. But the struggle has continued: As the central government's failure to control the investment spree indulged in by the local authorities in 2003–'07 shows, the latter have found a variety of ways to get around Beijing's diktat.

Response of local government–squeeze the peasant, sell his land

The local authorities initially responded to the central government's actions by increasing tax levies and extracting a number of "fees" and "contributions" from local enterprises and from the peasants. The center put a stop to this, however, in 1998 by implementing another reform, which came to be dubbed the "tax-for-fees policy." But this made the townships and counties bear down harder on the peasants. The total extrabudgetary revenues collected at subnational levels jumped from 53.2 billion yuan in 1982 to 315.5 billion yuan in 1999.[87]

The township and county authorities also sought to bridge the gap by going into debt. In all, they incurred five types of debt. They borrowed directly from the ministry of finance, from the Central Bank, the People's Bank of China, from international institutions, and from foreign investors; they ran up arrears of payment to their staff and deferred payment for the goods they bought, such as grain from the peasants; they borrowed through local financial institutions that they controlled to meet their current expenditure on public services and infrastructure; they floated informal credit institutions called rural credit foundations and borrowed from them; and they floated new enterprises with loans that they guaranteed, although the budget law expressly forbade them from doing so.[88] After 1998, their plight became so serious that that a study carried out in 2004 by two Chinese scholars, Tian Fa and Chenying Zhou, showed that the combined debt of the county, township, and village administrations in 2003 had reached one trillion yuan, or 8.3 percent of the GDP.[89]

But the local governments' most spectacular, and most socially damaging, foray was into the sale and commercialization of land. When, following the success of the original four special economic zones, which were set up in Schenzen, Zhuhai, Shantou, and Xiamen, in the 1980s, the central government permitted the other provinces to set up similar zones, a land-grab frenzy developed in which provincial, city, and prefecture authorities all participated with abandon. Between 1988 and 1993 they set up six thousand such special economic and development zones,[90] covering a total of fifteen thousand square kilometers. This was 1,600 square kilometers more than the entire urban area of the country in 1993. Four-fifths of this land was arable land, taken away from the farmers by virtue of their lack of individual title to it. In Guangdong province, the land taken out of cultivation amounted to half of all the arable land in the province. In addition to this there were so-called enclosed zones—development zones that had been carved out by the township- and village-level administrations for setting up township and village enterprises. No one had any precise estimate of how much land these enclosed zones had swallowed.[91]

The enclosure movement, for that is indeed what it was, was very largely speculative. None of the concerned authorities knew for certain which enterprises intended to move there and from where. This was "blind development," and it met the expected fate. A majority of the development zones never took off, while the land remained enclosed and fallow for the next decade and a half, until in 2005, under President Hu Jintao, 4,755 of them were disbanded and the land returned to the communes. This mounted to 70.1 percent of all the development zones that had been set up till then.

2001–2008: investment again out of control

The prolonged boom from 2001 till 2008 shows that the central government's efforts to regain control of the provincial and local governments has met with at best limited success. By 2001 the central government had tried just about every remedy it could think of to bring the economy under control. It had merged, closed, or transformed thousands of companies into limited liability companies to make them more market-oriented; laid off or transferred to the "non-state" sector forty million state employees; recaptured control of the banking system from local authorities; purged the banks of the bad debts; progressively introduced modern instruments of monetary control; allowed the rise of private banks; and brought foreign direct investment into the existing state and provincial banks to make their managers more commercially minded and accountable. These reforms had led to an improvement in the overall performance of the state sector and reduced losses in the banking system. But the reforms did not reach the core of the problem, which was the continuing divorce of power from responsibility in the state-owned sector—the power to take loans from the responsibility to pay them back. As a result, no sooner did the recession end, in 2001, than the Chinese economy began to repeat the mistakes of the early nineties all over again.

The recession/slowdown ended in 2001 and within a year China was powering forward again. But as had happened in 1992, within two short years of the turnaround history began to repeat itself. The Chinese economy began to overheat again. Bank lending grew at an accelerating rate toward the end of 2002, and during the first half of 2003 bank credit expanded by 23 percent, much too rapidly to be sustainable. Moreover, loans by state-owned banks increased more rapidly than those by other types of banks, accounting for 62 percent of the increase. Fixed investment had been growing strongly for several years under Zhu Rongji's program to counter the recession by promoting infrastructure construction, and it had already reached the extremely high level of 42 percent of gross domestic product (GDP) in 2002. Even so, fixed investment jumped further during the first half of 2003, increasing at a rate of 31 percent.

The cause, as in 1992–'94, was once again that the provincial administrations ran away with investment. During the first half of 2003, investment under the purview of local government increased 41.5 percent, while investment by the central government actually decreased by nearly 8 percent. By 2003, following an extremely rapid increase in investment, especially in the housing market, a bubble economy began to form once again.

In June 2003 the central government began to take yet more action to curb investment by the provincial and local authorities, issuing instructions to the banks to restrict lending to the real estate sector, and sharply curtailing permission to the local governments to set up new development zones, the prime vehicle for investment in real estate by the provincial and local governments. It also raised the deposit reserve ratio[92]—the minimum that the banks had to have on deposit with the Central Bank—from 6 to 7 percent, thereby reducing the amount that the banks could lend. Most important of all, it once again resorted to "informal window guidance"—i.e., physical control of the amount and direction of lending—to slow down the expansion of credit.[93] Initially these measures had little effect, for investment grew by 48 percent in the first quarter of 2004.[94] Only in the second and third quarters, when the government began to ration credit to the steel, cement, and other industries where it saw excess capacity developing, did the growth of investment slow down to between 20 and 30 percent. The growth of value added in industry also moderated from 14.2 percent in the fourth quarter of 2003 to 10.9 percent in the first nine months of 2004.[95]

But the slowdown did not last. Bank lending to industry and construction resumed the upward trend, forcing the People's Bank of China to raise the cash reserve ratio six times between June 2006 and April 2007, increasing from 7 to 10.5 percent. Yet total fixed investment, which had risen by 26 percent in 2005 over 2004, shot up by another 24 percent in 2006.[96]

Another increase was in the cards for 2007, because in January and February, bank credit grew by 37 percent over the same period of the previous year and at twice the average rate recorded in 2006.[97] Not surprisingly, in 2006 China's GDP grew by 10.7 percent, a full 2.7 percent more than the central government had planned for, and the highest growth that China had recorded in eleven years. Goldman Sachs predicted an even higher growth of 10.8 percent in 2007.[98]

The similarity between the boom that developed in 2003 and the boom of the early nineties is striking, but it does not stop with the rates of growth, investment, and bank credit. There was a similar buildup of unsold stocks across most of industry. In November 2006 the World Bank's Beijing office reported that unsold inventories had exceeded 15 percent of output in a quarter of the thirty-nine industrial sectors as early as the first half of 2004. In the automobile industry, 48 percent of production remained unsold in 2006.[99] In the first half of 2006, despite the curbs on lending for real estate projects that the central government had instituted, investment in such projects increased by 22 percent over the second half of 2005.[100] In 2006, despite every effort by Beijing to check investment in land and real estate, a "bubble" of unsold real estate had begun to develop once again. By 2008, well before China acknowledged that its economy was slowing down, real estate prices had begun to fall.

Chinese analysts persisted in regarding inflation as the prime danger arising from this runaway investment. "Investment in assets is excessive, and there is an oversupply of loans," a spokesman for China's National Bureau of Statistics, Zheng Jingping, said at a news conference. "In the long run, these will cause inflation. The government will be on guard for inflationary pressures."[101] Analysts for several international investment firms echoed this sentiment, but added that since China's inflation was still relatively moderate, especially in comparison to the early nineties, there was no immediate risk of a crash landing for the economy. Both groups remained oblivious to the real significance of the renewed hyperinvestment. This was an unambiguous demonstration of Beijing's loss of control. As in the early nineties, it was the provincial authorities that had run away with the bit between their teeth. And, as happened in the late 1990s, with the onset of recession in late 2008, it is Beijing, again, that is having to clean up the mess.

6 ENIGMAS EXPLAINED

SEEING CHINA'S GROWTH as a product of competition between the central and local party cadres to preempt resources for investment makes it possible to understand the two central paradoxes of the Chinese economy: How can an economy that grows so fast, and produces for export so cheaply, be so inefficient in its use of raw materials and energy? And why has an unprecedented alleviation of poverty not been able to prevent a sharp rise in social unrest? This chapter seeks to explain the first. The next chapter deals with the second.

The generally accepted explanation for China's wasteful use of inputs is that unlike most other mature and rapidly industrializing countries, its output comes not from a relatively small number of very large plants, but from a very large number of plants spread all over the country. The following table reveals the discrepancy and the impact it has had on China's industrial structure (see next page).

Even the five thousand cement plants in 2004 were an improvement over the situation that had existed earlier. According to the OECD, in 1996 there were eight thousand cement plants in China, as against 110 in the United States, fifty-one in Russia, fifty-eight in Brazil, and 106 in India.[102]

The inefficiency of China's industry arises from the smallness of individual plants and the obsolescence of their technology. There were, no doubt, a large number of obsolete and small

Table 6.1

**International Comparison of the Enterprise or Facility
in the Energy Intensive Industry (2004)**

CATEGORY	CHINA	FOREIGN
Coal Mines	28,000 with average annual output of 70,000 tons	9 in Germany, average annual output of 5.56 million tons
Refineries	56 with annual processing capacity of 4.19 million tons	6 in South Korea, annual processing capacity of 21.47 million tons
Blast Furnaces	263 with average annual steel production of 750,000 tons	29 in Japan, annual steel production of 2.83 million tons
Cement Factories	5,027 with average annual output of 190,000 tons	65 in Japan, average annual output of 1.14 million tons

Source: Wang Qingyi, China Security: Energy Conservation as Security (Washington DC: World Security Institute, China Program, 2006).

plants in China during the days of economic autarchy. But when the economy was liberalized, imports were freed, and foreign investment increased by leaps and bounds, competition should have forced the older plants to close down. That such large numbers of plants should continue to exist in every industry twenty-seven years after the economic reforms suggests we should look for another explanation. But the only other explanation is that the plants are relatively modern but are being forced to work at very low levels of capacity utilization. This will happen if there are too many competing plants, all trying to produce the same things. That is what the race to invest between the central and local cadres has brought about. China's prodigious consumption of raw materials and energy therefore reflects not inefficiencies in the production process, but a vast accumulation of very poorly used capital assets.

The waste is not occurring during the production process, but in the piling up of "dead" investment—not obsolete technology but the massive, and unnecessary, duplication of investment that has taken place after the winding down of centralized planning and devolution of investment power to the provinces in the 1980s.

Surveys of China's industrial structure have confirmed this duplication. In 1989, the industrial structure of twenty-two out of China's thirty-four provinces was 90 percent identical to that of China taken as a whole. In 1994, it was 90 percent identical in thirteen provinces and 80 percent identical in twenty-one. Seven years later, twenty-three out of thirty-four provinces manufactured washing machines, twenty-nine made television sets, and no fewer than twenty-seven assembled automobiles. In the mid-nineties, among the thirty-nine industrial sectors, the largest eight firms accounted for less than 10 percent of the market share in eighteen sectors.[103]

Every industry thus has a core of modern and efficient companies surrounded by a large penumbra of loss-making, inefficient enterprises. In 1999, fifteen out of 115 automobile companies accounted for 87 percent of the output of cars. The remainder produced anything from zero to a few thousand cars. In 2000, the steel industry had 1,570 independent companies, of which only four manufactured more than five million tons a year and another twenty-seven produced a million tons each. In 1997, the government announced a massive steel industry restructuring plan by which loss-making companies would be merged with profitable ones, to create four large enterprises that would produce 40 percent of the national output.[104] But as the comparison with Germany in the above table shows, by 2004 this had only partially resolved the problem of small size and obsolete technology.

Nor did things improve perceptibly in the late nineties. In 1999, in twenty-five major industrial product groups the largest eight firms together produced only 12.2 percent of the output. This was a marginal improvement over their 11.7 percent share in 1990. In nine product groups the share of the largest eight firms had actually declined. The negligible increase in consolidation of output shows how little the fate of these enterprises depended upon the dictates of the market.[105] For while the decision to establish these enterprises was taken by the local authorities in competition with Beijing, once they were up and running the local governments were as reluctant to close them down and take over the burden of compensating the laid-off workers as the central government.[106]

Waste and pollution

The rising raw materials intensity of China's growth has become a source of concern not only for international organizations and other outsiders, but for the Chinese central government. In August 2005, shortly after China formalized its eleventh five-year plan, Pan Yue, deputy environment minister, put the issue in stark terms in an interview in *Der Spiegel*: "We are using too many raw materials to sustain this growth," he said. "To produce goods worth [US] $10,000, for example, we need seven times more resources than Japan, nearly six times more than the US and, perhaps most embarrassing, nearly three times more than India."[107] He might have also added that China was using more than twice as much energy per dollar of GDP, measured in real consumption, as India.[108]

The eleventh plan set a target of bringing down the energy consumed per unit of incremental GDP by 20 percent—i.e., by 4 percent a year. The National Development and Reform Commission turned this into a set of concrete goals in a report published in August 2006. Central to it was a reduction of the consumption of coal by three hundred million metric tons a year, 13.5 percent of the energy consumed in 2005. But to do so, it warned, China would have to close down, or install antipollution equipment and otherwise modernize, the vast majority of its five hundred thousand small- and medium-sized coal-fired boilers. These consumed four hundred million tons of coal each year and were responsible for most of the country's serious atmospheric pollution. Up to seventy million tons could be saved by upgrading the technology and management of these boilers, the report said.

Just how difficult it would be to achieve the plan target was revealed when in the first half of 2006, the increase in energy consumption actually exceeded the growth of GDP by 0.8 percent.[109] The news caused a spate of emergency measures to be taken that, according to official estimates, ended by reducing energy consumption per unit of GDP by 1.79 percent in 2006 and 3.66 percent in 2007. Even if these figures are accurate, the reduction of energy intensity is lagging far behind target. As for closing down coal-fired boilers, the National Bureau of Statistics estimated that in two years the consumption of coal by these boilers had gone down by 32.6 million tons, or just over one-tenth of the targeted amount.[110]

Experts at the State Development and Reform Commission (SDRC) said it would take time for the energy saving measure the government was implementing to take effect, but other Chinese energy experts are not so sanguine, and do not believe the target can be met. On the contrary, Yu Cong, a researcher at the National Development and Reform Commission's Energy Research Institute, predicted that energy consumption in the mainland economy would rise to about 5.6 billion tons of standard coal equivalent in 2020, which is almost double a previous government projection. Ms. Yu put the blame on energy-hungry sectors, including iron and steel, building materials, and chemical and petrochemical industries, all of which had shown signs of rapid expansion in the first half of 2008.[111]

China's hunger for energy pales before its consumption of other key nonrenewable resources. The following table, which compares its consumption with that of the US and India, tells its own story.

Table 6.2

Share of China, India, and the US in World Consumption (in percent) of Key Raw Materials

METALS (2005)

	China	India	US
Aluminum	22.5	3.0	19.4
Copper	1.6	2.3	13.8
Lead	25.7	1.3	19.4
Nickel	15.2	0.9	9.5
Tin	33.3	2.2	12.1
Zinc	28.6	3.1	9.0
Iron ore	29.0	4.8	4.7
Steel production	31.5	3.5	8.5

ENERGY (2003)

	China	India	US
Coal	32.9	7.1	20.6
Oil	7.4	3.4	25.3
Energy (total)	12.6	3.6	23.4
Electricity generation	11.4	3.8	24.3

Source: Streifel 2006, cited in Winters and Yusuf, eds., Dancing with Giants.

With one-tenth of the world's GDP in purchasing power terms, China is consuming between one-third and one-sixth of the world's traded raw materials, including one-third of its coal, and one-eighth of its total energy. It consumes substantially more than the US of everything except crude oil, despite the fact that it has barely 15 percent of its GDP. And while this comparison is between dissimilar economies because the US is now largely a postindustrial society, the same cannot be said of the comparison with India.[112] With twice India's GDP, China consumes seven to twenty times as much of every important primary raw material that enters world trade.

Energy and the environment

Nowhere is the impending crisis more acute than in energy. According to the International Energy Agency, China and India are going to be responsible for most of the increase in energy consumption between now and 2030. The IEA's annual publication *World Energy Outlook 2007* predicts that if governments stick to existing scenarios for growth, the world's primary energy consumption will be more than 50 percent higher in 2030 than it was in 2006. China and India will account for 45 percent of this increase. This means that out of the fifteen billion tons of increase in the annual emission of carbon dioxide that will take place by 2030, China and India will account for almost seven billion tons, with China likely to contribute almost five billion tons of this increase.[113]

China's energy needs are rising sharply at precisely the moment when the world has begun to sense that it will soon run out of oil. China was a net exporter of oil till 1993. Since then, its imports have increased dramatically. In 2001 it imported sixty-six million tons. In 2004 the figure had risen to 101 million tons,[114] in 2005 to 143 million tons, and in 2006 to 158 million tons.[115] The International Energy Agency has estimated that based upon present trends, China could be importing ten million barrels a day or more than half a billion tons a year by 2030, five times what it imported in 2004.[116] By then, the world itself could be close to running out of oil.

High energy and raw materials use have combined to wreak havoc on China's environment. In September 2006 the National Bureau of Statistics and the State Environmental Protection Administration announced the first results of a long-term project to quantify the impact of growing pollution on the economy. It estimated that environmental damage cost the equivalent of 3 percent of economic output in 2004. It estimated that it would cost China about 1.08 trillion yuan ($136 billion) to clean up its deteriorating environment. This was equal to about 7 percent of gross domestic product.

"As China's GDP per capita reaches the range of $1,000–$3,000, society has experienced frequent conflicts and can no longer bear the social problems caused by environmental pollution," said the joint statement announcing the first results of the long-term project. "Although [China's] brand of high consumption, high pollution and high risk development has had a certain historical use, our economy has now hit a bottleneck for resource and energy use."[117]

"Soft landing," "slowdown," or "recession"–China's uneven growth

When decisions to produce and invest are made by hundreds of investors who do not know one another's plans and pay scant heed to signals from the market, huge surges of investment, and consequently the creation of large amounts of surplus capacity, cannot be avoided. It was therefore inevitable that the excesses of 1985–'88 and 1991–'95 would lead to the emergence of a generalized excess capacity, a mounting inventory of unsold goods, an increase in the losses of the state-owned enterprises, and eventually to a full-blown industrial recession. Signs of an economic downturn had begun to appear in 1988, but the imposition of ceilings on bank credit in 1988 in order to check soaring inflation, and the political crackdown after Tiananmen, make it difficult to separate the economic from the political causes of the short, sharp recession of 1989 and 1990.

However, there is no such ambiguity about the slowdown that occurred in 1995. China's National Bureau of Statistics estimated that in the first eleven months of 1996, the losses of the loss-making state-owned enterprises increased by 43.6 percent over the previous year to an estimated at $6.4 billion at the end of November.

The earnings of profitable SOEs were also down 49.3 percent to $5.9 billion. As recession strengthened its grip on the Chinese economy, the losses mounted. The Xinhua news agency reported that losses at the SOEs more than tripled in October and November, and a Beijing economist told the *South China Morning Post* that the December figures were likely to be even worse.[118] The following March, the *China Business Review* reported a World Bank estimate that 17 percent of China's GDP consisted of "unsaleable" SOE-manufactured goods.[119]

The strongest proof of recession came from the abrupt disappearance of inflation. For eighteen years between 1978 and 1995, China's National Bureau of Statistics had been accused, both within the country and abroad, of underestimating the rate of inflation. In its report *China 2020,* the World Bank constructed alternate indices of inflation for the economy as a whole, to better evaluate China's official claims of GDP. But all of a sudden, after rising by 11.6 percent per year between 1991 and 1996 by official estimates, consumer prices fell for 54 straight months beginning in 1997. In 2003, the consumer price index was still 1.6 percent below the 1997 figure of 102.8. Ex-factory prices and the investment deflator (average cost of new investment) also moved in tandem with the consumer price index.[120]

The empirical evidence of recession was overwhelming. Profits in manufacturing enterprises fell almost to zero, and one-third of the enterprises reported making losses.[121] In the first nine months of 1998, the consumption of electricity showed almost no change from the previous year. This suggests that manufacturing output was not growing by much.[122]

The slowdown in the growth of consumer demand was also unmistakable. There was a sharp drop in the sale of consumer goods across the board. Sales of automobiles grew by 4 percent from January to September 1998, against 26 percent in the same period of 1997.[123] Air traffic grew by 30 percent a year in 1994 and 1995, but slumped to 12 percent in 1996, 7.5 percent in 1997, and 6.3 percent in 1998.[124] This forced the government to ask Boeing and Airbus to postpone the delivery of forty-three aircraft that were scheduled for delivery in 1999. [125]

The sales of trucks fell by 2.2 percent from January to September 1998, and that of motorcycles by 22.4 percent.[126] The sales of other consumer durables also flattened out or declined, and producers and wholesalers were left with huge stocks of unsold goods.[127] This led to price deflation for the first time in China's post-reform history. To clear their stocks, manufacturers, wholesalers, and retailers resorted to price-cutting. So widespread was this trend that in October 1998, the retail price index fell for the first time ever, by 0.4 percent. The decline accelerated in November and by the end of that month, retail prices had fallen by 2.5 percent.[128] In the first five months of 1999, retail prices of consumer goods were 3.2 percent below the same period of 1998.[129]

Indirect evidence of the slowdown may be seen in the ever more anxious appeals to the Chinese to spend more. One favored explanation of the slowdown was that the government's attempt to "smash the iron rice bowl" had created a hitherto unknown insecurity in Chinese workers, especially after 1997, and they were responding to this by saving more than they did before out of their salaries.[130] In an effort to spur consumer spending, the government cut interest rates seven times between May 1996 and May 1999. This brought the rate down from 9 percent to well below 4 percent.[131] The government also reduced the down payment required for the purchase of automobiles and houses to 20 percent of the sale price.[132]

The worst hit was the real estate sector, where a sizable bubble had developed on the back of rampant land speculation and unrealistic expectations about continued growth. Shanghai, where one thousand skyscrapers had been built between 1990 and 1999, and five hundred more were scheduled to be completed by 2008, was teetering on the edge of a property collapse. In 1996 the Shanghai government brought down the price of commercial housing twice, a clear sign of flagging demand.[133] But this had no effect on the market. In 1997, 70 percent of the new housing constructed failed to find buyers. Not surprisingly, rents for office space fell by 50 percent in Shanghai, and 40 percent in Pudong city.[134] The following table charts the nationwide growth of the real estate bubble. It also shows that even in this sector growth had begun to slow down as early as 1996— i.e., well before the Asian financial crisis.

Table 6.3

Accumulation of Unsold Homes in 1994–'96 in China's Major Cities

YEAR	ACCUMULATION	ANNUAL INCREASE	RATE OF INCREASE
1994	32,890,000		
1995	50,310,000	17,420,000	52.96%
1996	71,350,000	9,320,000	15.02%

Source: "A Diagnosis of Unsold Commercial Homes," China Industrial and Commercial Time, July 30, 1998.

Not surprisingly, office rents fell by 40 to 50 percent in Beijing and other cities, too. There was also a huge mismatch between the housing that was being created and the housing that was needed. In all, seven million of the nine million square meters of unsold property created in 1997 was residential,[135] while the millions of migrant workers who had found jobs in Shanghai had nowhere to stay. Other cities in China were not much better off.

Their failure to build housing that people could afford, and their inability to sell what they had built, caused provinces and municipalities to run up huge losses. Apart from Shanghai, Guangdong, Zhejiang, and Guizhou, all the other provinces and municipalities of China suffered losses as high as 52 percent of their total invest-ment in the housing sector.[136] In all, it was estimated that at the end of 1997, when the long boom that began in 1991 had ended, China had 70 million square meters of vacant housing.[137]

It was not surprising that despite reports of 7.8 percent growth in 1997, President Jiang Zemin remarked in January 1999 that the country faced an economic slowdown,[138] and Premier Zhu Rongji told the tenth National People's Congress two months later that China faced a grim environment at home and abroad.[139]

But none of this truly fazed the Chinese government, which de-scribed the decline in growth rate that began in 1996 as a "soft land-ing" that the Chinese government had achieved after five years of torrid growth in which the GDP had increased by almost 12 per-cent per year. Those who accepted China's official statistics, with or without reservations, had no trouble in accepting this characteriza-tion of the economy's performance from 1996 till 2000, because the average growth rate from 1997 till 2000 fell only to 8 percent. But closer examination of the figures for these years shows that what China experienced was not a soft landing—not even a "slow-down," the OECD's definition of what happened, but something close to a full-fledged recession.

In the face of all this evidence the determined refusal of most Western economists to concede more than a mild economic slowdown in the late nineties is hard to understand. At a two-day conference on inequality in China's economy, held at Harvard in October 2006, Dwight Perkins of Harvard University dismissed the suggestion that China had concealed the depth of its recession by inflating its GDP estimates and cited several economists who believed that China was actually understating its rate of growth because of difficulties it was encountering in measuring the output of the services sector. He also dismissed a sharp decline in the growth of energy consumption as the product of concealment by local governments of the output of coal.

But one of the few economists who did assert that China experienced a recession in the late nineties was Thomas Rawski, then a professor at the University of Pittsburgh. In a series of articles written in 2001 and 2002, Rawski wondered how China had managed to increase its GDP between 1997 and 2000 by 24.7 percent, when its energy consumption declined by 12.8 percent. Rawski also pointed out several other anomalies. For instance, the official estimate of the growth of industrial production in 1998, 10.75 percent, was hard to reconcile with the fact that growth had exceeded 10 percent in only fourteen out of ninety-four main sectors of production, and had actually registered an absolute decline in fifty-three sectors. It was similarly hard to reconcile the increase in total fixed investment of 13.7 percent a year with an increase in consumption of steel and cement of 5 percent. Rawski concluded that China's actual rate of growth was not more than 2.2 percent in 1998, 2.5 percent in 1999, 3 percent in 2000, and 4 percent in 2001.[140]

Rawski's observations created a storm that took him by surprise. Yakov Berger, chief of research at the Russian Academy of Sciences' Institute of Far Eastern Affairs, described him as a "troublemaker."[141] A number of Chinese economists pointed out that GDP growth had exceeded the rise in energy consumption, in South Korea, Japan, and other countries, by a wide margin on several occasions in the seventies and eighties. Their argument, however, was not convincing because, as they also conceded, in the same period there were also several years in which energy consumption in East Asian countries had exceeded growth by a substantial margin. China's case was different because between 1978 and 1998 the growth of energy consumption had never exceeded the growth of GDP. On the contrary, the rise in energy efficiency in 1997 and 1998 was so great that China actually recorded a high positive growth rate in spite of an absolute decline in energy consumption.[142]

When tasked by Rawski and others to explain this seeming miracle, Chinese economists, and many other foreign students of the economy, attributed it to a deliberate underestimation of coal production and consumption. Coal production, they claimed, went underground after the central government asked the local administrations in 1997 to close down small coal mines because of their appalling safety record.[143] Coal accounted for 70 percent of the total consumption of energy in the second half of the nineties. Thus only a small level of concealment was needed to explain the sharp reversal of energy growth.

But this argument has lost some of its plausibility in recent years. Between 1996 and 2006 the National Bureau of Statistics revised its estimate of coal consumption repeatedly. In 2006 it increased its estimation of 2005 coal consumption by 30.7 percent without giving any explanation for the change. The NBS has also revised its data on total energy consumption upward several times. One can surmise, therefore, that most of the coal output that had initially not been declared was brought back into the data on energy consumption. Despite that, as Table 6.4 below shows, the anomaly that Rawski noticed remains. Between 1996 and 1998 the GDP allegedly grew by 16.4 percent while the consumption of energy *fell* by nearly five percent. And for six years after 1995, while the rate of growth of GDP averaged 8.1 percent, the growth of energy consumption, even after all the adjustments described above were made, averaged 1.1 percent. In short, seven-eighths of the increase in GDP in these years came from "invisible" sources. This is a little hard to swallow. Rawski's doubts remain valid.

What does the consumption of inputs have to say?

Energy is only one requirement for production, although the most important one. If the data on its consumption are changed from year to year and cannot be trusted, what does the consumption of other inputs have to say? Table 6.4 below shows how the consumption of seven crucial inputs—labor (employment), capital (total investment in fixed assets), total energy consumption, electrical energy consumption, steel, cement, and soda ash—all slowed down sharply after 1995, and in a few cases actually declined. Taken together, they leave no room for doubt that the Chinese economy did suffer from a sharp reduction of growth, if not an actual contraction, between 1997 and 2000. The recession, for that is what it was, lasted till 2000, and in some sectors of the economy till 2001.

Table 6.4

Consumption of Primary Inputs and Key Intermediate Products Used in Manufacture, 1978–2004

ANNUAL GROWTH IN PERCENT

Year	GDP	Employ- ment (industry)	Investment in FA∞	Consp energy total	Consp energy electrical	Consp of rolled steel	Consp of cement	Consp of soda ash
1978– '80	7.7	2.7		—	—			
1981– '85	11.0	5.1	24.0	5.0	—			
1986– '88	10.4	3.8*	23.2	6.6§	9.0**			
1989	4.2	-1.1§	-7.2	4.2	7.3			
1990	4.2	0.9§	2.4	1.8	6.2			
1991	9.1	2.5	23.8	5.1	9.2	9.5	18.5	8.1
1992	14.1	3.0	60.6	5.2	11.5	19.0	22.0	7.8
1993	13.1	2.1	45.4	6.3	11.0	16.6	20.0	18.5
1994	12.6	3.4	30.4	5.8	9.9	9.0	14	7.5

Year	GDP	Employ-ment (industry)	Investment in FA∞	Consp energy total	Consp energy electrical	Consp of rolled steel	Consp of cement	Consp of soda ash
1995	9.0	2.0	17.4	6.9	8.2	6.5	13	19.0
1996	9.8	-0.4	14.5	5.9	7.4	6.0	3.3	7.2
1998	7.8	-2.0	13.9	-4.1	2.8	7.6	7.4	2.3
1999	7.2	-2.5	5.1	-1.6 (1.2)	6.1	12.5	4.4	3.6
2000	8.4	-0.8	10.3	0.1 (3.5)	9.5	8.5	4.1	3.2
2001	7.2	+0.4	13.1	3.5 (3.3)	8.6	22.0	10.5	1.8
2002	8.9	2.8	16.9	9.9 (6.0)	11.6	20.0	9.5	5.3
2003	10.1	—	27.6	(15.3)	16.5	25.	18	16.7
2004	9.9	—	26.2	15.2 (16.1)	14.5	32.0	11.5	33
2005	10.2	—	26.7	—(9.9)	—(13.5)	19.2	10.2	8.6

Note: The figures in parentheses above are taken from National Bureau of Statistics of China, China Statistical Yearbook 2006. All the remaining figures are from China Statistical Yearbook 2005. The NBS has given no explanation for the very sharp "corrections" made to the data for 1999 and 2000 after the lapse of five and six years.

Two other indicators, this time indicators of demand, also confirm the occurrence of recession in the second half of the nineties. These are the ex-factory and consumer prices of all products. Both show that prices abruptly stopped rising in 1996 and, with only occasional lulls, fell continuously for the next five years, till the end of 2001. Ex-factory prices stopped rising first, a clear indication that demand was slackening, and resumed their upward movement only a year after consumer prices had begun to climb once more—i.e., after retailers had unloaded some of their old stocks and were confident once more that the recovery of demand was not a flash in the pan.

Table 6.5

Behavior of Prices, 1991–2004

ANNUAL GROWTH

Year	GDP	Consumer price	Ex-factory price
1991	9.1	3.4	6.2
1992	14.1	6.4	6.8
1993	13.1	14.7	24.3
1994	12.6	24.1	19.5
1995	9.0	17.1	14.9
1996	9.8	8.3	2.9
1997	8.6	2.8	-0.3
1998	7.8	-0.8	-4.1
1999	7.2	-1.4	-2.4
2000	8.4	+0.4	+2.8
2001	7.2	+ 0.7	-1.3
2002	8.9	-0.8	-2.2
2003	10.1	+0.9	2.3
2004	9.9	3.3	6.1

Source: National Bureau of Statistics of China, China Statistical Yearbook 2005.

In the tables above, both sets of data tell exactly the same story—China experienced an economic downturn sharp enough to be called a recession. They also show a complete absence of correlation between the NBS's estimates of GDP growth and of the consumption of inputs. The conclusion is therefore irrefutable: *Between 1997 and 2000, the growth of consumption of not a single input came anywhere near the claimed growth of output. What is more, at the height of the recession four of the indicators—industrial employment, energy consumption, and consumer and ex-factory prices—all went into negative territory.* It is difficult to see how this can be called a "slowdown," much less a "soft landing."

China's uneven growth did not end in 2000. The boom of 2001 to 2007 reversed itself in 2008. And as it had done in 1998, the government pinned the blame on an external financial crisis. In 1998, the Asian financial meltdown permitted it to admit that what it had originally described as a "soft landing" was in fact a "slowdown." In 2008, the Chinese government again readily acknowledged that the economy faced a "sharp slowdown," because it was able to place the blame upon the global financial crisis that had erupted in August with the collapse of the giant American investment bank Lehman Brothers and the worldwide recession that followed. But a close look at its data shows that as happened in the second half of the nineties, excess capacity and overproduction had begun to manifest itself as far back as at the end of 2004, and had become pronounced by early 2007.

Professor Zhou Qiren of Peking University's China Center for Economic Research pointed out, as far back as December 2005, that this was attributable not only to cyclical factors but also "structural factors." Chief of these was the emergence of China's unique kind of mixed economy, in which "private" enterprises had started to play a major role in the economy. According to him, the excess capacity was particularly marked in industries that were in the transition process from a planned economy to a market economy. Excess production capacity, he found, was concentrated neither in industries monopolized by state-owned enterprises nor in those dominated by private enterprise, but in an "intermediate" range of industries in which both types of enterprise were present. Although he did not seek an explanation, it is not difficult to surmise the reasons for this asymmetrical distribution of excess capacity. Sensitivity to signals from the market was highest in industries dominated by the private sector. At the other end of the spectrum, there was only a limited amount of excess capacity in the industries that were still monopolies of the state, because while these were not guided by the market, they were subject to the constraints of centralized planning. It was lowest in the "mixed" areas because these were the ones in which local and provincial governments had used their freedom to invest most liberally. The following table, assembled by him, shows that excess capacity was all-pervasive in a wide range of intermediate goods industries and in the automobile sector as far back as the end of 2004.[144]

Table 6.6
Production Overcapacity in Major Industries (2005)

Steel	Production capacity as of 2005: 480 million tons Production volume: 370 million tons Production capacity in excess: 100 million tons Plants under construction: 70 million tons Plants under planning: 80 million tons
Electrolytic aluminum	Production volume in 2005: 10.3 million tons (of which domestic demand is 6.02 million tons, external demand 1.02 million tons, and idle capacity 3.26 million tons) 11 construction projects underway and 14 under planning
Ferroalloy	Production capacity as of the end of September 2005: 22.13 million tons (24.97 million tons including plants under construction and planning) Demand in 2005: 12 million tons (capacity operating rate: 40%)
Charred coal	Production volume in 2005: 243 million tons (of which domestic and external demand accounts for 232 million tons and production in excess comes to 110 million tons) 240 projects for new construction or expansion of the existing facilities to add 390 coke ovens Production capacity is expected to increase by about 10 million

Carbide	Production volume in 2005: 10.43 million tons Average capacity operating rate: approx 60% Production capacity of plants under construction and planning: 12-22 million tons
Automobile	Production capacity as of 2005: 8 million units Units sold: 5.7 million units Production overcapacity: 2.3 million units Production capacity of plants under construction: 2.2 million units Production capacity of plants under planning: 8 million units

Sources: Compiled from media reports on statistics released by the National Development and Reform Commission

7 A PREDATORY STATE

HAD CHOPPY, ERRATIC, and wasteful growth been the only price China had to pay for unleashing the competition between cadres that propelled China's phenomenal growth, its benefits would have outweighed its drawbacks. But that competition's other effect has been to turn a society that prided itself on its egalitarianism and social cohesiveness into one of the most corrupt and unequal societies in the world. In 2006, China's per capita product was $2,010. But according to the National Bureau of Statistics, the rural registered population had a per capita income of $460 a year. Its migrant labor earned, on an average, $130 a month. Together, these two groups make up two-thirds of China's population. The remainder, those with urban *hukous* (residency permits), enjoyed incomes of close to $5,000 a year. The rural-urban income differential is not one to three, as the official statistics claim, or even one to six, as some economists have estimated, but more than one to ten. It is therefore no surprise that the World Bank's estimate of the Gini coefficient for China was 0.495, far in excess of the 0.463 for the US in 2007 and below only that of Mexico.[145]

Income disparities are vast even among those with urban *hukous*. This is brought out starkly by the sale of luxury cars (costing more than $50,000) in China. In 2007, 176,000 of these cars were sold in China, and the number was expected to go up to 233,000 in 2008.

By contrast, in India, which now has 123,000 millionaires (in US dollars) and where the Gini coefficient has also crept up to 0.365, only 3,500 such cars were sold in 2007.[146]

Like China's explosive growth, the rise of inequality is also a direct result of Beijing's loss of control over the activities of its cadres in the provinces. While the rest of the world applauded this loss of control as "liberalization" and "reform," within the Chinese historical perspective this was a return to a far older, but entirely familiar, pattern of governance. There is a Chinese proverb of the imperial days: "The mountain is high, the emperor is far away." In the eighties, and more strikingly in the nineties after Tiananmen, China's local leaders took advantage of the sudden weakening of the central government to revert to this age-old parable of governance with stunning swiftness. The arbitrary use of power by local cadres that resulted has become the single most potent cause of discontent.

Not all exercises of initiative by local cadres, even those in flagrant violation of central directives, are predatory. As the initial privatization of cultivation rights by local cadres in Anhui province in 1978 showed, local cadres manning township, village, and provincial governments frequently stretched, or ignored, Beijing's dictates, and took initiatives that the latter retrospectively sanctioned. But these were usually collective decisions, taken at a local level under the spur of distress or emergency, whereas the abuses that are eroding the legitimacy of the Chinese Communist Party and the state in the eyes of workers, peasants, sections of the intelligentsia, ex-soldiers, lawyers, and a section of the Communist Party itself are of a different kind. These have stemmed from what Chinese analysts call "the absolute power of the first-in-command." This pithy phrase refers to the complete fusion of the power to make laws, levy fees and taxes, assign and take away land, collectivize or not collectivize local enterprises, fix a variety of prices, determine local salary supplements and perquisites, enforce them, decide appeals, and inflict punishments. This power was summed up by a former mayor of Shenyang, Mu Suixin, in a pithy comment: "Central decrees and regulations have to be adapted once they reach me. I implement the ones I approve [of], and do not implement the ones I disapprove."

The power of the "first-in-command"

The party had not been free from corruption during the Communist era, but the inability to amass wealth had limited the types of illegal activities that cadres could indulge in, and the ways in which they could benefit. The commonest forms were the falsification of performance reports to please upper echelons of the party and vie for promotions, special postings, and privilege; hoarding goods to avoid shortages; and a variety of illicit activities intended to benefit the entire work unit. But corruption in its more familiar form appeared the moment China permitted the accumulation of income, and therefore wealth, in private hands. The very first step in that direction was the introduction of the household responsibility system in agriculture. For it allowed peasants not only to farm their own plots of land but to determine what they wanted to produce over and above what they had to supply to the state. The sale of this surplus created the first free market for food and freed workers from their bondage to the commune. This allowed them to migrate to the towns in search of work, thereby creating the first, rudimentary market for labor. But it also created the first "10,000-yuan" families in the countryside.

The central leadership was aware of the changes that the privatization of cultivation would bring about in rural society, and therefore took even this first step toward a market economy with considerable reluctance. Indeed, had there not been a succession of natural disasters in provinces like Szechuan and Anhui, in the late 1970s, the local cadres might never have mustered the courage to break the mold that the Cultural Revolution had created for agriculture.

The second concession to the market was spurred by mounting unemployment. Since the state had taken upon itself the responsibility of finding jobs for school and college graduates, especially in nonagricultural employment, the growing crisis revealed itself in all-pervasive overstaffing and underemployment. There was, however, a limit to how many people the state could employ to do any particular job. Thus, "confronting higher and higher levels of unemployment, the government had no choice but to free up people and allow them to make a living on their own in privately or township-owned enterprises that operated pretty much outside the state-owned sector."[147]

Beginning in 1983, the government passed a spate of laws that aimed at expanding the autonomy of families and enterprises, focusing responsibility for the performance of an enterprise on the plant director, and separating ownership from management, giving the enterprises their own legal identity and establishing a modern enterprise system.

But there was a vital difference between the unleashing of private incentive in agriculture and the unleashing of private incentive in industry. In the former the usufruct from the land went directly to the peasants who cultivated it. But outside agriculture, productive assets, even in the so-called non-state sector, continued to be owned by the state and managed by salary-earning cadres of the government and the party. So those whom the reforms "freed" to operate outside the state sector were not private entrepreneurs—that was to come several years later—but intermediaries acting in the name of the state. This was a situation that begged to be abused, and once the state ceased to frown upon the accumulation of wealth the abuse did not take long to develop. The exploitation of the power of the state by the individuals who wielded it was made fatally easy by the demise of the command economy. This freed local functionaries from the ironclad directives on what to produce and how much to surrender to the state procurement agencies. That was the genesis of the "first-in-command."

The first-in-command was no longer necessarily the party secretary, but could be the head of a local government, state agency, or public firm. The unique characteristic of this position was the first-in-command's almost complete lack of accountability to anyone but himself or herself. The rise of the "first-in-command" is an inevitable consequence of the state's retreat from centralized planning and its delegation of investment decisions to localities, firms, and markets. This began in 1984 when the center decided to delegate control rights over SOEs to the local governments. This transferred unprecedented discretionary power to local chief executives while simultaneously removing checks against their misuse. Yan Sun, professor of political science at the City University of New York, who has studied the rise of "number one" in considerable depth, concluded: "Except for centrally funded projects, local chief executives have taken over the approving power for critical sectors of the economy; at the firm, county, municipal and provincial levels. With the hierarchical relations of the Plan system gone, upper administrative echelons are left with few reliable channels to learn about routine violations by lower agencies. From land privatization to public projects, from financing to public levies, and from SOE reforms to development assistance, local chiefs can sign off approvals at the stroke of a pen." The emergence of a market economy and the resulting commercialization of state power created opportunities for self-enrichment that few of the first-in-commands were able to resist.

The myriad forms of corruption

Post-reform corruption did not start with the rise of the "first-in-command." The cadres' first forays into this new field were relatively innocent, when compared to what was to follow. One of the commonest early forms was for the director, the union leader, and the party representative in a factory to collude and invest the retained surpluses of their enterprise in setting up subsidiary enterprises—collectives—that were free from the price and distribution controls, and the social and welfare costs, that the parent plant was compelled to abide by. Typical of these new investments were light manufacturing units, shops, service centers, department stores, and real estate companies. The success of these enterprises, virtually a given before 1997, sharply increased the collective income of the enterprise.

The new ancillaries also became a favorite avenue for employing the relatives of enterprise directors, factory floor and union leaders, and party cadres assigned to the enterprise-level committees. Over time this practice proved not to be as innocuous as it had originally looked, for the diversion of the surplus of the parent enterprise to the subsidiary deprived the former of both the resources and the managerial attention that should have gone into modernization and changes in their product mix that could have helped them to remain competitive in an increasingly competitive market economy. This virtually guaranteed them a lingering death.

Perhaps the first individualized form of corruption was "arbitrage"—the purchase, by people in the right place at the right time, of goods at controlled prices and their sale in the free market. The opportunity for it arose from the system of dual pricing—one price for goods supplied under the five-year plan and another for those sold on the free market—that the central government adopted as part of its gradual shift from a planned to a market economy. This

created a long interregnum during which insiders in state enterprises made huge profits by procuring key inputs at the plan prices,
supposedly for their own enterprise, and selling a part of these to
users in the non-state sector at market prices. In an extraordinarily
candid book, *China: The Pitfalls of Development*, a Chinese scholar, He
Qinlian, estimated that in 1986 alone the price differential between
plan and free market prices created arbitrage opportunities worth
one hundred billion yuan. Seventy percent of this, she estimated,
ended up in private pockets. The "earnings" from arbitrage were
multiplied by investing in the share market, which was also rife
with insider and "sweetheart" deals. But, far more dangerously, it
was also invested in speculation in land. [148]

As planning continued to be wound up and economic decisions
devolved to the township, municipality of enterprise level, greed
multiplied and corruption became individualized. That was where
the "number one" became pivotal for success. Typical of this was
"asset stripping"—selling chunks of factory land, or profitable lines
of production within a state enterprise, to a newly established subsidiary, collective, or private enterprise, in which the control was
vested in a surrogate, usually a close relative, of the plant manager, a party chief, or a senior administration official. These sales
were made at throwaway prices, and the parent enterprise—i.e., the
state—was left to shoulder the losses.

Perhaps the most fertile source of "self-enrichment" was speculation in land. Between 1987 and 1992, state authorities at every
level from the province to the township acquired land to create
special economic zones and development zones, paying only minimal compensation to the peasants who were losing their land with
the intention of allotting or selling it to investors and real estate
developers. By 1992 no fewer than six thousand such zones had
been established, but more than half never took off. Many had
still not attracted a single investor when they were dissolved by the

government of President Hu Jintao in 2005. But this did not stop local governments from continuing to acquire land. To meet the demands of rapid urbanization, the central government ceded the power to determine land use to the local governments. This opened the way to millions of sweetheart deals between developers and local officials, which relentlessly ate into the land available to the peasants. Few of the latter received adequate compensation.

The government's decision to create a share market, capitalize the large- and medium-sized state-owned enterprises, and allow their shares to be traded in the market created another opportunity for personal enrichment. In enterprise after enterprise, the managers and party cadres colluded to undervalue the shares, buy or arrange to buy a significant portion, and allow the disproportionately high profits and dividends to push up their prices.

Even bank loans began to command a price. The fact that banking remained almost entirely a state monopoly, and that the funds of state-owned commercial banks' funds were preempted by the SOEs, created a premium on advances that bank managers were only too willing to appropriate. In a landmark study by two leading Chinese economists—the director of research at the People's Bank of China, Xie Ping, and his colleague Lu Lei—of the 3,561 bank employees, enterprise managers, farmers, and private businessmen whom they interviewed, 82.2 percent said that bank managers frequently or "quite often" took bribes to sanction loans. The average bribe amounted to 8.8 percent of the loans, paid either as an initial bribe or to "maintain relationships" with the bank afterward.

Corruption becomes entrenched

As the market economy matured the number of avenues multiplied, the amount of money involved in each transaction increased, the corruption rings became more elaborate and reached higher into the party and administration, and they endured longer before they were exposed and broken up. Two lists, compiled by Yan Sun, of the highest-ranking officials arrested and punished for corruption between 1986 and 1990 and 1992 and 2001, reflect the deepening hold of corruption upon the party and the administration, and the growing greed of the concerned officials. In the first period nine persons holding ranks of deputy minister and above (including provincial governors) were punished. But the bribes they accepted ranged from five thousand to thirty-eight thousand yuan. Most of the bribes were not in cash but were gifts, such as home electronics. Four of the nine did not engage in corruption personally. They were punished for tolerating corruption among their subordinates, business associates, and mistresses.

In the second period, there were thirteen such cases, but the bribes they took ranged from sixty-four thousand yuan to forty million yuan ($4.6 million), and twelve out of thirteen of them took their bribes in hard cash. In addition, two of them—Chen Xitong, mayor of Beijing for more than a dozen years, and his deputy mayor, Wang Baosheng (who was accused of accepting bribes totaling twenty-five million yuan but committed suicide before he could be sentenced)—built villas for their mistresses out of public money, at a cost of 35.21 million yuan. Finally, while the longest that any of the accused in the first period had remained in office before he was arrested was eight years, in the second period it was more than a dozen years—a clear indication that corruption had become more entrenched.

Sale of appointments

Another unmistakable indication of the way in which corruption is entrenching itself deep within the governmental system is the growing sale of appointments to coveted posts by the senior

officials, usually the "number ones." In early 2004, the party's committee on discipline issued a circular naming four senior cadres
who had sold 168 posts in the late nineties for close on three million yuan. The sale price varied from thirteen thousand to forty-
nine thousand yuan, roughly equivalent to a year's salary. Similarly,
a list of some of the worst office-sellers between 1995 and 2001
compiled by Yan Sun contained twelve more senior party cadres of
the level of mayors, party secretaries, governors, and their depu-
ties. Six of them received more than 1.2 million yuan for appointing, promoting, and transferring 1,015 officials. A seventh overruled
his colleagues and took forty thousand yuan to appoint a convicted
embezzler to a post in the anticorruption bureau from where he
could monitor and impede the progress of his own case. An eighth,
a deputy mayor in Anyang city in Henan province, took 139,620
yuan for eighteen promotions. One of these was to promote to the
post of deputy mayor a factory chief who had earlier been dismissed
for misconduct.

The willingness of these officials to raise and "invest" such a large
sum of money in securing a particular post reflects their confidence
that they would be able to recoup that amount and much more within
a short period of time. What is worse, the willingness of the senior
officials to accept these bribes means that they were beneficiaries of,
or were prepared to condone, the corruption that was to follow. Corruption had ceased to be an individual enterprise and was being carried out by organized networks of cadres in the government departments, in which each participant had his or her cut.

Two examples vividly illustrate the depths to which corruption
has poisoned the Chinese state: At the Zhengzhou railway station
three persons—the manager of the station's retail service corporation, an official from a provincial utility company, and a private
businessman—were able to secure extra allocations of space for
transporting cargo, and made millions of yuan by selling it to pri-

vate and non-state shippers. To persuade the railway officials to look the other way, they gave commissions to no fewer than fifty railway officials.

On December 27, 2005, a Beijing court convicted Tian Feng-shan, who had been the minister for land and resources till 2003, on seventeen charges of accepting bribes amounting to 4.4 million yuan ($543,000). Before he became a central minister, Tian Feng-shan had been the governor of Heilongjiang province, where he had run a well-oiled bribery machine from 1995 to 2000. This machine sold positions in government, arranged financing for projects, and reclassified farmland so that it could be taken away from the peasants and delivered to real estate developers—for a price. Tian was spared the death sentence because he confessed and helped the police recover some of the stolen assets, but the high office he held and the reputation he enjoyed in Heilongjiang suggest that the half-million dollars was only the tip of the iceberg. Tian has been the thinly veiled subject of a best-selling novel about corruption in Heilongjiang, *The Snow Leaves No Trace*. [149]

Tian came under police scrutiny when Ma Xiangdong, a fellow member of the Communist Party, confessed that he had paid Tian one hundred thousand yuan for arranging a loan and another eight hundred thousand yuan for appointing him the local party secretary. As party secretary, Ma Xiangdong made another twenty-four million yuan by selling other positions. As the case widened, it decimated the top level of the Heilongjiang administration. Among those fired or jailed were the president of the high court, the top prosecutor, the vice governor, the deputy head of the legislature, and at least ten mayors and vice mayors. Ma and another associate, Han Guizhi, were also given suspended death sentences, which were likely to be commuted to life imprisonment. But in Harbin, the capital of Heilongjiang, most people believed that many of the members of the corruption ring were still in positions of power.

Zhu Shengwen, a former deputy mayor of Harbin, reportedly committed suicide in jail. The official version of his death was that he threw himself out of a prison window, but his family was convinced that he was killed to prevent him from exposing more cases of embezzlement.

One of the most notorious cases of corruption at the highest level was that of Mu Suixin, the mayor of Shenyang, who enjoyed the power of the "number one" described earlier. Mu was given a suspended death sentence in 2001 along with his deputy mayor, Ma Xiangdong. He had been brought to book over his insistence on reallotting the land intended for an ethnic cultural hall to a known mafia gang leader to build a mall. He was convicted in 2000 of having accepted more than six million yuan (US $1.35 million) in bribes and having more than two million yuan in income he could not account for. In an interview he gave to a journalist after his death sentence was suspended, Mu said that he had drifted into corruption unwittingly by accepting a few presents and then growing to like it. "I thought that receiving bribes meant you had to strike a dirty deal with people in advance," he said. "But for my situation, it always happened afterwards—it was always that 'friends' came to see me and gave me money during holidays, when I was sick or at certain occasions. I never knew it was a crime."

But the truth was a lot uglier. Mu Suixin had run a corruption ring in Shenyang for several years. To do this he had recruited not only his deputy mayor, Ma Xiangdong, but also at least 120 officials of the Shenyang administration. These included the top prosecutor and the chief judge of Shenyang. Mu was denounced by Zhou Wei, a seventy-year-old former Communist Party official. For submitting and organizing petitions to the authorities about the corrupt activities of Shenyang's leaders, Zhou Wei had been sent by Mu off without trial to a labor camp in May 1999. Zhou Wei's alleged offense was "disrupting public order," and he regained his freedom only in April 2001, after Mu, Ma, and the others had been arrested and sent to jail. But there was considerable evidence that the corruption ring had been much larger, with intimate links to organized crime, and that several of its members were still at large—for Mu's arrest did not end the attacks on, and constant harassment of, Zhou Wei. Fearing that other officials who had been part of the corruption ring were still at large, Beijing moved the trials of the 120 officials to other cities.

Beijing's losing battle

In its attempt to curb corruption, the central government has given these and other similar cases wide publicity, but they are far from exceptional. According to the Chinese Communist Party's Central Commission for Discipline Inspection, nearly fifty thousand officials were prosecuted and punished in 2004 and 2005. More than a thousand cadres committed suicide, and eight thousand fled overseas.

As corruption has become more and more entrenched Beijing has made strenuous efforts to root it out and punish the perpetrators. Had it not done so, popular disenchantment would have been far more pronounced. But these efforts have been only partially successful. According to one study, after the decentralization of the early eighties, the central government directly monitored only seven thousand officials. Since government and party cadres were the first to benefit from the opportunities that the marketization of the economy created, it is not surprising that the reform era also saw the end of policing by ordinary citizens through denunciation.

The central government has attempted to control corruption among party cadres and in the administration, through three monitoring-cum-prosecution agencies, the Central Commission for Discipline Inspection of the Communist Party of China (CCDI), the Ministry of Supervision of the People's Republic of China (MoS), and the criminal justice system. The CCDI investigated allegations against party members, while the MoS investigated allegations against officials in the administration who were not party members. Administration officials who were also Communist Party members were investigated by both organizations. The CCDI was considerably more important and more effective than the MoS. The latter was established in 1949, disbanded in 1959, and reinstated in 1986, in a tacit admission that by then a large proportion of the officials in the state administration were no longer party members. It therefore lacked the continuity and experience of the CCDI. Both organizations paralleled the hierarchy of the administration, but their effectiveness was severely diluted by the overarching control of the Party. In theory, the local heads of the Ministry of Supervision and CCDI offices report both to the local party committee and to their own superiors. But in practice, they are required to seek the approval of the party committee before sending cases up to the next level of their organization for further investigation. This has deprived both organizations of most of their teeth. The local disciplinary committee of the CCDI is required to seek the approval of the party committee before it can send a case up to the next level of its own organization. There are similar restrictions upon the MoS offices.

The most serious drawback of this proviso is that it makes it virtually impossible to prosecute the "number one," for it requires the CCDI or MoS office to get the number one's permission to prosecute him or her. The feeling of invulnerability that this provision has given to the chief executives may explain why in Henan province three heads of the transport department were found indulging in the same malpractices within the short span of four years. The exposure and punishment of his predecessor did not deter the successor, because he simply could not believe that he was not invulnerable. This belief stemmed from the fact that the transport chief was also, concurrently, the head the party branch in Henan.

There are thousands of similar stories from all over China. The central government's determined, but so far unsuccessful, effort to maintain probity in public life has yielded a rich harvest of data on corruption. They reveal that the number of cases being investigated has grown from 39,000 in 1989 to 174,000 in 2001. Since there are about eleven million persons working in "public management and social organizations"—i.e., in posts manned by the bureaucracy or party—this means that as of 2001, one in sixty-three holders of public office or power was prosecuted *every year*. But the same data also reveal how few of the allegations of corruption are actually taken up for formal investigation, and how much fewer still are the number of convictions. They also show that the government agencies' reluctance to convict—and if they do convict, to punish—rises with the seniority of the accused.

Between January 1993 and June 1997, for instance, the government agencies investigated 731,000 allegations of corruption and penalized 669,000 offenders. The vast bulk of the punishments consisted of fines, demotions, and reparations. Only 121,500, or 18.2 percent, were expelled from the party, and only 37,500, or 5.6 percent, were convicted on criminal charges. By 2004 this figure had dropped to 2.9 percent.

Extortion–the real threat to the Chinese state

The pervasiveness of corruption—bribery, arbitrage, embezzlement, fraud, the selling of posts and favors, and smuggling—had already gone some way toward undermining the legitimacy of the Chinese political system in the eyes of its people even during the first decade and a half of reform, when it had seemed that there would be only winners and no losers. It vented itself mostly in cynicism, sarcasm, and black humor, expressed in doggerel verse and aphorisms. But rather than generate violent protest, let alone rebellion, it fueled efforts at reform. To the extent that a threat of rebellion exists in the Chinese political system today, it comes from the rapid spread of another form of predatory activity by the party cadres: extortion.

The crucial difference between the two types is that corrupt transactions of the kind listed above are essentially private and consensual, and do not involve the public at large. Extortion is the exact opposite; it is the forcible extraction of resources, money, or favors by cadres of the state using the power of the state. It does not result in mutual gain, and it occurs systemically, on a large scale, at the interface of the state and society. It is therefore rent-seeking in its purest form.

Extortion by officials occurs wherever there are laws that regulate the economic activity of the people, but it is most pervasive in the rural areas. One form of centralized extortion is a systematic under-pricing of agricultural produce. This was normal in the Communist era, and has resurfaced stubbornly from time to time during the re-form period. But its origins go further back in time, existing in the age-old relationship between town and country in China. A second form of centralized extortion, however, is new and is peculiarly a product of the capitalist transformation. This is the compulsory acquisition of private land, with inadequate, sometimes virtually non-existent compensation. This is being indulged in by both the center and the provinces, but it is ubiquitous in the latter. This has turned into the most potent cause of unrest in the countryside today.

Centralized extortion

Forced levies to meet the needs of the state had been a feature of every historical period in China, and had tended to reach crisis levels in the declining years of successive dynasties as other sources of revenue crumbled. The Nanjing government, after 1911, and the Kuomintang were no different. The Communists secured the support of the peasantry in part by declaring that they were not just committed to overthrowing the "three mountains" (imperialism, feudalism, and bureaucratic capitalism), but to simultaneously lifting the "burden [these had imposed] on the peasants." For the briefest of moments after the revolution the peasants did become masters of their own produce—land reforms between 1949 and 1952 enabled more than four-fifths of the rural population to gain control of the land they cultivated. But they lost their autonomy once again because of two initially unrelated developments. The first was the reappearance of taxation by local governments to meet those governments' administrative and developmental needs. The second was the pressure that the revolutionary government came under to industrialize and militarize itself during and after the Korean War. To minimize the cost, and maximize the efficiency, of tax collection the revolutionary government delegated the task to the local governments. To motivate them and also to enable them to carry out their functions, Beijing allowed them to raise additional taxes on agriculture up to a given proportion of the central levies. But as had happened before and was to happen again, the local governments showed a distressing tendency to become a law unto themselves. In a report dated October 21, 1952, based upon a survey of sixty-one townships, Liao Luyang, who looked after agricultural affairs in the Communist Party, concluded that the consolidated levies by the local governments on the peasants had already risen to over a fifth of their income.

Faced with rapidly rising peasant discontent, Mao Zedong issued several stern directives ordering local governments to bring local-added taxes down to a maximum of 15 and then 7 percent of the central tax on agriculture. But these had no effect. As a result, he was neither able to reduce the peasants' burden nor meet the central government's need for revenue to meet its external challenges. He "solved" both problems by collectivizing agriculture: in his own words, "it is hard to take hold of one's hair when it is scattered all over one's head, but easier when it is braided."

By degrees between 1952 and 1958, 130 million peasant families were gathered into seven million mutual aid groups, then into 790,000 rural cooperatives, and finally into 52,781 communes. By 1958, every last thing that the peasants owned, including their cattle and most household goods, belonged to the commune, which became the basic fiscal unit in the countryside. Nineteen-fifty-eight marked the beginning of the Great Leap Forward, which resulted in a catastrophic famine. And barely a decade later, the Great Leap Forward was followed by another period of severe disruption during the Cultural Revolution. By 1977, the living standards of the Chinese peasantry were worse than they had been in the early days of the PRC.

Decentralized extortion

The introduction of the household responsibility system in agriculture—in effect a return to private farming, in Anhui in 1978 and throughout China by 1980—transformed the peasants' lives. For six years, the return to private farming and a substantial increase in grain prices brought bliss to the peasantry, whose income grew by 15 percent a year. But the newfound affluence of a handful of farmers turned them once again into the natural targets of China's predatory power elite. While the central government returned tacitly to taxing the peasant by underpricing farm produce, it reawoke the greed of the local administrations, which too were once again free to levy taxes and determine expenditures within the broad, and necessarily vague, guidelines laid down by the center.

The infrastructure for this decentralized predation (i.e., extortion by local governments and cadres) was created in the very act of dissolving the communes. After the end of the Cultural Revolution, the fifty-thousand-plus communes were dissolved and their tasks taken over by some ninety-two thousand townships. In 1984–'85, these were brought under 61,766 township administrations. The rationale was exactly the same one Mao had used to collectivize agriculture in the early fifties. Agriculture was producing surpluses, and the surpluses had, once again, to be taxed. To do this efficiently the central government delegated the job to the townships. The township administrations were therefore endowed with both fiscal and administrative autonomy. Within a few short years they used this to replicate the entire bureaucratic structure of the provincial administration, with six governing branches—the party committee, government, disciplinary committee, people's congress, political consultative committee, and armed force department—to oversee all the normal functions of a government: finance, taxation, public security, industry and commerce, transportation, public health, grain administration, and agricultural technology (which included water conservancy, seeds, vegetation preservation, agricultural machinery, animal husbandry, food, and fishery). Husband-and-wife journalist team Chen Guidi and Wu Chuntao summed it up with a traditional Chinese proverb: "Though a sparrow is small in size, it has everything in its body."

The township administrations soon developed a life of their own. The number of Communist Party cadres they employed grew from 2.79 million in 1979 to 5.43 million in 1989, and further to eight million in 1997. The last figure included 1.269 million persons who had been laid off by the state-owned enterprises. By then, the township administrations were doing what state governments in India had been doing for four decades before 1991—create sinecures in the local bureaucracy to make up for the jobs that industry was no longer able to generate.

Each township and village administration replicated the departmental structure of the county administration. Each department and each of its offices had to have its complement of cars, office buildings, land lines, and mobile phones. Each senior official had to be similarly equipped. And all the townships had to cultivate relationships with bankers, entrepreneurs, senior officials, and visiting foreign investors through lavish entertainment. These "administrative expenses" became a huge fixed cost that the township governments had to meet, for no matter who else suffered, the cadres were the last to be laid off or have their perquisites reduced. The peasants summed up their plight, as usual, in pithy aphorisms: *"How many official hats does it take to crush a straw hat?"* and *"Too many dragons will cause a drought."*

To cover the growing expenses of local party and government organs and their subordinate agencies, the state added mandatory burdens on agriculture and peasants by way of different "red documents." These imposed taxes on agricultural specialties above and beyond the regular agricultural taxes; regulated the administrative charges and fees to be paid by peasants and laborers; framed guidelines for the creation of village reserves and planned township funds; laid down rules for the use of the accumulated revenue and interest thereon; and established the salaries of village cadres. The documents charged the township administrations with building schools in township and villages, implementing family planning, paying various allowances, training the people's militia, and constructing roads. All these demands were heaped on the peasants. By 1990, according to one estimate made in Anhui province, there were as many as 149 different kinds of levies on the peasants. Yet another aphorism began to make the rounds of China's rural areas:

A peasant mumbled while digging the ground with a shovel: "The first three shovelfuls are for turning in grain and taxes to the government; the next three shovelfuls go to the salaries of the commune director, the production brigade leader, and the production team leader; the following three shovelfuls go to those god-damned donations and wasteful banquets eaten by those sons of bitches; and only the tenth shovelful comes to me."

The effect of the levies on the peasants was summed up by Lu Xishiu, a veteran party cadre and a pioneer of agricultural reform in Anhui province, in a conversation with Chen Guidi and Wu Chuntao:

"Many of our cadres," Lu Xishiu said, "only see buildings without caring who built them; only see straight roadways without caring who paid for them! No sooner had our peasants improved their lives just a little bit than we started to devour them as if they were the "meat of Monk Tang." [In folk literature, Monk Tang's meat was desired because the one who ate it would become immortal!] Anyone can bully the peasants; they are so pitiful. In the past, the household-responsibility system that we started caused a national sensation and had a nationwide impact. . . . [But] what about now? The benefits brought by the household-responsibility system to the peasants have been taken away from them, little by little, by all levels of local government. Today, the situation can be summarized in this way: The state quota cannot be fulfilled, not enough can be reserved for the collectives, and nothing is left for the peasants themselves! . . . Who would have thought that our cadres today are so unfamiliar with and so negligent of our peasants, and that there are so few cadres who make friends with the peasants."

Between 1985 and 1991 the central government issued no fewer than four directives to curb the excessive taxation of peasants.[150]

These were some of the first efforts by the center to go over the heads of predatory local governments and somehow empower the peasants, but even that did not stop the imposition of fees and illegal levies upon the peasants. In 1991 the per capita net income of peasants nationwide increased by only 9.5 percent over the previous year in nominal terms—i.e., at current prices—but the "fees retained for village reserve and township overall planning" during the same period grew by 16.7 percent. 1991 also saw a change for the worse that relatively few noticed. From then on the fees, taxes, donations, and levies had to be paid in cash. Reviewing the causes for the continual rebirth of the same evils, Chen Guidi and Wu Chuntao found that

> [e]ach item that was suspended would inevitably affect the interests of some government agency or another and these agencies would soon create a different set of fees that were not included in the list of the explicitly prohibited ones. Even where items were explicitly banned, these agencies would still be able to find new bases for the reinstatement of these same items in a certain document released by the same agency, or in a certain speech drafted by the same agency and given by an official representing the interests of this agency. In some cases, these roundabout routes were not even needed; the documents were simply ignored and no action was taken at all to execute them.

But worse was still to come. When the central government drastically revised the taxation system in 1994 to snatch back the revenues that the local governments had appropriated, the impact upon the latter was little short of disastrous. Beijing tried to make up a part of the local governments' deficit, which amounted to a quarter of their overall expenditure, through tax transfers.[151] But, as Chen Guidi and Wu Chuntao succinctly note, the tax reform transferred the power to raise revenue upward, while the obligation to spend remained firmly anchored where it had been before—with the local governments. As a result, the provincial governments only passed on to the prefectures what they felt they could spare after meeting their needs; the prefectures did the same to the counties, and the counties did the same to the townships. Since all were strapped for cash, the townships received very little of the central money and were left to fend for themselves.[152]

The result was predictable. The county and township administrations not only ratcheted up permitted taxes, like the tax on agriculture and the tax on agricultural special products, but increased their exactions from the peasants and enterprises in their jurisdiction. Chen Guidi and Wu Chuntao reported, "According to the statistics of the Ministry of Agriculture, the two agricultural taxes (agricultural tax and tax on agricultural specialties) rose by 19.9 percent over the previous year in 1995; the 'three retained fees and five overall planned fees' levied on peasants rose 48.3 percent over the previous year; and all kinds of social burdens, including administrative and public institution fees, fines, fund-raising, and a requisition of donations rose by 52.22 percent over the previous year. In the very year after the so-called tax reforms, the burden on the peasants in one-third of all the provinces, autonomous regions, and cities directly under the central government exceeded the 5 percent limit stipulated by the state."

The political cost of the tax reform of 1994 became apparent a bare two years later when it was followed by the onset of recession in China. As the profits of the township and village enterprises (TVEs) dwindled and more and more of them were forced into loss, the township and village administrations responded by squeezing the peasants even harder. Chen Guidi and Wu Chuntao spent two years (between 2001 and 2003) investigating, and found that local governments exacted at least 269 various fees and charges.

Nor were the local governments the only agencies indulging in this time-honored practice. According to statistics Guidi and Chuntao gathered from the central government agency that monitors the burden on peasants, at the central level alone, government organs and agencies had issued or created at least ninety-three documents or items of charges, fund-raising, and requisitions of donation, involving twenty-four ministries, committees, offices, or bureaus.

Deepening insolvency has not prevented local administrations from undertaking extravagant, demonstrative expenditure. A favorite practice has been to build luxurious buildings to house themselves. These are allegedly always for a social purpose, for party offices, or for administrative, youth, hospitality, and entertainment centers. The buildings are being built not only in townships that have become rich or in the more advanced coastal regions, but, in a keeping-up-with-the-Joneses manner, in district centers of poverty-ridden provinces as well. One such building that drew Beijing's wrath was a five-story modern building with a manicured garden, built at Zhanjiang in inland Guangdong, that was supposed to be a poverty relief office. The building cost eleven million yuan ($1.45 million) and was built to provide office space for twenty employees. This epidemic of ostentatious official construction has made the central leadership issue a warning that if it is left unchecked, it could threaten the Communist Party's hold on power.

Predatory extortion has often become overtly criminal. A striking example is the way in which some party cadres abused the one-child family planning law to extort money from the peasants. Guidi and Chuntao described their experiences as follows:

[A] good policy like family planning can soon degenerate into many terrible local practices once it falls into the hands of village cadres. . . . A deputy chairman of the People's Congress of Anhui told us that a village in Tanxi county was found during their inspection tours to have fines of more than 3.1 million yuan within just a short month of shock inspections for family-planning purposes. That village was substituting fines for the law. Villagers were allowed to have more births if they paid fines; thus, birth permits became a cash cow. In the 1990s, Tanxi county had as many as 100,000 unregistered children (outside of the family-planning system). The judiciary of Lixin county publicized a particular case that ended in a light sentence for a shocking crime. From December 3, 1998 until May 1999 when the crime was disclosed, three cadres in Sunmiao township of that county, Lin Ming, Yuan Zhidong, and Li Peng, under the pretense of operating a population school, hired ruffians and acquired vehicles. On the false grounds of "birth beyond planning," "unauthorized birth," [and] "obstruction of official business," they took more than 200 innocent villagers away from their homes in the twenty-two villages of Sunmiao township and threw them into private jails. Through the horrendous means of illegal detention, they then extorted large amounts of money from the peasants. Their three private jail rooms were just as scary and dark in the daytime as at night, with all windows sealed and no lighting inside. The stench in the jail rooms was beyond belief as detainees had no washroom facilities. The jailed peasants brought their own blankets and were forced to sleep on the floor in their own filth. It was indeed a ghastly sight.

There was a single motive for imprisoning these peasants: money. Ru Zipei from Shuangmiao village, who had been a migrant worker in other places for many years, had some savings and thus became a major target of extortion. He was taken away on December 12, 1998, and was released eighteen days later after making a payment of 8,000 yuan. Three other migrant workers, Zhou Lixun, Zhou Lifu, and Zhou Guoyun, were taken away on the same day and detained for five days; before they were freed, they had to pay

10,000 yuan. Ma Yuerong, over sixty years of age, from Ruzhai village, had just suffered a house fire and had no money available; as a result, he was jailed for over 170 days. Because of the long detention, he almost lost his hearing. A pregnant woman named Ma Yin was accused of "unauthorized pregnancy" and gave birth to a child in the jail; there, she suffered all kinds of torture. When Ma Yin's father, Ma Xueyi, and her sister, Ma Sanyin, learned about this and went to the jail to visit her, they were also jailed on the grounds that they would act as prisoner substitutes for Ma Yin.

CHEN GUIDI AND Wu Chuntao had to pay for their courage and their devotion to their country. First published at the Beijing Book Fair in 2003, the first 100,000-copy print run of the full version of their book *The Life of China's Peasants* was sold out within a month. Then, in March 2004, after 150,000 copies had been sold, the authorities took it off the bookstore shelves. The book had been banned by the order of the propaganda department of the Central Committee of the Communist Party of China. Following the ban, an official, Zhang Xide, whom they had named in their investigations sued them on the grounds that their account of the "Baimiao Township incident" described in the book was defamatory. Zhang naturally brought up the case in the county of which he had been the party boss, so it was not entirely surprising that he won. The local court not only convicted them, but turned the case into a political indictment of the authors. What is more, the national media, which had hailed the book, suddenly went silent and did not cover the farcical court proceedings. The court proceedings ended in October 2004, but the court gave no verdict for more than a year. During this period, in December 2004, a newly appointed party secretary for Anhui province denounced the book. A party newspaper, which had been serializing the authors' next book on an uncorrupt judge, abruptly stopped doing so. A gang of hooligans pelted their two-room apartment with bricks. No one came to investigate. Shortly after that, Chen Guidi was asked to resign from his job. The stone-throwing continued night after night for twenty nights till the couple and their child fled from Hefei, the capital of Anhui, where they lived, and hid in a remote corner of the poor, southeastern province of Jiangxi.

Chen Guidi and his wife may have been persecuted, but their work did not go unnoticed. The 2004 *Blue Book of Chinese Society*, published by the Chinese Academy of Social Sciences, confirmed the rise of tension in the rural areas, and the close connection this had to the recessionary conditions that developed in the late nineties. "One of the chief sources of social tension," it concluded, "is the tendency of the politically well connected in the rural areas to take care of themselves and ignore the needs—or worse, actively harm the interests—of the remaining population."

In a significant admission, the *Blue Book* confirmed that the predatory relationship between cadres and peasants developed out of the freedom that the township administrations were given to manage their own budgets. In the years of plenty, between 1980 and 1995, they hired staff with abandon, only to have their revenues dry up, first because of the 1994 tax reforms and then because of the failure in the 1990s of a large proportion of the TVEs. The drying up of other sources of revenue had forced the majority of them into debt. Approximately one-third of the counties and two-thirds of townships were in debt. As a result, 80 percent of townships were facing difficulties in paying wages regularly. The *Blue Book* confirmed the findings of independent researchers that this forced the townships into extorting more and more money from the peasants. According to Zhao Shukai, a researcher at the State Council's Development Research Center, in 2004 the number of cadres at the township level was about three times what it had been in the 1980s. County and township governments accounted for 20 percent of total fiscal revenues, but supported 71 percent of public employees.

The *Blue Book* also conceded that the rising rural tension was a product of the conflict between cadres at every level of the local administration and the peasantry.

The peasants expressed their powerlessness by composing doggerel verse:

> *Seven hands, eight hands, everybody extends hands to the*
> *   peasants.*
> *You collect, I collect, he collects, and peasants are distraught;*
> *You solicit, I solicit, he solicits, and peasants are upset.*
> *Demand grain, demand money, and demand life;*
> *Guard against fire, guard against theft, and guard against cadres.*

Land-grab by party cadres—an enduring cause of discontent

The control that peasants regained over the use of their land in 1978–'80 proved short-lived. In 1986 the central government passed a land management law that allowed local village authorities to lease land to entrepreneurs. Following its policy of "fording the river by feeling the stones," the central government allowed Shenzhen to begin the experiment first, in 1987. Shenzen's successful auction of several pieces of land led, in 1989, to a decree, first by the National People's Congress and then by the State Council, allowing land to be leased to non-village, nonagricultural users.

The purpose of these laws was to start creating a land market that would meet the growing need for nonagricultural land. But the desire unleashed in the local party cadres to corner productive resources for their pet projects turned them into a potent new threat to the peasantry. The root cause was the local cadres' reluctance to surrender the power they enjoyed, by transferring ownership of the land back to the peasants. In the agricultural reforms of 1978–80, the local governments had transferred only the right to cultivate the land, i.e, decide what to produce, back to the farmer. Among these villages, 105 regarded the administrative villages as the owners and 119 held the small production groups as owners. In thirty-nine villages the land was owned by both the village and the small production group. In no village did an individual peasant own any land. As a result, when it became possible to sell land to industrialists and real estate developers, the decision rested in the hands of the cadres who controlled the village administration. What is more, since larger projects would require the surrender of land spread across several villages or small team holdings, the township or county cadres would also get into the act of selling the land.

Since there was no real land market, peasants found it difficult to estimate the value of the land that was being taken away from them. Being powerless, they got only what the cadres at the upper levels of local government deemed it necessary to pay them. The compensation was therefore not only small, but also totally arbitrary. In the suburban areas at the fringes of the cities and larger towns, it was customary to give peasants a regular salaried job as part of the compensation. But in one city in Szechuan province, for example, by 1993 more than twenty thousand peasants had failed to be allocated jobs after their land was taken away. In some villages in the suburbs of Shanghai, many peasants were not allocated jobs because there were not enough positions. Consequently, they received a two-hundred-yuan subsidy each month, which was less than their income from farming.

Things were no better when the compensation was entirely in cash. As investment from Hong Kong flowed into the Zhuhai, Shantou, Guangzhou, and Pearl River Delta areas, it sparked an instant frenzy to open up special economic zones (SEZs). Townships and municipalities in these provinces put vast tracts of land on the leasehold market. So great was the frenzy that in 1992 an estimated tenth of the entire capital raised in the Hong Kong market was sucked into these provinces. Their success caused the rest of the country to jump on the bandwagon. Between the end of 1992 and mid-1993 the entire country joined in the race to open SEZs. Money poured in from Taiwan and South Korea. In 1993, by some estimates, nine-tenths of the fresh capital flowing into China went into the real estate market.

It was the old story once again. No sooner had the central government created the tiniest crevice through which the local governments could make money, than the latter had rushed in pell-mell. Data published by Beijing's Ministry of Construction, and quoted by He Qinlian, showed that by March 1993, no fewer than six thousand SEZs had been opened. These had swallowed fifteen thousand square kilometers (1.5 million hectares) of land, more than the total urban area of China. This estimate did not include huge swaths of land that the township and village administrations had appropriated to create so-called development zones. There was a near-complete loss of control by Beijing over the provinces and by the latter over the townships and villages. The supply of land for SEZs and DZs so far exceeded demand that much of the land remained unutilized, and remains so till this day. Not surprisingly, the less attractive central provinces suffered the most. Hunan province, for example, enclosed 2,485 square kilometers of land in more than three hundred SEZs. The wire fencing went up, and the billboards advertising a glorious future adorned all the zones' approaches. But the province never found the resources to invest in the infrastructure. As a result, the billboards were all the development that took place.

What these SEZs did, irrevocably, was destroy farmland. The Ministry of Agriculture estimated that by the end of 1992, the SEZs had swallowed ten million *mu* (or 667,000 hectares) of farmland. A land ownership survey of the province of Guangdong in 1996 showed that local authorities had sequestered two hundred thousand acres of farmland for large-scale projects; this was half of the arable land in the province. Author Yongshun Cai also noted that by 1996, the amount of land acquired in the "zone frenzy" but left undeveloped totaled 280,000 acres, of which 53 percent was originally farmland. Half the idle farmland could no longer be converted back for farming purposes. In the process of this large-scale land conversion, many local governments occupied farmland at will and did not pay enough attention to compensation for peasants.

When local governments approach insolvency, but are in the grip of a land-enclosure frenzy, someone has to suffer. Needless to say, it was the peasants. Drawing upon a large number of surveys, Cai notes that county and prefectural governments would keep 30 percent or more of the lease proceeds to meet "expenses of sale." In some places, the take was high as 70 percent. In the nation as a whole between 1987 and 1994, "fees" collected from the leasing of land totaled 242 billion yuan, most of which the local governments kept in their extrabudgetary accounts. It was estimated that about 60 to 70 percent of the profits from land conversion went to the government or its agencies, and about 25 to 30 percent was collected by the village government—whereas peasants received about 10 percent.

The lack of a land market from which peasants can get a valuation of the land they are losing, combined with the absence of ownership rights, makes it almost impossible for them to resist summary eviction with little or no compensation. In provinces where industry has mushroomed, the peasants are at least able to fall back on nonagricultural employment to safeguard their incomes, and millions have emerged net gainers from the change. But even in these provinces, as the pattern of rural unrest shows, the dispossession has rankled. As Cai reported in 2003, "In Guangdong province [where half of the arable land was seized to set up SEZs], before 1992, petitions by peasants concerning land conversion accounted for half the total number of petitions." But the subsequent attempts at checking the frenzy did not stop the blind rush for land. "In 1998," Cai continued, "the Central State Council Letters and Visits Office received 460,000 letters and appeals from the whole country, of which issues concerning peasants accounted for two-thirds. Unauthorized fee collection, usurpation of farmland and corruption are the most common complaints. Some lower-level cadres admitted that peasant burdens and loss of farmland have been the two most serious issues that threaten stability in rural China."[153]

But the rising tide of protest has not stemmed the inexorable expropriation of land from the peasants. In a shocking admission in 2006, the director of law enforcement in the Ministry of Land and Resources, Zhang Xinbao, said there had been more than a million illegal changes of land use in the previous six years. A national land use survey conducted by the Ministry of Land and Resources in October 2006 and released in April 2007 showed that China had lost another 3,082 square kilometers of arable land in the first nine months of 2006 to nonagricultural uses. To the ministry's knowledge, 603 square kilometers of this—more than sixty thousand hectares—had been illegally appropriated by local governments for nonagricultural purposes in 131,000 separate cases. That was 131,000 more defrauded peasants. The ministry also issued a warning that the most recent losses had brought down the arable acreage in China to 1.226 million square kilometers. This was only twenty thousand square kilometers above the "danger level" of 1.206 million square kilometers, which the ministry considered the minimum that China needed to feed itself.

Stifling the people's right of protest

For more than two millennia, the Confucian state in China has bestowed absolute power on the emperor and his mandarins. But it has counterbalanced this by giving their subjects what is usually termed "the right to rightful resistance." What distinguishes "rightful" from simply "popular" resistance is the reliance of the former upon the laws and edicts passed by the state itself to point out the delinquencies of its officials. Two students of rightful resistance, Kevin J. O'Brien and Lianjiang Li, describe it as "a form of popular contention that employs the rhetoric and commitments of the powerful to curb the exercise [abuse] of power, [and] hinges on locating and exploiting divisions within the State."[154]

The People's Republic was every bit as much of an absolutist state as Imperial China. There was no separation of powers, and its minions exercised all the functions of government—legislative, executive, and judicial. The only way in which victims of the cadres' abuse of power could seek redress was the age-old one of petitioning higher authorities against the wrongdoings of their subordinates. But during the pre-reform days, and especially before the Cultural Revolution, the Communist Party was small, entry was difficult and required a proven commitment to egalitarian ideals, and the prohibition against accumulation of wealth ruled out the main incentive for the abuse of power. As a result, petitions against cadre abuse were rare.

The behavior of the cadres changed dramatically after Beijing permitted the accumulation of private property, and devolved the power to levy fees, collect taxes, and undertake investment to local governments. As conflicts between local cadres and peasants or workers multiplied, the central government was forced to codify the latter's right to seek redress. It did this in an amendment to the constitution in 1982. Article 41 of the amended document stated that citizens had the right to submit complaints or charges to state organs against any agency or functionary for violation of law or dereliction of duty.[155]

But as corruption, expropriation of land, and the levy of "extrabudgetary" fees and taxes multiplied, the number of complaints skyrocketed. In 1995 the provincial, county, and municipal offices of the State Letters and Visits Bureau received no fewer than 4.8 million petitions and complaints. More than three-quarters of these were presented by delegations of more than five persons. The central government was therefore compelled to impose restrictions upon the peasants' right to resist. In 1995 the bureau issued revised instructions that forbade villagers from sending delegations of more than five representatives when lodging a complaint, and made it necessary for them to pursue charges from level to level.

These strictures proved effective. A survey, carried out in 1998–'99, of petitioners who had managed to reach Beijing showed that only one in fifteen had bypassed the local levels of the bureaucracy. Six years later O'Brien and Li found, after carrying out a survey of 688 petitioners who reached Beijing in 2003–'04 and 2004–'05, that only eleven (i.e., one in sixty) had bypassed even a single level of the bureaucracy in filing their complaints.[156] And, whatever may have been the bureau's intention, these rules delivered the complainants, bound hand and foot, to their oppressors. For by then corruption had embraced virtually the entire local bureaucracy. The peasants' complaints were routinely handed over to the accused, who, being local officials, took their revenge upon them.[157]

But so heavy and arbitrary were the extractions from the peasants that the number of petitions kept multiplying. In 2000 the State Letters and Visits Bureau received 10.2 million petitions. And at the local level the cadres began to employ goons as local security staff and even members of triad gangs to discourage and wreak revenge upon those who had dared to protest. As Guidi and Chuntao have described, petitioners were threatened, beaten up, and occasionally killed. A standard mode of operation was to send the security staff to break grain bins, confiscate the grain, and smash or sequester the few consumer durables the peasants owned.[158] Not surprisingly, the peasants to began to organize themselves. From the mid-1990s, as it became apparent to the peasants that the corruption of the cadres had in fact destroyed their two-millennia-old right of rightful resistance, demonstrations and angry confrontations increasingly replaced the polite, civilized demands of the past. Not surprisingly, the number of incidents of mass protest that involved a disturbance of public order increased from 8,700 in 1993 and ten thousand in 1994 to seventy-four thousand in 2004 and eighty-seven thousand in 2005.

In May 2005, as a part of his campaign to restore social harmony, President Hu Jintao enacted new regulations that would make it easier and safer for peasants to register collective petitions. Among the more important of these was a strict injunction against punitive action toward a petitioner, and against the passing on of complaints to the accused. By abolishing all taxes on agriculture and removing the power of local governments to levy fees and ad hoc taxes, he also drastically reduced the scope for party cadres to abuse their power. But discontent has continued to rise and petitions to go unaddressed. There is now an entire township in Beijing inhabited by petitioners who have failed to obtain a hearing or redress, and are unable or unwilling to return home for fear of what awaits them. To quote Jonathan Watts of the *Guardian:*

> It is all too common a story. In the rubbish-strewn alleys of Fengtai, near South Beijing railway station, an entire community of petitioners has sprung up—some of them waiting for years in the hope of redress. Many are scarred, on crutches, blind or otherwise horribly maimed from industrial accidents, police beatings, and acid attacks. Most complain of being cheated of their land by developers and bribe-taking officials. Others tell of daughters raped by village chiefs, and factory bosses running off with workers' redundancy money. They are treated as trouble-makers who threaten communal unity. According to civil rights groups, fewer than one in 500 petitions is successful.[159]

8 HOW RECESSION HAS SHARPENED SOCIAL CONFLICT

WHETHER CHINA DID or did not acknowledge that it suffered a recession in the second half of the nineties would have been of only academic interest if the recession had not played such a crucial role in sharpening public discontent and eroding the legitimacy of the Communist Party. How this happened can explain why a country with such an astounding rate of growth should be suffering so much public discontent.

In the Western democracies, government and media's sustained criticism of the Chinese government's brutal suppression of the Tiananmen uprising have firmly implanted the belief that public discontent in China stems from the persistent denial of democracy to a rapidly modernizing and increasingly affluent society. This is a long way from the truth. Tiananmen was a turning point in China's political evolution for many reasons that are discussed later, but it played little or no part in stoking the massive outburst of discontent, particularly in the peasantry, that erupted in the second half of the nineties and continued for the next decade.

In 1988 and 1989, during the run-up to Tiananmen, China's peasants were, by and large, a contented lot. Although the central government had returned, three years earlier, to its pre-reform policy of giving priority to industrialization, and had begun once again to tax farmers indirectly by keeping down the procurement price of foodgrains, by then the peasants had benefited from seven years of unprecedented prosperity in which their income from farming had risen by 15 percent a year, and job opportunities in local industry—a vitally important additional source of family income—had multiplied at a mind-boggling pace. They therefore had little reason to take up cudgels against the Communist Party.

The Tiananmen uprising was sparked by a wholly urban discontent. It emerged out of a rapid growth of dissatisfaction among students and became a serious threat to the Communist Party when the students were backed by a significant portion of the workers and of the Communist Party itself. Its main cause was the burst of inflation in the mid-eighties brought on by the first wave of uncontrolled investment, a simultaneous decontrol of prices, and a slackening of economic growth in 1988 after seven years of dizzy growth, which suddenly made good jobs hard to find. In Guangzhou, the average disposable income of urban residents was 54 percent higher in nominal terms in the first quarter of 1988 than it had been a year earlier, but its distribution was already badly skewed. Seventy percent of the increase in electronics industry sales was accounted for by luxury goods such as television sets and music systems. But food prices, which had risen 10 percent in 1987, continued to increase rapidly in 1988, and the prices of vegetables had soared by 48.7 percent. To quote professor Richard Baum: "It was truly a 'crisis of incomplete reform.'" A survey of 2,300 families in thirty-three cities in 1987 reported a decline in the real purchasing power of urban workers for the first time since the reforms had begun.

At that time, practically everyone in nonagricultural occupations was a salary earner whose nominal income was only fitfully adjusted to the cost of living. Students, in particular, not only saw the purchasing power of their stipends melt away before their eyes, but witnessed the simultaneous rise of a new class of corrupt cadre-capitalists in the party who were amassing unheard-of wealth through graft and insider deals.

But with no rural backing, the uprising remained confined to Beijing, Shanghai, and a couple of dozen other cities, and was brought under control in less than a week. Another sharp burst of investment and proliferation of jobs, beginning in 1991, dampened the aftershocks. In 1993, at the end of what, with the exception of two turbulent years, can be called the Age of Contentment, there were only 8,700 public expressions of popular discontent, and nearly all involved only a handful of people.

But the situation changed dramatically for the worse in the second half of the nineties. The second recession, which began in 1996, catapulted hundreds of thousands, possibly millions, of the recently established urban and rural collectives into loss and slowed down the growth of business revenues and personal incomes. According to official data, the ratio of the profits earned by profit-making state-owned enterprises operated by the central ministries to the losses accrued by the loss-makers fell from 2.8 in 1993 and 1994 to 1.5 in 1996, 1997, and 1998. The non-state enterprises—i.e., the urban and rural collectives—fared a good deal worse. Data collected for more than 165,000 enterprises above a certain size show that their ratio of profits to losses had sunk to a low of 1.83 to 1 in 1998, but rose back to 10 and 9 to 1 in 2004 and 2005 after the economy entered its next boom. It is safe to presume that their profits had been equally high in the previous boom. Since the government relied on these revenues to meet a part of their mandated administrative and developmental expenses, this set off a scramble at every level within it to safeguard departmental revenues and protect personal incomes. The central government had already taken advantage of the tax reforms of 1994 to increase its share of tax revenues. Not only did it stick grimly to its share, but in 1997 it also enacted banking reforms that reduced the local governments' access to bank loans. Being at the end of the financial food chain, the township and village administrations were the worst sufferers. As the off-account profits of the small and medium-sized SOEs that had been turned over to them declined or turned into losses, and as the profits of the township and village enterprises fell, the revenues of the township administrations fell sharply. But the brunt of insolvency was not borne by the cadres who ran the administration and had sanctioned the investments of the boom years. These were still salaried employees of the state who enjoyed a wealth of perquisites. Vast numbers among them were cushioned by the wealth they had accumulated through kickbacks. The entire burden of adjustment fell upon the workers and peasants whom the cadres employed or oversaw. With no reduction in the tasks assigned to them (education, health, the maintenance of capital assets, and minor development projects), unable to cut salaries, and unwilling to economize on perquisites (such as new office buildings, automobiles, entertainment, and travel), the township administrations chose the only way of raising resources that remained open to them. This was to squeeze peasants and local enterprises ever harder to extract the funds they needed. So they resorted to delays in payment of pensions, stipends for laid-off workers, and health expenditure reimbursements for urban workers and the unemployed—and to ever heavier levies of ad hoc fees, taxes, and dues from the peasants.

In the provinces and prefectures that had not benefited from industrialization, this pushed the peasants back to the brink of poverty. The resulting discontent escaped notice for a long time because it did not develop all at once, but it rose steadily to an alarmingly high level.

Table 8.1

**Total Profits of Profit-Making Firms
and Losses of the Loss-Makers, 1990–2000
(in billions of yuan)**

Year	1990	1991	1992	1993	1994	1995	1996	1997	1998*	1999*	2000*
Profit	73.7	76.9	90.4	127.0	131.1	130.4	120.3	125.3	154.8	184.8	302.3
Loss	34.9	36.7	36.9	45.3	48.3	69.0	79.1	83.1	102.3	99.8	61.6
Ratio	2.1	2.1	2.4	2.8	2.7	2.0	1.5	1.5	1.5	2.2	4.9

Source: Carsten Holz and Tian Zhu,

*The absolute figures for profit and loss in these years are not comparable with those for the earlier years because the category "SOEs" was replaced by "SOEs and state-controlled shareholding companies."

Non-state enterprises

The non-state enterprises did not fare any better. A tabulation for 165,080 state and non-state enterprises above a designated size, given in a newly created database in the *China Statistical Yearbook 2005,* shows that this ratio was 1.83 in 1998, but rose to over 10 to 1 in 2004 and 9 to 1 in 2005, when the Chinese economy entered a boom and showed signs of overheating.[160]

Privatization: ideology or compulsion?

When President Jiang Zemin and Premier Zhu Rongji first announced plans, in 1997, to restructure the industrial sector, and privatize large parts of it, the beleaguered local governments found another way of shedding their mounting losses. This was to privatize hundreds of thousands, and then millions, of the local cooperative and collective enterprises that they had set up in the previous two decades.

How does one account for Jiang Zemin and Zhu Rongji's bad

timing? One explanation is that the recession of 1996–2000 caught them by surprise. They must have been aware that in 1996 industrial employment had actually shrunk for the first time since the beginning of the reforms, and investment in fixed assets (corresponding to gross fixed investment in Western accounting) had grown by only 14.5 percent, which was less than half the growth recorded two years earlier. But this had not deterred them, because they clearly believed that China had achieved a "soft landing" after four years of a virtually uncontrollable boom. They therefore expected the economy to continue growing and creating new jobs, to which those laid off by the SOEs could move. But the timing and pace of privatization in the nineties shows that, as with the introduction of the household responsibility system in agriculture and the devolution of taxation and investment powers in 1981–'83, privatization too was forced on the center by the local governments. This may have been another instance of the tail wagging the dog in the Chinese state.

The recession may well have played a crucial part in determining the timing of the 1997 decision. Township and municipal governments had begun to sell urban and rural collective enterprises to private owners in a small way in 1994. This had gathered momentum rapidly in 1995, 1996, and 1997—i.e., well before Jiang and Zhu made their initial announcement in September 1997, and even further ahead of their formal announcement of a three-year plan for reconstruction in 1998. As Table 6.4 in the previous chapter shows, the investment boom of the early nineties had begun to slacken in 1995. The resulting decline in demand would be felt first by the smallest, least well-known, or most remote enterprises. These would be the ones set up by the municipal, township, and village administrations. For them, privatization was a heaven-sent opportunity for getting these loss-making enterprises off their account books.

Retrenchment and unemployment

Privatization, and the transfer of enterprises from the state sector to the non-state sector, was accompanied by a large-scale retrenchment of workers in the state sector.[161] The government had expected that workers who lost their jobs in state-owned enterprises would soon get absorbed by the rapidly growing non-state and private sectors. That was why it announced only a three-year program to reduce the workforce in the SOEs, in 1998. But the recession invalidated the basic premise upon which this program was built—while the government was laying off workers from the SOEs, the non-state enterprises were also looking for ways to reduce their labor force. The economy had all but ceased to create new jobs.

As with so much else that happened during this period, the central government in China does not acknowledge this. Officially, there was an increase of 82.9 million urban jobs and a decline of 5.3 million jobs in the rural areas between 1995 and 2005.[162] Thus, 77.6 million new jobs were created in the decade after 1995.

But a closer examination of the employment data shows a huge discrepancy between the overall figures and the sectoral data. Over the same period, the *economically active* population increased from 688.5 million to 778.7 million, an increase of 90.2 million. But urban employment declined by 1.96 million while rural employment grew by 18.5 million. Even these figures are deceptive, because they give the impression that there was a net shift of economic activity from the cities to the townships and villages. This would have been welcome if it had been voluntary. But as authors John Wilson Lewis and Xue Litai pointed out in 2003, the return flow to the villages was anything but that. "[U]rban unemployment," they wrote, "forced tens of millions of rural immigrants back to their home villages and police repression failed to stem the rising tide of discontent."[163]

The sectoral data only account for 16.5 million out of the 90.2 million increase in the economically active population. So what did the remaining 73.7 million do? It is likely that they became migrant workers—casual or seasonal labor—who are included neither in the urban nor the rural tally, but are included in the total estimate of employment, which is obtained independently. A sample survey carried out by the National Bureau of Statistics in 2005 showed that the number of migrant workers who were holding down jobs in urban areas for more than six months in the year amounted to 145.8 million.[164] A decade earlier they had numbered about 80 million.[165] The increase in their number accounts for the major part of the discrepancy.

The ballooning of the migrant labor force is proof that nearly all of the new entrants into the labor between 1995 and 2005 market entered it at the bottom in jobs that were poorly paid, offered no employment security, and provided no welfare benefits. There is no tally of migrant workers who work for less than six months a year in the urban areas.[166]

The demise of the workers' state

In the state sector the decline in employment opportunities hit workers in the manufacturing industry especially hard, accounting for more than four-fifths of the layoffs.[167] To ease the pain of separation, the government passed new social security laws that came into force in 1998. Intended for permanent workers who were employed before the contract working system came into being in 1986, it guaranteed them 60 percent of their last paycheck for a transitional period of three years. The workers laid off under this scheme, called off-post *(xiagang)* workers, were to retain their health and retirement benefits. While the official media claimed spectacular success for the policy, a detailed sample survey carried out by three researchers in five large cities at the end of 2001 showed that the laid-off workers had suffered a considerable fall in their incomes even when they found jobs. They also faced modest wage and pension arrears, a steep fall in health benefits, and high arrears of reimbursement for their health expenses.[168]

While the denial of health benefits seriously impoverished workers who fell ill, the delay in the payment of their pensions aroused the greatest anger, for it affected all the former workers of an enterprise and compounded their feelings of betrayal. Since it was a grievance that all could share, it emboldened them to protest. In Benxi, a railroad, coal, and steel industry city of just under one million in Liaoning, all but one of more than twenty protests were triggered by pension arrears. The lone exception was a sit-in, in front of the city government office, to demand subsidies for *xiagang* workers who had been denied all benefits.[169] One typical Benxi coal miner—who had been jobless for ten years, had not received any payments from her former firm or the state, and had lost any health insurance coverage she once had—said that she would still not consider demonstrating in order to obtain the retrenchment benefits to which she was entitled, but would protest with great resolve if, upon reaching retirement age, her pension was delayed or withheld.[170]

Although it affected fewer people, it was the loss of health care benefits that did the most damage, for the illness of a single member could virtually bankrupt the entire family. The five-city study cited earlier revealed that only 56 percent of the laid-off workers continued to be covered in 2001, as against 69 percent in 1996. In three of the five cities, the coverage had fallen below 50 percent. The reason for the drop was that very few of the new employers offered health benefits. More than half of the respondents reported that they were dissatisfied with their condition.[171]

Overall, in 2000, the per capita income in the families of laid-off workers fell to just over half of their average pre-layoff income. In cities with dying industry, such as Changchun in the northeast, it fell by three-quarters.[172] Most of the laid-off workers were thrown back on their past savings and, when these ran out, were forced to borrow from, or live off, other members of their families. The workers did not take their sudden loss of security and status passively. By one frequently cited estimate, there were as many as sixty thousand protests by labor in 1998, and if a report in the *Far Eastern Economic Review* is to be believed, as many as one hundred thousand the following year. [173] Throughout the 1990s, the Ministry of Labor tallied thousands of public gatherings, strikes, petitions, and demonstrations each year; according to a trade union journal, 247 workers' demonstrations occurred in Henan during 1998 alone.[174] These demonstrations were carried out after securing the permission of the authorities, but not all of them remained orderly. The same report noted that more than half of the "incidents" in that province centered on some combination of wage arrears, pensions, and "livelihood difficulties," and that a further quarter (26 percent) were based on grievances involving "poor labor relations" or "illegal dismissals." Chinese enterprises cut back on separation benefits also by following the "last in, first out" layoff principle. Since pensions did not have to be paid until the workers attained the age of retirement this not only minimized their pension obligations but also postponed the need to pay them by several decades. A survey of Chinese and foreign newspapers from 1996 to April 2001 showed that it was mainly the younger laid-off workers who were able to find work once again. In 1998, only half of the laid-off workers were able to find new jobs. In 1999, the ratio fell to 35 percent. In 2000, it fell further to 26 percent, and in 2001 it dropped to a paltry 11 percent.[175]

It was only after 2001, when the recession ended and the economy began its next surge of growth, that the number of workers laid off from the SOEs began to decline. From 5.2 million in 2001, the number fell to 2.6 million in 2003.[176] But the workers' problems did not end. For the new surge in growth was markedly more capital-intensive, and created far fewer jobs, than the surges of the 1980s and 1990s. The restructuring that was begun with such optimism in 1998 has thus left a legacy of bitterness that haunts the Chinese state to this day. The workers captured this sentiment in satire:

> *In the '50s we helped people.*
> *In the '60s we criticized people.*
> *In the '70s we deceived people.*
> *In the '80s everybody hired everybody else.*
> *In the '90s we "slaughter"[177] whoever we see.*

The plight of migrant labor

The ones who suffered most in the cities from the onset of recession were not the laid-off *(xiagang)* workers of the state sector, but the hordes of migrant workers who had flooded into the cities during the decades of rapid industrial expansion. Migrant workers were the key to China's economic miracle in the eighties and nineties. By being the first to seize the opportunity created by the advent of a free market for food in the cities, they created the pool of available labor that Chinese industry needed for its rapid expansion. In the process, they prospered. Many ended as entrepreneurs; several became millionaires; and many more became respected managers of large enterprises.[178] The money they sent back to their homes lifted their families out of poverty. The skills and aspirations they developed cracked the shell of fatalism in their villages. But migrant workers enjoyed none of the protection that urban residents did. They did not even enjoy the rights they continued to have in their home counties. They were, in the truest sense, children of Karl Polanyi's "stark utopia," at the mercy of the market with nothing but their labor to sell. As a result, when the good times ended and boom turned into recession they were among the very first to feel the blow.

The *xiagang* workers lost secure, high-status jobs and had to take up insecure, low-status ones. But they did not lose the pensions, insurance, and welfare benefits that they had enjoyed under the Communist state. Nor did they lose their urban registration *(hukou)*, which entitled them to subsidized living quarters and schooling for their children. The migrant workers had none of these benefits. Two surveys, conducted in twelve cities in 2001 and 2005, covering 5,516 migrant households, showed that although their members jointly made almost as much as the families of urban *hukou* holders, they were able to do so only by working far, far harder. In the five largest cities included in the survey, the migrants earned an average of 4.6 yuan an hour, while the residents earned 14.7 yuan. In all twelve cities, nearly all the adults in migrant families worked, and each worked, on an average, for sixty-four hours a week. By contrast, very few resident families had more than one working adult member, and he or she worked on average for just over forty hours a week. Only by working so hard could migrant families overcome the difference in wage rates.[179]

The cause of this disparity is the household registration (or *hukou*) system, which, through most of the days of the Communist state, linked the civic rights enjoyed by the citizen to his or her place of residence. The *hukou* system is as old as China itself; its roots can be traced back to the Xia dynasty, which ruled from the twenty-first to the sixteenth century BC. Often modified but never annulled, it has remained a prime tool of governance in the Chinese state ever since. But in pre-Communist China it was used by successive dynasties for taxation, conscription, and the gathering of vital statistics only. Although a sharp urban-rural divide was a constant feature under all dynasties, the *hukou* system did not deny Chinese the freedom to move to and settle in any part of the country. This freedom was expressly reiterated by the PRC in 1949 and again in 1954, but its decision to concentrate on industrialization, which was of necessity urban-centered, led to what came to be called a "blind flow" of migrants from the villages into the towns.[180]

To check this, the PRC enacted a household registration regulation in 1958. Thenceforth, citizens enjoyed access to all public utilities and services only in their place of residence. This included employment, food coupons, housing, education for children, and health and old-age benefits. The *hukou* system chained the rural population to the villages and, since under the thrust for industrialization most of the jobs in the modern sector were being created in the cities, over time created a new kind of urban-rural divide that Chinese scholars increasingly compare to the caste system in India. The resemblance to the Indian caste system was reinforced by the fact that no matter where a child was born, he or she was given the *hukou* of the mother's original place of residence. While this condemned the rural population to relative poverty, it did not yet create an awareness of the glaring disparity between urban and rural living standards, since there was little scope for migration.

The opportunity to migrate to the cities appeared only after the restoration of private farming through the household responsibility system in 1978–'80 created large agricultural surpluses that the peasants were able to sell in the urban markets. This created a free market for food and loosened the iron grip of food rationing upon the freedom to move within China. Like most sections of society, migrant workers initially gained hugely from economic liberalization. By 1995 there were around eighty million such workers who spent more than two hundred days a year in urban areas,[181] sending $35 billion a year back to their families. Not only were they, themselves, earning up to seven times as much in industry as they had done in agriculture, but by moving out of the villages they also reduced the agriculture-dependent workforce and raised its average productivity by approximately a third.[182] But by the early nineties, the flood of rural migrants had awakened fears of another "blind wave" of farmers entering the cities, and created a backlash among the urban residents. This caused the city authorities to harden the *hukou* system in a variety of ways. Before they could secure work, migrants had to either be given a temporary residence permit or furnish a variety of permits: an identity card from the migrant's home county; a temporary residence certificate from the police in the city where the migrant worked, to be renewed each year; an employment certificate from the home county; and an employment card from the labor bureau of the city to which the person had migrated. These requirements were introduced by the Ministry of Public Security, ostensibly to keep a check on migration—but as with all similar laws, they became excellent pretexts for extortion by local authorities.

Unsurprisingly, therefore, migrants had to pay for each of these permits not only the stipulated fee but also a much larger "consideration" to the cadres manning the government bureaus. A sample survey by the Ministry of Labor in 1996 showed that instead of stipulated fees totaling twenty yuan, migrants were paying 223 yuan to get their cards. These levies cut into their already meager earnings, and forced them to work longer and longer hours to earn the minimum they needed to sustain themselves and their families back in the villages.[183]

Migrants were discriminated against in other subtle ways. In 1995, the Beijing municipal government enacted regulations aimed at tightening the control of housing rental to rural migrants. The regulation stipulated that any institution or person leasing a house to non-Beijing residents had to obtain a house-leasing certificate from the district or county government and renew the certificate annually. The house or apartment had to be privately owned, and certified by the police bureau as meeting stipulated safety standards. Even more odiously, the owner had to sign affidavits with police bureaus and family planning agencies accepting the responsibility for preventing over-quota births in the house or apartment. He or she also had to pay a fee equivalent to 2 percent of the annual rent.[184]

But the most deeply resented form of discrimination was practiced against migrants' children. Children with an urban *hukou* were, and remain, entitled to nine years of free schooling. But migrant families have to pay an annual fee ranging from three thousand to thirty thousand yuan per child to have their children enter public schools.[185] Most cannot afford the sum.

Beginning in 1996, as recession tightened its grip on the Chinese economy, the insecurity of the migrant laborers began to increase. Urban price and living standards data for 1996 showed that 37.5 percent of urban households reported a drop in living standards. The decline was unevenly distributed: While 54 percent of those in the lowest quintile experienced a fall, only 3.8 percent of those in the highest quintile did so. In 1997, the proportion of losers in the lowest quintile increased to 60 percent and in the highest to 20 percent. Since migrant workers fell squarely into the lowest quintile, they were the main victims of recession.

Chronic insecurity has told on the mental health of migrant workers. Several studies in the early 2000s showed that migrant workers and their families were suffering from chronic anxiety and depression, and that they were staying on in the urban jobs to which they had been assigned because conditions at home in the village were even worse. This became apparent in 2005 when the increase, in their families retained earnings and decline in arbitrary demands by local officials, after Hu Jintao abolished taxes on agriculture and took away the right of local governments to extract fees for services persuaded, large numbers of migrants did not return to the cities after their annual visit to their villages.[186] This was partly responsible for a shortage of labor that developed suddenly in 2006 and worsened in 2007.

For China's developing middle class and its core of social activists, the conditions in which migrants live and work is the most immediately visible proof of the dark side of the country's rapid development. Not surprisingly, therefore, as the recession of the late nineties entrenched the predatory behavior of the city authorities toward migrants, stories of their mistreatment began to appear in the newspapers with increasing frequency. One that shocked the entire country was that of Sun Zhigang, a college-educated fashion designer from Hubei province, whose wrongful arrest, detention, and custodial death in Guangzhou in April 2003 led to a national outcry that compelled a change of regulations governing the treatment of migrant workers by the Guangzhou administration. On April 25, 2003, a daily newspaper in Guangzhou published the following report:

> Sun was stopped on his way to an internet cafe by local police who asked him to show his identity card and temporary living permit. The temporary living permit (or *zanzhuzheng*) was a document then required for visiting workers from other provinces. Sun had forgotten to bring his identity card with him, and had not yet obtained a permit. As was then common practice, Guangzhou police took Sun to the local police station. Sun called his roommate, Cheng, from the police station on a mobile phone and asked Cheng to bring money for bail and Sun's identity card. Cheng did so, but was told by police that Sun could not be released on bail—most likely, Cheng learned, because Sun had "talked back" during his interrogation.
>
> The following day, Sun was transferred to a migrant detention center. Again, he called friends and asked for help. Sun's supervisor

went to the detention center to attempt to get Sun released on bail. However, he "was told to come back the following day, because staff were about to go off duty." Later that day, Sun's friends called the detention center again and learned that Sun had been transferred to the medical clinic within the detention center. Again, Sun's roommate Cheng tried to visit Sun in the clinic, but was turned away by staff who said that only family members could visit. On March 20th, Sun's friends called the clinic and learned that Sun had died of, reportedly, a heart attack. Sun's previous medical history had shown no sign of heart problems.

Sun's family and friends requested an autopsy of his body at Zhongshan University. The autopsy center of Guangzhou's Zhongshan University delivered a report on April 18th, indicating that Sun had died in shock and that he had been heavily beaten on the back and many other places on the body. Evidence of heavy hemorrhaging was found in the back and the muscles on his sides. A doctor who wished to remain anonymous told the reporter that Sun must have been beaten several times, for the hemorrhage was very unusual and serious.

Doctors from Zhongshan University were all stunned by the brutality. One of the doctors said that Sun was not only beaten on the back and buttocks, but that his knees were also burned. All the facts clearly showed that Sun was beaten to death.

It is reasonably certain that Sun Zhigang was being shaken down for a bribe by the police and died because he refused to pay. The public outcry unleashed by the story made the central government and the Guangzhou administration take rapid action. On June 10, 2003, the Guangzhou municipal intermediate court sentenced twelve persons to sentences ranging from three years' imprisonment to death. One person, the principal assailant in the hospital, was sentenced to death, and was an accomplice given a death sentence with two years' reprieve; two others received life sentences, and the remainder received between three and fifteen years in prison. Six other officials were sentenced to two years' imprisonment for their complicity.

Sun's case has triggered a major debate on the validity of the holding system and the two-decade-old Measures for Internment and Deportation of Urban Vagrants and Beggars. The holding measures, an administrative regulation issued by the State Council in 1982, the legal basis for internment and deportation by public security authorities.[187] By 2003 the powers they gave to the police and other city authorities had become widely used instruments for extortion from the poor. Sun resisted because he was well-educated and already had a job. But had he not been, and had he not had a group of friends and employers who valued him, his case would never have been investigated, let alone hit the headlines. The central government understood this and used the occasion to abolish the law permitting deportation altogether.

However, with no structural change in the *hukou* laws to give migrant workers residential rights in the cities, their persecution and exploitation by those in power has continued. In June 2008, between ten thousand and thirty thousand migrant workers rioted for three days in Guizhou, attacked and burned a police station, and destroyed twenty-nine cars, including police vehicles, because they believed that the police were trying to cover up the rape and murder of a teenage girl by the son of a city official. Weeks later in July, hundreds of migrant workers attacked another police station and smashed and burned government property in Kanmen, in Zhejiang province, after one of their number was severely beaten by the police.

One swallow does not a summer make. But in China they are beginning to darken the sky.

Distress in the provinces

In the rural areas, as more and more township and village enter-prises (TVEs) began to incur losses, the local governments had to choose between subsidizing them and cutting them loose. The seri-ous fiscal crisis that enveloped all tiers of the local administration would in any case have made them look for ways to reduce their fiscal burden. Handing the loss-making TVEs over to their workers and managers, who stood a better chance of turning them around than any outsider, was the best course open to them. A study of the privatization of 670 TVEs, carried out in fifteen randomly se-lected counties in two provinces, Zhejiang and Jiangsu,[188] showed that there was a marked rise in the rate of privatization between 1993 and 1998. Township leaders privatized only 8 percent of the firms under their control in 1993. But as the recession deepened in 1997 and 1998, the rate of privatization rose to 30 percent.[189] The three-year restructuring program announced by the govern-ment in 1998 gave this option the necessary legitimacy. Between 1993 and 2002, the number of collective enterprises decreased from 5,156,500 to 1,885,900. In the same period of time, the num-ber of registered private enterprises increased from 237,900 to 2,435,300.[190] The increase in the latter was a fraction of the decline in the former. While a majority of the loss-makers were no doubt folded into other enterprises, it is difficult to believe that many, perhaps several hundred thousand, did not simply stop functioning and get closed down.[191]

The workers in the TVEs had to bear the brunt of these changes. Large numbers not only found that the enterprises they worked in had been privatized, but that the township administrations had sequestered a part of their savings to confer this dubious benefit upon them.

Privatization meant ownership, which was initially welcomed. But ownership involved incurring risk. And as economic prospects darkened, the risks began to outweigh the benefits of ownership. Workers who had welcomed privatization when it began became increasingly reluctant to invest their savings, even in the enterprises where they worked and therefore knew best. The OECD did a detailed study of the first experiment in the complete privatization of 210 small- and medium-sized enterprises in Zhucheng, a town in Shandong. In 1994, the workers willingly bought between two and five shares in the enterprises on payment of one thousand yuan per share. But when profits began to flag, presumably because of the economic slowdown, many of them had second thoughts. Since the shares could not be sold to outsiders, most of the workers sold their shares to the managers, or to others within the enterprise, and managed to make a small profit.[192]

But as the recession deepened in 1996 and 1997, and more and more of the small and medium-sized enterprises began to fail, the sales of shares to the workers began to acquire a coercive tinge. In a similar sale in 1998, when the recession was at its height, workers in a seven-hundred-employee plant were forced to buy five thousand yuan worth of shares each, with the threat that if they did not do so, they would lose their jobs and be denied all the benefits that they were entitled to. In 1998, five thousand yuan was about ten months' salary. A hundred or so of the employees refused, and resorted to one of the early collective actions of the post-reform period.[193]

Insider privatization was only one of several tactics local administrations employed to cope with the declining viability of the collective enterprises they had set up during the boom years. Another was to encourage mergers and buyouts of weak enterprises by stronger non-state or private firms. This resulted in a dramatic decline in the total number of enterprises, deepening the fiscal crisis of the township administrations. Researcher Lynette Ong found that in one county in Szechuan province, where there had been 239 township enterprises in 1995, only thirty were left in 2003.[194] Most of the townships had set up TVEs not only to generate employment but to create an additional source of revenue, via the business tax, to finance their budgets. In the early nineties, the TVEs had not yet known failure on any significant scale. It had therefore seemed the right thing to do. As one township official told Ong: "Many collective enterprises were developed out of a 'me-too' mentality and ready access to financial capital. There was no viable business model to start with, [and] no due diligence conducted to ensure market demand for the products existed. And many township administrations set up enterprises and built more factories simply because their counterparts in other towns were doing so."

With their power to tax drastically reduced by the 1994 tax reforms, and their enterprises turning into loss-makers and requiring privatization, the township administrations turned in desperation to borrowing. Since the bank reforms of 1997 had also sharply reduced their access to credit from the state-owned banks, they established rural credit foundations (RCFs)—informal banks totally under their control—and offered astronomical rates of interest to raise savings from the better-off peasants and cadres. More than one-third of the loans these local informal banks disbursed went to the township enterprises, and one-sixth went to various government agencies; most of the borrowers defaulted. In the second half of the nineties, when a large proportion of the township enterprises collapsed, the RCFs became insolvent and had to be taken over by the central government. The poor again lost what little savings they had, for 70 percent of the deposits made with the RCFs had come from individual families.[195]

India

9 WHY WAS INDIA'S GROWTH SO SLOW?

GIVEN THAT INDIA had a fully developed national market and a thriving private sector by 1947, why did it remain among the slowest-growing economies in the world for a full forty years? Most economists place the blame at the door of India's first prime minister, Jawaharlal Nehru, and his fascination with Soviet-style central planning. In India the purpose of planning, the economists point out, was not to allocate resources and set production targets for state-owned enterprises, but to achieve the same result through an elaborate system of regulation imposed upon the private sector. These controls had the unintended effect of slowing down growth. It was only after they were removed that India was able to realize its true potential.

This explanation is not so much incorrect as incomplete, for it does not explain why India's GDP grew by barely 1.25 percent a year during the entire first half of the twentieth century, prior to the enactment of regulation-based planning. Nor does it explain why India stuck to this model of growth for a full two decades after it became clear that this had yielded neither efficient growth nor economic self-reliance. The explanation to the first puzzle lies in the impact of British colonialism; to the second lies in the rise to economic and political dominance of an intermediate class of property owners—an intermediate bourgeoisie—which, unlike its later counterpart in China, choked, instead of accelerated, growth.

Britain's neglect, if not active discouragement, of industrialization in its colonies is understandable. From the 1870s it faced rising tariffs against its manufactured exports to Europe, and had to find new markets for its products. It therefore kept the markets of its colonies firmly open to exports from the mother country. What is far less easy to understand is the continued discouragement of industrialization under an independent Indian government. The customary division of India's development into three phases obscures, instead of illuminates, the cause.

In this analysis the first phase, which lasted a brief ten years from 1947 to 1957, was one of a relatively open economy. During this period centralized planning, which began with the first five-year plan in 1951, was confined to setting a few important targets for growth. Outside the few sectors that had been reserved for development by the state, the central government made little effort to formulate detailed production plans. The second period, which began in with the second five-year plan in 1956–'57 and lasted till 1990–'91, was one of pronounced economic autarchy. India became an inward-looking economy that shunned the world market and focused all its energy on achieving self-reliance by minimizing imports. These policies slowed growth, made the economy inefficient, and led to a succession of five foreign exchange crises, between 1957 and 1991. The third phase began in 1991, when the government finally discarded its autarchic policies, went back to indicative planning, and made a conscious effort to link the economy to the global market. This segmentation of India's growth experience is a useful tool for highlighting the inefficiency of centrally planned economies and underlining the virtues of the open, export-led growth model that economists like I. M. D. Little, Maurice Scott, Jagdish N. Bhagwati, and Anne Krueger had begun advocating.[196] But other than blaming Nehru and his planners, it throws very little light on why India chose to adopt an autarchic growth model in the first place, and then persist with it for four decades. To understand this it is necessary to examine each of these phases of development in greater detail.

After the first "open" period from 1947 to 1957, the economy went through four distinct phases of autarchic development. These were 1957–'66, in which a centrally controlled command economy was built; 1966–'75, a period of half-baked socialism, in which the failure of the command economy was attributed to the lack of sufficient control instead of too much of it; 1975–'81, when the excessive control of previous period was reversed; and a fourth period, from 1981 to 1991, when even the government of Indira Gandhi was convinced of the need to abandon the command economy but, lacking the courage to take on the powerful vested interests that it had built up around it, carried out reforms "by stealth." The table below shows how the economy reacted to increased controls by slowing down and becoming less efficient, and to even small relaxations of control by immediately picking up its pace of growth. Of particular interest is the rise and later fall of the amount of capital that it needed to produce every extra dollar's worth of growth. This is reflected by the incremental capital to output ratio (ICOR) given below. The ICOR rose with every increase in controls and fell with every relaxation.

Table 9.1

Growth of GDP, Rate of Gross Domestic Capital Formation as a Percentage of GDP and the ICOR

Year*	1951–'56	1956–'66	1966–'75	1975–'81	1981–'91	1991–'92	1992–'97	1997–2002	2003–'07
GDP	3.7	3.3	3.3	4.3	5.5	1.4	6.8	6.3(6.0)	8.9
Cap formation	8.9	14.0	14.0	16.6	20.2	22.1	22.4	22.5	31
ICOR*	2.4	4.2	4.2	3.9	3.6	——	3.3	3.8	3.4

Source: Government of India's Economic Survey 2007–2008, Statistical Tables, Tables 1.4 and 1.5.
*The higher this incremental capital to output ratio is, the more inefficient the growth.

The causes of India's prolonged discouragement of industrialization have dominated economic policy debate for most of the past four decades. Foreign scholars, and a majority of Indian economists, put the entire blame upon the Nehru government's fascination with Soviet-style centralized planning and the dominance, in the Planning Commission and the major universities, of economists with a visceral distrust of the market. This view confuses correlation with causality. There can be no doubt that Nehru was impressed by the achievements of the Soviet Union, and that the Planning Commission was full of socialist-minded economists. But the reason the government gave up its relatively open economic policies of the first decade in favor of economic autarchy was entirely different: It was forced to do so by a severe foreign exchange crisis that hit the country in 1957. The crisis was brought on by the exhaustion of the foreign exchange reserves that it had built up in the form of sterling balances held in London, during the Second World War.

There had been a conflict within the Congress Party over its relationship to Indian industry ever since the twenties, the decade in which Indian industrialists had become its main financiers. The party therefore not only owed the industrialists a considerable debt, but its leaders had formed strong, durable links with the leaders of Indian business. This was a constant irritant to the younger generation of the party, who had been swept away by a wave of populist enthusiasm for socialism after the Bolshevik Revolution in Russia. This younger, more radical, wing of the party had found its idol in Pandit Jawaharlal Nehru.

At the time of independence the market was itself in considerable disrepute. Most of the decision-makers of the early fifties had lived through the economic crash of the 1930s and seen the harm that an unregulated market economy could do. India was not, therefore, the only place where theories of autarchic economic growth, in which centralized planning replaced the market as the instrument for securing an efficient allocation of resources, had become popular.

In India the yearning for an alternative to the market mechanism surfaced in 1949, when the Ministry of Industry proposed an industrial licensing system to ensure the efficient allocation of scarce resources and balanced economic development. This was incorporated in the Industries Act of 1951. The yearning surfaced again at an annual meeting of the Congress Party in 1954, held at Avadi. At this meeting, the left wing of the party scored a significant victory over the moderates by getting a resolution passed that called for the establishment of a "socialist pattern of society." This came to be known as the Avadi resolution.

But despite sustained pressure from this "ginger group" within the Congress, independent India's first government, under Nehru, did not adopt a closed economy model of development. The first Industrial Policy Resolution, promulgated in 1948, reserved only three industries for the state—defense, atomic energy, and the railways. In addition, it reserved the exclusive right to develop six other key industries: iron and steel, shipbuilding, mineral oils, coal, aircraft production, and telecommunications equipment. As for the private sector, the Nehru government gave it a substantial degree of protection in the form of a generalized set of tariffs (as against the case-by-case protection that the British had conceded), and assured it that there would be no talk of nationalization for the next ten years. Despite the government's awareness of the need to conserve foreign exchange, it placed few bans on imports because of the immense reserves that it had accumulated, as sterling balances held in London, during the war. By the end of the war in 1945, these reserves amounted to 2.5 billion pounds sterling. Even after two years of postwar reconstruction, and the division of the remaining sterling balance between India and Pakistan, on August 5, 1947 (ten days before independence), India still had foreign exchange reserves of 1.16 billion pounds (a little under five billion dollars),[197] more than two years' worth of imports.[198] The government's relaxed attitude toward imports was therefore easy to understand.

However, these reserves ran out in just ten years. First, the devaluation of the pound by 31 percent in 1949 forced India to make an equivalent devaluation of the rupee. This reduced the real value of its reserves by an equal amount. Second, heavy public sector investment in hydroelectric schemes, the rehabilitation and expansion of the railway system, and a variety of other infrastructure projects necessitated heavy imports that did not generate any corresponding exports. Last, importers of consumer goods, who had read the writing on the wall long before the government, went on a buying spree abroad. In 1957, the government found that the sterling balances were nearly exhausted, and brought the boom down on all except the most essential imports. India's move toward economic autarchy was therefore prompted less by ideology then by self-preservation.

Important shifts of economic policy are never devoid of political consequences. None of the policymakers of 1956 could have foreseen that their well-meaning but knee-jerk closure of imports would release not only economic but also political forces that would close the economy for the next four decades.

The shortages created by the sudden cutoff of imports created a sellers' market and huge windfall profits for the traders who had succeeded in obtaining import licenses before the closure was imposed. Many of them used these profits as seed capital to start manufacturing the very things they used to import. In many cases, their former suppliers arranged for them to obtain secondhand machinery to do so, occasionally donating such machinery as a mark of goodwill. This hectic import substitution led to a burst of investment. Industrial growth therefore averaged 9.5 percent between

1956 and 1965. But it also caused inflation and raised the cost of exports. Cutting off imports allowed the government to avoid devaluing the rupee yet again. As a result domestic inflation steadily eroded the competitiveness of India's exports. So the initial imbalance in India's foreign trade persisted and necessitated stricter and stricter controls on imports. By degrees this became the sole purpose, bordering upon an obsession, of the planning mechanism that the government had set up in 1949 to 1951.[199]

The ever greater complexity of planning lengthened the delay between identifying emerging demand and sanctioning investment to meet it. By the mid-sixties, these delays were exceeding a year in as many as one in six projects, and the ones held up were more often than not the largest investments.[200] This perpetuated the shortages in the economy and shielded the "intermediate" stratum of small manufacturers that had come into being after 1957 from competition. By degrees, therefore, this stratum was able to consolidate its identity and develop a common purpose—the perpetuation of these shortages. In this, the small manufacturers were joined by traders, who were able to extract exorbitant profits from the black market the shortages gave birth to.

Two other groups also shared this interest. The first were the farmers, who produced foodgrains and cash crops not for subsistence but for sale in the market. The second was the bureaucracy. Farmers with produce to sell had an interest in shortages because the demand for agricultural produce is "inelastic"—i.e., insensitive to price changes. As a result, a poor harvest actually increased the cash income of farmers who produced for the market, even though it reduced their yields. By the same token, a good harvest caused them to lose income precisely because it caused a disproportionate fall in prices. The only way that rich farmers could protect their incomes in bumper crop years was to get the government to set a minimum price for their produce and guarantee purchase at that price. They did this by taking advantage of a system that had been set up during the Second World War by the British, to procure food for the army facing the Japanese on the India–Burma border. This system of levy procurement was continued for a few years after independence, to tide over the disruption of food supplies caused by Partition, and then was all but given up in the 1950s. As the farmers began to exercise their political power in the sixties, the "procurement" system was given a fresh lease on life, but now with the altered purpose of providing a minimum support price for foodgrains and to build a buffer stock against inflation during bad harvest years.

The other group that developed a strong vested interest in controls, the bureaucracy, wanted to exert control for exactly the same reasons as those of the Chinese cadres in local government after 1981. More controls meant more permissions, and each permission commanded a "price." All these types of income are different forms of what Alfred Marshall, one of the founders of neoclassical economics at the turn of the twentieth century, had dubbed "quasi-rent"—i.e., not natural rent, which was obtained from land because its supply was necessarily limited, but rent obtained from manmade shortages. The closure of the economy after 1957 therefore created a class of "rent-seekers" with a powerful common interest in the capture of political power. For only by this means could it perpetuate the controls from which it derived its economic power. It is this common endeavor that, by degrees, turned the four groups that composed the intermediate strata into a distinct political class.

The consolidation of these four groups into an "intermediate class" did not happen immediately after the adoption of a regime of controls in 1957. Between 1957 and 1966, the high rate of growth of the Indian economy created enough new demand for everyone to prosper. The conflict of interest between the intermediate stratum of entrepreneurs and the large industrial houses remained dormant. This came to the surface only in 1966. A succession of external shocks—two wars in 1962 and 1965, followed immediately by two droughts in 1965 and 1966—precipitated a severe financial crisis for the government, at the same time that it ran out of foreign exchange for a second time.

The Sino-Indian Border War in 1962 ended in a humiliating defeat for the Indian army. The government responded by doubling expenditure on defense. A very large part of this had used foreign exchange. The war with Pakistan in 1965 led to a second surge in defense expenditure as the equipment lost in the hostilities had to be replaced.

The drought in 1965 brought the output of foodgrains down from eighty-nine million tons in 1964–'65 to seventy-two million tons in 1965–'66. To make matters still worse, it was followed the very next year by another drought, affecting about half of the country, which kept the output of foodgrains down to seventy-six million tons. The impact of these droughts was amplified by their having come after a prolonged period of near-stagnation in agricultural output.[201]

The financial crisis was caused mainly by the two wars and droughts, but the ground for it was prepared by the consistent rise of the government's nondevelopmental expenditures. The government did not allow the rise in defense expenditure to choke investment, but sharply increased taxation. The ratio of tax revenues to GDP, which had been a mere 6 percent of GDP in 1951–'52, rose to a peak of 14.1 percent in 1965–'66. As a result, government income rose from about twenty-one billion rupees in that year to thirty-two billion rupees in 1965–'66.[202]

But this last effort exhausted the taxable capacity of the country. During the next seven years, despite repeated increases in tax rates, the ratio of tax revenues to the GDP remained between 13.2 and 14.7 percent.[203] So when the government was forced to devalue the rupee by 36 percent in 1966, it was unable to raise the additional domestic resources that it needed to meet the equivalent rise in the rupee cost of the imported capital goods and raw materials it needed to implement its development plans. It was therefore forced to cut back its investment. The original draft of the fourth five-year plan, which was to cover the period 1966 to 1971, had envisaged a 40 percent increase in investment in real terms. But instead of accepting it, Indira Gandhi, who had become the prime minister in January 1966, decided to declare a "plan holiday" and cut back public investment sharply.

The "holiday" lasted for three years. During this period the average annual public investment fell in real terms by a third. The cut in orders from the government spread like a giant ripple through the rest of Indian industry. The main victims were other state-owned enterprises. The railway wagon industry, for instance, had built up a capacity of twenty-six thousand wagons a year. But the railways, their only buyer, reduced its orders from this figure to ten thousand wagons a year. The steel plants found themselves with a glut of steel. The Mining and Allied Machinery Corporation, designed to produce coal-mining machinery, found itself without a single order. Hindustan Machine Tools, one of the few profitable state-owned enterprises, plunged into the red and began to look for export orders. The sale of its machine tools fell from 546 million rupees in 1965–'66 to a mere 54.2 million rupees in 1970–'71.

During the second and third five-year plans the private sector had invested heavily in cement, chemicals, aluminium, copper, engineering, and other heavy industries. By 1966, the public sector accounted for about 60 percent of the total investment in the country, and accounted for purchases of about half the cement, one-third of the paper, and around half or a little more of the steel, aluminium, and copper sold in the country. The collapse of public sector demand sent many of the new investors in these industries into financial crisis. The two successive droughts also sharply reduced the demand for consumer goods and selected inputs from the rural sector, which lasted till the end of 1967. The conjunction created recessionary conditions in industry: Industrial growth fell from 9 percent per annum, between 1951 and 1964–'65, to 3 percent between 1965–'66 and 1972–'73, and the sellers' market that had existed ever since independence quite suddenly vanished.[204] Partly as a result of the decline in public investment and partly because of the slump in demand, the growth rate of steel, cement, and paper output fell from 12 percent a year between 1951–'52 and 1965–'66 to 1.4 percent, 5 percent, and 4 percent, respectively, during the next seven years. The recession persisted. Almost five years later, a study of 335 industries by the research bureau of the *Economic Times* showed that two out of every five industries was still working at less than three-fifths of its capacity.[205] By then, it was apparent that the decline in growth was not cyclical but structural.

The sudden disappearance of shortages and emergence of a buyers' market brought the dormant conflict of interest between the large industrial houses (LIHs) and the intermediate stratum of entrepreneurs out into the open. The LIHs were far better equipped to withstand the rigors of a lean market than the new entrepreneurs. They had established brand names, more modern technology, greater access to resources at lower rates of interest, and better-established marketing networks. It was therefore inevitable that, barring those few who managed to establish a niche in the market, the new entrepreneurs stood little chance of survival in the long run. The only way to improve their chances was to prevent the LIHs from growing.

By the end of the sixties it had become apparent, not only to economists but also to policymakers in the government, that the government's policies to promote growth were not succeeding. Despite an impressive increase in the savings rate of the economy, the growth of GDP had declined from 4.1 percent during the first five-year plan to 3.48 percent during the next decade. The reason was that the incremental capital to output ratio, the surest measure of the efficiency of investment, had risen from 2.8 to 4.2. In short, the economy was taking one and a half times as much capital to produce a unit of increase in the GDP as it had during the first five-year plan. In the next three years, as the plan holiday took hold, growth slowed down still further to 3.1 percent and became even more inefficient.

Soul-searching within the government

This touched off a spate of inquiries within the government.[206] The central issue should have been "Did growth decline because the strategy of growth had not been properly implemented, or was the strategy itself—the single-minded obsession with import substitution, and a determination to replace the market mechanism with centralized planning—wrong?" Instead, the debate remained centered on the deficiencies of the plans themselves, and the lack of correspondence between the targets set in them and the policies adopted by the government. Nor was there any categorical rejection, among economists, of the planning framework and its implicit distrust of the market.

The tenor of the debate can be judged from the fact that even Jagdish Bhagwati and Padma Desai, the most outspoken critics of the existing strategy, did not really question the government's choice of centralized planning, and the attempt to make India as self-reliant as possible, but reserved most of their criticism for the way in which the planning had been implemented. In a phrase that became famous, they concluded: "Indian economic policy suffered from a paradox of inadequate *and* excessive attention to detail. . . . The inadequacy related to a failure to work out in-depth programmes . . . But there were also failures arising from an excessive attention to detail and these were to be embodied mainly in the proliferation of ill-conceived and excessive direct physical control of investments (down to product level) and foreign trade."[207]

Bhagwati and Desai also criticized the lack of coherence between plan targets and economic policy: "While in-depth *planning* improved, in the sense of the [Leontief-type] models . . . the impact of this was seen nowhere in matching improvements in economic *policies* designed to accelerate the planned development." (emphasis added)[208] They did not take the additional step of questioning the "plethora of restrictions and regulations that had little economic rationale." Nor did they question the idea, which permeated policymaking in India at the time, that the function of economic policy was to *regulate*, as distinct from *stimulate*, economic growth.[209] Although Bhagwati was subsequently to build a compelling case against the import-substitution strategy, and advocate opening the economy and linking it to the world market, in the late sixties this still lay a few years in the future.[210]

The catalytic role of the Hazari report

Both inside and outside the government, the debate remained permeated with distrust of the private sector. This allowed the defenders of centralized planning and state enterprise to claim that the remedy for the slowdown of growth lay not in abandoning these dirigiste policies, but in enforcing them even more rigorously than before. To do this, they seized upon the findings of a study of the impact of industrial licensing on the growth of Indian industry, carried out by R. K. Hazari,[211] which showed that 80 percent of the licenses issued by the government had been cornered by about twenty large industrial houses (LIHs); instead of preventing the concentration of economic power, industrial licensing had actually promoted it.

Hazari went on to describe the many ways in which the LIHs had not only cornered licenses but prevented others from getting them. The Industries Act had laid down four objectives to be fulfilled by industrial licensing. Apart from the main goal of allocating scarce investable resources—mainly, finance and foreign exchange—on the basis of a central plan, these objectives were to protect cottage and small-scale industries, to prevent the concentration of economic power, and to ensure the even distribution of industry across the nation. In addition, there were six criteria used to determine which applications to accept. This meant that there were, in theory at least, twenty-four possible grounds for rejecting an application. But this surfeit of criteria could also be made to work the other way: It gave someone who had decided to give a license to a favored applicant as many as twenty-four reasons to advance in favor of his or her decision. In effect, therefore, the surfeit of objectives and criteria meant that there were no criteria. Applications were given on a first come, first served basis. This gave the LIHs a decided advantage.

However, the LIHs were not content with that advantage, and employed a variety of other strategies to corner licenses. One of these was to make several applications, often in the name of subsidiaries or dummy companies, for establishment of productive capacity in a single industry or product, and to exhaust the target for capacity creation set in the five-year plan. The LIH would then buy the license from the recipient, and decide when to implement the committed investment. Preempting capacity creation in this way not only eliminated competition, but enabled the LIH to maintain a sellers' market and reap monopoly profits indefinitely.

The cornering of licenses was made still easier by the government's practice of dealing with license applications sequentially on a first come, first served basis, instead of bunching them together and assessing them on the basis of clearly established economic and technical criteria. This opened the way for preemption because licenses continued to be given till the targeted capacity was exhausted.

Intensification of controls

Hazari's finding—that the LIHs were abusing the licensing system to prevent others from receiving permission to enter their chosen fields of investment—became the springboard from which a "ginger group" in the Congress Party, supported and exhorted by the Communists, launched an all-out offensive against "big business." The report's findings were heavily publicized in the press, and caused a wave of anger through the country. This was skillfully manipulated by the left to draw attention away from the deficiencies of the licensing system and put all the blame on the LIHs. In the process, they turned Hazari's own proposals for reform on their head. To prevent the abuses, Hazari had suggested a liberalization of the licensing procedures, and the abandonment of the first come, first served system. But instead, the left insisted that the remedy lay in closing off large swaths of industry to the LIHs altogether, making it harder for them to get licenses in other areas, and more difficult for them to raise resources to finance their investment.

The creation of an intermediate regime

This struggle between the small manufacturers and the large industrial houses, to corner the benefits derived from a regime of controls, might have remained inconclusive but for a succession of purely fortuitous developments in the political system. The first was the decision, made by Indira Gandhi's government in 1967 and implemented in 1970, to ban corporations from making donations to political parties. The second was a split in the Congress Party, in July 1969, into a left wing (strengthened by the powerful patronage of Indira Gandhi herself) and a right wing (dubbed the Organizational Congress or simply the Congress [O]), and the rout of the latter in the 1971 elections.

Political funding had been a vexed issue from the first days of independence, because of an inexcusable oversight by the framers of the Indian Constitution, who had made no provision for the financing of elections.[212] The Congress Party, which had built a strong relationship with the indigenous Indian industrialists during its freedom struggle, did not at first feel the pinch. But by 1962, Nehru's socialism had made many industrialists start looking for a political alternative. The surge of inflation in the mid-sixties pushed up the cost of fighting elections dramatically. In the general elections of 1967, the Congress Party suddenly found itself critically short of election funds.

Indira Gandhi could have responded to this in a constructive way by setting up a publicly monitored, state-financed election fund for distribution to recognized political parties, as is the practice in several western European countries. But she chose instead to put the blame upon the industrialists and the princely families (then another prime source of political funds) whom she accused of transferring their allegiance from the Congress Party to right-wing opposition parties. To punish them, she first abolished tax benefits on donations to political parties, and then promulgated a total ban on company donations. This came into effect in 1970.

The Congress Party's calculations were not exactly a secret. Since political parties would continue to need funds, they would have to go back to the very same sources that they had tapped before, i.e., the large industrial houses. Since it was in power not only at the federal level but also in the majority of the states, the

Congress Party would get the lion's share of the funds. But hence-forth it would be a transactional relationship—funding in exchange for favors. The Congress also made it clear that the task of collect-ing large amounts of cash to deliver to the party rested squarely with the enterprises. If they did not oblige the party, they would be made to suffer through the withdrawal of these same "favors." The opposition parties, with little or no prospect of coming to power, and unable to guarantee the donors immunity from prosecution, would find their funding drastically curtailed. This was the begin-ning of the predatory state in India. Indira Gandhi had little idea of the demons that she was releasing into the political and eco-nomic system.

The ban on company donations restricted the supply of funds to the political system, when the need was for the exact opposite. The resulting hole in political system finances created the avenue by which the new entrepreneurs could convert their immediate fi-nancial gains into political power. Not only had they made windfall profits for a decade, but because a good part of these had been made in the black market (India was rife with price controls), the profits were in cash. Even when their deals were not in cash, they had little difficulty in withdrawing large sums from their banks as chas, for as owners of private companies that were not obliged to publish their accounts or hold shareholders meetings, they did not have to account for their actions. Within a short period, therefore, there was a sea change in the backers of the Congress Party. While the large industrial houses continued to "donate" funds, increas-ingly under duress, more and more of the money began to come from traders' and manufacturers' associations, whose members pooled their donations in order to lobby for concessions.

The split in the Congress Party freed Mrs. Gandhi to follow a still more populist policy. For the next eighteen months she ruled with the help of the Communist Party of India. In January 1971, she campaigned on the catchy slogan of "Quit Poverty," promising a slew of populist measures, which her party, the Congress-Indira (Congress [I], for short), claimed would bring instant relief to the beleaguered poor. When the Congress (O) was routed in these elections, the link between large-scale industry and the Congress Party was finally broken.

Unlike China—where, in its never-ending battle to control the provincial governments, the state periodically washes its dirty linen in public, thereby giving researchers a wealth of information on the workings of the predator state—in India there is a virtual conspiracy of silence that stretches from the top of the political pyramid to its bottom. It is therefore seldom possible to expose precisely which lobbies were able to use their financial clout to affect what policies. But the spate of changes that occurred in the government's industrial policies between 1970 and 1973 provides unambiguous proof that the government had fallen in line with the needs of the intermediate class. In these years Indira Gandhi nationalized the private coal mining industry, the privately owned oil refining and marketing majors, about 86 percent of the private banking industry, and twenty-nine textile mills that had been losing money and which the owners wanted to sell for the value of the land on which they were located. These measures had mixed effects on the economy. For instance, after they were nationalized the commercial banks opened thousands of branches in the rural areas and in the smaller towns. They had fought shy of doing so while under private ownership.

But three new enactments tightened the government's stranglehold on private industry and accentuated the regime of shortages. The first was the Industrial Licensing Policy (Amendment) Act of 1970, which banned companies with total assets in excess of two hundred million rupees ($26.66 million) from investing in any but the "core" sector of industry, which included machine-building, steel, cement, nonferrous metals, and key chemicals. They were specifically banned from entering any new consumer goods industries except those in which they were already present, but even in these they remained subjected to the 5 percent growth limit of the existing industrial licensing system. At the other end of the scale, over seven hundred products were reserved for the small-scale sector. Nearly all of them were consumer goods. The small-scale sector, like the LIHs, was also defined in terms of a ceiling on investment.[213]

The second act was the Monopolies and Restrictive Trade Practices Act, passed in 1972. Even in its core sector, the act stipulated, an LIH could only expand if doing so did not turn it into a monopoly. Monopoly was defined as controlling more than one-third of the total output of the product. This was made still more restrictive by treating companies with interlocking boards as one.

The third act, passed in 1973, was by far the worst. Any company that borrowed funds from the investment banks (all of which were owned by the state) had to give them the option of converting 40 percent of the loan into equity. Needless to say, the banks were only interested in the highly profitable companies, while the owners of these companies were equally keen to keep them in their own hands. The result was that these companies stopped borrowing from the investment banks, and grew only at the pace that their internal accumulation of funds permitted.

Between them, the three enactments stopped investment by the LIHs except in niche markets utterly unconnected to their main areas of competence—niches such as tourism, hotels, and cargo liners. A fourth enactment, the Foreign Exchange Regulation Act, also put a virtual end to foreign direct investment.[214] The cumulative impact of these enactments, by a government that never missed a day without reaffirming its commitment to the poor, would have been comic had its consequences not been so devastating: Foreign private investment and invaluable technology and managerial expertise, which was flowing like the Yangtze in flood to East and Southeast Asia, was totally barred from coming to India. Within the country, the large industrial houses, which were efficient users of capital and had the financial, managerial, and marketing capabilities to respond quickly to demand, were virtually banned from investing in the areas of their core competence, in order to make sure that their investment was not wasted. Since public sector investment never fully recovered its momentum after the plan holiday, the end result of Mrs. Gandhi's populist brand of "socialism" was to further slow down growth.

All this created a fertile market for the sale of goods, produced in the small and medium-sized enterprises, of poor quality and reliability. This was the market space that the intermediate class had been looking for.

It did not take the government long to realize, however, that the new industrial licensing policy had gone too far. As the restrictions on investment by large private investors hardened, the rate of growth fell even further. From 3.43 percent between 1957 and 1966, it fell to 3.15 percent between 1966 and 1975. Instead of dispersing the ownership of industry by creating space for the emergence of new entrepreneurs, the new industrial licensing policy came close to blocking growth altogether. In the early seventies, to break this covert blockade, the government began to give large numbers of industrial licenses to "deserving," i.e., small, enterprises. The number of licenses issued grew, from around 800–1,100 a year during the second and third five-year plans to double that number in the fourth.[215] But after four years of this, the government found that only a handful of the licensees had been able to find the money, the technology, or the foreign collaborators to undertake the investment.

By then, the intermediate class was too well entrenched in the political system to be easily uprooted. From the sixties to the eighties it had succeeded in depicting itself as small, nationalist, and egalitarian. Indian movies dutifully projected this image by contrasting the small, struggling backyard manager with the evil *"seth"* or money financier. The Communist parties, which had appointed themselves conscience-keepers of the nation and protectors of the poor, lauded this class, describing it as the "national," as distinct from the "comprador," bourgeoisie. The Congress Party and the right-wing Hindu nationalist party Jana Sangh (later rechristened the Bharatiya Janata Party, or BJP) joined the chorus and depicted the mushroom growth of small enterprises as a diffusion of ownership and therefore egalitarian and "socialistic." For an entire decade after the publication of the Hazari report, the Congress government passed ever more restrictive laws against the retrenchment of labor, and the closure of insolvent factories. Retrenchment and closures had to have the permission of the central and the state government, and permission was seldom given. Not surprisingly, production continued to stagnate. Shortages became more acute, and traders and small manufacturers continued to thrive. For the next two decades, till well into the era of reform, India remained the perfect example of a "rent-seeking" society.

But there was nothing socialist or egalitarian about the intermediate class or the economy that it was bent upon creating. The intermediate class was a parasite. The income that fed it was obtained not by promoting growth but by choking it, not by creating surpluses but by creating shortages. Its wealth was based not on true profit but on rent—artificial profits derived from artificial shortages. For the class as a whole to prosper, it was necessary for the economy to sicken. By the mid-seventies, the harsh new industrial licensing laws had created shortages of every manner of product in the economy. So a black market flourished. In the seventies, and till well into the eighties, when controls on its production were partly lifted, cement, for example, was available for twelve rupees ($1.60) per bag of fifty kilograms if one had a license to purchase it.

But it was freely available for sixty rupees ($8.00) a bag in the black market.[216] Steel fetched a similar premium because the Tata Iron and Steel Company (TISCO), the sole remaining private producer, was prohibited from increasing its output, while the public sector's productivity was dismal and its product mix all wrong in relation to demand. Not surprisingly, a "backyard furnace" industry soon developed in the medium-scale sector, using pig iron bought from the integrated plants, and scrap iron from broken ships, for conversion in electric arc furnaces into the required types of steel.

As for labor, instead of giving it protection from arbitrary dismissals, the government did the opposite. Laws against retrenchment were progressively tightened till, in the Industrial Disputes (Amendment) Act, 1976, no employer who hired more than one hundred workers could retrench, or even close down, an enterprise without first appointing a works committee with other workers' representatives on it, and obtaining the permission of the government. Private employers therefore stopped hiring workers on the regular payroll and began recruiting them as casual or day labor for periods that ranged from a day to eleven months. Employment in the organized sector—i.e., those who had been lucky enough to get jobs before the laws meant to protect them were enacted—became a privileged class with pensions, life insurance, and health benefits under an employees' social insurance scheme. But their numbers remained virtually frozen after the end of the sixties. Employment in the private "organized" sector crawled up from 6.69 million in 1970 to 8.43 million in 2002. During this period, the labor force grew from 180 million to 397 million (1999–2000).[217] Thus almost the entire increase in the workforce was in what came to be called the "unorganized sector"—i.e., workers with no union protection, no bargaining power for wages, and no health, accident, life, or social security benefits whatsoever. What China did with its *hukou* system—protect its privileged state sector workers—the Indian government was able to accomplish with its stringent, overprotective labor laws.

1975–1991: reforms by stealth

It took yet another financial-cum-foreign exchange crisis, brought on by a drought in 1972 and a fourfold increase in the price of oil in 1973, to force the government to conclude that its autarchic model of growth was yielding neither growth nor self-reliance. This was the beginning of a two-decade-long effort to reform the economy by stealth.[218] Beginning in 1974, the government raised interest rates on bank deposits and began a long-drawn-out process of liberalizing the rules governing lending to the private sector. The collapse of the Bretton Woods system of global fixed currency exchange rates forced the government to peg the rupee to one or another currency. After experimenting briefly with pegging the rupee to the pound sterling and the dollar, in 1975 the Reserve Bank of India abandoned these in favor of a managed float. In theory, the Reserve Bank periodically changed the exchange rate with reference to a trade-weighted basket of convertible currencies. But in practice the only real change the Reserve Bank made was to devalue a dollar-linked rupee by the amount that inflation in India exceeded the average rate of inflation in the industrialized countries. From 1978 the government also progressively liberalized imports by lifting the ban on more and more previously prohibited imports and removing restrictions on the import of items that were previously on a "restricted" list.

In 1980, after another drought that coincided with another threefold increase in oil prices, the government drastically reduced subsidies on fertilizers by raising their prices, and eased the severity of industrial licensing by a process known as "broadbanding," in which a license to produce one product could automatically be used to produce all members of the related family of products. In 1981, it also began the process of lifting price and distribution controls on two key basic materials, steel and cement.

But so strong was the hold of the intermediate class upon the machinery of government and the political system that reforms, even when spurred by crises such as the ones that occurred in 1972–'73 and 1979–'80, remained minimal. The goal of successive governments remained to liberalize exchange rates, import and export controls, and industrial licensing just enough to give the economy another shot in the arm, but without disturbing the basic structure of protection and privilege created by controls, upon which the intermediate class depended for survival. In a striking phrase, Arvind Panagariya has called this phase of reforms "reforms by stealth." Panagariya attributed the need for stealth to the government's unwillingness to confront the powerful leftist lobby in the country, but he failed to ask from where the left drew its political power in a country where more than nine-tenths of the income earners were profiting from private enterprise.[219]

The revival of the share market, the development of a host of new types of equity and preference shares, and the removal of price controls acted as a tonic to industrial growth. Another round of "reforms by stealth" by Prime Minister Rajiv Gandhi in 1985, in which he further relaxed industrial licensing and slashed duties on capital goods imports, pushed the rate of industrial growth per decade up from 80 percent in 1961–'71 and 53 percent in 1971–'81 to 113 percent in 1981–'91.[220] But the economy remained far from open. The liberalization that had taken place was purely of the internal economy. The government did very little to open up the international trade and payments system. And although imports were greatly liberalized, the beneficial impact was partially offset by the decision of the bureaucracy (regularly embodied in the fine print of the budget papers) to levy still higher tariffs upon them.

As a result, the exchange rate remained overvalued. This kept the profit rate on domestic sales two to four times as high as the profit rate on exports.[221] Not surprisingly, exports remained a residual activity, or one that had to be kept alive with regular transfusions of export subsidies. The partial nature of the reforms therefore prevented the rise in industrial growth from being reflected in a rise in exports.[222] The balance of payments gap therefore widened rapidly and had to be covered by borrowing. India's external debt therefore increased from a modest $14 billion in 1984–'85 to $71 billion by May 1990. By then, international bankers had begun to warn India that they would not be able to continue funding its growing debt if they did not see reforms that promised to bring the external payments position back on an even keel.

The final crisis

It was against this background that Iraq's invasion of Kuwait in 1991 finally pushed India into insolvency. The invasion simultaneously pushed up oil prices, from around $18 a barrel to $31 a barrel, and cut off the remittances that had been coming back to India from about two hundred thousand Indian workers in Kuwait and Iraq. Estimates by the government showed that this would mean an additional loss of foreign exchange earnings of $4.2 billion in a full year.[223] That was sufficient for international bankers to stop further short-term lending to India. Thus the spurt in growth in the eighties within the framework of an autarchic economy itself precipitated the fourth and final foreign exchange crisis of the Indian command economy.

The first indication that the government had finally accepted the urgent need for a wholesale, as opposed to piecemeal, reform came in a paper submitted to Rajiv Gandhi by the special secretary for economic affairs, Montek Singh Ahluwalia, in the spring of 1989.

Gandhi apparently saw the logic of the paper, and the need for a second, much more thoroughgoing bout of reforms, straightaway (the first attempt had been in 1985), but felt that it would be wise to leave it till after the next elections, which were then only six to eight months away. With 413 out of 544 members of Parliament belonging to the Congress Party, he never seriously considered that he might not return to power.

In the December 1989 elections, nevertheless, the Congress Party was defeated and the country entered a period of unprecedented political weakness. A minority government under V. P. Singh was returned to power. Ahluwalia, who stayed on in the prime minister's office as special secretary (economic), submitted an enlarged version of his original paper to the new prime minister. As Rajiv Gandhi's finance minister, Singh had himself drawn the attention of the cabinet to the approaching but still distant threat of insolvency—but with only a quarter of the members of Parliament behind him, and dependent on both the left-wing Communist parties and the right-wing Bharatiya Janata Party to stay in power, Singh too shied away from attempting any bold reforms.

Political instability prolonged India's agony till June of 1991. V. P. Singh's government lasted only till November 1990, but his successor, Chandra Shekhar, with a party of fifty-five in Parliament and wholly dependent on the Congress Party to stay in power, proved even weaker. By January 1991 the outlines of the onrushing crisis were being discussed in the press almost every day, but the political system remained paralyzed, for the Congress Party was not prepared to back unpopular austerity measures that could ease the foreign exchange crisis, when it knew that this government's days were numbered. For four more months, the country had a caretaker government, and this period was stretched by another month when Rajiv Gandhi was assassinated.

All the while, the economic crisis continued to deepen. The fiscal deficit climbed to 8.4 percent of GDP, the external current account deficit climbed to 3.5 percent of GDP, inflation nudged 13 percent (which was double India's historical inflation rate), and foreign exchange reserves were down to $1.1 billion. Everyone knew that something drastic would have to be done, and secretly, every political party other than the Congress Party was relieved that it would not have to grasp the nettle of reform.

10 REFORMS AND THE DEMISE OF THE INTERMEDIATE REGIME

THE FIRST CHALLENGE to the intermediate regime came not from the economy but from the political system. Students in Gujarat were in the vanguard of this revolt. While their immediate grievance was the rampant corruption in the Congress government of their state, its underlying cause was a progressive weakening of the economy after two decades of relentless rent-seeking by the intermediate class. Slow growth had greatly exacerbated the problem of unemployment, and the students were its first victims. Till the early sixties there had been virtually no unemployment among the educated. After the economic crisis of the mid-sixties, students leaving college found, quite suddenly, that there were few jobs to be had, or at least few that they had been trained for and felt they were entitled to. Compounded by rapid inflation, their anxiety and sense of betrayal burst out in a succession of uncoordinated student riots across the country in 1966 and 1967. By 1973, when the growth rate had sunk to an all-time low of 3.15 percent, anxiety had given way to anger and a growing desire to hit back at the political system that had robbed them of their future.

The student movement that erupted in 1974, under the banner of a newly formed organization called the Navnirman Samiti, was far more widespread and better organized. Within weeks it had spread from Gujarat to the whole of northern India, for it had found a renowned patron in the veteran socialist leader Jayaprakash Narayan, the most respected political leader in the country after Jawaharlal Nehru. His support of the Navnirman Samiti secured the backing of a host of opposition parties across the country and turned it into a potent threat to the Congress Party. Apart from ensuring her political survival, the main purpose of the national emergency that Indira Gandhi declared on June 26, 1975, was to suppress this movement. Her first act, apart from indefinitely proroguing Parliament, was to put Narayan in jail. But the agitation convinced her that the challenge of mounting educated unemployment could only be met by increasing the rate of growth, and thereby of employment. To do this, she concluded reluctantly, the stranglehold of controls had to be relaxed. This provided the political rationale for the decade and a half of "reforms by stealth" that began in October 1974.

This covert strategy was only abandoned when Iraq invaded Kuwait. During the prolonged foreign exchange crisis that followed, India was able to avoid defaulting on the repayment of its international loans by pledging all of the gold it held in the vaults of the Reserve Bank of India. The humiliation that Indians suffered made them finally recognize, and reject, the hollow ideological foundations of the command economy.

Pledging its gold reserves gained India only a temporary reprieve. When the Congress Party returned to power in June 1991 under Prime Minister Narasimha Rao, most of this had been frittered away and India's foreign exchange reserves were sufficient only to cover ten days' worth of imports. The Rao government entered into a standby agreement with the International Monetary Fund and the World Bank in which it agreed to devalue the rupee, free the exchange rate, eliminate industrial licensing, do away with the remaining bans on imports, and lower and rationalize customs and excise duties. Above all, the government pledged itself to bringing down the fiscal deficit by cutting down government expenditure.

"Fording the Ganges by feeling the stones"

Like China, India too decided to "ford the river by feeling the stones." But its reasons for doing so were very different from those of China. During its thirty years of Communism, the People's Republic of China had all but destroyed the market mechanism and replaced it with an elaborate system of centralized production planning and distribution of five hundred broadly defined product categories. These covered more than nine-tenths of the country's output. When the PRC decided to abandon the command economy, it had to revive the market first. What is more, it had to revive not only the market for products but also that for labor, land, and capital. This could not be done overnight. Indeed, the market for capital is still largely monopolized by the state, and there is still no true market for land. Thus, China had no option but to proceed cautiously with reform.

India was under no such constraints, for it had never ceased to be anything but a market economy, even at the height of Indira Gandhi's socialism. Conventional wisdom therefore dictated that the government should have removed the obstacles to the market's free functioning as soon as possible, through the application of "shock therapy." The constraints that made Rao adopt a gradual approach and slow down the pace of economic reform were not economic, but political. The Congress Party had come back to power in June 1991 with only 232 members in a house of 544. Narasimha Rao himself was anything but a charismatic leader and had been propelled into the prime minister's seat by Rajiv Gandhi's assassination in May 1991. Rao was, moreover, a shy and introspective man who shunned the cameras, and seldom made any public statements of policy.

Rao could not even claim that his was a new government, forced to take drastic action by the errors of its predecessors. The Congress Party had been in power for all except four of the previous forty-four years. All the policies that had led to the crisis of 1991 were its creation. Rao could neither disclaim responsibility for the crisis nor ask the people for still more sacrifices. He could not even ask them to suspend judgment on what he planned to do till the fruits of his reforms began to ripen. On the contrary, he was especially vulnerable within his own party to the charge of betraying Nehruvian socialism, and the ideals of the Congress Party.

For a government placed as his was, a course of "shock therapy" would only have been possible if the crisis had erupted very suddenly, taken everyone by surprise, and led to a crash devaluation of the rupee. The very urgency of the crisis would then have justified recourse to drastic remedies. But in India, the crisis was confined to foreign exchange alone. At the time when it struck, in August 1990, India was at the peak of a two-and-a-half-year boom, and the growth rate of the manufacturing industry had reached an all-time high of 12.8 percent.[224] By June 1991, when the Congress Party came to power, the approach of the foreign exchange crisis had been visible for two years. Three prime ministers had already struggled with the issue of reform and shirked making more than cosmetic changes. But they all knew what needed to be done. So a consensus of sorts had emerged that some extraordinary measures would be needed to combat it. Thus, consensus, rather than leadership, strength, and charisma, paved the way even for the first burst of reforms.

The first task that the Rao government faced was to reassure India's foreign constituency—creditors, bankers, exporters who were holding their earnings abroad rather than repatriating them, and nonresident Indians, who had withdrawn more than a billion dollars between August 1990 and June 1991. The government had to show that it was taking control of the situation and was serious about reform. The first step it took, therefore, was to devalue the rupee by 25 percent.

Devaluation was not sufficient to make the IMF give its seal of approval. For that, India had to undertake two other sets of reforms—bringing down the fiscal deficit and freeing the external trade regime from its prohibitive duties and quantitative controls. To lower the fiscal deficit, the government had to reduce its spending. This would bring down inflation and reduce the volume of imports. Eliminating hurdles to imports, the IMF argued, would bring down the cost and improve the quality of India's manufactures. This would make it possible to increase its exports.

The government adopted a step-by-step, phased sequence of reform in all three areas. It set itself the target of bringing down the fiscal deficit of the central government from 8.4 percent of GDP in 1990–'91 to 5 percent. But it first said that this would be done in two years, then three, and finally in five years. These targets were not met.[225] The rationalization and lowering of import duties were not completed over four budgets, although by March 1996, the government was four-fifths of the way there. The peak rate of customs duty was brought down, from 300 percent before 1990–'91 to 65 percent in 1994 and 50 percent in 1994, and the average rate from 128 percent in 1990–'91 to 38.6 percent in 1996–'97.[226] Import restrictions on capital goods and intermediates were lifted completely in the first two budgets, but most curbs on the import of consumer goods remained in place. Finally, the number of import duties was brought down from several hundred to just twelve. There was a similar lowering and simplification of domestic indirect taxes (called excise duties). The average impact on costs of all import duties, measured as the ratio of their yield to the value of industrial output, declined from 10.2 percent in 1988–'89 to 7.1 percent in 1996–'97.[227]

The one area of reform in which the government had almost completed its task by March 1996 was the freeing of the external trade and payments regime. By the time the Narasimha Rao government fell from power in May 1996, India had a single, market-determined exchange rate. It had also met all the requirements of the IMF's Article VIII, for current account convertibility of the rupee. This liberalization, too, was carried out progressively over four budgets. However, the government had virtually ruled out capital account convertibility even before the onset of the East Asian crisis. The governor of the Reserve Bank of India and the finance minister were of the view that full convertibility would have to wait till the fiscal deficit was down to not more than 3 percent of the GDP, and inflation had been brought under control.

Sources of opposition

Opposition to the reforms came in India, initially, from practically every organized sector of society. These were a large section of industry; organized labor; farmers; fixed income earners, including the intelligentsia; and, most importantly, the central and state bureaucracies.

The opposition of fixed income groups, which included powerful opinion-makers such as journalists, professors, and schoolteachers, members of the armed forces, and pensioners, stemmed from their awareness that decontrol would—in the short run, at least—lead to inflation, and cut into their already limited incomes.

Organized labor, which made up approximately a quarter of the working class in 1991, was opposed to the reforms because it feared they would erode the absolute protection it had enjoyed from being laid off. Its opposition was exacerbated by the fact that the strongest trade unions were found in the public sector, which was the least competitive, and would suffer the most if the government stopped protecting it from internal and foreign competition.

In principle, farmers should have been in favor of reforms that lifted price and distribution controls. Numerous Indian economists, and those of the World Bank, had pointed out repeatedly to the government that its monopoly procurement of foodgrains—when combined with a complete ban on private exports, and severe restrictions on private trade even between food-surplus and deficit states within the country—kept prices down artificially, and therefore amounted to a heavy tax on the farmers. Decontrol of prices and distribution would therefore have raised their incomes. Despite this farmers remained, on balance, opposed to the above reforms because by 1991 they had come to depend heavily on very large government subsidies on inputs—power, diesel fuel, and fertilizers. These had been given initially to offset the rise in input prices that resulted from the steep increase in oil prices, and the rapid devaluation of the rupee in the 1970s. At that time the government had chosen not to offset the resulting increase in the cost of production by raising the procurement price for foodgrains, for fear of sparking inflation. By 1991, subsidies to the farm sector on these three accounts alone had ballooned to about 2.3 percent of the GDP.[228] From 1975 onward, the government got locked ever deeper into a system that subsidized farm inputs but taxed the farmer's output. By 1991, farmers were comfortable with this system and preferred it to an open market system because it gave them stable input and output prices, and therefore minimized the risks of cultivation.

Why industry opposed the reforms

The opposition from industry was the easiest to understand. By 1991, four decades of almost total protection from competition had

created a sheltered class of entrepreneurs that numbered in the
tens of thousands but ran, for the most part, small enterprises that
used obsolete technologies. Opening up the economy, and lowering customs duties, posed a dire threat to them. In 1990–'91, the
indigenous industrial class was potentially the most powerful opponent of thoroughgoing structural reform and had to be handled
with kid gloves.

Initially, industry adopted a "wait and see" attitude toward the
economic reforms. The abolition of industrial licensing gave them
the freedom to follow the market and invest wherever profits looked
most secure, a freedom that they had been dreaming of for four decades. But the reforms also opened them to competition from imported goods and from foreign investors. Opposition to the reforms
emerged only in 1993, two years after they commenced. It was led
by the "Bombay Club," a group of more than a dozen of the most
important Indian industrialists, many of them sons and heirs of
pioneers who had backed the Congress Party during the struggle
for independence. The club's principal spokesman was Rahul Bajaj,
chairman of Bajaj Motors—India's largest owner-managed, closely
held company, which produced more than 70 percent of all the
scooters and motorcycles in the country.[229] The Bombay Club rapidly forged links with the Hindu nationalist Bharatiya Janata Party
(BJP), which had opposed the opening of the economy to foreign
direct investment with the emotive slogan, "We want computer
chips, not potato chips," and had therefore been branded as pro-
tectionist. But the protection the BJP demanded was qualitatively
different from the demands to cut off imports, ban foreign investment, and curb monopolies that had resounded through the government in the late sixties and early seventies.

The demands that industrialists raised in the mid-nineties were
for "a level playing field for Indian enterprise." The origins of
these demands lay in the incomplete and ad hoc nature of Indian

reforms. In the eighties, as the succession of partial liberalizations of industrial licensing set off a boom in domestic investment, it soon became apparent that the ban on the import of consumer goods had ensured that profit margins in their manufacture for the domestic market were several times higher than in their manufacture for export. When piecemeal reforms began, consumer goods imports were the last to be liberalized. This gave rise to an anomalous situation. By 1993, the rules governing foreign investment had been sufficiently relaxed to allow a host of foreign companies to regain control of their previously moribund enterprises in India, or to enter and start up new ventures. Outside the computer-enabled services (IT-ES) sector, all but a few of these were in the manufacture of consumer goods. By not opening up the consumer goods industries to imports, but allowing foreign investment, the Rao government ensured that returns *to foreign investors* remained far higher in these industries than the return they could earn on others. What is more, these returns were only available in the domestic Indian market. Partial reforms thus biased foreign investment toward the consumer goods industries, and toward investment that tried to exploit the domestic market, instead of creating low-cost outsourcing facilities for products intended for the global market. Such investment brought foreign investors into direct conflict with the indigenous manufacturers, who saw the market into which they were at last free to expand being invaded by foreigners who suffered from none of the constraints that bound indigenous manufacturers down.

These constraints also arose from the incompleteness of reforms. The government's inability to carry the process of reforms through from the product to the factor markets had blocked most of the avenues normally available to entrepreneurs in their constant struggle to remain competitive. In 1993, and for several years thereafter, entrepreneurs were not allowed to sell surplus land to raise capital for expansion or modernization, to sell off branch companies or factories to make themselves "leaner and meaner," or to lay off surplus workers to cut down production costs. Companies that had hastily entered into partnership with foreign companies also found, to their chagrin, that when the time came to expand their share-holding base, the straitjacket that still existed in the rules that governed lending by the nationalized commercial banks (there were few others then) did not permit them to borrow money to invest in their own shares. So company after company was forced to allow the foreign partner to pick up its quota of shares, and be reduced to an insignificant minority partner. When a company tried to block the expansion, the foreign partner would decide to set up a wholly owned subsidiary in direct competition with the joint venture.[230]

The fears of Indian entrepreneurs were heightened when the Indian share markets were opened to foreign portfolio investors in 1993. This came at a time when twenty years of forced dilution of their shareholdings, to comply with the enactments of the early seventies, had left the promoters of most large Indian firms with only a tiny minority of the shares—often less than 10 percent. Opening up the share markets to foreign investors made the promoters vulnerable to takeover bids from foreign companies or consortia of nonresident Indians. The Bombay Club's demand for a "level playing field" was therefore understandable. It was not surprising that a deep vein of skepticism ran through the analyses of India's reforms at that time—but only five years were to pass before this skepticism was shown to be unfounded. The Rao government neutralized opposition to reform in five ways. First, it slowed down the pace of reforms to give those affected adversely by it time to adjust. Second, it sequenced the reforms carefully, doing those first that would restore balance to the economy and permit growth to be resumed. Third, it deliberately stimulated economic growth as a way of dissolving resistance to the more difficult structural reforms, in the full knowledge that all changes are easier to make when the market is expanding rather than when it is stagnant or contracting. Fourth, rather than closing down, or privatizing, existing state institutions straightaway, it decided to strengthen their financial and managerial foundations, and give them a chance to compete with a now-liberated private sector and foreign investors. If they survived, well and good. If not, their failure would provide the justification for their closure. Fifth, throughout the reform process, the government believed not only in being transparent, but noisy. The finance minister and others filled the media with declarations of what the government intended to do, *in the near future*. It appointed expert committees to go into every one of the more difficult structural reforms, and produce a report. These reports and statements aroused intense debates in the media, and gave everyone a chance to air his or her views. The deliberate use of a strongly independent, vigorous press to get people used to the idea of change, and to evolve a consensus, was another unique feature of Indian reforms. Far from enacting piecemeal reforms by stealth, as its predecessors had done after 1975, the government did everything in full view, and proclaimed its future intentions from the rooftops. This strategy was not thought out in advance but developed, little by little, through the constant interaction of economic compulsions with political constraints.

But gradual reform had its drawbacks, too. As the Chinese government had found, it proved far easier to reform the product market at home and the trade regime abroad than to reform the labor and capital markets. In India the strong opposition of organized labor, and the weakening of the central government that resulted from the end of the Congress Party's dominance of the political system in 1989, and its replacement by coalition governments at the federal level, stalled all labor law reform.

Opposition from the left-wing parties in Parliament and the intelligentsia stalled the privatization of state-owned enterprises. In the end, successive governments were left with no option but to give the SOEs time to adapt to a competitive economy (to their credit, the majority of them did do so).

Growth as a catalyst for reform

The caution with which the Indian government moved was only half the reason for the painless acceptance of the transition to an open, market economy. The other half was the government's awareness that opposition to the reforms would be easier to handle if demand was growing. Growth itself could therefore become a catalyst for reform.

The sustained opposition of the organized labor movement, underlined by sporadic strikes, continued till early 1994. But powerful opposition, not so much to reforms but to the way the government was enacting them, also surfaced without warning from owner-managers of Indian industry.

The owner-managers had been feeling increasingly insecure because while the government was bringing down tariff walls and allowing foreign companies with superior technology and managerial skills to invest in India freely, it was wary of deregulating the domestic market for labor, capital, and land, denying industrialists the freedom they needed to meet the challenge of an open economy. In October 1993, the Bombay Club held a meeting in Bombay and demanded a "level playing field" in relation to foreign companies. They asked the government to allow them first to issue blocks of shares at concessional prices to themselves, in order to increase their shareholding in the companies they were managing to a majority, as it had allowed already established foreign companies to do.

The government denied their request, but stopped the practice of allowing foreign companies to recapture their companies for a song. The industrialists were not mollified, because by then the foreign companies had done what they had set out to do. This opposition could have taken a serious turn, had it not been for the boom that developed in the economy in 1993.

The boom resulted not from following the advice of the IMF, but from ignoring it. The government did so because, after two years of sticking faithfully to the IMF's blueprint for reducing the fiscal deficit, to which it had committed itself by signing a standby agreement in 1991, it found that reducing government expenditure did not lower the fiscal deficit because it also lowered industry growth and, therefore, tax revenues. All that economic austerity was doing was to erode the support economic reform had enjoyed at the onset of the crisis. In the budget for 1993–'94, the government decided to relax controls on government spending by stepping up its planned investment sharply once again.[231]

The consequent rise in planned investment and a reduction of interest rates gave industrialists the necessary confidence to start investing once again. In the next three years—1993 till 1996—private corporate investment quadrupled, and the rate of industrial growth touched 16.2 percent in the first quarter of 1996. The return of the sellers' market dissolved most of the opposition, especially of big business but also of organized labor. State-owned and private companies introduced voluntary retirement schemes in which workers were encouraged to leave in exchange for handsome separation packages. Large numbers did so because there were other jobs to be had aplenty.

In this benign atmosphere, the government continued with its opening up of the economy. In successive budgets it lowered and simplified domestic taxation, and brought down customs duties still further. It made the rupee convertible on the current account, and continued to relax conditions on foreign direct investment till the conditions governing it became more liberal than those that prevailed in the majority of Southeast Asian countries. By 1997, the regime of controls that had choked India's growth for four decades had been all but destroyed.

The only section of society that remained unreconciled to the end of the intermediate regime was the bureaucracy. Senior civil servants in the central ministries of commerce, industry, and finance were fully persuaded of the need to abandon the command economy, but the change of heart was not shared by the lower reaches of the bureaucracy, particularly in the state governments. These made one final bid to block the dismantling of controls. Their opportunity arose when the Congress Party lost the 1996 elections and was replaced by a motley coalition of thirteen political parties that had christened itself the United Front.

The last gasp of the intermediate class

Ever since the Soviet Union collapsed and Eastern Europe began its hectic transition to capitalism, economists have been sharply divided on the role that government should play in the transition process. In the mid-nineties, there was an overwhelming consensus that government's most effective contribution would be simply to get out of the way of the transition and let the market take over. It took Russia's descent into chaos and the return of Communist parties to power in a majority of the former socialist states, through democratic elections in the late nineties, to weaken this belief. India's experience in the nineties strongly endorses the opposite view: that the transition has to be managed if it is to be orderly, and this requires a strong government that is committed to making the transition.[232]

The reforms proceeded smoothly till 1995 because the Rao government, although not quite in a majority, was confident about the need to carry them out. Self-doubt first arose when the Congress Party suffered two surprise defeats in the legislative assembly elections in Andhra Pradesh and Karnataka, two states it had always regarded as its bastions in the South. The soul-searching this set off led the administration to the facile but erroneous conclusion that the high rate of inflation throughout its tenure—a holdover from the crisis of 1990–'91—was the main reason for the setback. From then till the present day, the Congress Party has consistently considered taming inflation to be more important than stimulating growth. In May 1995, when the industrial boom was reaching its peak but inflation had touched 11 percent, the government sharply raised the interest rate and brought the boom to an end.

Slowing down the rise in prices did not save the Congress Party from defeat in the parliamentary elections of 1996. Its place was taken by the patchwork quilt of thirteen small parties, the United Front. When these thirteen parties went to the polls, not one of them had seriously expected that it would have to shoulder the responsibility of government. As a result, the Front had no ideology and no economic program. It did not even initially have a candidate for prime minister; it did not command a majority and was able to rule only with the grudging support of the Congress Party, which was keen to keep its main rival, the BJP, out of power.

The first thing the new government lost control of was its budget. When the new government came to power it faced two pressing problems: from where to find the money to pay the arrears of salaries and pensions owed to eighteen million civil servants to compensate for the erosion caused by inflation, and how to pass on a sharp increase in the price of crude oil and oil products to the consumer. The new finance minister, P. Chidambaram, proposed strong austerity measures and a substantial immediate rise in the prices of gasoline and diesel, but was forced to withdraw both proposals when he found himself facing an imminent revolt in the newly formed United Front. Others were quick to learn how weak the central government had become. It was in the resulting policy vacuum that the bureaucracy made its last bid to resuscitate elements of the command economy.

Three protracted conflicts between private investors and the central government's bureaucracy highlighted the latter's unwillingness to shed its dirigiste mindset. The first was the near-termination, in 1997, of a fifteen-year-old joint venture, between the Suzuki motorcar company of Japan and the government of India, to produce what was till 1996 India's only modern car, the Maruti. The second and third were the abandonment, in rapid succession, of two projects promoted by Tata, India's oldest and most respected industrial group. These were the establishment of a new international airport in Bangalore, which was rapidly becoming the IT hub of India, and the creation, in collaboration with Singapore Airlines, of India's first large private airline company.[233]

The airport project was sabotaged by officials who claimed that allowing foreign companies like the Raytheon Company of the United States, which worked closely with the Pentagon, to undertake the project would be a threat to national security. The Tata–Singapore Airlines project was scuttled by a temporary revival of the alliance between the bureaucrat, the politician, and the indigenous capitalist—the same alliance that had been responsible for India's slow growth till 1991.[234] Tata was convinced that its real opponent was a recently established Indian airline backed by investment from nonresident Indians and others living in the Gulf. This company, they believed, had established financial links with around two dozen members of Parliament, who kept objecting that the sudden incursion of a huge, extremely efficient, international airline into the hitherto-protected domestic market would hurt the state-owned Indian Airlines. The United Front government dilly-dallied till Singapore Airlines lost interest in the project.

While the travails of the Tata Group got their due share of attention in the media, it was the bureaucrats' dispute with Suzuki that caught the public's eye. For by 1992 the fast, fuel-efficient, and highly reliable Suzuki 800—introduced in India as the Maruti 800—had come to epitomize all that was good in economic liberalization. The dispute began, innocuously, with a minor misunderstanding at a board meeting in January 1993. The confrontation that ballooned out of this was finally headed off by Prime Minister Inder Kumar Gujral (who had taken over from H. D. Deve Gowda in 1997) during the very last days of the United Front government, in 1998. In the intervening six years it was misrepresented in the media in a wide variety of ways, by both the government and by Suzuki.

Disagreements began in 1993 when the board began to discuss plans for a major expansion of the Maruti plant—its second since 1982. While the Indian government directors wanted the company to indigenize the production of the Maruti car further, the Maruti directors wanted to maintain the company's dominance of the Indian market by introducing newer models with more powerful engines and added safety features. To justify their position, spokespeople of the government accused Suzuki of wanting to milk India by refusing to further indigenize the production of their cars, and to keep the import content high in order to engage in transfer pricing. The chairman and founder of Suzuki motors, O. Suzuki, was equally unsparing: In one outburst he went so far as to speculate that Indian officials and politicians were in the pay of other car majors, which were about to launch their own new models on the Indian market.[235] The conflict became prolonged because the government and Suzuki each owned 50 percent of the shares. Neither could overrule the other. The dispute became progressively uglier till, in June 1997, Suzuki threatened to withhold the transfer of any more technology to Maruti. That was when the prime minister's office finally stepped in to save the project and accepted Suzuki's proposals.

2003–the making of India Incorporated

In the end, the political instability that followed the defeat of the Congress Party, and the resurgence of bureaucratic foot-dragging, slowed down but could not stop the continued liberalization of the economy. Paradoxically, what overcame the last vestiges of resistance was the sudden onset of recession in 1997. As happened in China, the recession became a catalyst not only for economic but also for political change. The defeat of the Congress Party coincided with a sudden petering out of the boom in investment and growth that had begun in 1993.[236] The rate of industrial growth, which had touched 16.2 percent in the first quarter of 1996, fell to 3.25 percent in November. For the next six years it averaged five percent. This prolonged recession turned the sellers' market of 1993–'97 into a buyers' market. In the next six years tens of thousands of small and medium-sized enterprises sold out, merged with their peers, and modernized their operations, or went bankrupt and closed down.

The adjustment was all the more difficult because it had to be made in the teeth of a poor harvest in 1998, and a ban on foreign aid and various other sanctions that were imposed upon the country by the international community after it tested its nuclear weapons in May 1998. The Reserve Bank of India was obliged to raise interest rates in order to prevent an outflow of capital from the country. This prolonged the industrial recession, which had shown signs of easing toward the end of 1997, and forced still more of the small and medium-sized enterprises to modernize or perish. The industrial enterprises that survived the prolonged structural readjustment of 1997–2002 were leaner and more competitive than anyone could have imagined a few years earlier. An entire new generation of owner-managers had taken over from their parents. Most of them were highly educated, with degrees in management from some of the most prestigious institutes in the world. They were itching to prove their mettle, not solely in the domestic but also in the international market.

The performance of industry in the first nine months of 2002–'03 (April to December 2002) gave ample evidence of the change that had occurred. While the rate of industrial growth was a not-too-impressive 5.3 percent, corporate profits, especially for the larger companies, soared as never before.[237] What made their performance especially creditable was that these record profits had come at a time when demand was almost stagnant [238] and companies had been forced to cut their prices to compete with each other.[239] A good example was the cement industry. In 2002–'03 it recorded only a small increase in profits, but all of that increase had come from reduced costs of manufacture because it had matched a 10 percent increase in sales with a nearly 10 percent cut in the price of cement. The steel industry had been reducing costs and passing on the benefits to its customers by lowering prices since 2000. This had enabled it to become a substantial steel exporter for the first time in fifty years and sell more than a million tons of it abroad in the first nine months of 2002–'03. A similar quiet managerial revolution had been going on in nearly all industries.[240] By the time the recession ended in 2003, Indian industry had emerged from its chrysalis and India's transformation into a viable market economy was complete.

In May 2003, the National Democratic Alliance (NDA) government of Atal Behari Vajpayee, which had been reelected with a convincing majority in October 1999, decided to privatize its flagship enterprise, Maruti motors. To do this it sold 1 percent of its shares to its Japanese strategic partner, Suzuki motors, thus increasing the latter's shareholding to 51 percent, and sold another 18 percent of the shares to the public on the stock market. To the government's own surprise, Maruti's share offering was oversubscribed by thirteen times. Originally given a face value of a hundred rupees per share, the company was allowed under Indian law to add a premium of 25 percent because of the oversubscription, and sell them for 125 rupees per share. But when trading in these shares began, their price jumped to 168 rupees within minutes on the very first day.

This was the signal that everyone seemed to have been waiting for. Buoyed by the public's reaction, the government decided to give up the painful and often controversial effort to sell off public enterprises by finding a "strategic" partner who would buy a block of shares and take over their management, and announced that it would in future sell all public sector shares through public offerings on the stock market. A spate of new share offerings followed, and the public took up each of them with gusto. In the ten weeks that followed the sale of Maruti's shares, the Bombay (Mumbai) Stock Exchange's sensitive share price index (Sensex) rose seven hundred points to cross 3,700. The Sensex was based upon only the largest fifty companies, so what it did not capture was an even sharper recovery in the prices of shares of medium-sized companies. Hundreds of thousands of shareholders were able to take advantage of this to recover savings that had been lying moribund in old shares and reinvest them in newer, technologically more advanced, and therefore safer companies.

The transformation of the Indian entrepreneur from a defensive producer looking to the government to protect him or her from foreign and domestic competition into an outward-looking producer confident of his or her ability to defend the home market, and keen to compete in world markets, began not in the new millennium but with the onset of recession a good seven years earlier. The change of attitude became apparent in 1999 when a group of finance capitalists, nicknamed the "new Bombay Club," suggested to the government that it allow foreign direct investors to sell and issue some of their shares to the Indian public, so that Indians too could benefit from their higher levels of efficiency and profitability.[241] The NDA government conceded this demand, also, as part of a progressive decontrol of the share market. The Congress Party–led United Progressive Alliance (UPA), which returned to power in the elections of 2004 under the prime ministership of former finance minister Manmohan Singh, continued opening up the share markets. In 2007, foreign portfolio investment in the Indian share market exceeded $20.8 billion.[242]

Throughout the first decade of the twenty-first century the NDA and UPA governments continued to deregulate the remnants of industry, deregulate the services sector, lower and rationalize the domestic and import duty structures of the country, and open previously closed sectors like insurance and retail marketing to foreign investment. In the realm of domestic taxation, by far the most important reform was the switch by state governments from the archaic sales tax to the value-added tax.[243] Import duties also continued to be lowered, till in 2007–'08 the weighted average had come down to 10 percent, from over 30 percent in 1997–'98.[244]

The pieces come together

In the five years that followed the revival of investment and growth in 2003, the bits and pieces of India's piecemeal economic reforms finally came together. The growth of GDP accelerated to an average of 8.9 percent from 2003–'04 to 2007–'08. There was a palpable improvement in the quality of life, for the annual growth of consumption doubled from 2.6 percent a year in the eleven years between 1991–'92 and 2002–'03 to 5.1 percent in the next five years. The share of capital formation in the GDP rose from 25.2 percent in 2002–'03 to 35.9 percent in 2006–'07, a figure comparable to the most dynamic countries of Southeast Asia.

Employment also began to rise much faster. Between 1993–'94 and 1999–2000, employment in nonagricultural manufacture and services, excluding domestic service and employment in the government, had increased by about 22 percent, or 3 percent a year. Between 1999–2000 and 2004–'05 this almost doubled to more than five percent a year.[245]

Finally, the five-year period of sustained growth caused a surge in tax revenues. The combined tax revenues of the central and state governments increased from 14.4 percent of GDP to 17.8 percent in 2007–'08. Combined with a sharp reduction of the interest burden of the central and state governments because of the fall in interest rates after 2000, the overall fiscal deficit of the central and state governments fell from 9.5 percent of GDP in 2002–'03 to 5.5 percent in 2007–'08. But in judging the health of government finances, the more important indicator is the revenue deficit. The fiscal deficit includes the interest that the center and states have to pay on existing debt to the commercial banks, who are its principal lenders. Since these payments swell the banks' receipts and allow them to lend more, they do not affect the overall investment in the economy. But the revenue deficit is the actual excess of the government's consumption in the current year over its revenues. The government has to borrow to cover the difference. It is therefore the amount by which the government converts the public's savings into consumption. Better fiscal management and buoyant revenues brought the revenue down from 6.7 percent of the GDP in 2002 to 1.5 percent in 2008. This accounted, therefore, for more than a third of the increase of national savings (amounting to 14 percent of the GDP) that took place in these six years.[246]

China

11   THE INNATE CONSERVATISM OF CHINA'S REFORMS

2002 WAS A WATERSHED year for both China and India. In China it marked the resumption of very rapid growth after five years of recession, and the adoption, by the Sixteenth National Congress of the Communist Party of China, of President Jiang Zemin's doctrine of the Three Represents. By opening the party to private entrepreneurs, the doctrine formally buried the notion of class conflict upon which five decades of Communist ideology had been based. In India, also, the year marked not just the end of a parallel recession, but also the final demise of the socialist mindset that the intermediate class had thrived upon. Allowing only the efficient firms to survive, the recession ended the last vestiges of the struggle between "large" and "small" industry that had characterized the intermediate regime. Indians, too, shed inhibitions against becoming rich that had been bred into them by more than two millennia of Hindu philosophy, and embraced the "dharma" of capitalism—wealth equaled success and success was born of virtue. The media captured the triumph of capitalist values in a new phrase—*India Incorporated*. Both countries seemed to have navigated the shoals of early capitalism and seemed set on a fair course toward stable long-term growth. The sudden interest in forecasting their economic influence in the middle of the twenty-first century, reflected by the BRICs report and those of the US National Intelligence Council's 2020 Project, showed that this was a very widely shared view.

But in China there had been a change of leadership, and the new president, Hu Jintao, and prime minister, Wen Jiabao, did not share this complacency. In January 2006 the Chinese media reported that the number of "disturbances against public order" had risen from seventy-four thousand in 2004 to eighty-seven thousand in 2005. This was ten times the number of "incidents" in 1993.[247] Official publications like the *Blue Book of Chinese Society*, published by the Chinese Academy of Social Sciences, referred more and more frequently, and freely, to the threat that rising discontent posed to social stability.

In a country as vast as China, even eighty-seven thousand incidents do not sound like a great many. The Chinese government's own description of unrest, for one, is extremely broad and nonspecific. In the aforementioned release figures for social unrest in 2005, the Ministry of Public Security labeled them as "disturbances against public order." But the clarification issued by a ministry spokesman later revealed, possibly unwittingly, precisely why the Hu Jintao government was taking them so seriously. For he explained that the eighty-seven thousand number did not refer solely to mass protests but also to all criminal cases linked to public disorder, such as "mob gatherings, obstruction of justice, fighting and trouble-making."[248] In other words, the Ministry of Public Security was counting only those incidents that reflected a challenge to the authority of the state. What is more, the list included *only the challenges that could not be settled fairly amicably by the local authorities.* These were only the tip of a much larger iceberg. A parallel set of data constructed by Elizabeth Perry from China's Foreign Broadcast Information Service revealed that in 1993, the countryside witnessed some 1.7 million cases of resistance, primarily tax resistance, of which 6,230 cases were classified as "disturbances" *(naoshi)* that entailed severe damage to persons or property. The confrontations that year led to the death or injury of some 8,200 township and county officials.[249] Perry's enumeration of 6,230 *naoshi* is not far from the official tally for the year of 8,700 disturbances tabulated by the government and released during the tenure of Hu Jintao. It is reasonable to conclude, therefore, that the eighty-seven thousand in 2005 were challenges to the authority of the state of a similar degree of seriousness.

From "growth at any cost" to a "socially harmonious society"

The decision to highlight the rise of discontent was the beginning of a profound reorientation of policies in Beijing. Spearheaded by President Hu Jintao and Prime Minister Wen Jiabao, the move reflected their growing anxiety over the gradual erosion of the Communist Party's authority in the country. This loss touched a nerve that ran far deeper in the Chinese consciousness than the Communism that Mao Zedong had implanted. The fear of rebellion against a ruler who was perceived to be unjust had been a leitmotif of Chinese thought, through the ages,[250] and this did not change with the formation of the PRC in 1949. It underscored the ambivalence toward the market economy—attraction to its efficiency and repulsion from its inherent inequity—that characterized the policies of the Deng Xiaoping era[251] between 1978 and 1989. The relaxation of price and production controls, and the decentralization of investment decisions in the early eighties, led to a huge spurt in economic growth but also triggered rapid inflation, which impoverished students, professionals, and workers, and exacerbated corruption, which rewarded unscrupulous elements within the party. The resulting unrest culminated in the showdown at Tiananmen.

Tiananmen forced a choice upon the reformers. After much reflection, Deng Xiaoping concluded that the Communist Party had no choice but to push ahead with growth as fast as possible and hope that the gainers would sufficiently outnumber the losers to ensure political stability. Deng Xiaoping unveiled his choice during his southern tour of 1992. It was turned into formal policy by President Jiang Zemin and Premier Zhu Rongji in 1998. However, their timing could not have been worse, for their thrust toward structural reform and their reliance on the trickle-down effect of growth to resolve social contradictions coincided with the onset of a recession that lasted till the end of the decade. Most of the workers that they laid off in millions did not find new jobs, or had to make do with less well-paid and more insecure work.[252]

But the resulting rise in social unrest did not dampen Jiang Zemin's commitment to growth and modernization. In a landmark speech in July 2001, at the eightieth anniversary of the founding of the Communist Party of China (CPC), he sketched out his ideas on the challenges that the party would face in the coming years. Jiang Zemin developed his thesis in impeccably Marxist terms. Recalling the relationship between the economic base and the social and political superstructure of society, he warned that if the CPC did not adjust constantly to the changes in the former, it would become an "obstacle to the development of the productive forces and social progress." Jiang urged the party to recognize the economic and social differentiation that had set in as a result of economic reforms, and urged the party to change its structure accordingly. To make sure that the party remained the standard-bearer of this "advanced culture," Jiang proposed that membership be thrown open to China's new technocrats, managers, and outstanding entrepreneurs from the private sector.

Crisis of legitimacy

In July 2001, when Jiang made his groundbreaking speech, the party's senior leaders were aware that the CPC was facing a growing crisis of legitimacy. From the late nineties, highly regarded intellectuals like He Qinlian, Yu Shicun, and Sun Liping had been warning their readers that money and politics had become so inextricably intertwined that it had become impossible to combine growth with social justice; and that China was developing not a plural but a fractured society in which the middle class was being crushed between the very rich and the very poor.[253] Even writers who were more optimistic about China's capacity to meet the political challenges that had been thrown up by its rapid and cadre-initiated development readily recognized that the problems did exist.[254]

Officially, the leadership frowned on the outbursts of criticism from academics. He Qinlian's second book, *We Are Watching the Stars Above*, which was published in June 2001, was banned immediately. The central leaders first allowed Chen Guidi and Wu Chuntao's *The Life of China's Peasants*, to be published, but then hastily banned it. The authors were shunned, and hounded out of their hometown in 2004. But the leaders took the criticism sufficiently seriously to start their own investigation.

The results of a "millennium" survey of attitudes, compiled after interviewing three hundred thousand party members, gave the leaders a huge shock, for it revealed the moral decay that had crept into the Communist Party. The only part of the survey's findings that the leadership released to the public was that in Szechuan province 32 percent of the party cadres focused exclusively on what their superiors wanted, and not on service to the people. Since this was not, by itself, a shockingly high figure, analysts concluded that the party leaders had been shocked by what they had chosen not to reveal.[255]

But despite the growing discomfort in the Communist Party, it gave no significant response to the rising discontent in the country and animosity toward party cadres so long as Jiang Zemin remained its general secretary. Changes began only after Hu Jintao became president in spring 2003. These changes, too, took time to unfold. The party's tradition of emphasizing continuity discouraged even a hint of criticism of Hu's predecessor. The composition of party leadership after the Sixteenth National Congress also left the new president in no position to take a distinct line of his own. From 1999, the head of the Organization Department of the CPC Central Committee, and therefore the man responsible for most of the senior postings in the regional and central governments, was Zeng Qinghong—a close ally of Jiang Zemin from 1984, when Jiang was the mayor of Shanghai. After the Sixteenth National Congress, six of the nine members of the Politburo Standing Committee, and twelve out of the politburo's fifteen other members, either were recognized supporters of Jiang Zemin or favored his policies. Zeng Qinhong himself became Hu Jintao's vice president. Thus there was no reference to the impending crisis of legitimacy in a speech Hu Jintao gave on the Three Represents in 2002.[256]

Hu's first moves

But while he made no pronouncements, Hu Jintao and Premier Wen Jiabao unfolded a three-pronged strategy to reform and re-shape the Communist Party, address the immediate causes of discontent, and correct the underlying distortions in the structure of the state and party in which the discontent was ultimately rooted. Within weeks of ascending to the presidency, Hu launched a massive drive against corruption in the party and began to show an ostentatious and well-publicized concern for the plight of workers, peasants, the ailing, and the destitute.

Senior cadres who had prospered under the benign neglect of Jiang Zemin suddenly found themselves being investigated. So fierce was the drive that, according to the state-run *Wen Wei Po* daily, 1,252 party members killed themselves, 8,371 absconded, and 6,528 disappeared in the first half of 2003. Countless others were given the death penalty or sent to prison.[257]

Wen Jiabao, then still the vice premier, spent New Year's Eve 2003 sharing dumplings with coal miners five hundred meters belowground in a coal mine. This was the incumbent regime's way of showing that it intended to do something to bring down the extraordinarily high mortality rate in China's coal mines, which had claimed 59,543 lives in the decade between 1992 and 2001, a fatality rate ten times as high, per million tons of coal mined, as India's and 125 times as high as that of the US.[258] Eleven months later Wen became the first Chinese prime minister to visit AIDS patients in a Beijing hospital. He was followed a year later by Hu Jintao himself.[259] Such gestures of affinity with the commoners became an annual ritual.[260]

Wen Jiabao also prepared the party and the country for the coming changes of policy. In an address delivered to a party meeting in late December 2005, and released in Chinese newspapers three weeks later, Wen made a critical admission. "We absolutely cannot commit a historic error over land problems," he told the assembled delegates. "In some areas, illegal seizures of farmland without reasonable compensation have provoked uprisings. This is still a key source of instability in rural areas and even the whole society."[261] The Chinese newspapers published this statement less than a month later, on January 20, in a report that also disclosed that the number of public protests had risen by 13 percent to eighty-seven thousand in 2005, and the number of incidents in which public order was disturbed by 6.6 percent.[262] This dispelled any remaining doubt that important changes of domestic policy were in the offing.

Breaking the hold of the Shanghai gang

But substantial reform was far from easy. It required first a weakening of the power centers in the party that had fostered, and benefited most from, the growth-first policies of the previous decade, and then the induction of fresh cadres in senior posts who shared the president's vision and concerns. Hu Jintao unveiled his campaign for taking control of the government and party at the third plenary session of the Sixteenth Central Committee, in October 2003. There were three items on the agenda: a work report, some proposed revisions to the constitution, and a "Decision of the CCP Central Committee on Several Issues in Perfecting the Socialist Market Economy." This was the only document later made public, and in a quiet, unemphatic way, it made a complete break with the policies of Jiang Zemin. Whereas the Sixteenth National Congress the previous year—Jiang Zemin's last hurrah—endorsed the target of further quadrupling gross GDP, the third plenum emphasized the need to balance economic with social and cultural development. And whereas the Sixteenth National Congress report emphasized China's achievements, the third plenum focused on the problems that remained: " ... the relations of distribution have not been straightened out, rural incomes are increasing slowly, prominent contradictions persist in employment, increasing pressures are emerging from the resource environment, the overall competitiveness of the economy is not strong ... "[263]

But in implementing change, Hu faced two interconnected problems: First, most of the social discontent was being generated by the growth of inequality and the flowering of corruption and extortion. But the overwhelming proportion of these sins of commission and omission were being committed by local cadres, ranging from powerful provincial party bosses to millions of township and village cadres, over whom the central government had virtually no control. Hu Jintao's first major decision was to reestablish the central government's control over investment. In the beginning of 2004, he and Wen Jiabao adopted a "macroeconomic control" policy whose ostensible purpose was to prevent an overheating of the Chinese economy similar to what had occurred in 1993 and 1994 and to avoid "a financial bubble." This included sharp increases in the bank interest rate, physical limits on bank lending, much stricter central oversight over land use, and constant monitoring and limitation of fixed investment in key sectors showing signs of overheating, such as steel, cement, and real estate. Hu and Wen made it clear that the energy, technology, and education sectors were specifically exempted and that they intended to increase state investment in the agriculture, transportation, and social welfare sectors, especially in the less developed western and northeastern regions.[264] But both leaders emphasized that the central government was asking for a slowdown of investment in all sectors and regions of the country.

The city that epitomized defiance of the central government—that indeed had done so since shortly after the Tiananmen crisis—was Shanghai. Ever since Deng Xiaoping decided to develop Pudong, the eastern part of Shanghai, in 1990, Shanghai has been a focal point for modernization in the People's Republic of China (PRC). Since the mid-1990s Shanghai has become the showcase for China's coming-of-age. To finance this grandiose project, Shanghai received a large number of grants and loans from the central government; between 1990 and 2002, when Jiang Zemin was the general secretary of the CPC, Shanghai received 19.8 billion yuan more than did its main domestic competitor, Tianjin.

The deluge of state grants in turn stimulated more foreign direct investment (FDI) in the city. Between 1978 and 2001, 86 percent of the total FDI in China went to the cities of the eastern coast. By the end of 1999, 144 of the world's five hundred largest firms had invested in 511 projects in Shanghai. Another 110 had opened offices there. About two hundred foreign banks had opened branches or offices in the city. Unsurprisingly, Shanghai experienced the biggest building boom the world had ever seen. According to the Shanghai municipal government, in the early 1990s annual investment in the real estate sector was less than $120 million. In 2001 the figure reached $7.6 billion, "implying a compound annual growth rate of over 50 percent" during that decade.[265] While there were only three buildings in the city that exceeded twenty stories in height in 1980, and 152 in 1990, there were 1,478 in 2000, and 1,930 in 2003. In the late 1990s, three million laborers from the provinces were employed at the city's estimated twenty-one thousand construction sites.[266] A reporter for the *Wall Street Journal* was not exaggerating too much when he wrote in 1993, "What's going on in Shanghai, and up and down the China coast, might be the biggest construction project the planet has ever seen since the coral polyps built the Great Barrier Reef after the last Ice Age."[267]

But Shanghai's rebirth was taking place on the backs of the poor. With no ownership rights to the land on which their homes were built and the lands they tilled, they were unceremoniously ousted from the new construction sites. Data released by the municipal government showed that between 1992 and 1997, two million residents had to be relocated in order to pave the way for property development, half of them from the downtown area. But almost none could afford to move back when the construction was complete. A survey of eleven cities in Zhejiang province showed that 85 percent of those who had been displaced could not afford the housing prices in their cities. Small-scale public protests against official corruption, the wrongdoings of real estate companies, and the drastic dislocation of downtown residents had become a routine phenomenon in the coastal cities.

The rising dissent acquired political overtones because, in the eyes of a by now sizable public opinion, Shanghai's miraculous growth was taking place at the expense of other parts of the country. But Shanghai's party leaders were oblivious to the tide of ill will that was gathering in the party and among the intelligentsia, and remained obsessed with high-speed property development. In 2002 they restarted the construction of the Shanghai Global Financial Center, intended to be the tallest building in the world, which had been halted for four years in the wake of the Asian financial crisis. Mayor Han Zheng told the international media, a few months later, that the Shanghai property boom would surely continue for "a long time." Oblivious to, or possibly contemptuous of, the rising discontent, in mid-2003 the Shanghai municipal government decided to build "three new Pudongs within three years." Inspired by Shanghai fever, nearby cities such as Suzhou, Kunshan, Hangzhou, and Ningbo all set ambitious goals for economic growth.[268]

Shanghai was therefore one of the main centers, if not *the* epicenter, of the runaway boom; it was also the Jiang Zemin faction's power base. So that was where Hu Jintao decided to reassert Beijing's macroeconomic control in 2004. As a first step, the central government canceled four hundred billion yuan ($48 billion) worth of projects, including a theme park, a forty-kilometer undersea tunnel that would rival the UK–France Chunnel, a horse racing track, and several new subway lines. Beijing also canceled a thousand projects in Jiangsu province (in the Yangtze delta), including a proposed airport for Suzhou. Zhejiang was made to stop the construction of nineteen large steel, cement, and aluminum plants and 90 percent of its planned industrial parks. Beijing also sent investigation teams to the Yangtze delta to look into charges of illegal acquisition of land and finance to carry out industrial projects.[269]

The Communist Party in Shanghai opposed this drive from the very beginning. Its secretary, Chen Liangyu, voiced strong dissent in the politburo, at a meeting in June 2004, and accused Wen Jiabao of wanting to harm the interests of the Yangtze River Delta. Citing statistics and projections, he also claimed that putting brakes on investment would hamper future growth. Hu Jintao reportedly came to Wen's defense and rejected Chen's criticism, responding that the politburo had adopted this macroeconomic policy and that all local governments, including Shanghai, should therefore carry it out.

Chen Liangyu also resented and opposed the new leadership's ways of dealing with issues such as the accountability of government officials and the enforcement of measures to curb corruption and punish offenders. When, under pressure from Hu and the Central Commission for Discipline Inspection, Zhou Zhengyi, one of Shanghai's richest real estate tycoons, was arrested and charged with bank stock fraud and illicit property trading, the Shanghai courts sentenced him to only three years' imprisonment. What is more, the prosecutors carefully skirted what many analysts believed was the real issue in the indictment—the fact that in China, where all land was vested in the state, no real estate fraud was possible without the connivance of high government officials. The indictment of Zhou Zhengyi was therefore a veiled accusation against Chen Liangyu of adopting a laissez-faire attitude toward corruption. His open attack on the Hu-Wen team at the June 2004 politburo meeting therefore did not come as a surprise.[270]

An analysis of the speeches given by various leaders during the summer of 2004 showed that Hu Jintao and Wen Jiabao were not enamored of growth because they were fully aware of the backlash of discontent it tended to create. The Shanghai leadership, by contrast, had no such worries. While Wen Jiabao was asking for a continuation of curbs on investment into the second half of 2004, saying that the problem of overheating had not been solved, one of his own vice premiers, Huang Ju, did not hesitate to assert, at an international seminar in Beijing in May, that the macroeconomic controls had already had the desired effect and needed to be relaxed.[271]

Chen Liangyu and the "Shanghai gang" carried their contempt for Beijing to extraordinary lengths. Chen is reported to have said, "I have a dream."[272] But unlike Martin Luther King's, Chen's dream was not about equality but its opposite: He had set out to make Shanghai the premier city of Asia, if not the world. If this meant making it one of the most inegalitarian cities, he was prepared to pay the price. The deadline he had set himself was the 2010 World Expo, which was to be held in Shanghai. To achieve his goal he embarked upon a series of grandiose projects with a royal disregard for cost and return on investment. The "hai" in Shanghai, he used to lament, meant the ocean, but Shanghai had no beach. So the government shipped in 128,000 tons of sand from southern China to build a ten-kilometer-long beach in the suburbs. Not only did Chen Liangyu restart construction of the world's tallest building, which had been stopped after the Asian crisis, but he commissioned a $290 million world-class tennis complex and a $300 million Formula One race-track, both consciously designed to be among the most modern and best in the world. It did not matter to him that few Chinese owned cars, and fewer still played tennis.[273] So grandiose was the planning that the racetrack may have cost as much as $1.24 billion.[274]

Chen Liangyu finally overstepped himself when he announced plans to extend a thirty-kilometer magnetic levitation train linking Shanghai Airport to the Pudong economic zone. Built at a cost of $1.3 billion and opened for public service in January 2004, the train ranked as one of the biggest white elephants of all time, with an estimated payback period, if all went well, of more than 160 years.[275] Public discontent had been mounting steadily as the Shanghai government raced to complete its basket of mega-projects. Tens of thousands of longtime residents of the central parts had been evicted and resettled in remote suburbs. Inevitably, rumors of high-level corruption multiplied. The government's announcement that it intended to extend the maglev train to Hangzhou, at an estimated cost of $5 billion, proved to be the last straw. The public protests became so intense and continuous that Chen's government could not convene without massive security deployments worthy of a visit by a foreign head of state.[276]

The rising public discontent gave Hu Jintao the pretext that he needed to break the Shanghai gang's hold. On September 25, 2006, he dismissed Chen Liangyu from the position of party secretary and suspended him from membership of the Central Committee and the politburo, for possibly having siphoned off funds from a ten-billion-yuan social security fund, and sundry associated lesser charges. In May 2007, Chen's pet project—the maglev extension to Hangzhou—was canceled, and in July he was stripped of his membership in the Communist Party in preparation for a possible trial. By then other members of the Shanghai clique, including Vice President Zeng Qinghong and two vice premiers, had already begun to make their peace with Hu Jintao.[277]

Third rectification of the party

Breaking the hold of the Shanghai gang was only half the battle for the reform of the Chinese Communist Party. The other half was to remold it into a party dedicated to serving the people. To do this Hu Jintao began to systematically replace older retiring members of the politburo and other bodies with graduates of the China Youth League, the party's youth wing.[278] He also launched a sustained ideological campaign within the party. On January 5, 2005, the *People's Daily* published a lead editorial blandly titled "Educational Activities," in which it announced that the Chinese Communist Party was launching a new campaign to reeducate its cadres. The campaign would be mounted in three phases over eighteen months. As was their wont in important pronouncements, China's leaders used the editorial to stress a continuity of policy and absence of disagreement within the party. But in fact the announcement heralded a radical shift in the priorities of the Communist Party of China, away from its previous stress on rapid growth at virtually any cost, toward achieving growth with greater equity and social justice.

The ostensible purpose of the campaign was to reorganize the party along the lines sketched out by former president Jiang Zemin in his "Three Represents." But in reality it gave the new leadership an opportunity to assess the existing senior cadres at various levels of government and decide whom to reshuffle and replace. The reshuffle began immediately after the "reeducation." In the next twelve months the party replaced or reshuffled 170,000 senior members of party committees at four levels of government.[279]

The doors to self-criticism had been opened a little over three months earlier, in September, by the fourth plenum of the CPC, which had passed a resolution voicing the fear that the party was at a crucial juncture "at which the ongoing marketization of the economy, the pluralization of social interests, and the intensification of social contradictions have *threatened the ruling status of the party.*"[280](emphasis added) The *People's Daily* editorial that referred to it clearly reflected a decision by the leadership to draw the party cadres' and the country's attention to the changes that were imminent. A few days after the editorial appeared, Xinhua, China's official news agency, released a news item that left readers in no doubt that a major rectification campaign was in the offing. The news item was captioned "Opinions of the Chinese Communist Party Central Committee." It cited "the abuse of power and the moral degeneration of some party cadres, the weakness of many grassroots party organizations, and the inability of some leaders to deal effectively with complex social issues" to be the main threats to the party's authority. The leaders, it revealed, had resolved to "improve the education of the cadres, develop inner party democracy and enhance the capacity to govern."[281]

By the end of 2004 Hu had sufficiently consolidated his power to start shifting the locus of Chinese politics. In two speeches, on January 14 and 24, 2005, he made it clear that he intended to give primacy to improving the party's ability to govern, and "establish the party for the public and govern for the people."[282]

January also saw the publication, by official agencies, of data on social unrest in the country. While incidents involving violence and mass demonstrations had been reported with increasing frequency in the media, this was the first time that the state had collected information from across the nation and publicized it. The data came as a shock, for it showed an exponential growth in discontent, from 8,700 protests in 1993 and ten thousand in 1994 to eighty-seven thousand in 2005. In 2004, more than 3.5 million persons took part in seventy-four thousand protests. Hu Jintao used this information as a launch pad for a shift in the locus of government policy.

Harmonious society

In a highly publicized speech he gave at the Central Committee's Party School on February 19, 2005, at the opening of a seven-day training course for ministerial- and senior provincial-level cadres, Hu said:

> The CPC and the central government have made it an important task to build a harmonious society, which serve[s] the fundamental interests of the people. . . . it [is] important to balance the interests between different social groups, to avoid conflicts and to make sure people live a safe and happy life in a politically stable country. A harmonious society will feature democracy, the rule of law, equity, justice, sincerity, amity and vitality. Such a society will give full scope to people's talent and creativity, enable all the people to share

the social wealth brought by reform and development, and forge an ever closer relationship between the people and government. These things will result in lasting stability and unity.[283]

The term "harmonious society" was endorsed by the Comunist Party at its October 2006 plenum, and its content discussed extensively at the National People's Congress in March 2007. But it had a mixed reception. Within China it quickly became an omnibus phrase, used to justify whatever the speaker had in mind. Many scholars in the West concluded that Hu Jintao was a conservative who was determined to slow down China's hectic advance toward a market economy, and that he was invoking populist sentiment to weaken the Jiang Zemin faction within the party leadership. So a few weeks later, the leadership felt it necessary to spell out what it had in mind with greater precision. An editorial opinion in the *China Daily* did so on March 12, 2005:

A harmonious society includes a slew of elements: democracy, the rule of law, equity and justice, sincerity, amity and vitality. That calls for an alternative to single-minded pursuit of economic achievement at all costs. . . . In the trade-off between efficiency and equity, our policymakers have for a long time put more accent on the former. As a result, gross domestic product (GDP) has become an overriding gauge of political achievement. . . . After years of staggering economic growth, China's national strength has ballooned while its social undertakings have fallen way behind. . . .

At the core of the new concept lies the government's commitment to equity on the basis of the rule of law. To that end, it is vital for the government to revamp its governance. A heritage of the planned-economy regime, the government is still sometimes meddling in enterprises' business. Although administrative powers are subject to increasing constraints as the country embraces market-oriented reforms, the government remains a decisive force in allocating resources.

The government needs to make greater efforts to promote social equality by improving social security, employment, medical care, poverty reduction and education. It must especially devise policies to help rural areas develop faster to catch up with better-off urban regions. From the concept of the "harmonious society," China has begun a long march toward the right choice.[284]

Dual purpose of tax-for-fees reform

Many analysts have compared the downfall of Chen Liangyu with that of Chen Xitong, the mayor of Beijing, a decade earlier. Chen Xitong had been stripped of power by Jiang Zemin, in what had been widely perceived then as a bid to consolidate Jiang's, and Shanghai's, power at the center. Hu Jintao was accused of having done the same in reverse. But breaking the power of Shanghai was only a part of a much greater thrust to restore the legitimacy and authority of the Communist Party. Hu Jintao knew that nearly all the discontent was being triggered by the actions of local government officials and party cadres. These included the seizure of and the extraction of arbitrary and extortionate local taxes and fees, and an often brutal use of force to discourage villagers and other victims from taking the matter up to higher levels of party and government.[285] Hu and Premier Wen Jiabao therefore decided to strip the local governments of the powers that they were abusing in their dealings with the rural population. The reforms that Hu and Wen enacted had a dual purpose—to relieve the immediate burden on the rural population and to strip the local governments, particularly at the township and village level, of the powers to tax and invest. The most drastic of these reforms, enacted in stages between 2004 and 2006, were the tax-for-fees reform and the abolition of the agricultural tax.

The tax-for-fees reform (TFR) was intended to plug the loopholes that local governments had exploited in the 1994 tax reforms in order to continue taxing the peasants. First tried out in Anhui in 2000, and extended to twenty provinces on an experimental basis in 2002. In 2004, TFR replaced the multitude of fees, often illegal and arbitrary, that local authorities were levying on the peasantry with a single tax of 5 percent on agricultural cash crops other than tobacco. The reform had two goals. The first was to reduce the burden of levies on the rural population. The second was to force the local governments to reduce their bloated bureaucracies. According to newspaper reports, this reform dramatically reduced the exactions from the peasants.[286] But a more fundamental restructuring of center-province financial relations soon overtook TFR.

In 2004, the Yan'an municipal district in the province of Shaanxi, which had been among the first to introduce TFR, went a step further and also abolished the agricultural tax and the agricultural specialties tax—in short, all taxes on agriculture. The central government seized upon this opportunity to extol the performance of Yan'an and announced that it would eliminate all agricultural taxation in five years. However, so great was the response from the peasants that within months it brought this forward by three years to the beginning of 2006.[287]

It was able to do this because while the yield of the agricultural taxes had become an insignificant portion of the total revenue of the local governments,[288] they were steeply regressive. By 2005 they were contributing only a little more than 1 percent of the total revenues of the nation; their impact on incomes was most severe in the least industrialized parts of the country, and on the poorest families in each village. They were also difficult to extract, and therefore expensive to collect. Moreoever, the booming economy was filling the coffers of the central and provincial governments from other sources.

Agricultural taxes were abolished so soon after TFR that it is difficult to separate the social impact of the one from the other. According to official reports, in 2006 the number of public disturbances fell for the first time in more than a decade. The improvement in the rural areas was indirectly confirmed by the failure of large numbers of seasonal migrant workers who went back to their farms in 2006 to return for work to the cities. This caused a sudden and unexpected shortage of labor in many industrial towns.[289]

To a considerable extent, the TFR has also achieved its second purpose—of downsizing the rural administration.[290] But it was not an unmixed blessing. While the relief it has afforded to the peasants is palpable, it has also further eroded the fiscal autonomy of the township and village administrations without reducing their administrative responsibilities.[291] To compensate for this, in February 2006 Wen Jiabao announced that the center would transfer one hundred billion yuan directly to the county and lower levels of provincial administration, to compensate for the abolition of fees and waiver of the agriculture tax.[292] This was one of a slew of measures endorsed by the National People's Congress in March 2006. These included a promise to spend an overall 340 billion yuan on rural health, education, and infrastructure (14 percent more than in the previous year);[293] an exemption from income tax for anyone earning less than 1,600 yuan per month; and, most significantly, a strict ban on local governments expropriating peasants and assigning their land to industry free of cost or at throwaway prices.

But the experience of Yan'an suggests that TFR may provide only temporary relief from social discontent, because it has not solved the core problem that local governments have faced since 1994. This is what Chen Guidi and Wu Chuntao called the "upward movement of revenues and downward movement of responsibilities." As was described earlier, the 1994 reforms had plunged townships and town and village administrations into a financial crisis. The administrations had tried to make ends meet by levying an ever-expanding list of fees and administrative charges, and by borrowing ever more heavily from banks and rural credit institutions. Practically all of the extortionate impositions upon the peasants described in the last chapter sprang from the effort to cut the same coat (with silken lining, of course) out of a smaller amount of cloth.

By taking away most, if not all, revenue-raising powers, TFR has made this problem more, not less, acute. This was hidden in all but the least industrialized counties during the boom of 2001–2008 by the surge in tax revenues caused by the economic boom. With the onset of recession, as profits turn into losses and revenues dry up TFR could easily turn into a double-edged weapon. The poorer provinces and the less industrialized counties do not have even the reprieve granted to the industrialized counties by the economic boom. The party secretary of a township in Yan'an told a researcher that without the agriculture taxes its revenues were only thirty thousand yuan, but its expenses were two hundred thousand yuan. On average, in the poorer counties the two agricultural taxes used to contribute 30 percent of the total revenue.

A survey of Shaanxi province carried out in 2002 by the State Council's Development Research Center had shown that this was normal in the poorer provinces. The survey revealed that village committees were raising 78 percent of the total cost of education, while the county, provincial, and central administrations together met only 22 percent. If the bulk of this came from "off-budget" levies, then filling the gap left by abolishing both fees and taxes would have required at least a trebling of revenue transfers to them from the central government. A subsequent study by John James Kennedy suggests that the transfers did not come close to doing so. As a result, by 2003, the number of students in rural schools in

Yan'an had declined by 24 percent, and the number of schools by 15 percent.

Kennedy found that the reforms also forced the local administrations to cut back the already meager health benefits that the rural population enjoyed. As medical out-of-pocket expenses soared through the nineties, more and more people had come to rely upon the health care workers and rural doctors employed by the township and village administrations. After the reforms, the administrations lost their capacity to pay. As a result, the number of health workers in Shaanxi province declined from 15,365 to 2,813. The reforms also forced the township and village administrations to cut back three other important subsidies—on housing, coal, and grain.

In sum, Kennedy's research in Shaanxi confirmed that while the abolition of the right to levy fees would bring a great deal of relief to the peasants, it would also impair the local authorities' ability to provide essential services. Even where the greater control of the county and prefectural administrations led to a net improvement in these services, the TFR would reduce the autonomy of lower levels of local administration and, in the poorer provinces, turn the township and village administrations into mere shells.

A bunch of half measures

Once the party had officially endorsed the goal of creating a "harmonious society," Hu and Wen embarked upon other, substantial, urban and rural reforms. The most important of these was a decision to guarantee peasants the right to till their land for thirty years.[294] The government also committed itself to abolishing school fees in rural areas in 2006 and, in June 2007,[295] got the Standing Committee of the National People's Congress to pass a new labor law that would allow trade unions to engage in collective bargaining for the first time. It also required enterprises that laid off workers to "consult" with the unions first.[296] In 2006, the trade unions opened their doors to migrant workers. Their goal was to recruit eight million more migrant workers every year and to increase membership of the unions by thirty-three million by the end of 2008.[297]

Hu Jintao and Wen Jiabao's campaign to create a "new socialist countryside" is still gathering momentum, so it is too early to predict how effective it will be. But it is difficult to resist the suspicion that all they are doing is applying poultice to an open sore, instead of treating the infection. All of the measures described above are, in the end, half measures:

The tax-for-fees reform and the subsequent abolition of the agriculture taxes are providing only immediate relief without addressing the imbalance between local governments' revenues and their administrative expenditures, which has been the root cause of their exploitative behavior toward the peasants. The proposed abolition of school fees in the rural areas will worsen this imbalance. The struggle by the counties and townships to raise resources by any manner of means will therefore remain dormant only so long as the economy is enjoying a boom and the provincial revenues are rising rapidly. It will begin again the moment boom turns into recession, as happened in 1997.

The new property law unveiled at the March 2007 meeting of the National People's Congress was even more blatantly a half measure. While it gave thirty-year leasehold rights to farmers, it rejected the proposal to transfer full ownership rights to them.[298] It did not, therefore, significantly reduce the right of the local branches of the party to take over their land at short notice in exchange for wholly inadequate compensation.[299]

The right of collective bargaining granted to trade unions only requires enterprises to *consult* with the unions, and not, as some reformers had proposed, to obtain their consent. And even the thirty-three million unionized migrant workers at the end of 2006 made up only a sixth of the total number of such workers. Five-sixths remained outside the fold, and their numbers were slated to grow, for while the unions were mandated to recruit eight million more workers every year, the number of migrant workers was estimated to be growing by thirteen million each year.[300]

Under Hu Jintao, the central government has not only maintained but tightened its control of the Internet. Hu Jintao declared his intention to "purify" the Internet in a front-page article in the *People's Daily*.[301] He made this statement during a discussion, among senior party leaders, of ways to keep China's Internet community in check. "Whether we can cope with the Internet is a matter that affects the development of socialist culture, the security of information and the stability of the state," Hu said.

Reports on the impact of Hu Jintao's reforms suggest there has been a decline in the number of protests after 2005. These are probably correct, but it is difficult to know how far to trust them. Because the National Bureau of Statistics still relies mainly upon the self-reporting system for collecting data, Chinese statistics have been known to show dramatic results the moment the government has decided to politicize them. This happened with the estimates of GDP after 1997. It may have happened to estimates of energy consumption per dollar of GDP in the second half of 2006, when a 1 percent increase in the first half of the year suddenly turned into a 1.7 percent decline for the whole year. It may be happening to statistics on the number of mass protests taking place in the countryside. While the national media reported a 17 percent drop in the number of incidents in 2006, the 2006 social statistics announced in December 2007 by China's National Bureau of Statistics show that in 2006, public security entities handled 599,392 cases—such as "disturbances in social order, "disturbances in public spaces, "trouble-making activities," and "obstruction of public service execution"—among which 583,180 have been investigated and resolved.

This tabulation clearly uses different criteria from those that the Chinese Ministry of Public Security used to tabulate the rise in protests after 1993. But it confirms that social unrest remains very high in the country. Newspaper reports, including those by foreign journalists, also confirm that those which are taking place have become larger, more prolonged, and more violent. What is more, the abuse of power by the party cadres is not proving easy to uproot. The following examples show how little has actually changed so far in the rural areas:

- In October 2004, more than ten thousand farmers, whose land was slated to be submerged by a new dam in Ya'an, Szechuan, launched a vigorous protest against their forced relocation. Nervous authorities called in the People's Armed Police (PAP). The resulting clashes led to the deaths of at least one protester and two policemen.
- In April 2005, twenty thousand peasants from several villages in Huaxi township, Zhejiang province, who had been complaining for four years about industrial pollution from an industrial park that had ruined their agricultural livelihood, fought with police. Before the protests, local elected village councils and the township Communist Party secretary had made futile pleas to higher authorities to respond to the peasants' concerns. The factories were eventually shut down, but the protest leaders were arrested.
- In June 2005, about a hundred miles southwest of Beijing, approximately three hundred hired thugs attacked a group of farmers who had camped on disputed land that the local government had planned to use to build a power plant. The

farmers protested the lack of proper compensation for their land. Six villagers reportedly were killed in the attack, which was captured on video by a protester and shown on Chinese websites. Communist authorities fired the local party chief and mayor and returned the farmland.

- In July 2005, residents of Taishi village, near Guangzhou, capital of Guangdong province, submitted a petition to remove their village chief for plundering public funds. After one of their leaders was arrested, 1,500 villagers clashed with five hundred armed police. In September 2005, police seized government documents that villagers had been guarding to use in their legal case alleging official corruption, and shut down an Internet website that had been reporting on the unrest. Also in July 2005, farmers in Xinchang, two hunded kilometers south of Shanghai, attacked a pharmaceutical plant because of anger and lack of redress over pollution that it emitted.

- In the same month (July 2005), police beat up villagers who were protesting against pollution from a battery factory in Zhejiang province.

- In August 2005, unemployed residents of Daye, in Hubei province, attacked government offices and destroyed cars after police used dogs to break up a demonstration over an official plan to annex Daye to a larger city, Huangshi. In September 2005, a Chinese court sentenced ten persons to prison terms ranging from one to five years for their involvement in the protests.

- In December 2005, a dispute over the construction of an electricity-generating plant and related property seizures culminated in a violent clash in Dongzhou village near Shanwei city, Guangdong province, in which, according to different accounts, between three and twenty demonstrators were killed. Beijing suspended the deputy police chief of Shanwei, restricted movement in and out of the area, imposed a news blackout, and arrested three protest leaders. The year-long conflict included villagers filing formal complaints, setting up roadblocks, and kidnapping local officials; government officials visiting Dongzhou; local authorities detaining and releasing village leaders; and the mysterious death of a village accountant who had supported the farmers' demands.

- In January 2006, thousands of protesters clashed with police over inadequate compensation for farmland taken for industrial use in Panlong village, Sanjiao township, Guangdong province. A teenage girl was reportedly killed.[302]

- In March 2006, protest leader Feng Quisheng lost an election bid for the township people's congress. His supporters claimed that Feng's opponent engaged in vote-buying and that proxy votes were not accepted.

- In October 2006, as many as ten thousand students marched through the campus of a vocational college in Nanchang, the capital of Jiangxi province, after they heard reports in the state-run media that the college had deceived new students about their eventual qualification and had issued fake diplomas.[303] The demonstration reflected shock and a sudden loss of faith in their leaders, but its sheer size disturbed the authorities because it revealed organizational capacities that made the students a threat to the regime.

- In May 2007, an attempt by the local government to enforce strict population control by forcing women to have abortions sparked a violent clash between villagers and local police in Bobai county of the Guangxi autonomous region of southwestern China. Local officials resorted to compulsory abortion to meet targets set by their superiors after punitive fines, labeled a "social child-raising fee," ranging from five hundred to seventy thousand yuan, had failed to bring down illegal births sufficiently. The new "fee" had been imposed on families that had already paid an earlier fine for the violation of the birth control rules.

- When families objected strongly to the fee and refused to pay, witnesses said, they were detained, their homes searched, and valuables, including electronic items and motorcycles, were confiscated by the government. "Worst of all, the gangsters used hammers and iron rods to destroy people's homes, while threatening that the next time it would be with bulldozers," said a peasant who identified himself as Nong Sheng, in a letter faxed to a reporter in Beijing. According to reports posted on the Internet, as many as five persons, including three officials engaged in overseeing population control, were killed in the rioting, which went on for four days. Officials in Guangxi, in the meantime, boasted that they had collected 7.8 million yuan in "social child-raising fees" between February and the end of April.[304]
- In the single month of July 2007 in Chongqing, rioters took to the streets three times. In the third riot, early in July, an estimated five thousand persons participated, and went on a rampage that lasted for more than two days, killing one man and injuring ten others. The unrest began when villagers found that the government was offering three times as much by way of compensation for the extension of an industrial zone as they had received, three years earlier. What triggered the riot was their conviction that corruption had lain behind the low prices they had received three years earlier. The government shipped in a thousand policemen to put it down.[305]
- In the same month (July 2007), five thousand peasants clashed with the police in Shifang city in Szechuan, because effluents from a privatized brewery, they claimed, had halved their harvest.

These brief descriptions do not capture the depth of resentment and the resistance that is developing in the countryside. Two accounts of large protests that occurred in the Pearl River Delta in Guangdong, in 2004 and 2005, demonstrate vividly how the provincial authorities are losing the battle to keep dissent local. They also reflect the growing disillusionment of rural Chinese and the party's consequent loss of legitimacy.

The state viewed from below: Taishi

In October 2005, Lu Banglie, a social activist in Guangdong who had been helping villagers to assert their rights, was dragged out of a car when he arrived at a village called Taishi, beaten till he was unconscious, and left on the roadside. *Guardian* journalists, who were with him, escaped by taking to the fields. Six weeks later, Edward Cody of the *Washington Post* pieced together the full story of what had led to the brutal assault:[306]

> Construction cranes and factories had encroached on the banana plots and rice paddies of the surrounding villages as Guangzhou, capital of the Pearl River Delta's booming manufacturing region, swallowed up the rural surroundings. . . .
>
> Taishi, with just over 2,000 residents, benefited from the development along with the rest of southeastern China. The village administration took in $600,000 in 2004, triple its income of 2001. Each adult received about $100 in dividends from communal village land given over to factories assembling jewelry, clothing, shoes and electronic components.
>
> But two villagers, Feng Qiusheng and Liang Shusheng, began asking last May why the annual payments were not higher and why the village was deeply in debt. They demanded that Chen, the party secretary who had just taken over as village chief, open the accounts. Feng, 26, an accountant, wanted to go over the books himself. But Chen rejected that idea, along with the rest of their questions.
>
> In July, a new face showed up in Guangzhou, the huge nearby metropolis. He was Yang Maodong, 39, a former philosophy professor

and an experienced activist. Yang, a stocky, disheveled intellectual who spoke with rapid-fire intensity and wore the Chinese academic's traditional black-plastic-framed glasses, was a contributor to dissident Web sites and had written a book on the collapse of the Soviet Union. His political beliefs harked back to the democracy spirit of the Tiananmen Square protests in 1989. A natural organizer and unabashed nationalist, he had last been detained in April for his role in promoting anti-Japanese demonstrations in Beijing.

Given his background, it was not long before Yang made a connection with the angry peasants, including Feng, the young accountant who was challenging Chen's leadership of the village.

At a dinner in July organized by Yang in an inexpensive Guangzhou restaurant, Feng was also introduced to Lu, the peasant organizer who was later to be beaten. Lu was already gaining recognition for his activism. In 2003, he had endured beatings and used a five-day hunger strike to force out the leader of his own village, in Hubei province, on corruption charges. The government-run *China Youth Daily* had hailed him at the time as a "frontrunner of peasant grass-roots democracy." Eager to pursue his activism, he was immediately attracted to the fight over Taishi's leadership.

Lu, whose oily hair and ill-fitting black suit bespeak his peasant background, said he had come to Beijing in April and again in early July seeking guidance from more educated political activists about what to do next. One of the people he met during those consultations in the capital, he said in an interview, was Yang. And the subject of Taishi was already part of their conversation.

An activist leader, speaking on condition of anonymity, said Beijing-based community organizers had decided to lend support to Feng's cause soon after they heard of his challenge. For them, encouraging farmers to push for more democratic village elections was a longtime national goal, and Taishi seemed to fit the bill. They also reasoned this fast-growing region would be fertile ground, he said, because of its economic development and nearness to the relatively liberal atmosphere of Hong Kong.

Lu, the peasant organizer, moved to Guangzhou soon after talking with Yang. He found a job for about $65 a month in a factory manufacturing plastic Christmas trees. Although earning some badly needed money was his main motive for taking up residence here, Lu said it also meant he was on hand to offer advice when, in Taishi, the two peasants Feng and Liang decided to press a legal case for removing their village leader.

Yang and Lu, two veteran activists, quietly got involved in the struggle. They advised the Taishi villagers on what options were open to them under China's election laws, Lu said, and inspired them by recounting Lu's experience in booting out a corrupt leader back home in Hubei province. Basing their demand on the election law and its recall provision, Feng and Liang filed a formal recall motion on July 29. According to Lu and the district government, the motion was drafted with help from Lu and Yang.

It carried more than 400 signatures,[307] meeting the threshold of endorsement by 20 percent of Taishi's 1,500 registered voters.

Villagers gathered two days later in an open square. From atop a heap of bricks, as local reporters and other witnesses looked on, Feng read a section from Chinese law books saying village accounts must be published every six months and villagers had the right to recall Chen.

"The law will be our guardian," he vowed. . . .

An alarm bell rang in the village committee office on the evening of Aug. 3. Villagers who heard the noise rushed to the scene and, they recalled, surprised the village accountant and a companion in what looked like an attempt to spirit away the ledgers. Before the two could get away with the books, the villagers told reporters, a crowd gathered and prevented them from leaving. The accounts stayed put.

The next morning, police and district officials came to take the books away—to protect them, they said. Villagers called the Guangzhou Communist Party Discipline and Inspection Bureau, denouncing what they interpreted as an attempt to cover up malfeasance. But their calls elicited no response, they said. A group of elderly women moved into the three-story administration building and refused to budge. The ledgers would stay, they vowed.

As the sit-in continued, plainclothes security agents detained a protest leader as he rode his motorcycle down a village lane on Aug. 16. On hearing the news, hundreds of villagers poured out of their homes and surrounded the van into which the agents had stuffed the leader, blocking its passage.

After a several-hour confrontation during which the number of protesters swelled to more than 1,000, witnesses said, an estimated 500 riot police drove up in several dozen vehicles and waded into the crowd, swinging their batons. In Internet postings, villagers reported five of their number were arrested. A 16-year-old youth suffered a concussion, they said, and an 80-year-old peasant woman suffered a broken bone and had to be hospitalized. The sit-in continued, meanwhile, with the elderly women still refusing to leave. Within days, their numbers grew.

The district government two weeks later handed down a ruling that the recall motion was unacceptable because it was a photocopy, and the law demanded the original signatures. Outraged, a number of villagers, including elderly women, started a hunger strike outside the district headquarters building.

After several days, some of the hunger strikers were detained and later released on condition they return home, the protesters said. As they left custody about 3 p.m., they reported, officials gave them box lunches.

Despite the gesture, the atmosphere remained tense. As police moved in to make the arrests, one elderly woman threatened to blow up the building by igniting a canister of liquefied gas, according to witnesses. Yang sent messages to Chinese and foreign reporters recounting what was happening and urging them to visit. A reporter from the Hong Kong–based *South China Morning Post* showed up, and two youths smashed her car windows with rocks.

From that point on, things moved fast.

On Sept. 5, a delegation of villagers went to the district headquarters to present the original recall motion with the original signatures. But official patience had frayed. Activists later speculated that word had come down from Beijing that the uproar in Taishi— and the confluence of political activism with peasant outrage—had to be stopped. Although his role could not be determined, Premier Wen Jiabao visited the region Sept. 9–13 to confer with senior regional and city officials.

Beijing-based activists said they received warnings from the Civil Affairs Ministry about that time to back away from the Taishi dispute. "Everybody was scared," one of them recalled.

Back in Taishi, more than 50 vehicles drove up to the village administration building on Sept. 12 and disgorged hundreds of riot police, witnesses said. Swinging batons and training high pressure hoses on the elderly women inside, the police cleared the building and made way for district officials to take away the account books.

Nearly 50 protesters were taken into custody. The next day, Yang was also arrested as he drove to meet a crew from the Hong Kong-based Phoenix satellite television channel. Lu was urged to leave, but refused. "You know, he is just like a farmer; he is stubborn," said an activist who has worked with Lu.

Then, in a surprise turn of events, the district government announced that the recall motion was proved valid and villagers should choose an election committee to organize a new vote for village chief, scheduled for the middle of October. The protests should now stop, it said, and activists with "ulterior motives" should be ignored.

On first glance, this seemed like a triumph for the villagers. The official party newspaper, *People's Daily*, hailed the outcome as a model for village elections and pointed to signs of "a democratic environment built upon rationality and legality."

But then the district government arbitrarily chose all candidates for the seven-person election committee—and all were local officials loyal to Chen.

Outraged, the still-defiant villagers threatened to boycott the vote. Seeking to prevent more violence, the district government swiftly relented and allowed another slate to run as well. The vote was held on Sept. 16; all the unofficial candidates were elected and none of the government's slate.

The seven committee members now had four weeks to organize a new vote for village chief. But somewhere in the government and party bureaucracy—activists believe it was at a senior level in Beijing—officials had decided Chen would not be replaced, lest a precedent be set. . . .

Lu, who was in the village to monitor the Sept. 16 vote, was picked up by police the same day. After a long interrogation and a warning to clear out of the area, he was released that evening. In what they hoped was a farewell gesture, police officers bought him a pair of $12 shoes, he said later, to replace those that had come off during a brief struggle when he was taken into custody.

District officials announced shortly after the new election committee was chosen that their auditors had found no evidence of wrongdoing in the Taishi accounts. Party and government officials swiftly fanned out to persuade villagers to drop the struggle. Unless the recall motion was withdrawn, they suggested, detained relatives might stay in jail and people might lose their jobs.

The threats worked. The district government reported by the end of September that 396 out of 584 signatures were withdrawn.

The recall procedure therefore was invalid, it announced, and the vote scheduled for October was canceled.

Then guards wearing camouflage fatigues, but without official insignia, took up positions at streets leading into the village and began screening outsiders trying to enter and villagers trying to leave.

Villagers told the activists that the guards were unemployed men from surrounding villages paid $12 a day by Chen's head of security. The district government claimed in a statement that they were Taishi villagers who were upset at the uproar in their community. Two foreign reporters who drove up Oct. 7 to find out why the signatures were withdrawn were attacked by the guards and driven off.

It was the next night that Lu Banglie tried to drive in, along with a reporter from the *Guardian* newspaper ...

On that same night, according to Cody's *Washington Post* account, Lu was attacked and beaten senseless:

By the time Lu Banglie [entered the village] his photograph had already been distributed to local police stations. So when camouflage-clad men guarding the village entrance stopped his taxi and peered inside, Lu recalled, they immediately shouted, "It's him! It's him!" and yanked him out by the hair.

After dragging him to the side of the street, the guards set on Lu, kicking him and punching him until he passed out. . . . When Lu regained consciousness more than two hours later, he said, his body was bruised and hurting, his clothing smelled of urine, he was vomiting repeatedly, his vision was blurred and his memory had gone fuzzy. . . .

"We never imagined that we would be suppressed like this," Lu said.

In an interview nearly two weeks after his beating, Lu's lips were covered with scabs and his arms with bruises. His eyes were blurry at times and his head ached, he said, but he vowed to persist in organizing farmers to pick their own village leaders.

"I will definitely continue," he said, "but how to do it is the question now."

The state viewed from below: Xiangyang

The events at Xiangyang—one of the most backward but beautiful communities in Guangdong—highlight another ingredient of the gathering discontent in Chinese society. This is the progressive atrophy of citizens' age-old right of rightful resistance. This has been chronicled by Jonathan Watts of the *Guardian*, the journalist who had accompanied Lu Banglie to Taishi on the night when he was beaten unconscious.[308] Xiangyang is one of four villages in Yunfu, in the Pearl River Delta, whose farmland is inexorably being swallowed up by urbanization.

For the residents of the four villages in Yunfu, the loss of land was a calamity—wiping out all the gains they had made in the early days of China's economic reforms. When rural collectives were broken up in 1981, every villager in Xiangyang was given a little over half a mu (333 square metres) of farmland and permission to earn extra money in the cities between planting and harvesting seasons. There was enormous optimism that the good times were ahead.

But in 1997, the Yunfu township government confiscated more than a third of their land for development, paying compensation of 2600 pounds sterling per mu (666 square metres, or about a sixth of an acre). That was grudgingly accepted. The economy was growing so quickly that even with the quarter of a mu each family had left, they could still make a better living than in the days before the reforms. Growing vegetables, Mrs Wang and her husband could earn as much as 180 pounds a month—a good income for a Chinese farmer.

That changed completely on September 21 2004, when another huge tranche of village property was seized, leaving Mrs Wang too little land to make a living as a farmer and too little compensation to strike out into business. It took just one illness to plunge her family into poverty. Last year, her son needed emergency treatment for internal bleeding. Paying for his medical fees and prescription drugs used up all of the family's savings and pushed them into debt. . . .

Against such powerful local interests, what do peasants such as Mrs Wang do to seek justice? The answer has been the same for centuries: they travel to Beijing to make a direct appeal to the rulers of the nation. And in doing so, they become a member of China's most desperate underclass: the petitioners. This is probably the only group with lower social status than the peasantry. No one knows how many there are—it could be tens of thousands or tens of millions—but they all share the same belief in a benevolent central government that will correct the injustices carried out by local tyrants. It is a legacy of the imperial age. Up until 100 years ago, petitioners put their hopes in the emperor, who was believed to rule with the mandate of heaven. Since 1949, appeals for earthly, or divine, justice go by letter to the state council—the communist-controlled cabinet.

It is 2,460 kilometres from Xiangyang village to Tiananmen Square, but despite Mrs Wang's disability—since an accident in the 80s she has had trouble walking—she was determined to be part of the delegation that went to the capital. The villagers had never lodged a petition before, but they quickly organised themselves. Each family in the four communities dug deep into their pockets to raise the money to send a nine-member delegation to Beijing. On any other occasion, the 22-hour train journey through the plains of eastern China, across the Yangtze and Yellow rivers, would have been a source of wonder—none of the villagers had ever been to the capital before—but the mood was sombre. They were going to the only place where they thought they might receive fair treatment, but it was soon apparent that justice would be hard to find.

"When we arrived, we went to Tiananmen Square directly without having dinner, because we thought the National Petition Bureau was there," says Mrs Wang. It wasn't. By the time they found the right place, it was too late. They lodged at a . . . flophouse and tried again the next day. It was dispiriting and confusing. Mere peasants, the officials told them, should not be taking up so much important government time.

"The petition official was horrible," recalls Mrs Wang. "He told us, 'Don't come to me. There are more than 2,200 counties and cities in China. How can I deal with all of them?'"

Mrs Wang would never consider herself a rebel. But once she started petitioning, she was treated like one. On a second expensive and fruitless trip to Beijing, she and her fellow villagers were followed by Yunfu police and escorted back home. After six months, Mrs Wang's appeal for justice had got her nowhere. She was growing poorer by the day, and all the time she could see the developers working on the land that had been her life. When they started to construct a Honda showroom on the old cabbage patch, Mrs Wang's patience snapped. She joined the front line of a demonstration and was arrested by the police. It was the act that finally pushed her into the legal system, though not in the way she wanted. She spent 15 days in detention. She had lost her land and now she was being locked up for complaining about it. "That was the most unforgettable experience of my life," she says of her time on a penal production line, making rubber gloves. "We had to work without rest or they refused to feed us."

The distinctive feature of these, and countless other, confrontations is the violence with which the peasants' attempts to seek justice have been put down, and the unwillingness of even the Hu Jintao government in Beijing to redress a wrong for fear that it will set a precedent that could encourage many more demands for justice and redress. The fear, that the pressure that has already built up is too great to be reduced in a controlled manner, betrays the government's awareness that they are living on top of a volcano. Li Fan, a researcher at a private think tank in Beijing, summed up the government's dilemma:

> China's leaders speak of "serving the people" and "building a harmonious society." But Beijing also sees clearly that the survival of its regime depends on the local governments maintaining stability and order. Without that, who is left to protect the Party's kingdom?
>
> The central government tries to balance its support of local officials with its protection of the legitimate interests of common people. Sometimes Beijing punishes local governments in order to defuse popular tension; sometimes it allows local governments to pursue their interests freely. But as unrest continues to mount, how long will Beijing be able to strike this balance without real political reform?[309]

12 DEMOCRATIZATION WITH CHINESE CHARACTERISTICS—THE BRIDGE CHINA MUST CROSS

THE ONE REFORM that Hu Jintao and Wen Jiabao have assiduously steered clear of so far is democratization. There has been a liberal strain of thought within the Communist Party since 1986, when the first serious expressions of discontent occurred within the student community, that the party's monopoly on all forms of power—legislative, executive, and judicial—was not compatible with a market economy that had legalized the possession of private property. Once it was permissible to be rich, greed became an ineradicable ingredient of decision-making. Greed could be kept in check only by making the rulers accountable to the ruled. In October 1988, the Communist Party's theoretical journal *Seeking Truth* observed that official racketeering was an "ulcer" feeding upon the "sick system" of cadre corruption: "With the deepening of reform we have been trying to separate the party from the government, the functions of the government from those of the enterprise, and administrative power from managerial power."[310] But the totalitarian nature of the party made this virtually impossible. The party has made strenuous efforts to make its cadres accountable for their use of state power. But the lines of accountability run only upward to the next higher level of command. This explains the party's strenuous efforts to check corruption through severe punishment, including death. But by 2004 it was abundantly clear that even the prosecution of up to two hundred thousand party cadres a year was not applying enough of a brake to corruption and the abuse of state power for personal gain.

Both Hu and Wen were familiar with the arguments in favor of a greater degree of democracy in the relationship between state and society. Zhao Ziyang, who lost his premiership over his opposition to the use of force against the students in Tiananmen in 1989, reflected, fifteen years later, that "[t]he problem is . . . under a market economy, after property becomes legal . . . those with power will certainly use their control of the resources to turn society's wealth into their private wealth. These people become a huge entrenched interest . . . what China has is the worst form of Capitalism."[311] Zhao's insistence upon entering into a dialogue with the students at Tiananmen, and his agonized entreaties to the leadership not to use force, stemmed from this understanding of the threat that the rapid corruption of the party posed to its right to rule.

In a celebrated essay written in 1997 but never published in mainland China (it was eventually published in 2001 abroad, and circulated widely on the Internet), Wang Hui, one among the last batch of student demonstrators to leave Tiananmen on June 4, stressed the same issue:

> In China, as in other Third World countries, those who control domestic capital are in fact the same as those who control political power . . . The reforms the greater part of the populace hoped for and their ideals of democracy and the rule of law were for the purpose of guaranteeing social justice and the democratization of *economic* life through the restructuring of politics and the legal system (emphasis added). . . . [The 1989 social movement] was a

farewell to an old era and at the same time a protest against the inherent social contradictions of the new; it was [for students and intellectuals] an appeal for democracy and freedom even as it was [for the workers and salary earners] a demand for social equality and justice.[312]

Tiananmen was therefore an agitation for democracy not as an end in itself, but as a means of enforcing accountability upon an absolutist regime.[313]

By democracy, his translator Theodore Huters hastens to explain in his introduction, Wang Hui did not mean a template imported from abroad and imposed on the Chinese political system.[314] What the students had advocated, and what Zhao Ziyang, to his eternal credit, saw the need for, was to make the party accountable to the people. Zhao, who had had more interactions with the students and workers before Tiananmen than any other party leader, realized that accountability to the party had to be supplemented, and not necessarily replaced, by accountability to the people. This could be enforced by an institution *of* the state, but it had to be one that lay *outside* the party. For that, the party first had to cease to *be* the state.

In the light of China's experience, it is possible to lay out a minimum set of reforms that Beijing needs to enact to make the party, and the various levels of local government, accountable to the people. It needs to create an independent judiciary, staffed by trained lawyers, who are not members of the Communist Party, and whose independence and personal security is guaranteed by the constitution. It needs to hold elections to choose members of the local administration, not only at the village level as happens now, but at the township and county levels as well. These elections need to be genuinely open to non-party members, and not be a fig leaf for the party's continued monopoly of power. Beijing needs to supervise non-party members through a separate election commission set up directly by it. It needs to reinforce the voters' right of recall (which at present exists only at the village level, and there too largely in the breach), and extend it to the township and county levels. Finally, to reduce if not altogether stop the expropriation of land, it can give peasants the right to own, and not simply to cultivate, their land.

These reforms would not involve any significant dilution of the control of the Communist Party over the state. But they do require Beijing to draw a distinction between the central and local levels of the party, and to create an institutional framework within which the former are given the authority to hold the latter accountable for the correct execution of policy. However, these are precisely the reforms that Hu Jintao has steered the party away from. Instead, he has focused his energies on reforming the party and making it more fit to govern the country. To do that, he has singled out honest party chiefs who have shown themselves willing to "buck the system" and get things done.[315] He has replaced older cadres in high positions with younger incumbents drawn largely from the Chinese Communist Youth League.[316] And in January 2005, he launched a third party-rectification campaign in which, between June 2006 and June 2007, 170,000 senior party officials, at the levels of province, municipality, county, and town, were slated to be replaced.[317]

But apart from a single statement by Wen Jiabao, on the eve of Hu Jintao's visit to Britain in 2005, that the government intended to extend the election of committee members from the villages to the townships, there has been no mention of filling administrative posts at local levels, through elections.[318] As for creating a separate judiciary, in February 2007 the politburo emphatically rejected a proposal to establish a separate judiciary even though the proposed reform was nowhere near as far-reaching as has been suggested above. Instead, Luo Gan, a member of the politburo's standing committee, and China's top law and order official, said in a detailed speech on February 2, "Enemy forces are seeking to use China's legal system to Westernize and divide the country, and the Communist Party must fend them off by maintaining its dominance over lawyers, judges and prosecutors." The Communist Party's determination to retain its absolute monopoly of judicial power could not have been more explicitly stated.[319]

Instead, every measure that Hu and Wen have announced or enacted has been aimed at reinforcing the hold of the party on the state. All that has changed is their perception of how to do so. Whereas Deng Xiaoping (after 1992) and Jiang Zemin had relied upon the fruits of economic growth to overwhelm dissent, Hu realized that if the party was to retain the "mandate of heaven," the state had to actively promote not only rapid economic growth but also social equity and justice. But he realized that even under the best of circumstances, it would take some time for these reforms to change popular perceptions of the state and the party. In the meantime, where necessary, dissent would need to be suppressed.

In 2005, the central leadership therefore asked its provincial party and security officials to "produce" major decreases in the protests over the next two years. By degrees, through the accumulation of directives, a security strategy designed to suppress expressions of discontent took shape:

• Beijing began to put sustained pressure on local officials to bottle up protests and deal with them locally. It published nationwide rankings of the provinces with the most petitioners who brought their cases to Beijing, and enacted "petitioner responsibility systems" that punished officials if petitioners from their localities came to the capital, or if local conflicts turned into major protests. In theory, the adverse publicity was supposed to make delinquent provinces improve their local governments. But in practice it, and the penalties imposed upon failure to reduce the number of petitioners coming to Beijing, has only made the provincial authorities more determined to suppress the exercise of "rightful resistance." The politicization of data on social unrest after 2005 has made it difficult to assess the impact of these measures, but it is almost certain that physical intimidation, backed by penal levies and forced seizure of grain livestock and household goods, has increased.

- The media were admonished not to report protests without prior permission. This has in effect given the local authorities a carte blanche to prevent media persons from visiting protest sites, and to imprison journalists if they feel it necessary.
- Police forces were enjoined to use minimal violence, so as to avoid enraging protesters into retaliation. They were urged to try softer ways of managing, containing, and controlling crowds.
- The regime has come down heavily on activists and professional organizers of protest. Beijing has attacked itinerant petition organizers actively by detaining them, and passively by declining to punish local governments who hire thugs to beat or kill them.[320]

These directives have had an entirely predictable effect. As the *South China Morning Post* reported in April 2007,

> Officials in the prosperous mainland provinces of Jiangsu and Zhejiang are crowing about their success in preventing protests and riots. They claim to have substantially reduced the number that occurred last year and spoke with pride of their achievements at a national public security meeting held in Xian yesterday.
>
> There is nothing sophisticated about their method of creating the social harmony that President Hu Jintao and Premier Wen Jiabao are so eager for. All they needed was billions of yuan to toughen security.

This was used to provide surveillance equipment in as many places as possible and tens of thousands of extra police and guards. In effect, their solution to unrest is to monitor people more closely and whenever trouble breaks out, crush it with force. While in the eyes of the provincial officials this may be fulfilling the wishes of Mr. Hu and Mr. Wen, it is far from creating harmony. *Rather, it is preventing people with legitimate grievances from voicing their concerns.* (emphasis added)

Why have Chinese leaders, from Deng Xiaoping to Hu Jintao, been so determined to keep every shred of power within the Communist Party? Deng Xiaoping could be excused for having abandoned his protégé, Zhao Zhiyang, in 1989. He and his colleagues had been watching the unraveling of Poland and the growing disorder in the Soviet Union under the impact of glasnost and perestroika with horror, and were determined not to let the same thing happen in China. But after themselves calling attention to the dangerous increase in public discontent, why are Hu Jintao and Wen Jiabao showing the same adamant determination not to allow any dilution of the Communist Party's absolute hold on power?

A view widely held by pundits is that the threat is not as great as reports in the foreign media have made it out to be. According to Andrew G. Walder of Stanford University, it is virtually nonexistent. Although the number of incidents has undoubtedly risen during the last decade, they have, with very few exceptions, involved what he calls "politically nonstrategic"—i.e., marginal—sections of the population: laid-off and near-pension-age workers; migrant workers; and peasants. According to him, discontent poses no threat to a regime if it does not affect politically strategic sections of the population. In China, these are the forty-five million CPC cadres who hold no government office, and the multitudes of gainers from China's rapid development.[321]

Walder also points out that the grievances people are giving vent to are local ones, such as extortionate fees and taxes levied by local governments, forced appropriation of land by local authorities, and the denial of promised and sometimes mandated social benefits. He joins a long list of historians and political analysts in pointing out that the tradition of local protests—rightful resistance—is almost as old as that of empire in China, and that both can be traced back to the teachings of Confucius and his disciple Mencius. Chinese regimes have therefore seldom felt threatened by local eruptions of discontent, and have usually left it to the local authorities to provide redress.[322]

Walder's thesis, that the losers from China's market-led development are incapable of posing a risk to political stability, is based upon the somewhat tautological assumption that people seldom kill the goose that lays their golden eggs. He therefore assumes that the gainers from China's growth will tolerate the lapses of the party cadres and at least remain politically passive. So long as the gainers vastly outnumber the losers, and occupy strategically more important positions in society by virtue of superior organization, discontent at the margins is unable to develop into a coherent threat.

If Walder is right, then Hu Jintao's campaign to build a "harmonious society" is little more than a power play by a new leader, who is not from the prosperous coastal region of China, to reinforce his control of the party by playing up discontent and enacting populist measures to assuage it. But this belief has little empirical foundation.

As Walder himself concedes, in a society that is subject to sharp economic expansion and contraction, the dividing line between the gainers and losers can shift with disconcerting suddenness. Those who have experienced sudden, adverse, shifts in their status and prospects constitute the most volatile segment of the population. What is more, they are often already concentrated in urban areas or distressed industrial regions, and therefore far easier to mobilize than scattered and marginalized groups of losers. The French Revolution, for instance, was essentially an urban affair fanned by a sudden bout of inflation and led by a discontented new middle-class intelligentsia. The 80 percent of France that lived in abjectly poor villages with populations of less than two thousand remained uninvolved.

Chinese workers and peasants, too, have suffered several bouts of sudden impoverishment and loss of status in the past three decades. In the mid- and late eighties inflation caused a sharp decline in real income that impoverished students, workers, and civil servants, while a change in relative prices of outputs and inputs began to erode the newfound prosperity of the peasantry. In the late nineties the sharp loss of income and status by state workers, caused by the restructuring of state-owned industry, was compounded by recession, which played havoc with the lives of millions of migrant workers. To these triggers of unrest one can add extortionate taxation and fee extraction, the arbitrary takeover of peasants' land, and a progressive attrition of the right to demand redress that has been chronicled by Chen Guidi and Wu Chuntao, He Qinlian, and others.

The Chinese leadership's adamant refusal to consider any dilution of the Communist Party's hold on power is only partly rooted in the determination to hold on to power at any cost that characterizes authoritarian regimes in other parts of the world. Nor is it any longer rooted in the fear, which haunted the leadership in the late eighties and early nineties, of sharing the Soviet Union's fate. While both these motives have no doubt played their part, they have been immensely reinforced, but also to some extent humanized, by the profound hold of Confucian beliefs on the Chinese mind. "For more than two thousand years," wrote historian John King Fairbank, "the Confucian ideology was made the chief subject of study by the world's largest State. . . . Nowhere else have the sanctions of government power been based for so many centuries upon a single consistent pattern of ideas, attributed to a single sage."[323] Subsequent research has shown that the principles governing the relationship between the state and its subjects attributed to Confucius actually evolved over a period of time in a succession of commentaries, the most important of which was by one of his disciples, Mencius. It was Mencius who gave explicit shape to the idea, which had been implicit in the Confucian model of the state as a family, that while the subject owes absolute obedience to the ruler, the ruler must strive to make himself worthy of that obedience by being just, and guided by moral principles. This balancing of rights with obligations gave birth to the imperial Confucianism of the Han dynasty, a fully articulated philosophy of state-society relations that Fairbank called "government by moral prestige." This fundamental belief has so profoundly shaped Chinese thought that the People's Republic has incorporated it into its practices even while it has denigrated and rejected it in theory.

Embedded in Confucianism is the Chinese concept of law. This begins with the ancient idea, also found in the Hindu-Buddhist concept of dharma, that human actions have to harmonize with the order of nature. Since subservience to the natural order binds both the ruler and the ruled, the former is expected to regulate public behavior by setting a personal example of virtuous and moral conduct. From this spring three corollaries:

- Transgressions, to be punishable, have to be individual.
- If a transgression becomes general, i.e., systemic, it requires introspection by the ruler, debate, and accommodation so that all can return to the path of virtue.
- So long as the ruler is virtuous, an elaborate network of laws is not necessary. People will be guided by his example and by the norms of good citizenship, without need for regulation.

What if the ruler strays from the path of virtue and the people rebel? According to Mencius, the "mandate of heaven" will pass instantly to the successful rebel leader. Confucianism did not only provide a moral sanction for the exercise of absolute power by the ruler; it also created a parallel sanction for rebellion by the ruled, if the ruler violated the canons of morality in governance.[324]

"No country boasts a more enduring or more colorful history of rebellion and revolution than China," writes Elizabeth Perry. "The Chinese tradition of popular upheaval stretches back well beyond this century; indeed, records allow us to trace it as far back as 209 BCE when the Chen She Rebellion helped to topple the mighty Qin empire and give rise to the famous Han dynasty. Over the ensuing millennia, popular protest has formed a constant and consequential theme in Chinese political history."[325]

Perry's observations echo those of Chen Guidi and Wu Chuntao:

> Looking back at [China's] long history, we cannot find a single peasant uprising that was not related to the burden on peasants. From the Chen Sheng and Wu Guang uprising [of the Qin dynasty] to all other peasant uprisings that followed; from the Shang Yang Reform [of the Qin state] to all other reforms that came later, there was not one that was not related to peasants. Emperor Taizong's statement that "Water can carry boats, but it can also overwhelm boats" probably originates from Xun Zi. *Guan Zi* of the pre-Qin period is perhaps the earliest book in Chinese history that proposed alleviating the burden on peasants and correctly handling the relationship between state and peasant interests. Back then, it specified in many chapters, such as *"Quan xiu," "Ban fa,"* and *"Zhou he,"* that "taking from people with restraint and knowing when to stop adding burdens to them, even a small state can maintain stability; taking from people without restraint and not knowing when to stop adding burdens to them,

even a large state can be endangered. . . . When people do not have enough to make a living, orders will be disregarded; when people lead a miserable life, orders will be disobeyed."

The authors attribute the fall of the Kuomintang government to its relapse into age-old habits of predatory extortion:

> In the Republic of China in the 1930s, the Nationalist Party once proposed adopting a traditional policy of light taxation and invalidating exorbitant levies and taxes, but such a proposal had little effect because of continually increasing military expenses, domestic and foreign debt, a huge fiscal deficit, and an extremely corrupt political system. Close to the Liberation (the founding of the PRC in 1949), the enlightened local gentry who were capable of sustaining the moral tradition of an agricultural society gradually receded from the political stage in rural areas because they were unable to execute the government's unrestrained levying of taxes and fees from rural people, including themselves. Local tyrants, evil gentry, ruffians, and hooligans replaced them. They carried out government orders without any reservations, while at the same time enriching themselves. Therefore, self-administration in local rural communities collapsed under the rule of an evil gentry. The Republic's government dug its own grave while destroying the fundamental system that safeguarded the stability of China's agricultural society.[326]

Although the Communists tried to discredit Confucianism, all they really succeeded in doing was integrating its truths and precepts with their own. Chief of these were a fierce egalitarianism and a refusal to recognize the legitimacy of private ownership. In all other respects, they did very little to change the basic structure of Chinese society.

Thus not only did the People's Republic continue the *hukou* system, which separated the lowly peasant from the urban "elite" in Imperial China, they reinforced it by introducing a nation-wide food rationing system based upon one's registered place of residence. Nor could the central government resist the temptation to continue the extraction of surpluses from the peasantry. It did so by repeatedly setting prices that would turn the terms of trade between agriculture and industry against the former, by preempting up to 94 percent of the savings held in the banks to finance industrial development,[327] which by definition took place in urban areas, and by turning a blind eye for long periods to the unlawful extraction of surpluses from the peasants by the township governments.

The place of the mandarins was taken over seamlessly by the Communist Party cadres. In the decades before the Cultural Revolution, the party was highly selective in the recruitment of its cadres. Only those who had spent time in Communist youth organizations and passed an examination were inducted into the party. The new mandarins were the cadres of the central party and state organization in Beijing. They made the laws, and constituted the numerous inspection teams that Beijing regularly sent out to monitor their implementation and inquire into local grievances.

The place of the rural gentry in traditional China was taken by the various tiers of the local administration, particularly those at the township and village levels. These were party members too, especially after the Cultural Revolution, when membership of the party was greatly enlarged and conditions for entry made less severe. But they did not enjoy the almost imperial status of the central party cadres.

But by far the most striking example of continuity was the Communist Party's awareness of the umbilical connection between mass protest and political legitimacy. This remained intact through all the vicissitudes and changes of the twentieth century. To quote Perry once more:

> Sun Yatsen's "Three Principles of the People" helped inspire the 1911 Revolution that toppled two thousand years of imperial rule, while Mao Zedong's doctrine of "People's War" fueled the Communist victory in 1949—just as his subsequent call for "Continuing the Revolution" provided justification of a Cultural Revolution in the mid-1960s. Indeed, one of the principal differences between Chinese and Soviet communism lies in the former's emphasis on mass criticism and mass campaigns. Like Mencius's Mandate of Heaven, Mao's Mass Line insisted on the reciprocal linkage between leader and led in staking a claim to higher political morality. Whereas Stalin looked to the secret police to enforce top-down order, Mao repeatedly called upon the Chinese masses to engage in class struggle from below. This certainly did not mean that the People's Republic under Mao eschewed the use of state surveillance—quite the contrary—but it was unusual among communist countries in also requiring ordinary citizens to participate actively in government-sponsored campaigns.[328]

It is in the state's day-to-day dealings with its own people and with its own minions, the party cadres, that the enduring influence of Confucian philosophy is most evident. The first are characterized, as Perry notes, with what is for an authoritarian regime a remarkable degree of tolerance and latitude. The second, by a unique and unprecedented severity.

The most frequently remarked upon example is the central government's toleration of public dissent. As Perry notes, dissent is not simply tolerated; it is often quietly encouraged by senior members to bring problems to the notice of the leaders, in the hope that it will act as a springboard for changes of policy.[329] This encouragement takes innumerable forms. Central to all of this is a recognition of the people's right to rightful resistance. This is about as far from the spontaneous expression of public anger that one comes across in young democracies like India, where taking to the streets is the first thing that the discontented do, often even before they have fully articulated their grievance or the redress they seek. In China, confrontation with the state authorities is the last stage in the development of protest. It occurs only after all other methods of rightful resistance have been exhausted. Peasants, laid-off and migrant workers, and other disadvantaged groups who become the victims of bureaucratic indifference or predatory cadres have learned to use the existing laws (such as the 1994 ceiling on local taxes of 5 percent of the peasants' revenue) and the central government's directives as weapons of protest against the arbitrary actions of local governments. A class of social activists has also developed, composed mainly of educated villagers and workers, older party members, and professors, who help the protesters to frame their protest. When the protesters fail to get redress at the local level, they exercise their right, also guaranteed by the Chinese state, to appeal to higher authority.

The attitude of the central government toward such protests is benign, even though it is able to act upon only a fraction of the petitions it receives. But the attitude of the local administration is, with rare exceptions, the exact opposite. Confrontation usually develops only after they ignore or summarily reject these forms of protest. But local cadres use force to contain protest when persuasion and intimidation fail, not so much to snuff out the protest as to prevent the discontented from taking it higher up the party chain. For if they succeed, it is more than likely that Beijing will make the protest an "excuse for introspection," launch an inquiry, discipline the cadres, and change policies to the detriment of their power or capacity to make money. This is precisely what happened in the case of Sun Zhigang, the migrant worker who was beaten to death by the police.

Another striking contrast between the CPC, especially in the post-Mao era, and its European counterparts is its ambivalence toward criticism from writers, researchers, professors, and students. In the Soviet Union, dissident intellectuals were treated as threats to the state and silenced in a variety of ways, through being imprisoned, exiled, deprived of recognition, or denied the right to publish. Research on sensitive subjects was taboo. In China, the relationship between the state and the intelligentsia has been far more complicated. Three broad trends can be discerned. First, the Chinese leaders permit levels of inquiry and disclosure by academics that would have been unthinkable in the Soviet Union or Eastern Europe. The resulting criticism is taken as an important part of a process of constant introspection and reappraisal that owes next to nothing to Communist practice and a very great deal to the Confucian state. For instance, He Qinlian's pathbreaking book was given a glowing preface by a senior party leader, to facilitate its publication.[330] Chen Guidi and Wu Chuntao's book was published in mainland China in 2003, when it came in handy to reinforce Hu Jintao's advocacy of social justice. It was only when the book became a runaway best-seller and began to attract foreign attention that it was suddenly banned.

Second, reports issued by inquiry committees set up by the Communist Party or the State Council (and subsequently leaked to the media) are remarkably frank in their description of corruption, the abuse of power, and other causes of discontent. The *Blue Book* series on the condition of Chinese society, issued by the Chinese Academy of Social Sciences and cited earlier, are examples of state-sponsored critical appraisal. As was pointed out in the previous chapter, and as several of the remarks made by Hu and Wen show, many appraisals carried out within the party are even more critical. In fact, when the leaders decide to release some of the findings of these inquiries, it is invariably in a sanitized form compared to the original.[331]

Third: Closely related to the state's attitude toward its intellectuals is its attitude toward its students. While Tiananmen is remembered abroad as a "massacre," the fact, as Richard Baum has taken great pains to point out, is that relatively few people were killed and almost no students were harmed. In Tiananmen Square, in particular, there was no actual violence. The students dispersed voluntarily. Only one was killed on the square's outskirts when he was run over by a tank. Most of the actual killing took place in the streets and suburbs of the city as the PLA battled to prevent workers and urban salaried persons, including large numbers of party members, from joining the demonstration. In the soul-searching that followed, party leaders, almost without exception, felt that the students had been "misled." The antidote to future student unrest, the party decided, was not to make an example of the ringleaders by shooting or severely punishing them, as happened in Hungary after the crushing of the 1956 uprising, but to enroll students into the party in much larger numbers![332]

In sharp contrast, the Chinese state's conduct toward its own party cadres reflects none of the toleration it has shown to dissidents. Year after year, it has prosecuted up to two hundred thousand of them for a wide range of crimes.[333] The punishment it has meted out has been proportionate not only to the seriousness of the crime but also to the seniority of the delinquent official. China has the distinction of being by far the most frequent user of the death penalty. Human rights groups estimate that anywhere from five thousand to twelve thousand persons are put to death every year.[334]

But a distinctive feature of the use of capital punishment has been its extension from serious and violent crimes, like treason, murder, rape, and drug trafficking, to cover an ever-widening spectrum of economic crimes. The courts have regularly handed out scores of death sentences, and while, under a law passed in 1983, some condemned persons have been reprieved for cooperating with the government in rooting out the criminal networks to which they had belonged, a large number of senior cadres have paid the ultimate penalty. These include governors of provinces, mayors of cities, and cabinet ministers, or people of equivalent rank. How seriously the government takes the punishing of corrupt officials may be gauged from the fact that in just four months, between June and September 2006, the prosecutor's office of the central government framed charges of corruption and other economic crimes against four party secretaries of various provinces; two deputy mayors, including that of Beijing; and their immediate subordinates. The highest-ranking of these was Chen Liangyu, who, in addition to being the party secretary of Shanghai, was also a member of the CPC's politburo and the highest-ranking official to be dismissed and arrested. At the end of September one of these, Lei Yuanli, deputy mayor of Chenzhou, had already been sentenced to death, albeit with a two-year reprieve.[335]

In 2007 the government sentenced, and this time did not reprieve, another very senior official of the party secretary level. This was Zheng Xiaoyu, the head of China's State Food and Drug Administration. Zheng, who had been pronounced guilty of accepting bribes to certify substandard drugs, was executed on July 10, 2007.

THE PROFOUND IMPRINT of Confucian philosophy on the day-to-day working of the Communist Party is impossible to ignore. Whether the transgression in question is murder, smuggling, drug trafficking, the abuse of official power for personal enrichment, or acceptance of bribes, these are individual transgressions, and so should be, and therefore are, punished severely. On the other hand, social protest, by groups of people, comes under the category of general, or systemic, transgression. The state needs to examine whether their causes are local, or are symptoms of a deeper, systemic malaise. The state is therefore ambivalent toward protests by groups because, while it is keen not to let them spiral out of control, it needs to learn more about their causes in order to determine whether "reflection" and "rectification" has become necessary.

Although the People's Republic is as authoritarian a state as any that Europe has given birth to, the relationship between it and society is as different as it can be within the authoritarian framework. European tyrants have, with very few exceptions, laid the blame for social unrest upon the ruled. The Chinese state—and the PRC is no exception—has at least entertained the suspicion that the blame might rest with the ruler. This is because European authoritarianism traces its antecedents back to the Divine Right of Kings. In China it traces its ancestry to Imperial Confucianism, at whose center lies the belief that the perfectly just and virtuous ruler does not need to resort to coercion to command obedience. In practical terms, this translates into a profound reluctance to use force against the people. Baum's account of the buildup to, and the aftermath of, the Tiananmen crisis highlights not the regime's brutality but the lengths to which it was prepared to go to avoid violence.

Tiananmen 1989–the first crisis of legitimacy

The students' movement that ended in the alleged massacre in Tiananmen Square started on April 16, 1989, one day after veteran leader Hu Yaobang's death. But its origins lay in a rash of student protests that had broken out in December 1986, when several hundred students gathered at the University of Science and Technology of China (USTC) in Hefei, to protest against their exclusion from the selection of the head of the campus students' union and of students' representatives to the Provincial People's Congress. The students were incensed because this happened just days after a 1979 electoral law had been amended to make it more democratic. The university authorities had simply ignored the law.

These demonstrations had spread rapidly to Jiao Tong and Tongji universities in Shanghai and then to Peking University in Beijing. Although the immediate demand of the students was political, an important underlying cause of their anger was the rapid increase in inflation, which was, among other things, eroding the value of their stipends, and the rise of corruption in the state and party. Fang Li Zhi, an astrophysicist from USTC, had made a series of speeches at these and other campuses a year earlier, during which he had made impassioned attacks on the corruption in the party.[336]

In South Korea, till the end of the eighties, student demonstrations were routinely put down by riot police, often with a substantial loss of life. In India, during the first serious confrontation between students and the state in 1966, the police opened fire upon the demonstrators on several occasions, and caused a number of deaths. The confrontation took place after a drought in 1965, followed by a war with Pakistan, had pushed prices up by 20 percent in a single year, and a decade of slow economic growth had worsened the prospects of finding a job, adding to the instability of the student community.

But in China in 1986, the state's response to the appearance of wall posters asking for democracy in Jiao Tong University was to send Jiang Zemin, then the mayor of Shanghai, to the university on December 10 to reason with the students and plead for stability and unity. When he was heckled and asked a student his name, the meeting grew rowdy and the protest spread to Fudan and other universities and colleges in the city. But neither there, nor at any other place where the disturbances occurred, did a single student lose his life. Baum concludes that "despite scattered arrests and sporadic use of intimidation tactics by public security forces, local authorities generally refrained from using excessive force to quell student protests."[337]

Two years later, when the student demonstrations that culminated at Tiananmen began, continuing inflation and corruption had immensely increased the students' alienation from the state and the party. The state had widened income differentials in urban society so rapidly that it had left all but the beneficiaries stunned.

On April 16, several hundred students from various Beijing universities marched to Tiananmen Square to lay wreaths at the foot of the Monument to the People's Heroes. Over the next days the mourners swelled to tens of thousands. As many as ten thousand tried to gain entry into Zhongnanhai, the exclusive compound adjoining the Forbidden City that housed the People's Republic's leaders. This led to the first clash between them and soldiers guarding the compound. Several students were injured in hand-to-hand fighting, but none was killed. The police used no firearms.

Between April 18 and 20, the first autonomous nonofficial student body (gaozilian) was set up at Peking University. Thus far, nearly everyone involved had been a student, but on the night of April 21, they were joined by crowds of people who had come to mourn Hu Yaobang. On the next day, a Saturday, despite official warnings to clear the square, one hundred thousand people gathered quietly for the funeral ceremony. Following a misunderstanding as to whether or not the government had indeed agreed to hold a dialogue with the students after the funeral ceremony, students angrily surged toward the Great Hall of the People, but were pushed back by the now greatly reinforced police. A few students were hit with batons. Once again, in sharp contrast to what would have happened almost anywhere else in the world when police faced a hundred thousand demonstrators, no firearms were in evidence, let alone used. But the mere fact that force had been used against them came as a shock to the students. Many broke down in tears.

Tiananmen was to remain "occupied" for the next six weeks. As the government's subsequent behavior was to show, it would have infinitely preferred to wear out the students' patience till they all melted away, had it not been for the way in which the protest began to spread to other sections of the population. Between April 22 and 25 the students' movement spread, as they organized themselves into autonomous federations in Shanghai, Tianjin, Nanjing, Wuhan, and elsewhere. On April 20, a newly formed Beijing Workers' Autonomous Federation *(gongzilian)* issued a manifesto, blaming "dictatorial bureaucrats" for social ills ranging from soaring inflation and a sharp drop in living standards to "expropriating the minimal income of the people for their own use." The manifesto exhorted the citizens of Beijing, and specifically the police and firefighters, to "stand on the side of the people and justice" and not become "tools of the people's enemies."[338] China's leaders suddenly found themselves face to face with their worst nightmare.

At an urgent meeting held on April 22, the politburo decided that the best course was to stand firm. Its members were heavily influenced by the events in Poland, where initial concessions had only strengthened the uprising till it swept away the Communist state. This was communicated to the people in a *People's Daily* editorial on April 26. The editorial accused the students of a planned conspiracy incited by "a small number of people with ulterior motives" whose intention was to "sow dissension among the people, plunge the entire country into chaos, and sabotage the political situation of stability and unity." The attack on the students' patriotism had the opposite of the expected result. The Beijing Students' Autonomous Federation *(gaozilian)* immediately called for "patriotic marches" on Tiananmen to support "socialist order," in opposition to "bureaucracy, corruption and special privilege." The very next day the number of students who marched to Tiananmen doubled.[339]

Baum's research shows that Deng Xiaoping contemplated the use of the military as a last resort at the April 22 meeting of the politburo.[340] But from then till the showdown on June 4, the government followed a two-track strategy of trying to persuade the students to drop their agitation, while at the same time preparing the military to move into Beijing if the need arose. Its most important conciliatory effort was a meeting of Li Peng and several other leaders with leaders of the students' hunger strike on May 18. The meeting went badly, with Li Peng urging them to withdraw the hunger strike and the fasting students adamant that their demand to be considered a patriotic and democratic movement, and not "troublemakers," as they were dubbed in the April 26 editorial, be accepted first. The very next night the government promulgated martial law in Beijing.

Like the April 26 editorial, the declaration of martial law had the opposite of the desired effect. Workers, who had by and large stayed clear of the students' movement before the hunger strike, now began to join *gongzilian* in very large numbers. Its membership rose from around two thousand, where it had stagnated for a month, to ten thousand in days after the hunger strike and the declaration of martial law. Large numbers of party cadres and residents of Beijing began to join the movement, as well. According to an assessment made by the party organization after the crackdown, more than ten thousand party members from the central party organization and government departments in Beijing had taken part in the May demonstrations. Throughout the nation, approximately eight hundred thousand party members, out of a membership of forty-five million, had joined the movement. Another ninety thousand had requested permission to leave the party.[341]

On the night of May 29, students from Beijing's Central Arts

Academy assembled a thirty-five-foot-high statue of a woman carrying a torch in both hands, directly in front of Mao Zedong's portrait, which is suspended from the top of the Gate of Heavenly Peace. The next day, three hundred thousand residents of Beijing came to the square to see the "Goddess of Democracy." This created the pretext for the military crackdown that was probably planned shortly after the declaration of martial law. Even then, the government was almost shamefaced about its decision to use force. The troops entered Beijing unarmed. The arms were sent in separate, unmarked buses and trucks. And although it was the students who had spearheaded the uprising, the government went out of its way to treat them gently. This was not accidental. Baum observes that "historically students formed an elite substratum within the Chinese political order; even in contemporary times they have been shielded from severe state reprisals in all but the most extreme circumstances."[342]

It did not extend any such courtesy, however, to the workers and the *shimin* (citizens). Most of the killing took place on a three-kilometer stretch of road leading to Tiananmen from the west. On this road, which was thereafter called the Blood Road, the soldiers repeatedly opened fire upon workers and civilians who had joined the protest. As one worker in Beijing put it, "You know, with students it is nothing; they arrest you for a couple of days and let you go. But when we workers get arrested, they shoot us . . . the government is ruthless towards us workers."[343]

Yet, given the magnitude of the protest/confrontation and its prolonged duration, the number of deaths was remarkably small. The best available estimate of civilian deaths ranges from 1,000 to 2,600. Of these, only thirty-five were students and only one of these was actually killed in Tiananmen Square, which was evacuated peacefully by the last student holdouts some time after 5:00 a.m.[344] Nearly all of these casualties occurred on the single night of June 3–4. But the extent to which the military and police tried to control the students and workers without the use of arms is revealed by the fact that that there were several dozen soldiers and public security personnel killed, and six thousand injured. This could not have happened if they had not tried to control the crowds using nonlethal weapons at close quarters.[345]

The regime's treatment of the dissidents also reflects its enormous reluctance to impose extreme penalties. As the news of the Tiananmen crackdown spread, protests and demonstrations occurred in several other cities. To bring this under control, a by now seriously disturbed government hastily put at least thirty-five persons to death in five cities. The purpose was blatantly deterrent, for most of the condemned were workers or unemployed youth and migrants without an urban *hukou,* who had, allegedly, been caught committing various acts of violence during the uprising in early June. Contrary to persistent rumors, not one of those executed was a student.[346]

The Tiananmen upheaval lasted for six weeks. It began in Beijing but spread to five cities. Half a dozen others saw antigovernment outbursts of protest. After the crackdown there were antigovernment demonstrations in 123 cities. Beginning with students, they were joined by tens of thousands of workers, then by the salaried classes, and finally by one in fifty members of the Communist Party. Faced with a threat to its very existence, no other regime would have hesitated to pull out all the stops in order to restore its authority. But the Chinese government proved an exception in this respect too. It was, from the start, defensive about its use of violence. It put the blame for its onset on the students and the *shimin,* claiming that it was they who had attacked the soldiers as they made their way into Beijing. The political commissar of the Twenty-seventh Division, which led the way into the square, was put on television to tell the people that neither it nor any other unit had shot down students on the square. He described in detail the assaults on the military that had occurred on the road as the populace tried to block the soldiers' way. The fact that in addition to the six soldiers killed and six thousand injured, sixty-five army trucks and forty-seven armored personnel carriers had been totally destroyed, and 485 other vehicles damaged,[347] suggests that the soldiers did not fire until they felt very gravely threatened.

The CPC's profound reluctance to use force is in stark contrast to the way in which Communist regimes in Eastern Europe dealt with their students and dissidents. A comparison with the Hungarian uprising of 1956 is instructive. The Hungarian political police, the AVH, felt absolutely no qualms about opening fire from inside buildings on unarmed student demonstrators. Peter Fryer, then the foreign correspondent of the British Communist newspaper *Daily Worker*, described the first two attacks:

> It began with a students' demonstration, partly to show the students' sympathy for the people of Poland, who that weekend, through Gomulka and the Central Committee of the Polish United Workers' Party, had resolutely rebuffed an attempt by an unprecedented delegation of Soviet leaders to get tough with them. . . .
>
> First Gero had gone on the wireless to make an address which, "poured oil on the flames." He had called the demonstrators (now joined by workers from the factories, to which the students had sent delegations) counter-revolutionaries—"hostile elements" trying to disturb "the present political order in Hungary" . . .
>
> Secondly, the crowds which had gathered outside the radio station to ask that students' demands be broadcast were fired on by AVH men, 300 of whom were in the building. This was, without question, the spark that turned peaceful demonstrations into a revolution.

A similar incident took place in Magyarovar. A peaceful demonstration of five thousand, inspired by the events in Budapest, marched to the AVH headquarters and demanded they remove the red star, symbol of the Soviet occupation. The AVH replied with a hail of machine gun fire, killing eighty. The crowd went to the army barracks, demanded and received weapons, and stormed and took the AVH headquarters. Thousands of Hungarians were killed in the uprising that followed, and two hundred thousand fled to the West.

In China, the first batch of executions was not followed by a systematic purge. On the contrary, the government treated the dissidents throughout with kid gloves. This was especially true of students and intellectuals. Arrests began on June 6, but the authorities proceeded at a snail's pace, selecting only the most prominent of the dissidents till, on June 11, the Supreme People's Court instructed the Ministry of Public Security "not to be hamstrung by details." The pace of arrests then picked up, but in the end, the total did not exceed four thousand, and only 1,730 were sent to prison. In 1991, at the height of the Persian Gulf crisis, the government tried and convicted thirty-five imprisoned intellectuals and let go seventy-six. Those convicted received sentences ranging from two to thirteen years, but almost all were later released after showing "sincere repentance" for their actions. Only two, who insisted to the end that they had committed no crime, served out their full thirteen-year sentences.[348] The Confucian principle of reflection and self-analysis surfaced once again in the government's treatment of the party members who had revolted. Out of the eight hundred thousand, in the end only 13,254 were required to undergo party discipline, and fewer still, only 1,179, were actually punished.[349]

The government's almost immediate switch to the defensive allowed, if it did not actually encourage, the students and workers to continue expressing their anger. Not surprisingly, unrest continued to simmer throughout the fateful summer of 1989. But Beijing preferred to live with it rather than crack down again and again. On July 23, students in Beijing held renewed demonstrations. As they marched down the roads, they sang the songs of the revolution. But to these they added a touch of satire by coupling the songs with current advertising jingles about pesticides. No one had any doubt about who were the pests and who were the pest-killers. But the government took no action against the demonstrators. Instead, it decided to preempt the possibility of future outbreaks of the same kind. Three weeks later, it removed the reform-minded head of Peking University and replaced him with a hard-liner. It also sharply reduced the intake of students into the humanities, and sent the entire 1989 batch of students out to do a year's compulsory military service.

The party also went into an orgy of "reflection." The conflict within it was not an orthodox ideological one, centered upon plan versus market or state versus private ownership of productive assets. Accounts of the debates that raged make it clear that the fierce debate within the party revolved around the corruption that was destroying the party's right to rule. No one denied that the economic reforms were responsible for it, as well as for the rapid inflation that was impoverishing the workers, salaried classes, and intellectuals, and rapidly widening income differences in what had, till a decade earlier, been a highly egalitarian society. But opinion was sharply divided on who was to blame, and how best to prevent the rot from reaching any deeper.

The old guard of the party, which had reasserted itself when the government was of two minds about how to deal with the students, put all of the blame for the uprising upon the policies of bourgeois liberalism that had been pursued under the stewardship of Zhao Ziyang. It blamed Zhao Ziyang and the liberal reformers in the politburo for first having gone too far and too fast toward a market economy, and then wanting to go still further, toward some form of democratization, to solve the problems it had created. This was tantamount to an attempt to bring down the party itself. However, contrary to a commonly held interpretation abroad, this was not simply a last-ditch attempt by an irredentist Communist old guard to go back to the old days of absolute centralized power. The real targets of the conservatives' anger were the local governments, who were almost entirely responsible both for the uncontrolled investment that had fueled inflation and for the wholesale corruption that had precipitated the Tiananmen crisis. They pointed out, correctly, that this would not have been possible had administrative and financial powers not been devolved to the provincial and lower levels of government in 1983 and 1984, and they put the blame for it upon Hu Yaobang and Zhao Ziyang. While this dissimilar duo were the official scapegoats, few had any doubt that this was a barely veiled attack on Deng Xiaoping himself.

The way to repair the damage, as Li Peng strongly urged at the fifth plenum of the Thirteenth Central Committee in November 1989, was to strongly centralize investment decision-making by bringing all but a small part of it back under the central plan and *slowing down growth!* There could be no more unequivocal proof that the conservatives regarded the explosive growth—resulting from the local governments' scramble to corner the resources that had been the prerogative of the center alone in the pre-reform days—as the principal threat to China's stability.

It was left to Deng Xiaoping to find a middle way that would maintain the unity of the party and repair the damage that Tiananmen had done. In retrospect, it is possible to see that this was the pivotal moment when the future of China could have been rewritten. Deng had two clear alternatives to choose from, and the soul-searching during and after the crisis had etched these out more sharply than they had ever been presented before. Both the by now discredited liberals and the ascendant conservatives agreed on one thing: They wanted the causes of the corruption and allied sicknesses to be tackled at the root, and not papered over with half measures.

The liberals wanted the system of accountability within the party to be supplemented by accountability to the people, which meant moving in stages toward a Chinese version of democracy. The conservatives wanted to root out the causes too, but to them the root cause was the greed and indiscipline of the local administrations. Their economic powers had to be drastically curtailed; they had to be confined, once again, to the task of implementation and supervision alone. If this meant a slowing down of growth, then so be it.

Deng could have chosen the liberal option. As was pointed out above, he did not have to move far toward Western-style democracy, nor significantly weaken the party's monopoly of power, to make the provincial and local administrations accountable to the people. But Deng, ever the unifier, decided instead to define a middle road that the party could unite around once again. He stepped in decisively to stop the vilification of the students and the scapegoating of Zhao Ziyang. The students had to be educated, not punished, he said. Their fault was not that they did not know the four cardinal principles (Deng's formulation of a socialist market economy with continued one-party rule), but that they did not know them well enough. Zhao Ziyang had gone too far in propitiating the students, but his actions were not born out of bourgeois liberalism or counterrevolution. They were simply mistakes born of his anxiety to avert the use of force. Deng therefore asked Jiang Zemin not to "throw mud" at Zhao Ziyang anymore.[350]

Deng also explicitly rejected Li Peng's proposal to recentralize planning. But he conceded the core of the conservatives' fears that if corruption was not rooted out of the party then, coming on top of the inevitable inflation and widening of income and wealth gaps, it contained the potential to destroy the Communist Party's mandate to rule. But the solution lay not in simply taking all economic powers away from the local governments and returning to centralized planning, as Li Peng was urging the party to do, but in purging the state and party of corruption. With this, Deng inaugurated a fierce anticorruption drive in the party that led to more than three hundred thousand arrests in the next eighteen months.[351]

In 1989, with the reform process discredited and the old guard back in control of the politburo in Beijing, Deng can be excused for not having come out in defense of the liberal option that his own protégé, Zhao Ziyang, had been advocating. But the effect of his middle-roading was very different from what he had hoped for. With Beijing's hold on the state further weakened by its need to use force, the provincial governments read into his decision to oppose the recentralization of economic power an encouragement to continue appropriating the resources of the state in order to push ahead with locally conceived programs of development. That is why the huge rebound in investment and growth of the early nineties began not after Deng Xiaoping's southern tour in 1992, but a year earlier, in 1991.

From 1991 the Chinese Communist Party has sought to silence students by inducting them into the party in much larger numbers, and has relied upon the well-being spread by rapid growth to make the masses accept the moral blemishes that capitalism is putting upon the face of the Chinese state. To still the pangs of conscience and make these more acceptable, it has regularly punished tens of thousands of corrupt cadres every year, putting several hundred, at least, to a well-publicized death.

The rise of the neoconservative state

With the benefit of hindsight, it is difficult not to conclude that Tiananmen marked the end of the struggle to maintain a moral, i.e., Confucian, state.[352] At the fifth plenum of the Thirteenth

Central Committee in 1989, Deng had rejected the conservatives' proposal to deprive the local cadres of the opportunity to strike corrupt deals by stripping the local governments of their financial autonomy—but their ideas crept insidiously back into the party's policies under the guise of neoconservatism. Over the next decade and a half, the center reasserted its control over investment decision-making partly by taking back the economic power that it had ceded to the local governments in 1983–'84, and partly by preempting resources for a succession of very large projects in the central, western, and northeastern regions of the country.[353]

To consolidate its claim to legitimacy, the CPC followed a two-pronged strategy. The first was to continue Deng Xiaoping's 1978 policy of opening the doors of the Communist Party to all those who were prepared to accept its discipline and work for it. By 2007 the party had 73.4 million members, an increase of thirteen million over the numbers of a decade earlier.

The second prong was the party's never-ending bid to remake itself. The most important change was made by President Jiang Zemin when, under his policy of the Three Represents, he opened the doors of the party to private sector entrepreneurs. But he did so selectively. The vast majority of the private entrepreneurs and managers who were accepted belonged to the high-technology and financial sectors of the economy, where a number of highly educated engineers and economists had set up their own enterprises and succeeded. In addition, the party continued to replace old-guard, working-class, less-than-high-school-educated cadres with younger, highly educated technocrats. The transformation of the party's leadership was dramatic: In 1982, less than 20 percent of provincial CPC chiefs had more than a high school education. In 2006, over 97 percent held advanced degrees. The country's highest political body, the Politburo Standing Committee, contained nine engineers educated at China's elite universities and technical institutes, compared with the Long Marchers who had held these offices in the eighties. Even at the local level, it is no longer uncommon for party secretaries, governors, and mayors to hold PhDs.[354]

But the legitimacy that these measures were intended to build—indeed, were capable of building—was based upon the cooptation of the rising elite in a new, capitalist society. It had little to do with the mandate of heaven, which had to be earned through virtuous and just conduct. That is what Wang Hui meant when he wrote, eight years later, that Tiananmen had been the farewell to an old era. The question of democratizing the party to rid it of corruption was never raised again.

Fifteen years after Tiananmen, Hu Jintao faced the same choice that Deng had faced in 1989. In the intervening years, corruption had embedded itself still deeper into the state. Local governments had reacted to the progressive withdrawal of economic autonomy by finding ingenious and often illegal ways of getting around the restrictions. The four-year recession after 1996 had deepened discontent among former state sector workers and migrants in the cities. It had also cut into the local governments' financial resources and made them bear down still harder upon the peasants. All this had combined to increase public discontent to the point where Hu Jintao and the new politburo could no longer ignore the threat it posed to the stability of the state. *And yet, he too made exactly the same choice Deng had made in 1989.*

Shunning all proposals to democratize China by extending elections, and by establishing an independent judiciary, he too chose to rely upon the same methods—a drive against corruption, harsher punishments to the guilty, and a renewed bid to remake the party to maintain its advanced nature. Even his abolition of agriculture taxes and school fees upon the rural population was a byproduct of the continuing desire to clip the wings of the local governments and thereby eliminate their capacity to abuse their power.

Only too aware that change from within without institutional reform can easily be frustrated and will, even when successful, take time, Hu Jintao has had no option but to try and suppress protest till his reforms take hold. The key to success here is to keep the protesters localized and prevent them from forming lateral links. To quote Perry once more:

> History suggests that a key to the success of such undertakings [challenging the Mandate of Heaven] lay in bridging the (often state-imposed) categories that set various groups of people against one another. Such divisions, although responsible for much of the unrest that has colored the Chinese past, also posed serious obstacles to concerted popular imagination and action against the state. To overcome these hurdles required the intervention of farsighted individuals, who often issued from the lower rungs of the intelligentsia or local elite. Whether drawn from the ranks of students, teachers, militia captains, religious masters, bandit chieftains, or Communist cadres, such leaders have played a catalytic role in converting ongoing strategies of competition into large-scale political movements. The state, too, was a critical variable in the equation; a poorly executed repression effort could stimulate, rather than stymie, the spirit of political protest.

Beijing has delegated the task of addressing grievances to the local authorities. But the emergence of a capitalist state has rendered these short-term Confucian remedies inoperative. The Confucian tradition required local authorities to assess the causes of discontent and win over the aggrieved by explaining why the steps they were taking were necessary and compensating them fairly for the losses they incurred. When the cause turned out to be injustice, or self-enrichment at the cost of the peasantry, tradition would have required the local authorities to take action against erring officials. But both persuasion and the punishment of delinquent officials work when the grievances are individual; they cease to work when official delinquency becomes systemic. That is when the state needs to indulge in reflection, and a reappraisal of its policies. If, for some reason, it cannot, then coercion becomes its sole remaining option. But it is no longer a short-term option, because the greedy get greedier and more entrenched in power. As the causes of discontent become generalized, and endure, it becomes more and more difficult to prevent the victims from forming lateral links and organizing themselves.

That is what is now happening in China. The Internet and the mobile phone are defeating the efforts of the state to keep the victims separated. Controlling even the official media is proving less and less easy. This explains Hu Jintao's allergy to the Internet, the increasingly frequent harassment of journalists working for the foreign media, and the imprisonment of as many as thirty-three journalists. But perhaps the most telltale sign of the Chinese government's growing anxiety is its severe repression of the Falun Gong in July 2001. For in traditional China, the lateral aggregation of rebellious forces usually took place under the banner of religious reform movements. The fact that tens of thousands of Falun Gong members were able to congregate without any warning in Tiananmen Square showed the leadership how easy the mobilization of dissidents had become.

India

13 INDIA: THE CHALLENGE OF THE FUTURE

CHINA'S ECONOMIC REFORMS have yielded extraordinarily rapid growth but created a predatory "intermediate" state that it does not know how to reform. India's economic reforms, by contrast, have accelerated economic growth by dismantling the major part of a predatory, rent-seeking, intermediate regime. Does this mean that India's transition to capitalism is more advanced and more sustainable than that of China? Such a conclusion would be premature, for the sudden acceleration of growth that has followed the dismantling of the command economy has given birth to a set of new threats to stability. And these have surfaced precisely when the democratic system has lost most of its capacity to reconcile social conflict. The evidence of this is a spreading rash of challenges to the authority of the Indian state, in six states across the breadth of central India.[355] These are being spearheaded by a newly formed Marxist party, the CPI (Maoist), and constitute the first challenge that is rooted purely in economic deprivation.

These new challenges have arisen from three mutually reinforcing developments. The Green Revolution, which pushed India's output of foodgrains up from eighty million tons in 1961–'66 to over 210 million tons in 2002–'07, has run out of steam. This has happened just when, under the spur of economic liberalization, there has been a shift in the focus of economic policy away from agriculture and rural development, and toward industry and external trade. The third factor is the rapid development of a "growth is God" capitalist ethos that glorifies wealth, turns a blind eye on how it was obtained, and openly jeers at the older virtues of simplicity, austerity, and fraternity. This change of ethos has turned the poor into "the other" and effectively dehumanized them. The first development has created a profound crisis in the countryside; the second has made the central and state governments adopt policies that have deepened the crisis; and the third has sown an insensitivity in the state that has made it turn away from the problems of the poor and treat their outbursts of discontent as a law and order problem, and not as a symptom of malaise in the state itself. The overall effect of these developments has been to make the poor feel abandoned. This is now becoming the seedbed of revolt.

The crisis in the countryside

Why was India an oasis of political stability for four decades, between 1951 and 1991, when it was experiencing one of the lowest rates of growth in the world? And why is India facing its first fully fledged challenge to the state based purely on class struggle, during the years when its rate of growth has exceeded 9 percent a year? The answer to the first question is the enormous increase that the Green Revolution brought, not only to farmers' incomes but also to employment and therefore to the incomes of the poor across the country. Although the new high-yielding and labor-intensive agricultural technologies could be adopted only where there was an assured supply of water (in about two-fifths of the country), the revolution sucked in labor from every other part of the country and transformed the lives of the immigrant workers. As a result, although the economy grew slowly, the benefits of growth were spread widely. The poor therefore remained, by and large, content.

The very base of this contentment evaporated when the stimulus to growth given by the Green Revolution became exhausted in the late nineties. This happened so suddenly that it took the policymakers, and most analysts, by surprise. Agricultural growth fell from over 4 percent a year, between 1992 and 1997, to 1.7 percent in the next five years. The yields per hectare across a range of products peaked simultaneously in 2000–'01 or 2001–'02, and in several crops they began to decline. In 2006–'07, the yield of rice per hectare was only 2.5 percent higher than in 2001–'02, an improvement entirely attributable to a better monsoon. After rising steadily for more than thirty years, the per hectare yield of wheat declined by almost four percent in these five years.[356]

The following table shows the sudden end of the Green Revolution in the first years of this century.

Table 13.1

Index Numbers of Yield of Some Principal Crops

Crop	1970–'71	1980–'81	1990–'91	2001–'02	2006–'07
Rice	90.2	107.7	140.2	167.5	171.4
Wheat	82.4	102.8	143.8	174.1	168.4
Cotton	66.7	95.4	140.8	116.5	264.3
Sugar cane	88.8	104.6	118.3	121.8	128.6
Potatoes	92.6	102.9	133.8	153.0	133.3

Source: Government of India's Economic Survey 2007–2008, Statistical Table 1.11.

The Green Revolution ended in spite of the farmers' best efforts to keep it alive. Year after year, they used more and more fertilizers in a desperate bid to coax a little more crop from the land, but their efforts were in vain. In 2006–'07 they applied 25 percent more fertilizer per hectare than they had done in 2001–'02.[357] But as the table above shows, except in cotton, it had no effect whatsoever on the yield. Needless to say, their profits have been squeezed. But this is not the sole cause of their growing distress. The post-reform period has seen a sharp rise in other costs as well. Chief of these has been the cost of electricity, diesel, and public transport following the near-elimination of subsidies on diesel fuel and an attempt by the state electricity boards to reduce their losses on the supply of electricity to agriculture.

Farmers have tried to safeguard the growth of their incomes by switching from cereals to cash crops and, more recently, from nonperishable to very high value perishable crops like fruit, vegetables, and flowers. There has been a 2.5 percent decline in the area under cereal crops since 1980–'81, and a 41 percent rise in the area under cash crops.[358] But this has proceeded at a snail's pace because the switch has been fraught with risk. To succeed, farmers need to have an assured supply of water, and to apply carefully calibrated doses of fertilizers and pesticides. These ventures need large working capital loans, and to stand a chance of paying these back, or at least not being destroyed by them, they need security against the vagaries of nature and those of the market. Had the central and state governments devoted the same concentrated attention to this secondary and tertiary Green Revolution, the agricultural crisis would never have taken place, for they would have been able to meet these needs by supplying assured concessional financing for an initial startup period, crop insurance, a cooperative marketing infrastructure, and a measure of price support. All of these measures exist on the statute books. Many work exceptionally well—such as the Himachal Pradesh State Cooperative Marketing and Consumers' Federation, which has an established network of collection points where it buys the fruits and vegetables produced by farmers in the remote Himalayas every day and sells them to wholesalers and retailers in every part of the country. But the shift of focus away from agriculture to industry and exports has brought this kind of infrastructure development to an almost complete halt. Agricultural extension has fallen into disrepair, and what little remains functions perfunctorily, with no one to hold the concerned officials accountable.

What was worse, wherever obligations to the rural sector clashed with obligations to trade or industry, the former were immediately overlooked. Thus, for instance, when the central government instructed the nationalized banks to lower their ratio of nonperforming loans and improve their capital adequacy ratios, agriculture was the first area in which they cut lending and hardened conditions. When the central government allowed private companies to enter the insurance industry, the state-owned Life Insurance Corporation of India responded by discontinuing its least profitable insurance schemes, most of which were originally designed to serve the rural and urban poor.

It was inevitable that the distribution of income would become more unequal. But this is the least of the changes that liberalization has wrought in the social fabric. A far more disturbing change has gone virtually unnoticed: *The poor have not only grown poorer, but their lives have grown more insecure.* The first signs of this change came in the mid-nineties, when farmers began to commit suicide in the thousands every year. By the government's own estimates, more than one hundred thousand farmers committed suicide between 1998 and 2003.[359] The vast majority of the deaths occurred in four states of India—Maharashtra, Andhra Pradesh, Karnataka, and Punjab. The deaths caught the attention of the media and the government in the late nineties. The investigations that followed revealed a complex set of causes, all of which could be traced back to a collapse of the financial, technological, and marketing support system on which agriculture depended, an increase in input costs following the attenuation of subsidies on agricultural inputs, and a reduction in protection to their output following India's accession to the Uruguay round of tariff agreements. In the words of P. Sainath, one of the most perceptive and committed reporters on the crisis in Indian agriculture,

> The rural landscape is a shambles. Agricultural credit and finance systems have collapsed. Taking their place are new entities that can make the village moneylender seem relatively less coercive. Prices have pushed most inputs beyond the reach of the small farmer. For many, the move from food crops to cash crops proved fatal. In some cases, the shift was towards high-outlay, water-guzzling crops such as sugar cane. All this, in an era of huge power tariff hikes. A steady shrinking of local democracy further deepened the chaos.[360]

A striking example of how agriculture has been pushed into crisis by a growing tendency to favor industry is the Indian government's refusal to take advantage of the bound tariffs on cotton to which it committed itself with the WTO. In the days of the command economy, cotton, grown mostly in Punjab and Gujarat, was called the white gold of India. After the Green Revolution its cultivation had spread to Punjab and parts of Haryana, where it turned farmers with as little as five hectares of land into millionaires overnight. The reason was a ban on the import of raw cotton and, in Maharashtra in particular, a monopoly procurement scheme that offered somewhat more than fair prices to the farmer.

But India's decision to lift all quantitative controls on the import of raw cotton in 2000, as a part of its obligations to the WTO, turned cotton from a boon into a curse. Already faced with rising input prices in the nineties, the farmers now had to compete against an unrestricted flow of imported cotton. To avoid being completely outpriced, the Maharashtra government had to bring down its procurement price for cotton. Between 2000 and 2004, this came down by 43 percent. Caught in a nutcracker, farmers responded in the only way they knew, by trying to produce more and more for sale. They sank tube wells, spent more on fertilizers, switched to transgenic seeds, and bought new machinery in a desperate effort to produce more and more.

Sainath has captured the frenzy and desperation of the farmers in one unforgettable paragraph:

> Musampally has more borewells than people. This village in Nalgonda district has barely 2000 acres under cultivation. But it boasts over 6,000 borewells—two to every human being. Over 85 percent of these wells have failed. The rest are in decline. The desperate search for water has bankrupted a once prosperous village. Borewells loom large in the latest round of farmers' suicides in Andhra Pradesh. All those who took their lives had run up huge debts. A hefty chunk of this money (borrowed at interest rates of 36 percent and above) was spent on borewells. Just 12 households that have suffered suicides recently had invested in 52 of them. All but four or five failed. They had spent close to Rs. 8 lakhs on these. And that is not counting the cost of pump sets.[361]

And they succeeded. For yields per hectare more than doubled between 2001 and 2007—a striking contrast to the rest of agriculture. The farmers achieved the near-impossible, only to come face to face with the middleman, and with the hard realities of economics. For when demand is inelastic, producing more means earning less per unit. And demand for cotton had become extremely inelastic, because with exports in mind, the textile mills had switched most of their production to different varieties of cotton, long and extra-long staple cotton, most of which had to be imported. As a result, by 2004 two-thirds of the raw cotton input into the textiles industry was coming from abroad. The last and unkindest cut was delivered by the government. Whereas under its tariff-binding agreement with the WTO India was entitled to levy a 90 percent import duty on raw cotton imports, in 2003 it was levying a tariff of only 5 percent. The reason was not hard to discern. Industry did not want high tariffs, because these would raise the cost of production. And by 2004, in the best traditions of capitalism, industry was ruling government instead of the other way around. It is no surprise that the highest incidence of suicides has been in Maharashtra's cotton-growing areas, and among cotton farmers in Punjab.

The denial of protection against agricultural imports that other countries feel no compunction in subsidizing is not confined to cotton. Since 2000, when India removed the last of its quantitative restrictions on agricultural imports, the government has not only kept its tariffs below the bound rates but also tended to bring them down yet further. Only one significant crop, soybean oil, enjoyed the full protection that it merited under India's agreements with the WTO. The case of cotton is especially egregious, because in this farmers have been denied protection despite the fact that the US continues to give $13 billion of subsidies to its cotton farmers, who produce almost entirely for export.[362]

The response of the poor

India's poorer peasants had become aware that agriculture offered them a limited, and increasingly insecure, future as far back as the early nineties. They reacted to the challenge in ways that showed a touching faith in the future of their country. The first response was to send children between five and fourteen to school instead of sending them to work alongside their parents in the fields. Largely as a result, between 1994 and 2000 the agricultural labor force declined for the first time in living memory.[363] What made women take this step was a realization that their children would have to seek employment outside agriculture when they grew up. To ensure this, more and more families began to shun the state schools and to send their children to private schools, paying forty to 150 rupees a month (one to three dollars), so that they could get a better education and learn English.[364] They began to save, some of them consciously for the first time. A part of their saving took the form of having fewer children. As a result, to the surprise of demographers, birthrates began to fall in the nineties, not only in states with high female literacy but also in those without it.[365] When researchers asked the women why they were adopting birth control, women in these states said that it was to give their living children a better chance in life.

Fortunately for them, there were jobs to be had. In 2002, the five-year-long recession ended, and in the very next year growth exceeded 8 percent, not to drop below 9 percent for the next five years. These first three post-recession years were sufficient to push the growth of nonagricultural jobs up by 4.7 percent a year between 1999 and 2005.[366] Thus most of those who came into the labor market were able to find work. But just about all the new jobs are in the unorganized, or informal, sector, where workers have no protection whatever, whether it be against sickness, unemployment, accident and disability, or old age. To make matters worse, half of the workers in this sector do not work directly for the employer, but are hired by contractors who keep a part of their wages. A particularly damaging lacuna is the absence of maternity benefits for pregnant and nursing mothers. More than 92 percent of the women workers in the country work in the unorganized sector. When they become pregnant and have to stop work, they lose their incomes, just when their bodies need added nutrition. This is one of the main reasons why 35 percent of all the underdeveloped children of the world are to be found in India.

The flood of job-seekers into the nonagricultural unorganized sector has immensely widened the already rising income gap between the rich and the poor in the country. So great has been the pressure of job-seekers that it has allowed employers to bring down the real wages even in the organized sector. The National Sample Survey found that between 1999 and 2005, only urban males in the unorganized sector had been able to hold on to their real wages. All other categories of workers—urban female, and rural male and female—had suffered a decline in real wages.

The pressure of job-seekers has allowed employers in the organized sectors to appropriate virtually the entire increase in productivity since the reforms began to take hold. For much of the 1980s, the share of wages in the product of the organized sector had hovered around 30 percent, but by 2003–'04 this percentage had shrunk by half. As a result, the average real wage in the organized sector in the three years ending in 2003–'04 was 11 percent lower than in the triennium ending in 1995–'96.[367] This happened during a period when the productivity per worker increased from three times the productivity of a worker in the unorganized sector to seven times. None of the benefits accrued to organized labor.[368]

The developments described above have brought about a profound change in Indian society. In fifteen short years they have swept away a large part of what remained of traditional attitudes and traditional values. The main repercussions have been an inherited fatalism that has made the poor passive, and a willingness to rely upon the largesse of the joint family to tide over hard times. Anthropologists have been warning their readers that the joint family is breaking down under the twin pressures of rising numbers and rising aspirations. Today, people want something more for their children than what they have known, and they are increasingly anxious about who will look after them when they are too old to work. Nor are they prepared to accept dispossession, and expropriation by the state in the name of development, in the way that their forebears were in the early decades of independence. There is thus a tension in society and a potential for conflict that traditional India never knew.

It is against this background that new conflicts have begun to emerge. Chief among these is the growing conflict between the new aggressive capitalist class, allied with the remnants of the intermediate regime in the rural areas—the coalition of local bureaucrats, police, politicians, well-off farmers, and local contractors and traders who have not been affected by the dismantling of controls on industry and trade—and the poorest of the poor. The latter group's members include the submarginal land owners, sharecroppers, and landless laborers, and above all the tribal populations that inhabit the mineral- and forest-rich areas of central and northeastern India. What makes India's future less than secure is the drastic decline in the central government's capacity to play the arbiter's role, make the hard decisions, and on occasion take the coercive action needed to resolve issues.

The collapse of central power

The most striking feature of the federal government's decline is its loss of control over the framing and execution of national policy. The root causes can be traced back to a structural flaw in Indian democracy, whose full consequences came to light only after the Congress Party lost its dominance of the Indian political system in the late eighties. Rajiv Gandhi's government, which stayed in power from 1984 to 1989, was the last one at the center to be backed by a party with an absolute majority in Parliament. When the Congress Party came back to power in 1991 under Narasimha Rao, it was fifty-eight seats short of an absolute majority and had to rely upon by-election victories and understandings with small parties to stay in power. But the decline of the Congress did not see the rise of another dominant party. Instead, "dominant party democracy" gave way to rule by shifting, unstable coalitions, whose capacity for directing economic or social change has been fatally weakened by recurring conflicts of interest between their members.

In theory coalition rule should have been a transitory phenomenon. India had adopted the simple majority, "first past the post" system of voting, which magnifies the number of seats won by the largest party in relation to its share of the vote and correspondingly shrinks the number of seats won by smaller parties. Over time this forces small parties to sink their differences with their immediate political neighbors in order to enlarge their share of the vote and make a credible bid for power. This creates a two-party system, or a bipolar system dominated by two stable coalitions of parties. But not only has this not happened in India; it cannot happen. The first past the post system originated in Britain, which is a unitary state with only one legislature. Like the US, India adopted it for use in a federal state. Over fourteen general elections, the simple majority voting system has created two stable parties or coalitions in the state legislatures. But in the very act of doing so it has ensured that there will be a multiplicity of small parties at the center. For each party that is well-entrenched in a state has been able to translate its hold on the vote there into a small but stable number of seats in the Lok Sabha (lower house of Parliament). As a result, in the parliamentary elections of 1999 there were no fewer than sixty-three recognized political parties in the fray.[369] Simple majority voting therefore yields very different results in federal democracies than in unitary ones, precisely because it works in the same way in both. This has been hidden from view in the US, the only other large federal democracy, because of the need to vote for a single president of the United States. But the looseness of the Republican and

Democratic parties, and the constant cross-voting in both houses of Congress, reflects the extent to which senators and congresspeople are able to rely on their secure backing in their home states to flout their party's wishes in Washington.

Coalitions in which the largest party has to woo or bribe, but cannot threaten, its smaller parties in order to enact changes of policy are by nature weak. But in India, the federal government's capacity to frame coherent economic and social policies has been further vitiated by the separation of central from state elections that took place in 1971.[370] As the Congress Party lost control of more and more state assemblies in the seventies and eighties, and short-lived coalition governments began to take its place, the timing of state legislative assembly elections also became erratic. Soon there were elections in one part of the country or another every year. At no time, therefore, were all the members of a coalition government in New Delhi free from the pressures of electoral politics. This compounded the difficulty of maintaining cohesion in coalitions on policy issues.[371]

State governments recapture industrialization

As happened in China in 1981–'83, the coincidence of economic reforms with the rapid weakening of the central government has transferred to the state governments much of the power to initiate industrial investment. Before the 1991 reforms, although industry was a state subject, the concentration of the bulk of investment in the federally administered five-year plans had effectively divested the states of control over industrial investment. The plethora of conditions that private investors had to meet, under the industrial licensing, antimonopoly, and exchange control legislation that had been passed between 1949 and 1974, gave Delhi total control over both public and private investment.

The repeal or drastic relaxation of these laws freed private investors. But they soon learned that they could go nowhere without the
active support of the state governments. These controlled their access to land (purchases of more than five hectares had to be preceded
by permission and a change of land use by the state government), to
power, and to transport systems. But dealing with the state governments also gave them countervailing power, because if one state was
not prepared to accept their terms they would threaten to take their
project to another. As had happened in China, money rapidly ce-
mented the relationship between the large corporate sector and the
state governments. Within less than a decade, the latter went from
opposing the large corporations to becoming their allies in the framing of statewide development plans.

Special economic zones: going the China way?

As happened in China between 1988 and 1992, the strength of this
connection was suddenly revealed by the way in which state governments converted a well-meaning effort by the federal government to set up special economic zones, modeled on China's, into a
land grab for personal profit. The idea was a brainchild of a former
commerce and industry minister, Murasoli Maran, who announced
it in the NDA government's import-export policy in March 2000.
It was, however, implemented by Kamal Nath, Maran's successor in
the commerce ministry, in 2006, and it exempted investors in SEZs
from all manners of local and indirect taxes, giving them an income
tax holiday that would last on a diminishing scale for fifteen years.
Nath claimed that the SEZs would draw in $25 billion of invest-
ment and create five hundred thousand jobs in three years.[372] The
center's initial estimates were that the SEZs would occupy about
145,000 hectares of land. But to its surprise, the state governments
began to set up one SEZ a day and had already earmarked more

than half a million hectares for them.[373] In their hurry, they made short shrift of the guidelines that the center had laid down for the acquisition of land. These specified that the states had to acquire only barren or single-cropped land, and that the proportion of double-cropped land could not exceed 10 percent.[374] But the politician–SEZ developer nexus led to the earmarking of prime agricultural land. The site would invariably be chosen by the industrialists, with the state playing the passive role of facilitator.[375]

The closeness of the nexus that had developed between members of the state government and the SEZ developers was revealed when, on November 3, 2006, Indiabulls Infrastructure Limited, a newly created subsidiary of a financial services company, issued a corporate announcement that it had obtained "in-principle approval" to establish an SEZ south of Mumbai, and invited prospective buyers to contact the company. It did so even before the state government had notified the owners that it was acquiring their land, before any compensation had been offered or accepted, and before the Maharashtra government had received the federal government's clearance for the project. Indiabulls' supreme confidence that it would have no problems on these fronts reflected its supreme faith in its influence over the Maharashtra government, and over Maharashtra's ability to deliver on its part of the bargain.[376]

Unbalancing growth

Another indication of the shift of control over industrial investment from the center to the states was the former's announcement of a scheme to establish two "industrial corridors." Granted in-principle approval in August 2007 by the central cabinet, the first is to be a gigantic 1,483-kilometer-long industrial corridor connecting Delhi and Mumbai. This is to be developed in collaboration with Japan, with a projected investment of $100 billion; the second is to be between Chennai and Bangalore, and designed to attract $50 billion. But in sharp contrast to the pre-reform period and the early years of reform, it was understood from the start that the center's role was mainly to legitimize these projects and open the gates for their financing by the financial institutions. Private investors will do the bulk of the investing.

In theory, the Delhi–Mumbai corridor is expected to promote industrialization in six states.[377] But the bulk of the investment will be concentrated in the already highly industrialized states of Maharashtra and Gujarat, and in the national capital region around Delhi. Any illusions the center may have held that all states would benefit equally were dispelled by Narendra Modi, the chief minister of Gujarat, who boasted, during his campaign for the state assembly elections in Gujarat in December 2007, that fully one-third of the investment envisaged would come to Gujarat.

The significant difference between this grandiose scheme and previous announcements of investment plans was that they, and indeed the entire concept of industrial corridors, had been dreamed up by a combination of large industry, real estate developers, and state governments, mainly those of Gujarat, Maharashtra, Tamil Nadu, Karnataka, and Delhi. Not to be outdone by Gujarat, the Maharashtra government announced that it had invited and received tenders for constructing not one but six magnetic levitation train routes in and around Mumbai, to run over more than two hundred kilometers. Based on the cost of the Shanghai maglev, these will cost between eight and ten billion Euros. That is three-quarters of the capital budget for India's entire 110,000-kilometer railway system in the tenth five-year plan. Maharashtra had not consulted the central Planning Commission, much less sought the center's agreement, before announcing the project.

Concentrating so much investment in a relatively small part of the country will not matter if it is financed solely by foreign capital. But in contrast to China, where on average half of the investment in joint ventures has been raised abroad, in India the foreign component of "foreign" direct investment can be as low as one-sixth. The balance is raised by issuing shares and taking loans in the Indian capital markets. Thus, the debilitation of the center has given aggressive, better-developed states the opportunity to preempt the nation's savings.

As profitability has become the sole determinant of investment, the income gap between various parts of the country has widened rapidly. The growth rate ranges from 12–14 percent in Gujarat and Maharashtra to 3–4 percent in Bihar, Orissa, Jharkhand, Chhattisgarh, and the northeastern states. Not surprisingly, the per capita income of Gujarat is more than three times that of Bihar. Six states—Karnataka, Tamil Nadu, Andhra Pradesh, Punjab, Haryana, and Delhi—have recorded above-average rates of growth. The rest of the country, including the two most populous states of Uttar Pradesh and Madhya Pradesh, falls substantially below the national average. The long-term threat this widening gap poses to the unity of India cannot be underestimated.

The triumph of the capitalist ethos

The other casualty of the shift from a command economy to a market economy has been the genuine, even if much abused, concern for the poor that had underpinned the effort to build a "socialist mixed economy" in the fifties and sixties. Its place has been taken by an increasingly self-righteous identification of financial success with virtue, and an increasing impatience with the complaints of the poor and with those who insist on voicing them on their behalf. The media have captured this spirit accurately, albeit in a spirit of celebration rather than criticism. They regularly headline the number of Indians in *Fortune*'s list of the richest men in the world.

They also headline the highest starting salaries offered to management institute graduates by Indian and foreign companies, and have turned this into a race between the institutes.

Fully aware of the market value of the degrees they hand out, the management institutes now charge fees that bear absolutely no relation to the cost of the education they provide. In an uncritical emulation of the American business schools, they expect those whom they admit to their programs to get bank loans to fund their education.

If being rich is a sign of success, and success is virtuous, then flaunting wealth is no longer a vice. Consumerism has therefore gained a stranglehold on the urban middle class. The ethos of personal austerity that had been a hallmark of earlier generations of Indian entrepreneurs has disappeared altogether. This has, not coincidentally, been facilitated by a relaxation, during the NDA regime, of the rules government sets for foreign direct investment to permit single-brand retailing in India. This has led to the arrival of Mercedes, BMW, Chanel, Hugo Boss, Swarovski, Montblanc, Louis Vuitton, and most of the other global brands. The availability of shirts that cost $400, ties that cost $150 and more, fountain pens that cost upward of $500, and automobiles that cost up to a million dollars has, unavoidably, fueled the appetite for salary increases in the Indian managerial class. It may be this, rather than a sudden shortage of managerial talent, that has made the salaries of business managers rise at double-digit rates every year since the beginning of the current decade.

When Prime Minister Manmohan Singh cautioned business to curb its appetite for salary increases in a speech in Mumbai in 2007, the *Financial Express,* one of the leading financial dailies in the country, published a news analysis piece pointing out that in 2006 salaries had risen by an average of 13 percent, and top executive salaries by about 30 percent, but post-tax profits had risen by 68 percent, so the prime minister had no cause for complaint. The authors did not suggest that managers' salaries should be reduced when the companies they ran made a loss. The Indian elite has thus taken Deng Xiaoping's much-misquoted dictum "getting rich is glorious" very much to heart.[378]

Not surprisingly, the income gap in the nonagricultural sector has widened dramatically. While managerial salaries have risen by double-digit figures since 2003, real wages of labor in organized industry have stagnated or declined because of a weakening of trade unions and the increasing pressure of demand for jobs in the organized sector. As a result, between 1993 and 2005 the share of wages in the net sales revenue of industrial enterprises has halved. This is in spite of a sharp rise of labor productivity in the organized sector, which has increased the gap between it and productivity in the unorganized sector from 4 to 1 in 1993 to 7 to 1 in 2004.[379] The difference has been absorbed into profits and managerial incomes.

From developmental to predatory state

The third flaw in Indian democracy is the failure, by the framers of the Indian Constitution, to provide for a legal system for funding electoral and associated political activity by recognized political parties. This is the loophole by which, in the sixties and seventies, the intermediate class was able to convert its newfound economic power into political power. But the loophole's other, far more deadly, effect was to replace the Nehruvian "developmental state," of the early years after independence, with a predatory, kleptocratic state in which the purpose of those who sought power was to enrich themselves at the state's expense.

In sharp contrast to China, where local governments are responsible for most of the predatory behavior of the state, in India blame is to be found almost equally at the center and in the states. The origins of the predatory state in India lie in the omission of a system of legal funding for political parties from the Indian Constitution. Every candidate who secures a party's nomination has then to find the funds to fight the election. In the pre-reform period, when Indira Gandhi split the Congress Party in 1969 and broke its seven-decade-old link with Indian big business, it was not only the self-employed traders, manufacturers, and rich farmers of the intermediate class that filled this gap. Opposition parties also enlisted mafia gangs and musclemen to capture election booths and coerce entire communities who were known to be against their candidates into staying away from the polling booths. All of these had eventually to be accommodated in the political system, and all commanded a price. The most honest of candidates had to find ways of paying back the people who loaned him, or her, the money to fight the elections.

By degrees, the purpose of elections therefore became to make money. Over the ensuing decades this created a vicious circle: The more the state forsook developmentalism in favor of predation, the more rapidly did it lose legitimacy in the eyes of the people. The loss of legitimacy shortened the life of succeeding governments, and increased the temptation felt by its members to privatize the services of the state by taking kickbacks, commissions, and bribes. In the end this has led to "clientelism"—the construction of coalitions of interests that come together with the express purpose of robbing the state.

A revealing example of state governments' predatory behavior in India is the perversion of the public distribution system for foodgrains from an instrument designed to protect the poor into one designed to enrich the well-off peasant proprietor who produces foodgrains for the market. In the late summer of 2001, the Vajpayee government was severely criticized in the media for allowing starvation deaths to take place in Orissa and some other parts of the country, when his government was sitting on a sixty-million-ton mountain of foodgrains supposedly destined for subsidized public distribution. Put on the defensive by the criticism, the government defended itself in Parliament by pointing out that the fault lay not with the central government but with the states. The center was delivering the foodgrains destined for the "fair price" shops all the way to railheads and other distribution centers in the food-deficit states. But the state governments were not picking up the foodgrains and transporting them the short remaining distance to the ration shops.

Why were they not doing so, and why was the central government holding sixty million tons of buffer stocks in the first place? The answer to the second question was that the bulk of the rice and up to 86 percent of the wheat that the center procured came from just two states, Punjab and Haryana. The governments of these states had long since given up any pretense of following a contra-cyclical policy designed to prevent a crash in market prices in bumper crop years, and had been raising procurement prices year after year irrespective of whether the harvest was good or bad. Their goal was to push up the floor price of foodgrains in the market and ensure a rising income for the farmers—by definition, those with larger land holdings—who had a surplus of foodgrains to sell. But these higher floor prices meant that marginal farmers, agricultural laborers, and the increasing number of nonagricultural workers in rural areas, who had to buy all or a part of their foodgrains in the local market, had to pay more, and suffered a decline in their real income. The constant upward revision of "procurement" prices by the surplus states, and the reluctance of the food-deficit states to distribute the grain supplied to them by the central government, therefore exemplified the rise of a predator state.

The opposite was happening in the food-deficit states. Since picking up the food sent by the center from the railhead and transporting it to their warehouses and ration shops involved some cost, they preferred to minimize the amount they lifted from the railhead. To do this they found ever more ingenious ways of discouraging the poor from buying their requirements at the ration shops. Typical of these stratagems was requiring families with ration cards that identified them as being below the poverty line, and therefore eligible for a further reduction in price, to buy a month's rations at a time. Since most of these families earned money from day to day, they were in no position to do so. The food-deficit states then sold some of the unused allocations for the below-poverty-line families back to the central government as grain "procured" by them for the public distribution system.[380] This was the classic behavior of the predator state. Everyone gained—the ruling party and the rich farmers in the grain surplus states, the governments of the grain-deficit states, and the corrupt employees of the public distribution system. Only the consumers lost, and the poorest among them risked starving to death.

Such predatory behavior is all-pervasive. Political parties in the central and state governments vie with each other to grant subsidies on fertilizers, power, irrigation, and road transport in publicly owned buses. The public distribution system remains unreformed: the stiffness of the state governments' and concerned food ministry officials' opposition may be judged from the fact that Manmohan Singh's finance minister, P. Chidambaram, announced his government's intention to replace the present corrupt ration shop system with a food stamp system, in 2004—but it was only in 2008 that he was able to announce the agreement of one state government to try it out as an experimental measure.

One form of predatory behavior in India actually masquerades as charity. This is the indiscriminate offer of subsidies on all products produced by state-owned enterprises or subject to price-setting by it. What this actually does is to transfer the losses of these enterprises to the shoulders of taxpayers, who are mainly urban and belong to the middle or affluent classes. The payoff for the political parties that form the government comes in the form of votes that they hope will prolong their hold on power. One area in which such predatory behavior is rampant is the indiscriminate subsidization of electricity. Here, in a holdover from the alliances of the intermediate regime, the state governments have allied themselves with well-to-do farmers, small industrialists, and service providers to rob the state itself of the revenues that are its due. On average, a fifth of the power generated is stolen outright. The state governments sell another one-third to agriculturists at an average tariff that is a tenth of its cost of production. A large part of this power is actually consumed by small industrialists and shopkeepers who take advantage of the fact that their enterprises are located on what is classified as agricultural land, and by farmers rich enough to own air-conditioned farmhouses.

The federal government is also not above wooing the powerful fertilizer lobby in this way. When the Vajpayee government lifted the ban on fertilizer imports at the beginning of the new millennium, to fulfill India's commitments under the Uruguay round, it immediately made sure that subsidies on locally manufactured fertilizer would remain high enough to discourage imports. As a result, an estimated two-thirds of the fertilizer subsidy now goes not to the farmers in whose name it is regularly renewed, but to local manufacturers who have "gold-plated" their capital costs in order to inflate their cost of production and increase the subsidy they are entitled to.[381]

Two-fifths of the subsidy on kerosene goes not to the rural poor who supposedly use it as a cooking fuel, but to adulterators of gasoline and diesel and to smugglers who ship it out from Bihar and Bengal to Nepal and Bangladesh. In November 2005, a crooked petrol pump owner who had been adulterating diesel with kerosene was caught by Manjunath Shanmugham, an inspector for the Indian Oil Corporation who, instead of accepting the hefty bribe he was offered, decided to report the dealer to his head office. This led to his murder on the petrol pump premises. In the furor that followed, the *Indian Express* unearthed the following facts:

> [In 2005] kerosene [cost] Rs. 10 per litre [25 US cents]. Diesel [cost] Rs. 32. By mixing 400 litres of kerosene into 600 litres of diesel the dealer makes a profit of Rs. 9,468 [$236]. Had they sold pure diesel they would have made Rs. 509!

A study, published in 2005 by the National Council of Applied Economic Research, a Delhi-based organization that specializes in market research and economic forecasting, estimated that 39 percent of the fourteen billion liters of kerosene sold in the country every year was being used to adulterate diesel or being smuggled to Nepal and Bangladesh, yielding illicit profits of more than $3 billion a year to the adulterators. This was not far short of the profit before tax that was expected by Reliance Industries, India's largest private corporation, in 2005–'06.[382]

Predatory extortion—mistakenly described as corruption—has become a way of life for all but a small minority of civil servants in the state and central bureaucracies. Kickbacks are mandatory in virtually every transaction between a public servant and a member of the public. For any private company, whether Indian or foreign, entering a business in which the state might be even peripherally involved has become a nightmare. Every time an official is transferred, or there is a change of government, they have to start negotiations afresh with the successor to work out a fresh kickback.

It is not only projects, government purchases, and large companies that are being regularly ripped off. Preying upon individuals has become the order of the day. Whether one wants a water or power connection, a telephone or power line repaired, a building permit or a completion certificate; whether one wants to draw one's own pension or obtain a tax refund, or simply obtain an income tax clearance certificate, one must first pay a "private cess" to concerned petty officials.

As in China, rings of corruption have developed that involve virtually everyone in a government office, from the "number one" downward. Unlike China's bureaucracy, however, the Indian bureaucracy has been rendered immune from accountability for misdemeanors and misconduct. Two articles of the Indian Constitution[383] make it next to impossible to dismiss a civil servant, except in cases of proven criminal misconduct. To prosecute a civil servant for damage he or she has inflicted on the plaintiff through acts of negligence or omission, such as delaying payments or issue of licenses and permits, requires a waiver of immunity from the government. This is seldom given. As a result, no civil servant can be punished in any significant way for not performing the tasks assigned to him or her. Corrupt officials have lost no time in taking advantage of their near-immunity. In every department, therefore, they charge a "fee" for not delaying the processing of applications.

As in China, corruption and extortion have become more entrenched with the passage of time and an increase in officials' greed. No one dares to challenge the predators, and in particular no one dares to try to prosecute them—because while one's chances of obtaining redress are slim, the retaliation of the bureaucracy is an absolute certainty. Indian democracy has therefore created a paradox: The people have the power to change their political leaders, and in their desperation they are doing it with a regularity that has earned their perpetual discontent a name for itself—the anti-incumbency factor. But their powerlessness in the face of the bureaucracy, and the economic interests with which it is enmeshed, is absolute. The doggerel verse that Chinese peasants composed to describe the local cadres of the Communist Party is every bit as applicable to the relationship between the state and the people in India:

If you lined up the cadres and shot them one by one, someone would certainly be wronged.

If you shot every other one of the cadres, someone would certainly escape due punishment.[384]

Spreading challenge to the state—an illustration

The steady increase in predation by the bureaucracy and its allies in the intermediate class, and the absolute powerlessness of the poor to obtain redress through legal expedients, explains the rapid spread of armed challenges to state authority across India. An example of how predation directly feeds insurgency is provided by the nexus between timber smugglers and militants in Kashmir. In the mountains that surround Kashmir valley, where land is scarce and unemployment is rife, felling trees illegally and extracting the timber at night has become the sole source of cash income for a growing number of families. Since the sound of chopping and sawing carries a long way in the mountains, forest guards invariably come to know of the tree-felling. The smugglers regularly pay up to half of what they receive from the sale of the timber to middlemen, to bribe their way past forest officials and police checkposts on the way to the collection centers. The only years in which the smugglers were relatively free of extortion were 1990 through 2005, when the mountains were infested with insurgents. The militants therefore regularly received shelter and, on occasion, support from the village poor. The return of peace to the mountains in 2005 following accords between India and Pakistan led to a withdrawal of the militants from many of these areas. This threw the villagers back into the arms of the police and forestry officials once more.[385]

14 FADING VISION OF EQUITY

THE VALUES OF a self-righteous capitalist class have begun to permeate the Indian state. As a result, the state governments have begun to exhibit the same impatience with the problems of the poor that is now freely aired by the urban middle class. A single incident in January 2006, reported in the print media, served to highlight the change. When the central government had set up the Rourkela steel plant in the late fifties, it had fenced in several thousand hectares of "waste" lands that, it alleged, belonged to no one. Most of this land was never used and lay fallow for the next half a century. In 2005, tribal people of Kalinganagar, a resettled township in Jaipur district, whose forebears had been driven off the land began to demand the return of the unused portion to them. Instead of negotiating, the Orissa government tried to arrest them. When they resisted and became violent the police opened fire upon them, killing twelve.[386]

The treatment meted out to the tribal people at Rourkela was only one straw in the changing political wind. At Singur, in West Bengal, when some farmers protested against the forcible acquisition of their land for a small car project initiated by Tata's oldest and best-known industrial group, and tried to prevent the police from fencing the land, the West Bengal government sent in its police repeatedly to force the barricades open. To do so, they broke a few heads but did not open fire on anyone. But the West Bengal government's restraint broke down when faced by a similar agitation at the site of a proposed chemical industry hub at Nandigram. The hub was to be developed by the Salim Group, a Malaysian conglomerate, and needed ten thousand acres, ten times as much land as the Tata small car project in Singur. Although the government had not publicized the land acquisition, the villagers of Nandigram got to know of its intentions and formed an organization to fight the government, the Bhumi Ucched Pratirodh Committee (BUPC). After an initial violent confrontation with the state government officials who had called a village meeting in January 2007, the BUPC cut off all roads and other access routes to their land. The administration responded by sending in around three thousand policemen to break the BUPC's resistance on March 14, 2007. But the villagers found out they were coming and amassed a crowd of roughly two thousand villagers at the entry points into Nandigram, with women and children forming the front ranks. In the resulting mayhem, the police opened fire on the crowd and killed at least fourteen people.

A detailed account of the confrontation, given on March 25 by Angad Choudhury, a Kolkata-based journalist, reveals strong similarities between the way that the Left Front (Communist) government of West Bengal dealt with the Nandigram protest, and the way that local authorities have been dealing with land-based protests in China. In sharp contrast to the rest of India, where ruling party cadres almost never come to the aid of the government, at Nandigram (and in Singur, the previous year), the Communist Party cadres were as much involved in suppressing the agitation as the police.

"Nandigram," Choudhury wrote,

> had been out of bounds for CPM and West Bengal police for the past several months—since the fateful day in January 2007 when

the "popular" uprising happened. This is something that severely challenged the [authority] of the CPM party as well as the state administration which is anyway the executive arm of the CPM party. There had been several open threats from the party. Binoy Kongar, the leader of the CPM's farmer lobby had threatened that he [would] make life hell for the people of Nandigram . . . by surrounding Nandigram with CPM panchayats [village councils]. Though he was censured by the party top brass, there was no way of ignoring the undercurrent of animosity that existed in and around Nandigram.

Mr. Prasad Ranjan Roy, Home Secretary in the West Bengal Government announced that there would be police action in Nandigram as soon as possible. The police top brass went into a huddle and the blueprint was prepared.

Almost 3,000 policemen were mobilized for the operation, though officially the number was put at 700. Police from adjoining districts supplemented the local police. Local peacekeepers/mob chasers were joined by companies of rapid action force and commandos. In addition to standard batons and .303 rifles, the police were equipped with semi automatic weapons and INSAS assault rifles. Advanced mob dispersing equipment like water cannons, multiple barrel tear gas launchers etc were not part of the equipment assembled by the police. There has not been any satisfactory answer from the police or the state administration as to why the invading force was equipped with killer weapons rather than mob dispersing equipment. . . . There was a tacit understanding that the CPM party cadres would follow the police into Nandigram for the mop up action. The police would break the resistance and establish state's control and the CPM party would re-occupy the villages . . .

On 14th March, the police marched into the villages in four columns. The action started around 10:30 am. They faced stiff resistance in two areas—sonachura and adhikaripara. The local resistance kept the women and kids on the front to deter the police. The police claimed that they first requested the mob to disperse, then lobbed tear gas shells and only then opened fire. The locals [deny this]. They [said] that the police announcement and the tear gas shelling was done as a matter of record, almost as an excuse to open fire. What we know is that only 15 minutes lapsed between the first announcement and the first round being fired.

[The] Media [were] blocked out of the action zone. CPM activists built a cordon around Nandigram to keep everybody out. The local CPM MP, Lakshman Seth and other MLAs were responsible for this cordon. Media people were stopped at a distance of 17 km from Nandigram and were politely requested to come back in 3 days when the situation would be under control. Each car/bike reaching the cordon was stopped, people body-searched at times and movement allowed/restricted on the basis of identification. The blockade lasted the whole day while the police action continued and the world condemned. By 12 noon there was official confirmation of two deaths. Soon the figure went up to 5 and then 14. Unofficial sources put the estimate at 22. So far 14 bodies have been recovered.

By 12 noon the first visual [footage] reached a local TV channel and within seconds the world saw what CPM wanted to hide at any cost. We saw police firing on a crowd that consisted of women. We couldn't see children. We saw men and women running for life. We saw two bodies falling down. We didn't see any retaliation, as police claimed. Final count—14 dead, 10 died of bullet injuries, 2 from "pipe gun" injuries, 1 from bomb injuries and 1 from "sharp cutting injuries."

By late afternoon the horror of Nandigram was well documented. The government first attempted to make light of the matter. Then backtracked. The Governor, who also happens to be Mahatma Gandhi's grandson issued a press note. He asked a pertinent question—why would Indians be fired upon by the Indian security forces? He described the incident as chilling. The Kolkata High Court on 15th March issued a suo moto order directing CBI to investigate. The Chief Minister made a statement in the Assembly—expressing regret but did not tender any apology.

[The Central Bureau of Investigation (which comes under the central government)] reached Nandigram on the 15th. They found many evidences and gaping holes in the police claims. The police had claimed that they had fired a total of 37 rounds including 10 rounds in the air. CBI said 10 people (out of 14) died of bullet injuries and between 30 to 35 people sustained bullet injuries. The police figures didn't add up. More importantly they found empty shells of .315 cartridges. The police do not use these cartridges, so who did? And in a swooping raid in a brick kiln, they arrested 10 CPM activists with about 10 guns, and about 800 rounds of live ammunition, CPM flags & pamphlets etc etc. CBI has submitted their report to the High Court. State CID has started their own investigation. More enquiries will follow.[387]

Concern for equity at the center

As in China, the new capitalist spirit is far more in evidence in the state capitals than in New Delhi. Like President Hu Jintao, Manmohan Singh recognized the need to reconcile growth with equity, in order to maintain political stability. This vision was enshrined in a National Common Minimum Programme (NCMP). To send the message that this was not just a list of pious intentions, Singh said in one of his first televised statements that the UPA intended to implement the NCMP "in letter and in spirit." The very first goal of the NCMP, "to preserve, protect and promote social harmony," was echoed by Hu Jintao, perhaps unconsciously, in his landmark speech of February 2005.

The purpose of the twenty-four-page program was:

- To ensure that the economy grows at least seven to eight percent per year in a sustained manner over a decade and beyond, and in a manner that generates employment so that each family is assured of a safe and viable livelihood.
- To enhance the welfare and well-being of farmers, farm labor, and workers, particularly those in the unorganized sector, and to assure a secure future for their families in every respect.
- To fully empower women politically, educationally, economically, and legally.

In concrete terms, these goals were translated into a national employment guarantee scheme that would guarantee one hundred days of manual labor, at the stipulated minimum wage of the state, to one member of every family beneath the poverty line. The government also promised a reduction of interest rates on farm loans, a refinancing of rural cooperative banks to increase their lending capacity, and eight "technology missions" named after the late prime minister Rajiv Gandhi; these would promote horticulture and facilitate agricultural diversification, improve drinking water supply, rural housing, and roads, and increase telephone, power, and Internet connections. To facilitate more investment in agriculture, rural health, and education, the central government increased its planned allocations for these sectors. To meet the cost, it decided to levy a surtax on personal incomes and corporate profits.

With the aid of these levies, Manmohan Singh's government more than trebled the planned allocations for health, education, and rural development—from an average of $8.5 billion a year, under the NDA government headed by Atal Behari Vajpayee, to $30 billion in 2008–'09. In his budget speech on February 28, 2008,

Finance Minister P. Chidambaram summed up his government's achievements in these fields during the first four years of the United Progressive Alliance government as follows:

- Agricultural credit doubled in the first two years and almost doubled again to 2.4 trillion rupees in 2007–'08.
- The National Rural Employment Guarantee Act proved a historic measure for empowerment of the scheduled castes and tribes (the bottom quarter of Indian society) and for women.
- The school midday meal scheme reached 114 million children.
- The National Rural Health Mission strengthened the primary health centers and made 8,756 into twenty-four-hour medical centers.
- A girls' residential schooling scheme started by the government had already enrolled 182,000 girls in residential schools.
- Over one thousand days, another government program, "Bharat Nirman," had constructed 4.113 million rural houses, provided drinking water connections to 290,000 households, provided forty-two thousand villages with electricity and fifty-two thousand villages with a telephone connection, and connected seventeen thousand households to an all-weather road.

These absolute numbers look impressive, so it becomes all the more difficult to explain how India slipped in the United Nations Development Program's human development index from 126th in 2003 to 128th in 2007. One explanation could be the sheer vastness of the problem: India has three-quarters of a million villages, and around 120 million rural households. Even the above achievements only touch its fringes. What is more, while they do represent an increase in the pace at which essential services are being provided, the difference is not sufficiently striking to offset the effect of rising prices, widening income gaps, and the steady appropriation of natural resources—which the poor had access to previously as "free gods of nature"—for developmental purposes.

There could, however, be another explanation: that the vast resources allocated by the central government for rural development have probably not reached the rural poor, and that the achievements cited above are state government concoctions accepted uncritically by the center in its desperation to believe that it has succeeded in mating growth with equity. Had even half of the funds provided by the Planning Commission's Rural Development Division in the previous ten five-year plans actually reached the intended beneficiaries, there would have been shelter, safe drinking water, and hygienic, private sanitation for all of them long ago. But the lion's share of these funds have been regularly trapped by the "impermeable layer" of the intermediate regime in the rural areas and prevented from filtering any further down. Instead, the intermediate regime has used the funds intended for rural development to create a structure of political power in the villages, designed to perpetuate the regime's dominance. In rural India, parliamentary constituencies are roughly coterminous with administrative districts, while the constituencies of state legislatures encompass the village development "blocks"—i.e., groups of one hundred to 150 villages. Over the years the MP (members of Parliament), the MLA (members of the legislative assembly), the chairpersons, members of the Zilla Parishad (the District Development Council), the block development officers (BDOs), and the *pradhans* (heads of the village councils) have all been woven into a single clientelist network that allocates funds preferentially for villages and areas of the constituency that have voted them into power. The contracts, in turn, are given to contractors who are prepared to give hefty kickbacks to these officials, who then use these to meet the expenses of staying in power,

The first person to expose this was Prime Minister Rajiv Gandhi, who declared during his address to the centennial meeting of the Congress Party in Mumbai in 1985 that only 15 percent of the funds allocated for poverty alleviation programs filtered down to the beneficiaries. He based his conclusion on a report he had recently received on poverty eradication programs in Bihar.[388] When the Congress Party returned to power in 2004 as the main constituent of the United Progressive Alliance, it was aware that it had to break through this impermeable layer if it was to reach the people. It tried to do this by inserting a clause in the National Common Minimum Programme that the additional central allocations for education, health, and rural development would be devolved directly to the village councils (*panchayats*). But the Left Front, which was in power in the states of West Bengal and Kerala, would have none of it. The Congress Party was therefore forced to accept defeat, and it adopted a face-saving compromise in which the funds would be channeled to the *panchayats* through the state governments. This one change in terminology sufficed to keep the power of the intermediate regime intact. The state governments also refused to be held accountable to the central Planning Commission for the way they spent the funds. So Chidambaram had to make do with the estimates of work done that they chose to send to the central government departments.

The National Rural Employment Guarantee Act

One program which the government has taken pains to monitor is the National Rural Employment Guarantee Act (NREGA). To get around the state governments, it has employed nongovernmental organizations (NGOs) to submit periodic reports from different parts of the country. But the first monitoring report submitted to the central government in 2006 summed up the shortcomings of the NREGA as follows:

There is a general tendency to keep spending low through a combination of measures that violate the NREG Act in letter and spirit. This is through low coverage of the eligible population in notified districts, unfulfilled entitlements even of the registered population, inadequate administrative capabilities and little effort to overcome deficiencies in manpower, skills and training, impermissible restrictions on eligibility, verification, works, etc.

There are systemic forces at work which result in invisibilising women's work through a focus on productivity-linked earth works and high productivity requirements. The urge to save costs and make additional assets by exploiting existing gender biases that already invisibilise women's work and pay her less/nothing for her labour is the most important underlying factor behind the continued clubbing together of easily divisible tasks and low payment. In a sense, women's labour at public worksites gets treated almost in the same way as women's work in the household. Unfortunately, administrative laziness has exacerbated this situation further whereby difficulty in computing women's work has resulted in not being recognized as independent work.[389]

To make matters worse, a number of NGOs have reported widespread corruption in the administration of the scheme. A study of one hundred villages in six districts of Orissa in May and June 2007, by the Delhi-based Centre for Environment and Food Security, showed that

[a]s per the NREGP [National Rural Employment Guarantee Programme] Implementation Status Report for the Financial Year 2006–7[390] the total number of job cards issued in Orissa was 2,593,194. Orissa was able to provide 79.9 million person-days of employment to 1,394,169 households spread over 19 districts of the state. . . . But, our experience in 100 villages of Orissa suggests that

all these claims are bogus and manufactured only in official records in order to siphon NREGP funds. . . .

[W]e could not find a single case where entries in the job cards are correct and match with the actual number of workdays physically verified with the villagers. Out of the 100 sample villages covered for this survey, 18 villages have not received any job card, 37 villages have not received any job under NREGP even after 16 months of launch of the scheme, 11 villages have received neither job cards nor any job, job cards of 23 villages were lying with VLWs (Village Level Workers) and JEs (Junior Engineers) for more than 6–8 months against the will of card holders.

In 25 villages, only half, one third or partial wage payments were made. In 20 villages, we found scandalous difference in the number of workdays recorded in the job cards and the number of actual workdays given to the workers. There are 3 villages where no wage payments have been made even after 4–8 months of the works done. We found 6 villages in Kashipur block of Rayagada district where NREGP work was being done without any job cards being issued to the villagers. . . .

Our back of the envelop calculations suggest that less than 2 crore person-days of employment has been provided on the ground and more than 6 crore person-days of employment has been provided only in the pages of false job cards and fabricated muster rolls. We could not find a single family in the 100 sample villages who had actually got 100 days of wage employment. We found very few families who had got 40–60 days of wage employment.[391]

Orissa is by no means unique. There is a general consensus, based on successive monitoring reports, that a sizable portion of NREGP funding is being siphoned off by corrupt officials. In spite of that, by March 2008 the NREGP had been extended to the entire country and was expected to cost 160 billion rupees ($4 billion) a year.

The inherent conservatism of India's "inclusive growth"

It is far too early to judge how the programs and "missions" will improve people's lives. But even if they do, their ability to contain, let alone reduce, social discontent, is questionable. For all these measures are essentially redistributive and therefore paternalistic: It is the government that will find the money for them by taxing the better-off, and the government that will dole it out. They will therefore accentuate the dependency of the people. Not a single one of the measures implemented so far has had the objective of empowering the poor so that they can look after themselves. In sum, none of them is intended to alter the balance of power between the rich and poor.

The UPA government's drive to promote "inclusive growth" is a mirror image of President Hu Jintao's drive to create a "socially harmonious society." Just as the Hu Jintao regime angrily dismissed proposals made before the Seventeenth National Congress to create an independent judiciary, the Manmohan Singh government has shied away from each and every measure that could empower the poor and thereby reduce the rich-poor gap. Both of these governments are quintessentially conservative, for they share an aversion to any reforms that will dilute the power of the newly empowered bourgeoisie and enhance that of the emerging proletariat.

The profoundly conservative bias in the Manmohan Singh government was reflected not in what it did but in what it carefully refrained from doing. The first was its halfhearted, token implementation of its promise in the NCMP to "assure a secure future" for workers in the unorganized sector and their families. The second was its refusal to even consider legislation that would end the impoverishment of the rural and tribal poor through their alienation from the land.

Aversion to social insurance

The NCMP's promise arose out of the UPA coalition's awareness that there had been a profound change in the nature of employment in the country in the nineties, a change that was gaining momentum in the first decade of the twenty-first century. The growth of employment, which had declined sharply from 2.04 percent between 1983 and 1994 to 0.98 percent between 1994 and 2000, had accelerated sharply with the end of the recession to 2.6 percent a year between 1999 and 2005. This was much faster than the rate of population growth, but it masked a profound change in the type of employment that was being generated and a decline in its quality and security. The main change was that the agricultural labor force had stopped growing. Between 1983 and 1994, the agricultural workforce had grown by 1.51 percent a year. But between 1994 and 2000, it had actually declined by 0.34 percent every year. By 2000, there were five million fewer agricultural workers than there had been in 1994. An examination of the workforce by age group revealed that the main cause was that families had taken children between five and fourteen out of the workforce and sent them to school. What is more, most of these families were bypassing the moribund state schools and sending their children to private schools where they could learn English, paying fifty to 150 rupees a month. Between 1999 and 2005, as the long spurt in productivity caused by the Green Revolution ended, the workforce in agriculture had begun to grow again, but at less than 1 percent a year. The reason was obvious: Farm families wanted their children to do nonagricultural work.

Not surprisingly, therefore, nearly all the growth of employment during this eleven-year period, between 1994 and 2005, had taken place in industry and the services. Between 1999 and 2005, this employment grew by 4.7 percent a year. Anecdotal evidence suggests that this growth had been accompanied by a substantial rise in the real incomes of unorganized sector workers in several occupations, a growth that has gone unnoticed because it is not easy to record.[392] But there is also some evidence that as industry and service workers' numbers increase they are having to compete for the available work, and therefore face an increase in uncertainty. This is reflected in an increase in the proportion of the Indian workforce classified as "casual workers"—i.e., workers who float in and out of unemployment—from 29.6 percent in 1987–'88 to 33.2 percent in 1999–2000. This competition is likely to remain muted during periods of high growth, such as the one India experienced between 1992 and 1997, and again between 2003 and 2008. But it will sharpen dramatically when growth slows down, whether for structural or cyclical reasons. When that happens, these workers will be completely at the mercy of market forces—victims of Polanyi's stark utopia—for they enjoy no social security benefits whatever: no health, disability, or medical insurance, no maternity benefits, and no old age pensions.[393]

In 2004 the central government set up a national commission, headed by economist-turned-bureaucrat Arjun Sengupta, to examine the problems of the unorganized sector and suggest, among other things, how to provide unorganized sector workers with social insurance. The commission took two years to submit its recommendations, and these turned out to be woefully inadequate. Its life, accident, and disability insurance proposals were minimal (although still a big step up from the total insecurity in which the working poor lived); its recommendations for maternity benefits and an old age pension, for workers beyond the age of sixty, were an exercise in tokenism. Pregnant women were to receive one thousand rupees ($25) as a onetime maternity benefit per child. Workers would receive two hundred rupees a month ($5.00) as an old age pension. Neither of these sums bore any relationship to actual needs. The thousand-rupee proposal was based on the assumption that all the pregnant women would be able to have their children in primary health centers or district hospitals, free of cost, and would face no complications. It blithely ignored the fact that a large proportion of the former were nonfunctional, with absent doctors and nurses, and medicines present only in their account books. It also ignored the need for a supplementary source of income during pregnancy. The need arises are to be found from the fact that 92 percent of India's working women in the unorganized sector doing, for the most part, backbreaking labor in the fields or on construction sites. The minimum that they earn is sixty rupees ($1.25) per day, or 1,800 rupees in a full month. When they became pregnant they had to choose between quitting work for some months and losing this income at just the time when their bodies needed added nutrition, or continuing to work for as long as they could, leaving their bodies and babies to fight for the nutrition they could provide.[394]

The minimum benefit that women working in the unorganized sector needed was sufficient money to hire a midwife and buy the increasingly expensive medicines that they would need, even in a primary health center, and a replacement of the income they lost by staying home, for three months before and three after the birth of their child. In the same way, the minimum old age pension that workers and their spouses needed in 2005, if they were to meet just their need for food and a minimum of clothing and not become a burden on their children, was five hundred rupees a month in the rural areas and up to 1,500 rupees in the towns.

The Sengupta committee turned a blind eye to these needs. But it made up for these shortcomings in large part by proposing one radical departure from the conservative paternalism of the Indian state: It proposed that only workers who paid a contribution of a rupee a day—i.e., 365 rupees ($9) per year—would be eligible for the social security benefits (equal amounts were to be paid by the employers and the government). This put the commission squarely on the side of empowerment. The uniform experience of more than three score of social insurance schemes, designed for workers in different unorganized industries, had shown that workers who made no contribution to the scheme often did not even know of its existence, let alone believe that they were entitled to some benefits under it. As a result, even the inadequate sums that came into them from employers and state governments remained very largely unutilized.[395] The commission had recognized this vitally important flaw in earlier schemes.

A close examination of the Sengupta commission's report also revealed why it had proposed such paltry benefits. In a superabundance of caution it had used the "secured fund" method of determining old age pensions and maternity benefits, in which the insured accumulates all the funds out of which he or she will draw insurance him- or herself. This was based on the Employees' Provident Fund Scheme for government servants that had been framed by the British, both for the UK and for India. Had the commission adopted the "unsecured fund" approach that is used by life and general insurance companies, in which insurers balance the annual premium receipts against annual claim disbursements and raise the insurance premiums if the disbursements begin to exceed a stipulated proportion of the premium receipts, the same pension fund would have comfortably provided the minimum needed social security defined above.

But the government summarily rejected even the ultra-cautious recommendations of the Sengupta commission. In the budget for 2008–'09 the finance minister, P. Chidambaram, announced a token two-hundred-rupee-a-month old age pension and a minimal health insurance scheme, but limited eligibility to families below the poverty line. The Planning Commission turned its face resolutely against making the pension fund an unsecured fund, citing the funding difficulties faced by Germany and the US, which had adopted the unsecured, "pay as you go" principle of funding, and choosing to ignore the fact that these had arisen in Germany only 120 years after Bismarck introduced social security in 1870.[396] Most significant of all, the government rejected the proposal to make the beneficiaries pay a contribution to the fund and chose to fund it entirely out of tax revenues. It therefore remained firmly on the side of redistribution.

Classical immiseration–the alienation of land

The government's lack of interest in providing social security to the workforce only denies workers what they do not have. But its takeover of land for special economic zones, infrastructures, and mines takes away from them what they still have. While the former allows insecurity to grow, the latter creates insecurity, and with it a growing rage against the state itself. The way in which the alienation of farmers from their land by state governments intent upon promoting industrialization became a national issue has already been described. What had angered the public was that for almost the first time in India's post-independence history, the state was acquiring land not for a public purpose, such as a road or a power station from which all would benefit, but in order to hand it over to private interests who would make money from its use. There could not have been a more blatant intervention by the state on behalf of the bourgeoisie, for not only did it take away the right of the landowners to decide whether or not they wanted to sell it, and to determine its price, but it also cut them off from all the profits that would accrue in the future from the land's use. A government that proclaimed its commitment to the poor at every opportunity should have been aware of the way in which the poor would view its actions, but for eight months after it passed the Special Economic

Zones Act the central government remained blissfully unaware of the political consequences of its decision, not to mention its impact on the lives of the affected persons. It took a year of protests by farmers at Singur and Nandigram in West Bengal, and a wave of public anger, sparked by police violence that killed more than a dozen protesters in Nandigram, for Prime Minister Manmohan Singh to announce, in December 2006, that his government would bring out new guidelines for the approval of SEZs within 90 days. But when these were announced they turned out to be minimal and disappointing; most significantly of all, they hewed to the conservative principle of "letting the market decide." They took the state governments out of the land acquisition process altogether and made real estate developers deal directly with the landowners. They restored the power of the farmers to refuse to sell and, if they agreed, to determine the price of their land. But they did nothing to ensure that the farmers received a part of the profits that would accrue to the ultimate users of the land, as dividends or a royalty. The guidelines continued to evade the issue of empowerment, for they did nothing to entitle those who had surrendered their land to a share of its future yields under its new use. They therefore failed to make those who lost their land stakeholders in the industrialization of the country.

The revised guidelines also carefully omitted the acquisition of land by the state for public purposes, such as the building of highways and hydroelectric and thermal power plants. And in a not-so-inadvertent omission, they left out the acquisition of land for establishing coal, iron ore, bauxite, and other mines. This had been treated as a public purpose in the past because since 1956 the development of all of these industries had fallen exclusively within the purview of the public sector. In 2007 the government conveniently forgot that the private sector had been allowed back into all of them. The new guidelines therefore amounted to cosmetic surgery and no more.

Maoism—the rebirth of class struggle

For "public purposes" land continues to be acquired under an act, passed by the British colonial government in 1894, that allowed the provinces (now state governments) to take over even privately owned land at throwaway prices. After independence, as more and more farmers began to fight the acquisition of their land in the courts, a succession of judgments drove up the acquisition price, to market and even above market levels, but the benefits were limited to those who had a clear title to the land that was being acquired. This left out huge tracts of land over which the poor—mainly *adivasis* (tribal people)—had enjoyed traditional usage rights. After six decades of steady immiseration, as forests have been felled and land taken over to sink mines and build roads, dams, and power stations, these people have taken to armed struggle to defend what is left.

The country got a wakeup call in November 2005, when five hundred armed "Naxalites" descended upon the town of Jehanabad in Bihar, drove away the local police, broke into their armory, seized their weapons, freed more than a hundred of their compatriots from the jail, and left the town without having hurt a single civilian.

The Naxalite movement had begun in West Bengal in the late sixties, but had been infiltrated by the Bengal police and crushed. Its leaders had taken refuge in the jungles of the adjoining states, Orissa, South Bihar (now Jharkhand), Andhra Pradesh, and eastern Madhya Pradesh (now Chhattisgarh). For the next three decades it had remained a fringe movement, present in about a quarter of the districts of the country, but making little dent on the lives of people outside a few pockets of influence.

All this changed on September 21, 2004, when twenty-six scattered Naxalite groups came together to form the Communist Party of India (Maoist). This time, behind the tired exhortations to wage "class struggle" and "revolution," they had a definite agenda. It was to stop the alienation of land from the tribals, the *harijans* (untouchables), and the marginal farmers—the poorest of the poor—in the name of development. The Maoists made it clear that what the government, the media, and the intelligentsia called "development" was expropriation. Instead of making the poor its beneficiaries, it made them its victims.

For the first time in decades the Maoists began to draw mass support from the jungle dwellers and the rural landless poor. Jehanabad was only a beginning. Since then groups of armed Maoists have hijacked trains and buses, and fought pitched battles with large contingents of police in Jharkhand, Chhattisgarh, Bihar, and Orissa.

The movement grew so rapidly that barely two years after Jehanabad, Prime Minister Manmohan Singh described it as the most serious threat that India faced. But all that the state governments asked for was more modern weapons, money to reinforce and fortify police stations and to train the armed constabulary, and the dispatch of the central government's paramilitary forces to help them fight the "terrorists."

But repressive policies are not achieving much success. In an encounter in the state of Chhattisgarh in June 2007, an informer offered to lead a police party to a large Naxalite encampment, but led it into an ambush instead in which twenty-five policemen lost their lives. The arms that the Maoists seized from the slain policemen showed that behind the facade of "police action," the state government has declared virtual war upon the Maoists. For these were frontline weapons so far provided only to the Indian army and paramilitary forces operating in insurgency-affected areas like Kashmir—AK-47s, and the new ultra-light and accurate INSAS infantry rifles. The encounter also showed that the Maoists had the upper hand.

In another concerted set of attacks in Orissa, in March 2008, Maoists seized 1,600 rifles and machine guns and tens of thousands of rounds of ammunition. By then they were so well-stocked that they took away only the automatic weapons, leaving behind two-thirds of the rifles after destroying them.

The Maoists also have no dearth of funds. Gadchiroli, a single district of Maharashtra, contributed $3.5 million to the war chest in 2006.[397] One of the few successes of the police, in 2008, yielded information that the government would have much preferred not to believe. This occurred in January 2008, when the Jharkhand police captured a senior Maoist leader. Papers seized from him showed that the Maoists were collecting $15 million *a month* in exactions from the public and had not only forged links with the Maoists in Nepal and the Tamil Tigers in Sri Lanka, but had been exploring ties with Al-Qaeda–linked groups in Pakistan.

The Maoists have gained a following because the poor are becoming convinced that they can obtain no redress from the democratic system. After fourteen general elections and an equal number of state elections, they know that their elected representatives have only to reach the state capital to put up their "for sale" signs. But this is a revolt born out of despair. The pamphlets of the People's War Group (PWG); the Maoist Communist Centre of India; and their amalgam, the Communist Party of India (Maoist) are striking for their complete absence of hope. When one has hope, one dreams. And the dreams get converted into manifestoes. But although Maoist leaders advocate "protracted armed struggle" and "annihilation of class enemies" and urge the use of extreme violence to secure "organizational goals," these goals have remained undefined. Beyond "the seizure of power" there is no vision of the future and no answer to the most pressing questions that any political movement must face: What will the power they acquire be used for? What kind of society will they create? How will they set about doing so? On these issues, the pamphlets say not a word.

Their leaders know that they cannot hope to capture the Indian state, and that the most they can do is create temporary safe havens in pockets of the country in which to survive. They also know that the only way to finance their parallel government in these transient mini-states is to extort money from local shopkeepers and petty landowners under the threat of death—in short, to become another instrument of oppression of the poor. That is what the PWG and the newly formed CPI (Maoist) have been doing. But they draw their strength from the all-pervasive hopelessness of the tribal poor and the rage that it constantly feeds.

The sources of this rage are revealed by the Maoists' areas of strength. In 2006 the Ministry of Home Affairs conceded that "Naxalism" had gained a foothold in 156 districts in thirteen states spread over roughly a quarter of the country. Their presence was notional in several states, like Punjab, Haryana, Rajasthan, and Himachal. However, in a contiguous core area stretching across almost 1,500 kilometers in the center of the country, comprising districts in Maharashtra, Andhra Pradesh, Madhya Pradesh, Chhattisgarh, Jharkhand, Bihar, Orissa, and adjoining West Bengal, the Maoists increasingly rule the countryside, at night if not in the day.

This area shares several characteristics: Its people are not merely poor, but have also been neglected by their governments for decades. It is relatively rich in both mineral and forest resources. Its agriculture is for the most part rainfed and precarious. A disproportionately high share of the population is tribal. The most relevant issue in this region, though, is not poverty; it is not even political disempowerment. It is the victimization of an identifiable segment of Indian society by the forces of capitalist development.

Orissa, for instance, accounts for around 30 percent of India's iron ore deposits. The ore is high-grade hematite, with a minimum of 58 percent iron content. Orissa's proven recoverable reserves amount to about 1.5 billion tons, with another 1.5 billion tons probably recoverable. Virtually all of the ore is to be found in areas inhabited by Orissa's tribal population. In 2003 and 2004 alone, the Orissa government received around forty offers from Indian and foreign parties to establish new steel plants in the state, with a total proposed capacity of over forty-four million tons a year.[398]

Tribals have also been the main, although not only, victims of the various hydroelectric schemes that the central and state governments have launched. Every one of the villages in Maharashtra and Gujarat and fifty-three of the villages in Madhya Pradesh that are being submerged by the Narmada hydroelectric project are tribal villages.[399] Some idea of the trouble that lies in store for the government may be had from the fact that in 2005, the UPA government had identified no fewer than 399 sites for future hydroelectric projects. Seventy-eight of these were in the northeastern region, which has been in the grip of several localized insurgencies for half a century.

Not surprisingly, there has been a steady rise in the level of violence in the Naxalist-affected states; in 2007, violent incidents in these states claimed the lives of twice as many policemen and paramilitary personnel—214 compared to 133—as in the whole of 2006.[400] Chhattisgarh and Jharkhand, the two most thickly forested states, with the highest proportion of tribal to total population, have emerged as the centers of the Maoist insurgency. In 2007 they accounted for 68 percent of the incidents (almost a thousand), and three-quarters of the casualties among India's security forces.[401]

Bastar district in Chhattisgarh, an area that had become synonymous with the exploitation of tribal peoples by traders and land grabbers as far back as the 1970s, has emerged as the most important training ground for CPI (Maoist) cadres from across the country. In 2007 the People's Liberation Guerrilla Army (PLGA), the military wing of the CPI (Maoist), was running four camps in the forests of the region, where cadres from several states were being trained in carrying out attacks and planting explosives. The Chhattisgarh police estimated that 1,500–2,000 cadres were present in these camps at any given time. Intelligence reports and seized documents suggested that apart from locally recruited cadres, Maoist extremists from other states, including Maharashtra, Jharkhand, Andhra Pradesh, Bihar, and West Bengal, were also being trained. Apart from eight to ten thousand armed PLGA and *jan* (people's) militia in the region, there were also twenty-five to thirty-five thousand Maoist sympathizers or *Sangham* members. According to the police chief, Bastar was ideal for such camps, as the cadres could be given "'on the job training' through real attacks on security forces, planting of explosives, and blowing up of government buildings and infrastructure."[402]

Despite the growing seriousness of the Maoist threat, the Indian corporate sector, and virtually the entire political leadership of the country, continues to play ostrich to it. Some weeks after Manmohan Singh warned a conference of state home ministers and police chiefs that the Maoist threat was the most serious that India faced, Shivraj Patil—the home minister in Singh's own cabinet, hailing from Singh's own party—declared in a television interview that this was the personal opinion of the prime minister and one that he did not share.[403] At most, a dozen of the Naxalist-affected states' 1,385 incidents in the first eleven months of 2007 made the national press. The reporting on Maoism has consisted almost entirely of reproductions of press releases from the police and home ministries of the concerned states. There has been little, if any, independent investigation of Maoism by journalists, and less than

a handful of interviews of its leaders. There has been little analysis of the causes of its resurgence, and the goal of its leaders and
followers.

Apart from linking up with other insurgent groups, in 2007 the
Maoists began to expand their base of recruitment by championing
the cause of landholders who were losing their land to industry.
Reports by the Bengal state police repeatedly referred to the presence of Maoists among the protesters at Singur and Nandigram.
This could have been a police attempt to explain the scale of violence, and to exonerate themselves for their role in provoking it,
but it would be unwise to assume that the claim is entirely specious.
Maoism, and the struggle over land that has inspired its resurgence,
is a time bomb waiting to go off.

Conclusion

15   RUNNING OUT OF TIME

THE PRECEDING DESCRIPTION of China and India's transition from autarchic to market economies reveals similarities in their trajectories of growth, experiences that have hitherto remained unnoticed.

- Contrary to the universal belief that India decided to dismantle its command economy thirteen years after China, in 1991, the first decisive retreat from the command economy was made by Indira Gandhi's government in 1980, a little more than a year after China began the reform of its agriculture and set up its first four special economic zones.
- Neither country took this momentous first step without a great deal of hesitation. In China, it led to more than a decade of *fang* (letting go) and *shou* (tightening up) policies as the Communist Party under Deng Xiaoping experimented gingerly with additional doses of reform and then drew hastily back to minimize their social backlash. India was forced onto the reform path by domestic inflation and an externally triggered foreign exchange crisis in 1980–81, but this, and a previous foreign exchange rate-cum-inflationary crisis in 1972–73, only gave birth to "reforms by stealth," in which successive governments surreptitiously widened

the area of operation of the free market, while maintaining an elaborate pretense of continuity with previous policies.

- Both countries only abandoned their attempt to reconcile the future with the past, and opted wholeheartedly for market-directed growth, in the early nineties. Deng Xiaoping signaled this with his summer tour of the South in 1992; Narasimha Rao did it in India a year earlier, after elections brought his party, the Indian National Congress, back to power.

- Both countries eschewed shock therapy and opted for gradual reform. This yielded immediate results and gave them a five-year spell of rapid growth, from 1991 to 1996 in China and from 1992 to 1997 in India.

- Both countries experienced recessions from 1997 to 2002.

- Both countries went into another spell of hectic growth after 2002.

- Both countries experienced a slackening of growth in 2007, and this sharpened into a cyclical economic downturn in 2008. Both countries blamed this upon the global financial crisis and the recession in the industrialized countries, but there is abundant evidence that growth in virtually every producer goods sector, from machinery to intermediate goods to real estate, had begun to decline well before the crisis began.

These similarities extend into the political sphere as well:

- In both countries, the attempt to force the pace of industrialization and economic development has led to the development of highly predatory systems of government.

- In their attempts to cushion the impact of rapid industrialization upon the sections of the poor whom it has hurt, both have relied almost entirely on the redistribution route to social justice and tried to use government revenues to provide a safety net for the poor.

Neither country has so far come even close to trying the alternative route, which is to make the poor stakeholders in development so that they acquire the power, or the legal right, to share automatically in the fruits of development. In Europe, Japan, and the US, this was the route that eventually created both democracy and the welfare state. But so far, both the Chinese and the post-1991 Indian governments have relied only on economic redistribution and are still only tinkering with the creation of entitlements, such as pensions and social insurance, for the poor.[404]

Where experience of the two countries has diverged sharply is in the way this conflict has affected economic and social change. The "creative destruction" of the past has been far more rapid in China than in India. The authoritarian nature of the Chinese state ensured that the struggle between the state and the local cadres would remain mainly economic. It therefore led to a race to monopolize investment. The democratic nature of the Indian state ensured that the struggle immediately became political. The goal of the two strata of capitalists, large industry and the small businesses, became to capture political power to enact policies that furthered their interests. India's slow growth was the outcome of the initial victory of the intermediate class. The acceleration of its growth to Chinese levels after 2003 was the outcome of the demise of the intermediate regime and the capture of political power at the center by "large" Indian capital.

A work in progress

But precisely because a capitalist transformation is never limited to economics alone, the transformation is far from complete. For neither country has completed its other half. This is the building of political institutions that will reconcile the interests of the winners and losers from development on an ongoing basis. China has not taken even the first steps in this direction. Proposals to make the judiciary independent of the Communist Party have been sternly discouraged. Although elections to village councils have been open to non-party members for some time, in practice this provision has been ineffective because candidates have first to be approved by the local party committees. This has allowed them to perpetuate their stranglehold on power in a variety of ways. One common method is to approve the nominations of only as many candidates as there are seats to be filled.[405] As was demonstrated by the runaway expansion of investment by the provincial administration between 2002 and 2008, local party committees have also, to a considerable extent, frustrated Beijing's attempts to free bank managers and officials of the Ministry of Public Security from the control of the local party secretary and make them answerable only to the next higher level of command in their own service. Thus, seen from the viewpoint of the people, the power of the party cadres remains more or less absolute, for they remain vested with not only legislative, executive, and judicial power but also economic power. It is the resulting feeling of helplessness that is spilling over into a rising tide of discontent. President Hu Jintao's drive to build a socially harmonious society has gained China only a temporary respite. While officially the number of incidents of mass protest has come down in 2006, it is difficult to tell to what extent this reduction is genuine and to what extent it is the result of a greater determination on the part of local authorities to settle matters, by no matter what means, at their level and therefore avoid having to report a failure to curb social discontent. Even the 59,392 cases of mass protest in 2006 compiled by the National Bureau of Statistics show that the level of discontent remains high.[406]

India, by contrast, looks far better placed, for it already has a strong democratic system and therefore has the institutions that it needs to manage social conflict. These can no longer be used to restrict competition and slow down growth because it has already broken the back of the resistance posed by the intermediate regime to economic development. India is therefore all set to achieve very rapid growth within the framework of democracy. But this advantage is in danger of being lost because of the central government's sudden loss of capacity, following the end of the dominance of the Congress Party in 1989, to engineer social change and manage conflict. The asymmetries here are no less striking than the symmetries in the two countries' economic development:

- China's leaders are fully aware of dangers that their country is facing. What they are looking for are ways to contain the rising social discontent without making any drastic change in the existing political system. The same cannot be said of India. With only a handful of exceptions, its entire political leadership is blissfully unaware of the dangers that lie ahead. India's release from the crippling constraints of the intermediate regime is still too recent for it to do anything but savor it and revel in its "Chinese" growth rate. India is therefore extremely reluctant to acknowledge that the sharp rise in social protest in the country since the dawn of the new century could be a product of this same accelerated growth.

- As the dismissal and imprisonment of Chen Liangyu, the powerful party secretary of Shanghai, showed, China's central government in Beijing retains the power, in the final analysis, to force recalcitrant provincial and municipal governments in line with its wishes. But India's central government has lost most of its capacity to discipline the state governments in any significant way. Although the Indian Constitution allows the center to dismiss a state government whose functioning has been severely impaired, the rampant misuse of this provision by a succession of governments between 1966 and 1991 led to a powerful backlash that culminated in a landmark judgment of the Supreme Court of India in 1994, which curtailed the power of the center to end a state president's rule by detailing almost a dozen circumstances in which the declaration of would not be justified, and making any future use of this clause of the constitution subject to a judicial review.[407]

• Although local party bosses in China frequently behave like warlords of an earlier time, Beijing retains the power to hold them accountable for their actions. In India, by contrast, the constitution virtually guarantees civil servants immunity from prosecution without the explicit permission of the president of India or the governor of the concerned state, except in cases of criminal misconduct.[408] One consequence of this has been to make it impossible for even bureaucrats' seniors to take action against bureaucrats for not carrying out their duties. A virtual carte blanche has been conferred upon officials to indulge in corruption and extortion. As a result, whereas Chinese government agencies investigated 731,000 allegations of corruption and penalized 669,000 offenders between January 1993 and June 1997—an average of almost 200,000 a year—India's Central Vigilance Commission investigated a total of 22,517 allegations between 1997 and 2000, a similar length of time. In 2006, out of 4,683 investigations, 2,442 led to some form of punishment. Only 150 offenders were actually prosecuted. The figures speak for themselves.[409]

China—first steps toward political reform

Although President Hu Jintao avoided, indeed discouraged, proposals for political reform during his first four years in office, by 2007 he and Prime Minister Wen Jiabao were convinced that redistributive reforms would only buy them time. However, they preferred to wait till the Seventeenth Party Congress in 2007 was over, and to obtain informal feedback from the delegates, before proceeding down this thorny path. The first signs of what could be an epic change came in a statement by Hu Jintao at the Seventeenth Party Congress: "We will spread the practice in which candidates for leading positions in primary party organizations are recommended both by party members and the public in an open manner and by the party organization at the next higher level, gradually extend direct election of leading members in primary party organizations to more places, and explore various ways to expand inner-party democracy at the primary level."[410] However, within weeks of the end of the Party Congress, the Central Committee's Party School published a book titled *The Fifteen-Year Assault: A Research Report on China's Political Reform, 2006–2020,* which discussed and, in several of its chapters, outlined a program for political reform extending over the next fifteen years,[411] showing that preparations for the shift had been underway for some time.

The book begins with a candid admission that, beginning in the 1990s, as market reforms have deepened, "the interests of individuals and government departments have become increasingly integrated, with the result that corruption has followed, economic policies are distorted, and the people—particularly the poor—are increasingly unhappy." It calls for a cautious and controlled process of reform to usher in the rule of law, a greater role for NGOs, an acceptance of the role of religion in society, and a greater role for the people's congresses at various levels.

It devotes an entire chapter to discussing the meaning of the "rule of law." Its author, Wang Changjiang, reinterprets it to mean that the cadres should be accountable not only to their seniors within the Communist Party, but also to the people. Noting that state power belongs to the people (according to the PRC Constitution), Wang argues that the party has got around this by resorting to a variety of stratagems that have evoked cynicism among the people and discredited the party. The most commonly used stratagem is to present to the people for election at any level exactly the number of candidates (all, of course, drawn from the party) as the number of seats to be filled. This, he points out, has made the people ridicule the election process and wonder why the party is unable to generate more talent. Accountability to the people can be introduced, he concludes, by putting up more than one candidate per seat.[412]

The reform that Wang proposes is minimal and reflects how wary the political leadership is of any move that will dilute Communist Party control over the functions of the state. Wang builds his case for reform by citing the experience of Pingchang—a remote county, in a mountainous, rural part of Szechuan province, that introduced direct elections. In 2001 a quarter of Pingchang's 970,000 people were below the poverty line of 930 yuan a year (thirty cents a day). The pressure of demand for jobs had led to the creation of a bloated bureaucracy that, in 2001, employed 4,760 persons against an authorized strength of 1,093. These people were employed through the expedient of multiplying the number of municipal and township offices. Since each of these duplicated the departmental structure of the county office, and since each of the offices spent lavishly on entertainment and perks, administrative costs ballooned. By 2001 the sixty-one towns and townships had accumulated a debt of 5.5 billion yuan. When the state began to eliminate agricultural taxes and unauthorized fees after 2002, the combined revenues of the townships fell from 1.4 billion yuan to 30 million yuan.

Pingchang county was therefore broke. But the party committee decided that it could not embark upon the drastic pruning of the administration that was needed without the support of the people. It therefore went ahead on its own with an experiment, in a single township, in electing officials through direct elections, out of panels of candidates recommended by the party. The experiment proved a success, and direct elections were extended to the entire county by the end of 2004. By 2006 Pingchang had reduced the number of government employees by 40 percent and drastically reduced the number of offices. It also cut entertainment expenses by 3 to 4 million yuan a year. As a result, the individual tax burden on the people fell from 162.8 yuan to 24.3 yuan.

The Pingchang case study was intended to demonstrate how the greater legitimacy that a modicum of democracy gave to county and township councils would make it easier for them to make difficult decisions. But it also inadvertently revealed how difficult it would be to implement similar administrative reforms across the entire country. For much of the debt that the county had accumulated consisted of money borrowed from its own residents. Many of these lenders had accumulated the money through graft and embezzlement and were lending it back to the county at high rates of interest in what was essentially an elaborate money-laundering system of which the county officials were an integral part.

The state of Pingchang's finances in 2001 is typical of the majority of counties in the country. Breaking this network down on a nationwide scale is therefore likely to prove extremely difficult. But Pingchang's success also shows that letting the people choose their representatives may be the only way to break the entrenched rings of crime and corruption that have developed in China's local government.[413]

India–shoring up the crumbling center

India already has a sophisticated democratic system in place. Over the sixty years of its independence, it has developed an extraordinary array of institutions, in its Planning Commission, its five-year Finance Commissions, its autonomous districts and development councils, and its democratically elected *panchayats* (village councils), which regularly harmonize interstate and intrastate relations.[414] While several of these institutions, like the National Development Council (NDC) and the Inter-State Council, were not needed so long as the Congress Party ruled both the center and all the state governments (from 1947 to 1967), they gained in importance as the Congress Party lost control of more and more state assemblies to its political rivals in the seventies and eighties.

In the post-reform period, as dominant party democracy has given way to coalition rule at the center and a wide dispersion of political power between national, regional, and single-state parties, the federal government has used these institutions to build consensus on policies and thereby compensate for the erosion of their power to make and implement national policy. These include not only the NDC and the Inter-State Council but also a host of ad hoc center-state consultative conferences such as the annual governors' meetings and periodic meetings of the state home ministers, power ministers, and police chiefs. The process has been excruciatingly slow but has achieved some important successes, notably the passage of an Electricity Act in 2001 that ended the absolute monopoly of the state governments over power distribution and opened the way for the private sector to step in and the acceptance by the state governments of a number of important financial reforms, including the introduction of the value-added tax, in 2007.

But as the discussion of India's ubiquitous subsidies in the previous chapter showed, what India has not yet found is a way to restore the central government's capacity to frame and implement national policies that involve making immediate sacrifices for long-term gain. As in the case of China, it is far easier to outline the political reforms that will do this than to discern how they can be enacted. The center could regain its preeminence if a national party emerged once again that was capable of winning an absolute majority of seats in the Parliament. But since it is most unlikely that one party will ever dominate national politics again, the only alternative is to make constitutional changes that will give coalition governments at the center the stability and cohesion that will enable them to implement policies that require sacrifices in the short term for long-term political or economic gain, once more.

In theory at least, two constitutional reforms could restore much of the power that the center had once enjoyed—without running the risk of its abuse. These are the reunification of central and state elections and the state's creation of a system for the funding of elections and associated political activities of recognized political parties.[415]

Reuniting central and state elections would give coalition governments in New Delhi a five-year respite from having one or more of their members facing tests of popularity every year in one state or another. This would reduce the capacity of smaller parties within the coalition to dictate terms to the entire coalition. Simultaneous state assembly and parliamentary elections would also halve the need for funds to fight them and to run the party machine in the intervening years. This would reduce the dependence of political parties on special interests and enhance their capacity to make decisions based on the public interest.

The establishment of a state fund to meet the election expenses of recognized political parties will further reduce this dependence. Taken together, these reforms would restore much of the capacity to mediate economic and social conflict in the country that the center has lost. But both reforms require the lawmakers to reform themselves. As of now, there is little evidence of any desire among them to do so.

Running out of time

Both China and India are running out of time. If *The Fifteen-Year Assault* is any indicator, the Chinese government believes that it has this much time and more in which to enact sufficient democratic reform to allow communities to establish and maintain their own social equilibrium. But even in 2007, when the economy was booming and another economic downturn was only a theoretical certainty, this time period had seemed too long. By repealing agricultural taxation and most local fees, introducing a minimal rural health insurance system, and increasing the compensation paid to peasants for the loss of their land, the government had only stemmed the rise of social conflict for some time. It had been able to do this without bankrupting the local administrations because the prolonged boom from 2002 had increased provincial revenues threefold between 2000 and 2006. But given the uncoordinated nature of investment in China and the consequent inevitability of overinvestment, another sharp downturn of the kind China experienced after 1995 was unavoidable. This was likely to set off, once again, the chain reaction that China had experienced after 1995: a slowdown in the growth of tax and non-tax revenues; a decline in the capacity of provincial governments to replace the funds that the township administrations had lost through the abolition of agricultural taxes and fees; and a consequent, desperate effort by the poorer township and village administrations to make good the deficit by imposing a variety of clandestine fees and fines to which the central and higher levels of provincial government would have no option but to turn a blind eye. This chain reaction would, in any case, have ended by transferring most of the social burden of reduced incomes and increased insecurity onto the shoulders of the poorest elements in society, but the global recession has made it a good deal worse.

THE GLOBAL DOWNTURN arrived in 2008, but the Chinese economy had begun to slow down well before its onset. As described earlier, substantial excess capacity had appeared in the economy as early as the end of 2004. By the end of 2006 the automobile industry was producing far more than it could sell. In 2008 the real estate industry found itself facing a sharp fall in demand for housing and office space. Steel producers cut back drastically on their orders for inputs. In October 2008, ninety million tons of iron ore—enough to meet the raw material needs of the steel industry for two months—had piled up in China's ports because steel plants was being forced to cut production. There had been a similar sharp fall in the demand for copper, nickel, and a number of other metals. Steel producers were also trying to renegotiate the prices of raw materials with their suppliers.[416] Indian iron ore producers who were exporting a third of their ninety million tons of annual output to China found virtually no orders for 2009 and a demand to lower their prices substantially for the already contracted supplies in 2008. The collapse of demand for steel had forced one brand-new giant steel plant, built at a cost of twenty-eight billion yuan, to stop production altogether.[417] The decline in the capital goods industries had already set in well before the global financial crisis.

The global recession greatly increased the severity of the economic downturn in China.

Sixty-seven thousand factories were shut down in the first half of 2008. The total for the year was expected, in October 2008, to exceed one hundred thousand.[418] More than ten thousand of the firms closed in the first half of the year were textile companies.[419] China's status as the preeminent center of outsourced manufacture in the world made it especially vulnerable to the global slowdown. Chen Cheng-jen, chairman of the Federation of Hong Kong Industries, made the gloomy estimate that by January a quarter of small and medium-size Hong Kong–invested companies in the Pearl River Delta would have closed down. This would throw 2.5 million workers out of work.[420]

By March 2009 his gloomy prediction had been fully vindicated. A survey carried out in that month by the National Bureau of Statistics showed that of the seventy million migrant workers who had returned to their villages for the Chinese new year, 14 million had lost their jobs before going home and not returned. Only about one in five of those who did not return to the cities had found jobs in their villages and townships, but at a considerably lower income. Of the 56 million who returned 11 million had been unable to find jobs and were unemployed at the time of the survey. For the families of the workers the loss of the migrant's job has meant not only a substantial decline in income but also an extra mouth to feed. The impact has been greater in provinces and counties where there is little or no industry. A detailed survey in one primarily agricultural province, Henan, showed that only 4 million of the 9.5 million who had returned for the new year had gone back to the cities. The remaining 5.5 million had remained behind with their families. About one in twenty of these found that their land cultivation rights had been reassigned. This had led to a sharp rise in the number of disputes in the villages.[421]

Most of the workers who have been laid off are migrants from the rural areas, and this is lending a sharp new edge to the popular discontent, one that was not much in evidence a decade ago. For in addition to losing the source of cash income on which the workers' families in the villages have grown to depend, the mass layoffs are a brutal and unwelcome reminder of the depths of their powerlessness in a society where the poor have been powerless since the beginning of time. For the government, the disaffected migrant workers spell a special threat to stability. Over the years, entire townships have developed on the fringes of the cities where those without an urban *hukou* are forced to live. The inhabitants have developed both aspirations to a better life and a collective consciousness that cannot be handled in the traditional way by localizing and isolating discontent. Large numbers have, moreover, brought their children to live with them and have put them through urban schools at immense cost to themselves. These children are imbued with little of the passivity of their parents. Sending any significant number of workers back to their home villages to become a burden on the families that they had, till lately, been supporting is one way of spreading the discontent to the peasantry.

China's response to recession has been heroic. When it announced in November 2008 that it intended to pump an additional 4 trillion yuan ($586 billion) into the economy, mainly in infrastructure and industrial projects, several China watchers received this commitment with polite disbelief. But by the end of March, a bare five months later, far more than the 4 trillion yuan worth of projects were already in the pipeline.

Beijing has not relied upon the private sector to secure this enormous jump in investment. Instead it has gone back to a modified version of the system of centralized planning that had been in force till the early eighties. Under a new directive issued in November titled simply Document 18, 2008, the central leadership informed the provinces that it intended to spent 1.3 trillion yuan through its ministries and required them to submit projects worth the remaining 2.7 billion to it for vetting and approval. The document has also promised them "block" grants to fund a part of the cost of the approved projects and has given them an unambiguous mandate to raise the rest through bank loans. The response of the local governments has been staggering. By the end of the year, eighteen provinces had submitted projects for approval worth 25 trillion yuan, leaving Beijing with the unenviable task of choosing from among them and assigning priorities. One infallible indicator of the speed of implementation is the rise in total bank credit. In the first quarter 2008 it had grown by 5.3 percent of the nominal

GDP. In the first quarter of 2009 it grew by 15.3 percent. The difference amounted to 4.6 trillion yuan!

This enormous rise in bank credit reflects the sheer speed with which the central, provincial, and local governments have identified and taken up new projects. The central government expected to spend no more than 1,100 billion yuan in 2008–09 (beginning in the fourth quarter of 2008). Of this it intended to provide 500 billion yuan from its funds and leave it to the local authorities to raise the remaining 600 billion. But in a manner that has already been described at some length in earlier chapters, the local authorities have not waited for central disbursements to reach them but have gone ahead with their projects on the basis of bank loans that they intend to reimburse later. Beijing has facilitated this by simultaneously restoring much of the power of local party secretaries to mandate bank loans from the local bank managers (who are also members of the party) that it had taken away with its banking reforms in 1998.[422]

The 4-trillion-yuan package demonstrates yet again the extraordinary capacity of China's "cadre-capitalism" to ramp up investment and growth. But it also reveals how this type of growth simultaneously feeds political discontent. Only 9 percent of the 4 trillion yuan is earmarked for boosting household consumption. More than three-quarters is to be spent on infrastructure projects. The central government is therefore repeating the strategy that it used to fight the unacknowledged recession of the nineties. Infrastructure projects are highly capital intensive. Most of the money is disbursed over several years and goes to machinery and construction companies. The immediate impact on household incomes is therefore small. The experience of the nineties should have taught Beijing how slowly such spending revives demand. When Premier Zhu Rongji unveiled his 200 billion yuan a year investment package in 1997, but the economy took till 2001 to turn the corner.

The plan had nonetheless made sense in 1997, because investment in the infrastructure, and in the modernization of industry (which is to absorb 12 percent of the stimulus package this time) is an investment in the future. China was therefore able to use the recession to build infrastructure comparable to that of Southeast Asia, and increase China's attractiveness to foreign investors. Zhu Rongji's investment plan therefore catapulted China into major power status. But repeating the exercise makes little economic sense today. China has had more than a decade of sustained investment in infrastructure projects. It has modernized its ports, roads, and airports and given its major cities first world roads, water supply and sanitation systems. The increase in its power generation capacity can be judged from the fact that in five years, from 2003 to 2008 it added ninety thousand megawatts of coal-based thermal power plants to its power grid. This was more than the entire coal-based generating capacity of India. Still more investment in infrastructure cannot fail to yield rapidly diminishing returns.

Chinese leaders have never worried overmuch about economic viability, because they have been able to order banks to provide the funds for new projects.[423] But if these projects are not intended to recover their costs on their own, then they have to be financed by the public. In China the dependence on bank lending has meant a one-way draft on the peoples' savings. This is extracted by depressing real wages in order to keep consumption low. But the concentration on infrastructure spending impoverishes the peasantry more than the urban dwellers because the bulk of the money goes into the purchase of steel, cement, and machinery, which is produced in urban centers. A decade of such spending has already widened the urban-rural income gap dramatically. An even bigger infrastructure investment package may not only further depress, or at least slow down the growth of consumption, but do so more in the villages than the towns.

Political impact

In Chapter 8 we described how the slowdown/recession of 1996–2001 increased discontent sharply, especially in the rural areas. But there had been very little discontent before 1996. When the slowdown began China had enjoyed eighteen years of almost uninterrupted growth, and thanks to the agricultural reforms of 1978–84, its benefits had been fairly evenly distributed. The situation is very different today. After reporting that the number of "mass incidents" rose from 8,700 in 1993 to 87,000 in 2005, the government stopped releasing comprehensive data. But according to the journal *Liaowang*, there were 90,000 cases of "mass incidents" in 2006, and the trend was rising. The *Blue Book* for 2009[424] also reported that there were "more than" 80,000 mass incidents in 2007. Aware that attempts to increase growth and employment through infrastructure spending may again not prevent popular discontent from rising, the central leadership is attempting to restrict even the limited freedom of expression and association that Chinese civic and human rights groups have won for themselves. Both Amnesty International and the US State Department noted that human rights abuses by the State had worsened in 2008.[425] But Beijing's growing nervousness was revealed most clearly by a sweeping directive it issued in June 2009, requiring all personal computers sold in China to be fitted with software that will allow the government to update computers with a list of banned websites.[426] Ostensibly this is intended to let the authorities filter out pornography and other "unhealthy" information, but few are deceived by this pretense. In recent years as China has strengthened its surveillance of mobile phones, dissident groups have turned increasingly to the Internet. The proprietary software that Beijing requires computer manufacturers to install will not only screen out politically undesirable websites but also identify those who try to log onto them. Growing discontent and increasing repression feed off each other. China's stability in the future has therefore become less certain.

India

While China has concentrated on reviving growth, India has remained preoccupied by a desire to control inflation, even though this has meant sacrificing growth. The preoccupation first arose when the economy went into a boom in 2006. In the first quarter of 2007 industrial growth rose to 12 percent a year. But fearing that too high a growth rate would trigger inflation, the Reserve Bank of India began to raise interest rates in order to curb the demand for consumer credit and reign in the real estate sector. After several successive moves designed to tighten the supply of credit in the money market, it had forced down the growth of industry to seven percent in the first quarter of 2008. In normal circumstances this might have been the time to relax controls on credit and let the interest rate drop once more, but the global inflation, which was spurred by a rise in oil and food prices, hit India at just that moment. With the next general elections less than a year away, so great was the government's fear of the political fallout of rising prices that it clamped monetary controls designed to restrict credit and raise interest rates, even though it knew that the inflation was being caused by international shortages over which it had no control. This drove industrial growth down even more steeply. In the third quarter of 2008 (July–September) industrial growth had fallen to 4.7 percent. That was when the global recession struck the Indian economy. In the next six months industrial growth has just about zero.[427]

The global recession was almost as cruel to India's exports as it was to China's. These fell by 13 percent between October and December and by 27 percent in the first quarter of 2009. In April 2009 the fall grew more steeply to 33.2 percent.[428] Since external trade is the most labor-intensive sector of the Indian economy, the effect on employment was severe. A survey carried out by the Federation of Indian Export Organisations in January concluded that by the end of March up to ten million people were likely to lose their jobs.[429]

Despite this, the government has continued to assign a higher priority to not allowing inflation to rear its head in the future than to kick-starting an economic recovery. When inflation turned negative in the first week of June 2009 for the first time in thirty years, Indian financial dailies rushed to clarify that this was only because the change in prices was being measured from the peak of the commodity price-based inflation of the first months of 2008.[430] Far from seeing this fall as an opportunity to stimulate the economy without running the danger of inflation, the government immediately announced that it would not change its policies because the fall was purely statistical. In its estimate, inflation would pick up again toward the end of the year.[431]

In sharp contrast to the exhortations of Chinese leaders to "make every second count"[432] in the fight against recession, Indian analysts and spokesmen have looked for signs of recovery in every little spark of new demand.[433] Evidence that the recession is not going to be V-shaped, i.e., short-lived, but L-shaped, i.e., a sharp dip followed by a long, slow crawl upward, has made no dent in the government's thinking.[434] Just as the jump in China's investment was heralded by a huge rise in bank lending, the deepening of recession in India is being signaled by a contraction in the credit being advanced to borrowers by the commercial banks. A sharp contraction in November 2008 was brushed off by the Indian policymakers as an inevitable consequence of the shock administered by the global recession. But the volume of credit has fallen again in absolute terms by Rs. 37,000 crores ($7.5 billion) in the six weeks between April 10 and May 22. In keeping with the reluctance to believe that India was actually faring rather badly in its fight against recession, analysts in the government were still trying to make sense of what was happening, but economists outside the government had come to the conclusion that the corporate sector was reluctant to invest because the cost of borrowing was far too high.

The contrast with June 2009, when the rate of inflation had fallen to minus 1.6 percent after hovering around one percent for six weeks, the prime lending rate for loans to the commercial borrowers still ranged from 13 percent for blue chip companies to 17 percent for marginal borrowers. The real cost of borrowing was therefore 12 to 16 percent. Large numbers of borrowers were not qualifying for loans even at the 17 percent rate and were being turned away by the banks. Here too the contrast with China, where the central government had restored the right of local party committees to more or less order banks to advance the needed credit, could not have been more striking.

The Manmohan Singh government was aware of the need to provide a fiscal stimulus to the economy from the early days of the global recession. But its efforts have been thwarted by the fiscal conservatism of the Reserve Bank of India and by its own unwillingness to break an understanding, made by the Narasimha Rao government with the Reserve Bank in 1993, that the finance ministry would leave the management of money supply entirely to the Reserve Bank and never again cover its budget deficits by resorting to deficit financing, i.e., printing new money. As a result, although it increased its own spending by no less than seven percent of the GDP in an effort to stimulate demand, it covered the rise in spending by borrowing from the commercial banks. As a result, instead of issuing the budgeted government bonds worth Rs. 1.33 trillion ($30 billion) by issuing government bonds for the market to buy, it raised Rs. 3.26 trillion ($75 billion). The flood of bonds released into the market lowered their prices and took the interest earned on them up to a peak of 7 percent in February–March 2009.

When banks can earn risk free returns of 6 to 7 percent by simply buying government bonds, they feel little need to lower their interest rates to private borrowers. The government's massive borrowing programme, which it intends to repeat in 2009–10 has therefore crowded private borrowers out of the money market by raising the cost of borrowing to prohibitive levels. As a result in June 2009, India found itself firmly headed towards stagflation. Consumer demand had been stimulated by the huge surge of government spending, but the mode of finance had brought investment to a near halt. As a result industrial growth remained zero and the growth of GDP was propelled almost entirely by much less reliable and possibly overestimated growth in the services sector.

First signs of a political turnaround

To nearly everyone's surprise, this had little or no adverse effect on the government's performance in the ensuing national elections. The Congress party increased its share of the vote by 2.3 percent to 28.6 percent and the number of seats it won from 145 seats in 2004 to 206 in 2009. Since this was only 64 short on an absolute majority, the Congress was able to form a far more cohesive government than in 2004.

Analysts were surprised because the Congress had lost most of the state assembly elections held during the previous five years. In the preceding five years, from 1999 till 2004, the BJP-led NDA government had suffered a similar fate and then gone on to suffer defeat in the 2004 elections. The reason why the Congress was able to buck this powerful trend, dubbed the "anti-incumbency factor," was debated for weeks afterwards, but all were unanimous on two counts: The electorate had voted for stability and performance and against divisive politics that relied mainly on whipping up caste or communal animosity.[435] The common feature of both these rejections was the voters' quest for security and predictability in their lives. This was not a new development, but had been apparent since the early nineties when the Quinquennial surveys by the National Sample Survey revealed a rush in rural areas to pull children off the fields and send them to school. Investigations by journalists revealed that the parents, in even the poorest families, were preferring to send their children to private schools where they would be able to learn English, instead of the state schooling system. The quest for security was also visible in a rapid and somewhat surprising spread of family planning even among uneducated women in northern India. Behind both lay the erosion of the Hindu United Family under the twin pressures of rising aspirations and stagnant or slow-growing incomes. This had forced the urban and rural poor to confront a terrifying new question: "Who will look after us when we are too old to work?" Safeguarding the future for their children had therefore become a matter of supreme importance.

The change this had wrought in voters' choices first revealed itself in the weakening of the anti-incumbency factor in state assembly elections. Beginning in the late nineties, in Madhya Pradesh, Delhi and Gujarat voters returned the same party to power once, then twice, and then three times. It was revealed in a sudden rejection of caste-based voting in Bihar in 2005 that brought in a development-minded party to power. The 2009 parliamentary elections saw a further weakening, if not disappearance, of the anti-incumbency factor in Andhra Pradesh, Tamil Nadu, Bihar, and Orissa. In all of these states the return of the ruling party could be traced in large measure to its largely successful effort to ensure that various benefits promised by the state actually reached the poor.[436] The Congress under Dr. Manmohan Singh owed its success to the fact that it had understood, and tried to meet, the evolving need for security and employment. Its efforts had been sporadic, often not well thought out. But the voters had not doubted its sincerity.

The 2009 election may also end the progressive marginalization of the very poor because it has seen the rise of a non-Marxist political party, the Trinamul Congress, that had broken the hold of the Left Front on Bengal by openly championing the cause of tribals and sharecroppers who have been the main victims of the rush to seize land for development projects that has been the seed bed of the Maoist uprising in ventral India. The inclusion of the Trinamul Congress in the central government has opened the way for the center to seek an alternative to force to end the Maoist revolt.

To sum up, projections of China's and India's future—such as those made by Goldman Sachs in its BRICs report, and by the US's National Intelligence Council—fail to take into account the fact that the two countries are not simply undergoing rapid economic growth, but undergoing a transformation into capitalist states. This is not only an economic but also a political change, pregnant with conflict between winners and losers from the transformation. The future will not be assured for either country until it succeeds in harmonizing their interests. Both countries have become increasingly aware of the need. But China lacks the political institutions that can perform this task, while India, which has them, has allowed many of them to atrophy through neglect or get corrupted till they have all but ceased to function.

Setting these problems right is a huge challenge, and the ability of the two countries to surmount them in time to contain rising social unrest cannot be taken for granted. But the great global recession that hit the world in September 2008 has made it harder to do so.

END NOTES

[1] Energy Information Administration: Official Energy Statistics from the US Government, "Annual Oil Market Chronology," http://www.eia.doe.gov/emeu/cabs/AOMC/Overview.html. Accessed February 9, 2008.

[2] In all, seven explanations have been put forward to explain the end of the "golden age of capitalism." For a detailed examination of all of them, see Prem Shankar Jha, Chapter 4 of *The Twilight of the Nation State: Globalisation, Chaos and War* (London: Pluto Press, 2006), 51–80.

[3] Paul Krugman, *The Age of Diminished Expectations* (Cambridge, MA: MIT Press, 1990).

[4] Prepared by Dominic Wilson and Roopa Purushothaman. Goldman Sachs, Global Economic Paper No. 99.

[5] This is called the purchasing power parity (PPP) rate of exchange. For developing countries, the PPP-based GDP is nearly always a good deal higher than the GDP based on market rates of exchange.

[6] National Intelligence Council, *Rising Powers: The Changing Geopolitical Landscape,* December 2004.

[7] For a broad defense of this strategy, see Richard L. Armitage and Joseph S. Nye Jr., "Stop Getting Mad, America. Get Smart," *Washington Post*, December 9, 2007.

[8] Robert Kagan, "The Illusion of 'Managing' China," *Washington Post*, May 15, 2005.

[9] The term "container," as conceptualized by the eminent French historian Braudel, refers to the social, economic, and political unit that is large enough to organize and contain all the interrelated functions of capitalism—finance, production, and marketing. While the linkages that

define this unit are primarily economic, the need for a secure environment within which to operate turns it into a political and military unit as well. See Jha, Chapter 1 of *The Twilight of the Nation State*, for a more detailed discussion of the concept.

[10] Karl Polanyi, *The Great Transformation* (Boston: Beacon Press, 1954).

[11] Kagan, "The Illusion of 'Managing' China."

[12] Robert Kagan, "End of Dreams, Return of History," *Policy Review*, August–September 2007.

[13] Gordon G. Chang, "Geithner in Beijing," *Forbes*, June 4, 2009, http://www.forbes.com/2009/06/04/china-treasury-geithner-opinions-columnists-beijing-wang-qishang.html. The Chinese, Geithner said, backed the Obama administration's stimulus program, understood the temporary need for enlarged federal budget deficits, and supported the dollar's dominant role in the global economy. Summing up his short stay, Geithner said, "I've actually found a lot of confidence here in China, justifiable confidence, in the strength and resilience and dynamism of the American economy."

[14] National Intelligence Council, *Rising Powers*.

[15] Aurelia George Mulgan, "Hegemonic Angst Driving America's Containment Policy in Asia," *Canberra Times*, March 16, 2006. At the time of writing, Mulgan was a professor at the Australian Defence Force Academy at the University of New South Wales.

[16] Aida AKl, "Containing China?", Voice of America newscast, August 7, 2006, http://www.voanews.com/english/archive/2006-08/US-India-China2006-08-07-voa68.cfm

[17] The phrase was coined by Karl Polanyi half a century ago in *The Great Transformation*, his seminal study of the capitalist transformation in Britain.

[18] Susan L. Shirk, a former assistant secretary of state in the US State Department, gives a telling example of the kind of event that could trigger a war between China and Taiwan and drag the US in. Referring to her days in the State Department, she writes, "I can still imagine receiving the dreaded phone call from the State Department Operations Center: 'The Pentagon has just informed us that a Chinese SU-27 jet fighter and a Taiwanese F-16 have collided in the Taiwan Strait.'" Shirk, *China: Fragile Superpower* (New York: Oxford University Press, 2007), 1.

[19] *Economist*, "The Great Divide," March 3, 2005.

[20] Ibid.

[21] Partly because of a 17 percent upward revision of its GDP estimates following an exhaustive economic census, carried out in 2005.

[22] The data for 1978 has been taken from Minxin Pei, *China's Trapped Transition: The Limits of Developmental Autocracy* (Cambridge, MA: Harvard University Press, 2006), pp. 2–3. Those for 2006 come from *China Statistical Yearbook 2007,* Table 10.1.

[23] Nirupam Bajpai and Nandita Dasgupta, "FDI to China and India: The Definitional Differences," *Hindu Business Line,* May 15, 2004.

[24] L. Alan Winters and Shahid Yusuf, eds., *Dancing with Giants: China, India, and the Global Economy* (Washington DC: World Bank and the Institute of Policy Studies, 2006), 11.

[25] Wilson and Purushothaman, *Dreaming with BRICs.*

[26] Yasheng Huang and Tarun Khanna, "Can India Overtake China?" *Foreign Policy,* July 1, 2003.

[27] Under Indian law any shareholder with 26 percent or more of the equity can block a vote on the board that makes fundamental changes to the structure and business of the company. He or she can, for instance, prevent the company from being sold, prevent it from issuing blocks of shares to existing shareholders at nominal prices, or prevent it from radically changing the nature of the business. Since the debt to equity ratio in a typical manufacturing enterprise is around two to one, this means that a little over 8 percent of total investment can give an investor a controlling interest in the firm.

[28] Winters and Yusuf, eds., *Dancing with Giants,* 5.

[29] Vivek Bharati, "China's Economic Resurgence and Flexible Coalitions" (paper presented at the Power Realignments in Asia conference, New Delhi, December 15–17, 2006).

[30] Oded Shenkar, *The Chinese Century: The Rising Chinese Economy and Its Impact on the Global Economy, the Balance of Power, and Your Job* (Upper Saddle River, NJ: Wharton School Publishing, 2005), 2.

[31] Ibid., 3.

[32] Nicholas Lardy, "The Economic Architecture of China in Southeast and Central Asia" (seminar paper for the CASI-ORF conference, New Delhi, December 15–17, 2006).

[33] *China Statistical Yearbook 2005,* table 18.7.

[34] The very first example of outsourcing manufacture may have been

when GE moved production of steam irons to Singapore in 1955, after closing a plant in Los Angeles. See Barry Bluestone and Bennett Harrison, *The Deindustrialization of America: Plant Closings, Community Abandonment, and the Dismantling of Basic Industry* (New York: Basic Books, 1982), 26.

[35] James T. Areddy, "China's Export Machine Threatened by Rising Costs," *Wall Street Journal,* June 30, 2008.

[36] Rediff, "India's Software Exports to Cross $40 Billion," February 11, 2008, http://in.rediff.com/money/2008/feb/11nass.htm. Accessed February 14, 2008.

[37] Ibid.

[38] *Employment Potential in the IT Industry,* MacKinsey study commissioned by NASSCOM for the period 1999–2008, fig. 4.

[39] Ibid.

[40] Meera Mitra, *It's Only Business! India's Corporate Social Responsiveness in a Globalized World* (New Delhi: Oxford University Press, 2007).

[41] The Visveswaraya Trust.

[42] Minxin Pei, *China's Trapped Transition: The Limits of Developmental Autocracy* (Cambridge and London: Harvard University Press, 2006).

[43] Winters and Yusuf, eds., *Dancing with Giants,* Introduction.

[44] James A. Dorn, "On Ownership with Chinese Characteristics: Private Property Rights and Land Reform in the PRC" (statement before the Congressional-Executive Commission on China Issues Roundtable, February 3, 2003). Dorn outlines the most recent institutional reforms as follows:

- Qualified foreign institutional investors will be allowed to buy equity stakes in SOEs through the A-share (local currency) stock exchanges in Shanghai and Shenzhen;
- Strategic foreign investors will be allowed for the first time to buy the nontradeable shares of listed and unlisted SOEs [state-owned enterprises];
- Foreign joint-venture investment funds will begin operation;
- Private commercial banks are being established in rural areas;
- China's first civil code has been drafted, including an entire chapter dedicated to the protection of private property rights;
- Chinas top judge, Xiao Yang, president of the Supreme People's Court, has called for safeguarding private property rights and told a national conference in Beijing: "Efforts should

be made to enhance awareness of the need for equal protection of all subjects in the marketplace."

- Farmers will have more secure land-use rights as a result of the Rural Land Contracting Law adopted in August 2002;
- Shenzhen, the first SEZ in China, is embarking on a bold political experiment, with Beijing's approval, to limit the power of the local cadres, introduce checks and balances, and cultivate the rule of law.
- A new think tank devoted to studying political reform is planned for the Central Party School in Beijing;
- Numerous rules and regulations not in conformity with WTO norms are being scrapped and there are plans to streamline the central government's complex bureaucracy.

All those reforms are being driven by the need to be competitive in an increasingly global economy. To attract and retain capital in the future, China will have to continue to improve its institutional infrastructure.

[45] Sachs, Varshney, and Bajpai, eds., *India in the Era of Economic Reforms* (New York and New Delhi: Oxford University Press, 1999), preface to the paperback edition.

[46] Kate Xiao Zhou, "From Political Society to Economic Society: The Evolution of Civil Rights in China," in *China's Future: Constructive Partner or Emerging Threat?*, eds. Ted Galen Carpenter and James A. Dorn (Washington DC: Cato Institute, 2000), 29–48.

[47] World Bank, *China 2020: Development Challenges in the New Century*, September 18, 1997.

[48] This consisted of a barter economy in which state-owned enterprises exchanged their surplus, or "above-plan," output with each other in increasingly complex chains of exchange, at semiannual "buyers' conferences." See Gene Tidrick and Chen Jiyuan, eds., *China's Industrial Reform* (New York: Oxford University Press, 1987).

[49] from a long-term average of 4.4 percent to 9.5 percent. The first figure is higher than official estimates, which were then for the net material product, i.e., those estimates excluded important parts of the services sector. This was calculated by Angus Maddison.

[50] China and India provide additional proof of the incompleteness of classical Marxist analysis as a framework for understanding the evolution

of capitalism. For the motive force behind their social and economic evolution has not been the much-overworked conflict between capital and labor, but one between two strata (or controllers) of capital. It therefore suggests the need for a more complex explicatory model than the one provided by Marx's theory of social classes.

[51] *China Statistical Yearbook 2007,* table 14.1.

[52] Irfan Habib, "Potentialities of Capitalistic Development in the Economy of Mughal India," in *Essays in Indian History: Towards a Marxist Perspective* (New Delhi: Tulika, 1995).

[53] William Foster, ed., *The English Factories in India, 1618–1669* (13 vols), published by Oxford University Press between 1906 and 1927, p. 310, and Owen C. Kail, *The Dutch in India* (Delhi: Macmillan India, 1981), 73.

Similarly, during the fight among the sons of Mughal emperor Shahjehan for the throne when Shahjehan fell ill, Prince Murad forcibly extracted 5.5 lakhs of rupees from Shantidas. Such was his influence that when Aurungzeb became the emperor, he returned one lakh of rupees of Murad's "loan" as a token of goodwill.

The House of Jagat Seth, in Eastern India, enjoyed similar relations with Farrukhsiyar, one of the later Mughal rulers, whose claim to the throne it largely financed in 1712, and with Farrukhsiyar's governor in Bengal, Murshid Quli Khan. Farrukhsiyar granted the head of the House of Jagat Seth the hereditary title of "treasurer-general of Bengal," but to obtain it he had to pay Murshid Quli Khan five lakhs of rupees. Since his wealth was estimated to be in the region of eight *crores* of rupees, this was not an unduly onerous burden. See J. H. Little, *House of Jagat Seth* (Calcutta: Calcutta Historical Society, 1967), vi, vii, etc., and Om Prakash, *The Dutch East India Company and the Economy of Bengal, 1630–1720* (Princeton, NJ: Princeton University Press, 1985), 58–60.

[54] Foster, *The English Factories in India, 1618–1669,* 310, and Kail, *The Dutch in India,* 73.

[55] Fernand Braudel, *Civilization and Capitalism, 15th–18th Century: The Perspective of the World, Vol. III* (London: Collins/Fontana Press, 1988), 120–121. The estimate was made by Doge Mocenigo, in 1421.

[56] The first gold ducat struck in Italy was the *zecchino d'oro,* in 1284. It was worth nine shillings sterling—i.e., 0.45 pounds. This made it worth about six Indian silver rupees (http://www.taxfreegold.co.uk/austriandu-catsinfo.html).

[57] Amiya Kumar Bagchi, "De-Industrialization in India in the Nineteenth Century: Some Theoretical Implications," *Journal of Development Studies,* January 1976.

[58] Government of India, *Economic Survey 2006–2007,* box 7.1, 138.

[59] J. L. Van Zanden, "Tracing the Beginning of the Kuznets Curve: Western Europe During the Early Modern Period," *Economic History Review* 48, no. 4 (1995): 643–664.

[60] Karl Marx and Friedrich Engels, *The Communist Manifesto,* 1848.

[61] Michal Kalecki, "Social and Economic Aspects of Intermediate Regimes," in *Selected Essays on the Economic Growth of the Socialist and the Mixed Economy* (Cambridge: Cambridge University Press, 1972), 162–169. For a thorough discussion of the literature on intermediate regimes, see Barbara Harriss-White, *India Working: Essays on Society and Economy* (Cambridge: Cambridge University Press, 2003), Chapter 3.

[62] Kalecki, "Social and Economic Aspects of Intermediate Regimes," 162.

[63] K. N. Raj, "The Politics and Economics of Intermediate Regimes," *Economic and Political Weekly,* July 7, 1973. The topic is addressed more fully by Prem Shankar Jha *(The Twilight of the Nation State)* and Barbara Harriss-White *(India Working).*

[64] The idea of casting big business houses as victims in an intermediate regime has been difficult for most analysts to swallow. E. M. S. Namboodiripad, the Communist leader of Kerala in the seventies and eighties, and economist Pranab Bardhan flatly rejected it and defined the dominant class in Indian society to include big business and the bureaucracy, in addition to the rich farmer. Harriss-White is also deeply uncomfortable with the notion. It is the crude division of the bourgeoisie into "big" and "small," a division made without reference to the need to define a central line of conflict, that is responsible for this confusion.

[65] Harriss-White, *India Working,* 59.

[66] The Rajiv Gandhi government knew that a foreign exchange crisis was brewing in 1987. It therefore framed a long-term fiscal policy for drastic tax reform though a simplification and lowering of rates. But it did not have the courage to implement the policy in a forthright manner. In 1989 Rajiv Gandhi accepted a more detailed plan for the opening up of the economy, lowering of tax rates, and devaluation of the rupee prepared by his economic adviser Montek Singh Ahluwalia, but postponed its implementation until after the next election. When the Congress Party lost that

election, Gandhi's successor, V. P. Singh, wrestled with the proposals and eventually announced a new industrial policy that involved a very small additional liberalization of industrial licensing and no opening up of the external sector. Even that was shot down by leftist members of Singh's own planning commission. (The author was a member of the prime minister's office at the time and was privy to all of the above.)

[67] A rare exception for its time was Lynn T. White III, *Unstately Power*, vol. 1, *Local Causes of China's Intellectual, Legal and Governmental Reforms* (Armonk, NY: M.E. Sharpe, 1998).

[68] World Bank, *China: Reform and the Role of the Plan in the Nineties* (Washington DC, 1992), 37–42. See also *China 2020*.

[69] Polanyi, *The Great Transformation*. See also Will Hutton, *The State We're In: Why Britain Is in Crisis and How to Overcome It* (London: Vintage Books, 1996).

[70] It took the Asian financial crisis to jolt Beijing into changing this law and placing all bank branches under a newly formed Central Finance Work Committee. (Victor Shih, "Dealing with Non-Performing Loans: Political Constraints and Financial Policies in China," *China Quarterly*, 2004: 933).

[71] Angus Maddison, *Chinese Economic Performance in the Long Run* (Paris: Development Centre of the OECD, 1998), 81.

[72] Ibid.

[73] Pei, *China's Trapped Transition*.

[74] Organisation for Economic Co-operation and Development (OECD), *China in the World Economy: The Domestic Policy Challenges* (Paris: OECD Publications, 2002), 134.

[75] Among the authors are Lynn T. White, *Unstately Power* (Armonk, NY: M. E. Sharpe, 1998); Daniel Kelliher, *Peasant Power in China* (New Haven, CT: Yale University Press, 1992); and Dali L.Yang, *Calamity and Reform in China: State, Rural Society, and Institutional Change Since the Great Leap Famine* (Stanford, CA.: Stanford University Press, 1996). A very similar account is offered in Kate Xiao Zhou, *How the Farmers Changed China: Power of the People* (Boulder, CO: Westview, 1996). Others who have recognized this development and dwelt on aspects of its consequences for China's economic policies are Mancur Olson, *Power and Prosperity: Outgrowing Communist and Capitalist Dictatorships* (New York: Basic Books, 2000) and Victor Nee and Lian Peng, "Sleeping with the Enemy: A Dynamic Model of

Declining Political Commitment in State Socialism," *Theory and Society* 32, no. 2: 253–296.

[76] Hongye Zhang, Xiaofeng Li, and Xiaomei Shao, "Impacts of China's Rural Land Policy and Administration on Rural Economy and Grain Production," *Review of Policy Research* 23, no. 2 (2006). Although the key reform, of fixing a quota of grain for delivery by the commune to the government, and leaving the use of the balance of the land to be determined by the commune, was implemented in 1979, it took the center four more years, till 1983, to legalize the further devolution of commune targets into village and family targets, and consequently the transfer of decision-making on how to use the land, down from the commune to the family.

[77] Yi-Min Li, "Economic Institutional Change in Post-Mao China: Reflections on the Triggering," *The Chinese Economy* 35, no. 3 (May–June 2002): 26–51, footnote 46.

[78] Ibid.

[79] Nee and Peng, "Sleeping with the Enemy."

[80] Pei, *China's Trapped Transition*, 126.

[81] Ibid., 127.

[82] Ibid., 128.

[83] Roy Bahl, *Fiscal Policy in China—Taxation and Intergovernmental Fiscal Relations* (Burlingame, CA: 1990 Institute, 1999).

[84] Holst and Tian Zhu, 74, table 3.

[85] Vivek B. Arora and John Norregaard, "Intergovernmental Fiscal Relations: The Chinese System in Perspective," IMF staff working paper WP/97/129 (October 1997), 25, table 3. Estimates of extrabudgetary revenues are necessarily imprecise, because of the opacity of the accounting practices followed. The OECD made a more conservative estimate of about 8 to 10 percent of GDP (OECD, *China in the World Economy*, 638).

[86] Lynette H. Ong, "The Political Economy of Township Government Debt, Township Enterprises, and Rural Financial Institutions in China," *China Quarterly* 186 (2006): 377–400.

[87] Ray Yep, "Can 'Tax-for-Fee' Reform Reduce Rural Tension in China? The Process, Progress and Limitations," *China Quarterly* 177 (2004): 42–70.

[88] Ibid.

[89] Cited by Ong, "The Political Economy of Township Government Debt."

[90] The World Bank's publication *China 2020* puts the figure at 9,000, but this includes a variety of economic zones developed at lower levels of the local government.

[91] He Qinlian, *China's Pitfall*, Chapter 2.

[92] In Indian parlance, the cash reserve ratio.

[93] Barry Naughton, "An Economic Bubble? Chinese Policy Adapts to Rapidly Changing Conditions," *China Leadership Monitor*, no. 9, Winter 2004.

[94] *China Update*, World Bank Office, Beijing, November 2004.

[95] Ibid.

[96] Yoshikuni Sugiyama, "China's Economy Sways the World," *Yomiuri Shimbun*, March 21, 2007.

[97] Cary Huang and Jane Cai, "Central Bank Lifts Reserve Ratio to 10.5 Percent," *South China Morning Post*, April 6, 2007.

[98] Cary Huang, "Economy Rebounds from Slowdown," *South China Morning Post*, March 31, 2007.

[99] *China Update*, 3.

[100] Peter S. Goodman, "Chinese Growth Exceeds Forecasts; Rapid Rate Adds to Fear of Overheating," *Washington Post*, July 19, 2006.

[101] Ibid.

[102] OECD, *China in the World Economy*, 15.

[103] Pei, *China's Trapped Transition*, 129.

[104] Ibid., 177–178.

[105] Ibid., 167.

[106] Ibid.

[107] Frank Ching, "The Price of Chasing Figures," *South China Morning Post*, August 17, 2005.

[108] In 2004 China consumed 9,080 Btu per $2,000 of PPP GDP, against India's 4,205. Energy Information Administration, Official Energy Statistics from the US Government, Energy Information Annual 2004, table E1.

[109] Cary Huang, "Mainland's Progress on Goals for Energy Efficiency 'Not Promising,'" *South China Morning Post*, August 5, 2006.

[110] Xinhua, "Energy Consumption Per Unit of GDP Continues to Fall," July 15, 2008, http://www.chinadaily.com.cn/bizchina/2008-07/15/content_6847891.htm. Accessed July 17, 2008.

[111] Shi Jiang Tao, "Unbridled Growth Dents Hopes Energy Targets Will Be Met," *South China Morning Post,* July 20, 2006.

[112] The structure of China's GDP is more heavily slanted toward manufacture than India's, and India's service sector accounts for marginally more of the economy than those of other countries with similar levels of income, but these differences do not come close to accounting for the immense difference in per dollar use of raw materials. See Winters and Yusuf, eds., *Dancing with Giants.*

[113] Lynne Kiesling, "China and India Energy Predictions from the IEA," http://www.knowledgeproblem.com/archives/002274.html. Accessed July 23, 2008.

[114] Wang Qingyi, "Energy Conservation as Security," *China Security,* published by the World Security Institute, China Program.

[115] Sources: Winters and Yusuf, eds., *Dancing with Giants; Shenzen Daily,* "Oil Imports Expected to Rise 10.2%," January 8, 2007.

[116] Tom Holland, "Hu Boldly Struts into the Minefield of Energy Efficiency," *South China Morning Post,* October 14, 2005.

[117] Richard McGregor, "Report Finds Pollution in China Cost 3% of Economic Output in 2004," *Financial Times,* Asia Edition, September 8, 2006.

[118] *South China Morning Post* (Hong Kong), January 2, 1997.

[119] *China Business Review,* March 1, 1997.

[120] Economists, and they are the majority, who accept the official data ascribe the sudden change to the Asian financial meltdown, which occurred in July 1997. While the Asian crisis did have an effect, it was almost entirely upon exports, which rose by only 0.4 percent in 1998 after rising by 20 percent the previous year. But the slowdown in exports was more than offset by an actual decline in imports. This left the trade surplus pretty much unaffected. Indeed, 1997 and 1998 saw healthy trade surpluses of 335 and 360 billion yuan, which were of the same order as the surpluses recorded in all but one of the preceding years. For foreign trade to reduce aggregate domestic demand and therefore push down prices, there has to be a trade deficit. This condition was not fulfilled in 1998 or 1999.

[121] OECD, *China in the World Economy,* 15.

[122] Seth Faison, *International Herald Tribune,* January 1, 1999.

[123] Ibid.

[124] Seth Faison, "China's Cutback Surprises Boeing and Airbus," *International Herald Tribune*, February 10, 1999.

[125] Ibid.

[126] Xinhua, "Chinese Truck, Motorcycle Production Up," October 26, 1998.

[127] Li Jianlin, "Economy Good Despite Severe Crisis and Flood," *China Daily*, December 30, 1998. Jianlin, citing economists of the Chinese Academy of Social Sciences, writes: "It is widely recognized that the root cause for the low efficiency of China's economy lies in overly duplicated industrial structures and overflowing similar products, which have brought a pervasive glut relative to household consumption demands in the domestic market."

[128] Jianlin, "Economy Good Despite Severe Crisis and Flood."

[129] Xinhua, "China Sees Stable Economic Growth," June 15, 1999.

[130] Reuters, "High Savings Rate Cuts into Chinese Economy," *International Herald Tribune*, March 6–7, 1999.

[131] Xinhua, "News Analysis: Interest Rate Cut to Benefit Economic Growth," June 10, 1999.

[132] Ibid.

[133] He Qinlian, *Zhongguo de xianjing* [*China: The Pitfalls of Modernization*] (Hong Kong: Mingjing chubanshe, 1998), Chapter 2.

[134] Nicholas R. Lardy, "China and the Asian Contagion," *Foreign Affairs*, July/August 1998, 82.

[135] Joshua Cooper Ramo, "The Shanghai Bubble," *Foreign Policy*, Summer 1998.

[136] He Qinlian, op. cit 88, footnote 21. Quoting the *Guangdong-HK Information Daily*, July 7, 1996.

[137] Ramo, "The Shanghai Bubble."

[138] Elizabeth Rosenthal, *International Herald Tribune*, January 16–17, 1999.

[139] Ibid.

[140] Thomas Rawski, "What's Happening to China's Growth Statistics," *China Economic Review* 12, no. 4 (2001): 298–302. See also Prem Shankar Jha, *The Perilous Road to the Market: The Political Economy of Reform in Russia, India and China*, Chapter 10, "China's Undeclared Recession" (London: Pluto Books, 2002), 135–148.

[141] Yakov Berger, "On the Fidelity of China's Economic Growth and the 'Chinese Threat,'" *Far Eastern Affairs* 31, no. 1 (2003): 46–63.

[142] This explanation was put forward by Ren Ruoen, professor of economics at the Administration Institute of the Beijing University of Aviation and Aeronautics. Quoted by Yakov Berger, "On the Fidelity of China's Economic Growth and the 'Chinese Threat.'"

[143] See, for example, Barry Naughton, "The New Common Economic Program: China's Eleventh Five Year Plan and What It Means," *China Leadership Monitor*, no. 16 (2005): 1–10. Naughton asserts that just as the decline in total energy consumption by 19 percent and in coal consumption by 29 percent while GDP grew by 36 percent between 1996 and 2000 was "preposterous," the increase in coal consumption by 18 percent a year and in total energy consumption by 15 percent a year between 2000 and 2004 is equally preposterous. His logic is not easy to follow because what makes the first set of figures preposterous was the fact that GDP and energy consumption were moving in opposite directions. This is not so in the second period. Naughton seems to believe that, having at last got a credible figure for coal consumption in 2005, the Chinese have been correcting their data for coal consumption by loading the whole of the correction onto the figures for 2001–'04. Why they should do that instead of smoothing out the data from 1996 onward is not easy to understand.

[144] Zhou Qiren, "*Channeng guosheng de yuanyin*" ["Causes of Production Overcapacity"], December 10, 2005, issue of *Jinji guancha bao*, and "*Zailun channeng guosheng*" ["Reexamination of Production Overcapacity"], January 16, 2006, issue of *Jinji guancha bao*. Cited by Chi Hung Kwan, "Excess Production Capacity Is the Result of Not Only Cyclical but Also Structural Factors," *China in Transition*, June 28, 2006.

[145] This was .528 in 2004.

[146] Reuters, Hindu *Business Line*, September 3, 2008.

[147] Qinlian, *Zhongguo de xianjing* [*China: The Pitfalls of Modernization*], Chapter 3.

[148] Qinlian's *China: The Pitfalls of Modernization* was first titled *China: The Pitfalls of Development* when it was translated, but not published, by M. E. Sharpe, Inc.

[149] Jonathan Watts, "Sleaze Exposed in China as Former Minister Is Jailed," *Guardian*, December 28, 2005.

[150] According to the Hindu *Business Line*, "[t]hese were a 'Circular Proscribing Arbitrary Requisition of Donations and Arbitrary Fund-Raising from Peasants,' issued in 1985; a 'Circular on Effectively Reducing the Burden on the Peasants,' issued by the State Council in February 1990; a 'Decision on Resolutely Terminating Arbitrary Fund-Raising, Arbitrary Fines, and All Kinds of Requisition of Donations' taken by the Central Committee and the State Council in September of the same year; and Order No. 92 of the State Council that promulgated the legally binding 'Regulation of Fees Payable by Peasants and Administration of Peasant Labor,' released on December 17, 1991. The Li Peng government took the highly unusual step of departing from the normal practice of circulating the Order only within the party and the government and making it a public document."

[151] The details of the 1994 tax reform are given in Chapter 5.

[152] Beijing was aware of the townships' plight. To enable them to carry out their responsibilities the government passed a law that "allowed" the townships to spend the "surplus collected on their own programmes and assured them that the excess of their expenditures over revenue would be compensated." This was, probably correctly, interpreted by the townships as a green light to raise fresh resources locally through the exercise of the powers that remained with them.

[153] Yongshun Cai, "Collective Ownership or Cadres' Ownership? The Non-agricultural Use of Farmland in China," *China Quarterly* 175 (2003).

[154] Kevin J. O'Brien and Lianjiang Li, *Rightful Resistance in Rural China* (Cambridge: Cambridge University Press, 2006), 2.

[155] Ibid., 31.

[156] Ibid., 31 and 32, footnote 4.

[157] For five moving accounts of the way in which peasants have been victimized for having dared to seek redress, see Chen Guidi and Wu Chuntao, *Will the Boat Sink the Water? The Life of China's Peasants,* trans. Zhu Hong (New York: Public Affairs, 2006).

[158] Ibid. See particularly Chapters 1–3 and pages 68–69.

[159] Jonathan Watts, "The Big Steal," *Guardian,* May 27, 2006.

[160] *China Statistical Yearbook 2006*, table 13.5. The profits in 2005 were 1.134 trillion yuan, against losses of 124 billion yuan.

[161] Judith Banister, "Manufacturing Employment and Compensation in China" (report prepared for the US Department of Labor, Bureau of Labour Statisitcs, December 2004). Two articles based on the report can

be accessed at http://www.bls.gov/opub/mlr/2005/07/art2full.pdf and http://www.bls.gov/opub/mlr/2005/08/art3full.pdf.

[162] *China Statistical Yearbook 2006*, table 5.1.

[163] John W. Lewis and Xue Litai, "Social Change and Political Reform in China: Meeting the Challenge of Success," *China Quarterly* 176 (2003): 926–942.

[164] *China Statistical Yearbook 2006*, Table 4.9. Population by sex, household registration, and region (2005). The table gives the actual results of a sample survey of 1.325 percent of the workforce. The estimated total number of migrant workers has been calculated accordingly.

[165] World Bank, *China 2020*, 45. The definition used here is slightly different. It is "those who live outside their home counties for more than 200 days in a year," i.e., slightly more than six months.

[166] The following tables give the growth of employment in the urban and rural areas:

Changes in Urban Employment, 1995–2005 (by main sectors)

Year Total Urban total SOEs Collect-ives Lim. Liability cos. Share-holding cos. Private Cos. HK & foreign cos. Self-employ-ed 1995 680.65 190.40 112.61 31.47— 6.20 5.13 17.09 2005 758.25 273.61 64.88 8.10 17.50 6.99 34.58 12.45 27.78 change +77.6 +82.9—47.8 -23.4 +17.5 +5.35 +28.38 +7.32 +10.69

Changes in Rural Employment, 1995–2005 (by sectors)

Year Total TVEs Private Self-employed 1995 490.25 128.62 4.71 30.54 2005 484.94 142.72 23.66 21.23 Change—5.3 +14.1 +19—9.3

Source for both tables: *China Statistical Yearbook 2006*, Table 5.1.

[167] Partly because of a 17 percent upward revision of its GDP estimates following an exhaustive economic census, carried out in 2005.

[168] John Giles, Albert Park, and Fang Cai, "How Has Economic Restructuring Affected China's Urban Workers?" *China Quarterly* 185 (2006): 61–95.

[169] William Hurst and Kevin J. O'Brien, "China's Contentious Pensioners," *China Quarterly* 170 (2002): 345–360.

[170] Ibid., 350.

[171] Lewis and Litai, "Social Change and Political Reform in China."

[172] Pei, *China's Trapped Transition: The Limits of Developmental Autocracy*, 199.

[173] Dorothy J. Solinger, "State and Society in Urban China in the Wake of the 16th Party Congress," *China Quarterly* 176 (2003): 943–959; Jiang Xueqin, "Fighting to Organize," *Far Eastern Economic Review*, September 6,

2001, 72–75. These figures are higher than the ones published officially in 2004 and 2005. The reason is that the definition used by the government is more restrictive, because it only refers to incidents of mass protest in which there is a serious, often violent, confrontation between the people and the authorities.

[174] Hurst and O'Brien, "China's Contentious Pensioners," 345–360.

[175] Pei, *China's Trapped Transition: The Limits of Developmental Autocracy*, 200.

[176] Ibid., 94.

[177] Slaughter is used here metaphorically as an omnibus term to refer to all the ways in which the workers have been deprived of their livelihoods and their rights by the cadres.

[178] Guidi and Chuntas, *Will the Boat Sink the Water?* 199–203.

[179] Albert Park and Dewen Wang, "Migration and Urban Poverty and Inequality in China" (paper presented at a conference on the "Rural-Urban Gap in the PRC" at Harvard University, organized by the Fairbank Center for East Asian Research, October 6–8, 2006).

[180] Zhu Lijiang, "The *Hukou* System of the People's Republic of China: A Critical Appraisal under International Standards of Internal Movement and Residence," *Chinese Journal of International Law* 2, no. 2 (2003): 519–565.

[181] Estimates of the size of the migrant labor force vary widely because of the different definitions in use. Based on its 2001 household survey base, the Ministry of Agriculture estimated that there were 88 million rural migrants in 2001, of whom 55 percent came from the central region and 34 percent from the western region. Of these 88 million, nearly 90 percent went to urban areas (including nearby townships), with 82 percent moving to the eastern region. Most of the people who went to the eastern region found jobs and stayed in townships and county towns; migrants who went to provincial capitals and other large metropolitan areas were less than 30 percent of the total. However, these figures do not include construction workers in the townships, who numbered 27 million, and those who came to the cities and townships as dependents of migrants, who numbered 20 million. See Huang Ping and Frank N. Pieke, "China Migration Country Study" (paper presented at the Regional Conference on Migration, Development and Pro-Poor Policy Choices in Asia, jointly organized by the Refugee and Migratory Movements Research Unit, Bangladesh, and the UK Department for International Development,

Dhaka, Bangladesh, June 22–24, 2003). This and all other conference papers are available from http://www.livelihoods.org. The most comprehensive estimate was made by the 2005 national sample survey conducted by the NBS, and mentioned earlier, which gave an estimate of 147.5 million.

[182] World Bank, *China 2020*, 45. The estimate comes from Sarah Cook, "Surplus Labour and Productivity in Chinese Agriculture: Evidence from Household Survey Data," *Journal of Development Studies* 35 (1999): 16–44.

[183] Yaohui Zhao, "Rural-Urban Migration in China: The Past and Present," in Chinese Rural Labor Flows, ed. Loraine West and Yaohui Zhao (Berkeley, CA: Institute for East Asian Studies, University of California, 2000).

[184] Ibid.

[185] Belton M. Fleisher and Dennis T. Yang, "Labor Laws and Regulations in China," *China Economic Review* 14 (2003): 426–433.

[186] Lei Guang and Lu Zheng, "Migration as the Second-best Option: Local Power and Off-farm Employment, China Quarterly 181 (2005): 22–45. See also Chow Chung-yan, "Textile Factory Sees Migrant Labour Returning to the Land," *South China Morning Post*, September 23, 2005, and "Labour Shortage Threatening Industrial Growth," *South China Morning Post*, May 26, 2005.

[187] *China Daily*, "Man's Brutal Killers Receive Punishment," October 6, 2003.

[188] Hongbin Li and Scott Rozelle, "Privatizing Rural China: Insider Privatization, Innovative Contracts and the Performance of Township Enterprises," *China Quarterly* 176 (2003): 981–1005.

[189] Ibid.

[190] Joseph Fewsmith, "Continuing Pressures on Social Order," *China Leadership Monitor*, no. 10 (Spring 2004).

[191] This would have been relatively easy in the non-state sector, where contract work was the rule, and there were no commitments of the state to its employees safeguarded by the constitution of the PRC.

[192] OECD, *China in the World Economy*, 45.

[193] Yongshun Cai, "The Resistance of Chinese Laid-off Workers in the Reform Period," *China Quarterly* 170 (2002): 327–344.

[194] Ong, "The Political Economy of Township Government Dept."

[195] Ibid.

[196] Bhagwati, *Essays in Honour of Manmohan Singh*.

[197] Letter from the British Chancellor of the Exchequer, Hugh Dalton, written to reject an Indian request for 47.5 million pounds to be released from the balances to cover expenses till the end of 1947, quoted in Suniti Kumr Ghosh, "The Transfer of Power: Real or Formal?" *Aspects of India's Economy, no. 43 (July 2007)*.

[198] Since by conventional estimates India's GDP in 1948–'49, the first full year after independence, was Rs. 86.5 billion, or 6.5 billion pounds (Government of India, *Economic Survey 1967–1968*).

[199] Jagdish N. Bhagwati and Padma Desai, *India: Planning for Industrialization: Industrialization and Trade Policies Since 1951* (New York: Oxford University Press, 1970), Chapter 4. See also Francine Frankel, *India's Political Economy, 1947-1975: The Gradual Revolution* (Princeton, NJ: Princeton University Press, 1978; New Delhi: Oxford University Press, 1980).

[200] Ibid., 262.

[201] Bhagwati and Desai, *India: Planning for Industrialization*, 68. Between 1951–'52 and 1965–'66, the area under cultivation increased by 22 percent and the yield per hectare by 18.3 percent.

[202] Ibid.

[203] Ibid.

[204] Ibid., 9. These data are all taken from the Government of India, *Economic Survey 1974–1975*.

[205] Ibid., 66–67. For an overlapping but somewhat different period, Isher Ahluwalia's calculations confirm this sharp decline. In terms of net value added, the industrial growth rate fell from 8 percent a year between 1951–'65, to 5.7 percent between 1966–'67 and 1979–'80. Capital goods fell from 15.4 to 6.6 percent and basic goods (steel, cement, etc.) from 11 to 5.9 percent (21).

[206] Three were of special importance: The Monopolies Inquiry Commission report of 1965; the Ninth Report of the Estimates Committee of the Fourth Lok Sabha (Parliament), 1967–'68; and the Report of the Mathur Study Team. All are extensively referred to in Bhagwati and Desai, *India: Planning for Industrialization*.

[207] Bhagwati and Desai, *India: Planning for Industrialization*, 5–6.

[208] Ibid., 5.

[209] Ibid., 499.

[210] Jagdish N. Bhagwati and T. N. Srinivasan, *Foreign Trade Regimes and Economic Development: India* (New York: National Bureau of Economic Research, 1975; New Delhi: Oxford and IBH Publishing Company, 1976).

[211] R. K. Hazari, *Industrial Planning and Licensing Policy* (report prepared for the Planning Commission, Government of India, 1967).

[212] This was an oversight that had resulted from the constitution makers' decision to use the British-drafted Government of India Act of 1935 as the base upon which to build the new constitution. The 1935 constitution had a property qualification for voting that disenfranchised all but 6 to 8 percent of the adult population of the country. With only a handful of voters to mobilize, the British drafters had not even considered the problem of electoral finance. But the Indian Constitution adopted universal franchise for all above the age of twenty-one. As a result, in 1951 Indian candidates for Parliament had to cover constituencies spread over an average of 6,000 square kilometers and 400,000 voters. From the beginning elections were prohibitively expensive and they became more expensive with each passing year.

[213] Not coincidentally, as will be shown later, the reservation of items for production only by the small-scale sector began in 1967 with forty-seven items in the list. At its peak in 1984 the number had climbed to 873.

[214] In India, FDI did not include the reinvested profits of foreign companies reinvested within the country. One reason may have been the enactment by Indira Gandhi's government of laws that also banned their repatriation. This classification was only changed in 2004, by when there were no restrictions left on profit repatriation.

[215] Prem Shankar Jha, *India: A Political Economy of Stagnation* (Bombay and New York: Oxford University Press, 1980), 83–84, and Bhagwati and Desai, *India: Planning for Industrialization*, Chapter 13.

[216] In 1981 A. R. Antulay, the Congress chief minister of Maharashtra, lost his job because he had imposed an "informal" levy on builders in Bombay (now Mumbai) of Rs. 40 per bag of cement, to be paid into a legally registered trust controlled by him. Had he kept the money in cash, no one would have been the wiser. Antulay paid, in fact, for trying to set up a legal source of political funding through illegal funding.

[217] Data for 1970 are taken from Centre for Monitoring the Indian Economy, *Basic Statistics Relating to the Indian Economy*, August 1994, tables 9.1 and 9.7. Data for 1999–2000 are taken from *Report of Task Force on Employment Opportunities*, Planning Commission, Government of India, 2001, chaired by M. S. Ahluwalia. Data for 2002 are taken from Government of India, *Economic Survey 2003–2004*, table S-50.

[218] The term "reforms by stealth" was coined in the 1990s by Arvind Panagariya.

[219] Arvind Panagariya, "The Triumph of India's Market Reforms: The Record of the 1980s and 1990s," *Policy Analysis*, no. 554 (2005). A detailed description of the succession of economic crises that hit the Indian economy between 1957 and 1991 is to be found in Vijay Joshi and I. M. D. Little, India: Macroeconomics and Political Economy 1964-1991(Washington DC: World Bank, 1994).

[220] Government of India, *Economic Survey 1998–1999*, s-1, table 1.

[221] This was the finding of a report prepared by D. V. Kapur, then a member of the Planning Commission.

[222] Even with the help of subsidies and devaluation, exports grew by 114 percent between 1981 and 1991, against 113 percent growth of industry. This was not sufficient to prevent the external payments gap from widening. Some idea of the growth rate needed to sustain an 8.2 percent annual increase in industrial output can be taken from the experience of 1992–'93 to 1995–'96. In these years an average industrial growth rate of 9.1 percent was accompanied by a 20 percent growth of exports. The balance of payments deficit still widened from 0.4 percent of GDP in 1993–'04 to 1.6 percent in 1995–'06. (Centre for Monitoring Indian Economy, monthly reviews of the Indian economy).

[223] This and the preceding figures were given to Prime Minister V. P. Singh by then-Finance Secretary Bimal Jalan some weeks after the invasion, to justify the imposition of yet another blanket ban on all but the most essential imports. As an adviser to the prime minister, the author received a copy.

[224] This was the first estimate released by the Central Statistical Office, in August 1990. As in the case of all Indian statistics, this has been revised marginally more than once since then.

[225] In 1995–'96 the Centre's fiscal deficit was still 5.9 percent of GDP. This figure, taken from the *Economic Survey 1997–1998* (21) is markedly different from the estimate, published by the government in its *Economic Survey 1999–2000*, of 4.3 percent of the GDP. The difference is explained by two changes made in the basis of calculation. In 1998, the government shifted the base year for calculation of the GDP from 1980–'81 to 1993–'94. The resulting GDP series was about 11 percent higher than the old, and reflected the fuller inclusion of a host of new industries and

services. This change lowered the ratio of fiscal deficit to GDP by a corresponding amount. In 1999 the government shifted borrowings made under the Small Savings scheme and transferred to the State governments, out of the Centre's gross borrowing. This further reduced the Centre's fiscal deficit by about 0.6 percent, but increased the States' deficit by the same amount.

[226] Government of India, *Economic Survey 1995-1996*, 31.

[227] Centre For Monitoring the Indian Economy, "Monthly Review of the Indian Economy," February 1997, 140.

[228] World Bank, "India – Country Economic Memorandum: Five Years of Stabilization and Reform: The Challenges Ahead," August 1996, 77–78.

[229] Rahul Bajaj is the grandson of Jamnalal Bajaj, who founded the company in 1926 and was one of the staunchest supporters of the Congress Party before independence.

[230] Indian industrialists managed to get the government to issue a notification requiring the foreign partner to obtain the company's permission—a permission seldom given. The practice was finally abolished in 2006.

[231] In 1992, while presenting the budget, the government had promised to bring it down from 6.5 to 5 percent of GDP. In actual fact, it was finding it hard to get down to even 5.7 percent, and although this was the figure eventually given in the budget, the government had resort to all kinds of sleight of hand to get there. For a detailed description of the debates that preceded the government's decision to renege on its agreement with the IMF, see Prem Shankar Jha, *The Perilous Road to the Market: A Political Economy of Reform in Russia, India and China* (London: Pluto Books, 2002), 186–187.

[232] This argument has been made in considerable detail by Jha in *The Perilous Road to the Market: A Political Economy of Reform in Russia, India and China*. See especially the introduction and the conclusion.

[233] While the Suzuki venture was eventually saved, Tatas abandoned their airport project on June 25, 1998, and their airline project on September 3, 1998.

[234] Jha, *The Perilous Road to the Market*, 214–221.

[235] As of the end of 1998, there were no less than 11 other models of foreign cars being made or assembled in India.

[236] This was not a coincidence. The Congress brought about a premature end of the boom in its efforts to curb inflation, which had climbed

back to 11.1 percent in May 1995, a level close to what had prevailed in early 1991. It did so by savagely tightening the supply of money. This pushed up the real interest rate sharply and triggered a decline in private investment that went on till 2002–'03. See Jha, *The Perilous Road to the Market*, Chapter 14, 201–203.

[237] In a sample of 1,700 companies, 908 of them, accounting for 82 percent of total production, recorded a 66 percent jump in their net profit over the previous year.

[238] Government of India, *Economic Survey 2003–2004*, table 1.3. Real consumption growth declined from 7.4 percent in 1998–'99 to 7.1 percent in 1999–2000 to 2.4 percent in 2000–'01. Thanks to a good harvest it rose to 5.3 percent in 2001–'02, but fell again to 2.3 percent in 2002–'03. In real terms, the growth rate of private consumption reduced from 5.5 percent in 1999–2000 to 2.2 percent in 2000–'01. See section: "Review of Developments: Demand Factors."

[239] An analysis of the accounts of the profit-making companies in the sample referred to above showed that while a third of the increase in profits had come from a sharp decline in the cost of borrowing following successive reductions of interest rates over the previous two years, fully two-thirds had been earned by cutting costs, and a vastly improved management of inventories.

[240] These are based upon periodic profitability studies carried out by the Confederation of Indian Industries and published in the economic dailies. The data used here were published in the *Business Standard* and cited by the author in articles in the *Hindu* on March 21, 2003, and July 20, 2003.

[241] Sucheta Dalal, "Investors are Now Demanding a Voice," *Indian Express*, May 30, 1999.

[242] Government of India, *Economic Survey 2007–2008*, 100, table 5.21.

[243] The value-added tax is the main instrument for raising revenues in the countries of the European Union and other parts of the world except the US. It differs from the sales tax in one important respect: The seller of the final product, let us say an automobile, deducts the value-added tax that has been paid by all his suppliers of parts, materials, and components. There is thus no double taxation of the latter—first when they are produced and sold, and then when they are sold again as a part of the automobile.

[244] Government of India, *Economic Survey 2007–2008*, 21, figure 2.4.

[245] Planning Commission, Government of India, *Report of Task Force on Employment Opportunities*, 2001, table 2.5, and *11ᵗʰ Plan Approach Paper*, 2006. The dark side of the increase is that almost all of it has taken place in the unorganized sector where workers have no social security. Their plight is as bad as, and in many cases worse than, that of the migrant workers in China.

[246] The following table summarizes the performance of the economy in all important parameters since 2003.

Table 10.1
India's Economic performance:
Growth Rates of Key Indicators, 2003–2008

Year	2003-4	2004-5	2005-6	2006-7	2007-8*
GDP(99-00)	8.6	7.5	9.4	9.6	8.7
P. cap GDP	6.8	6.6	7.6	8.1	7.2
p.c.consp	4.2	3.6	7.0	5.6	5.3
Industr.Prod	7.0	8.4	8.2	11.6	9.0
Gr.capital form	27.7	30.6	33.4	33.8	n.a
Fixed cap. Form	24.7	27.1	29.2	30.6	32.6
Inflation(WPI)	5.1	4.1	5.9	4.1	n.a.
Inflation(CPI)	4.2	4.9	6.7	5.5	n.a.
Exports	3o.8	23.4	22.6	21.6	n.a
Imports	42.7	33.8	24.5	25.9	n.a.

Source: Government of India, Economic Survey 2007–2008, Chapter 1: "Overview of Economy" and statistical tables in appendix.

[247] There were 8,700 incidents in 1993. However, this and other figures need to be treated with caution. There are varying definitions of social unrest, and Chinese officials use different ones at different times. The figures of 8,700 in 1993 and 87,000 in 2005 were compiled by the Ministry of Public Security.

[248] Mike Monteleone, *Knocking from Within: Contemporary Social Unrest and its Consequences for a Stable China* (Department of East Asian Languages and Civilizations, University of Chicago, Spring 2006).

[249] Elizabeth J. Perry, "Challenging the Mandate of Heaven: Popular Protest in Modern China," *Critical Asian Studies* 33 (2001): 163–180.

[250] This has been captured by Lucien W. and Mary W. Pye in the ques-

tions they pose at the beginning of their book, *Asian Power and Politics: The Cultural Dimensions of Authority* (Cambridge, MA: Belknap Press of Harvard University Press, 1988), 33–34. "Does the culture tend to conceive of primitive power as . . . something that belonged to the distant past? Or is primitive power a continuous, lurking danger, ready to surface with any faltering of established authority? Is it something that lies ahead, as society slowly becomes more degenerate and as rulers leave the way of righteousness? . . . In contrast to the West, traditional Asian countries have generally not located primitive power in the distant past but have thought of it more as an ever-lurking danger in the future."

[251] Richard Baum, *Burying Mao: Chinese Politics in the Age of Deng Xiaoping* (Princeton, NJ: Princeton University Press, 1994), 5.

[252] Details of the recession are given in Chapter 3, and the way in which it aggravated social discontent in Chapter 5.

[253] Joseph Fewsmith, "Social Issues Move to Center Stage," *China Leadership Monitor*, no. 3, Summer 2002.

[254] Ibid.

[255] Ibid. One possibility, in the light of what followed, is that the decay of values was far more pronounced in the eastern coastal provinces such as Guangzhou and Shanghai, but since these were the seats of power within the CCP during the Jiang Zemin regime, the leaders were in no position to be more specific. Szechuan was, by contrast , a not very prosperous, not very influential central province, and could easily be singled out. Its only problem was that the magnitude of dereliction was unimpressive.

[256] Joseph Fewsmith, "The 16th Party Congress: Implications for Understanding Chinese Politics," *China Leadership Monitor*, no. 5, Winter 2003, 43–53.

[257] Jonathan Watts, "Corruption Crackdown Led to Hundreds of Communist Party Suicides," *Guardian*, January 30, 2004.

[258] Tim Wright, "The Political Economy of Coal Mine Disasters: 'Your Rice or Your Life?'" *China Quarterly* 179 (2004): 629–646.

[259] *China Daily*, "Hu visits Aids patients in Beijing," December 1, 2004.

[260] Wen Jiabao spent his New Year's Eve 2005 having dinner with the families of AIDS patients, and a few weeks later, on February 15, 2005, Hu Jintao celebrated the Spring Festival, China's most important family reunion, with villagers in an impoverished village in Guizhou province. Wen Jiabao spent the 2005 Spring Festival in a village in Henan province where a large number of blood donors had contracted AIDS from infected

needles. 261 Joseph Kahn, "Chinese Premier Says Seizing Peasants' Land Provokes Unrest," *New York Times,* January 21, 2006.

[261] Joseph Kahn, "Chinese Premier Says Seizing Peasants' Land Provokes Unrest," *New York Times,* January 21, 2006.

[262] Deutsche Presse-Agentur, "Chinese Premier Alarmed over Rural Unrest, Calls for Reforms," January 20, 2006.

[263] Joseph Fewsmith, "The Third Plenary Session of the 16th Central Committee," *China Leadership Monitor,* no. 9, Winter 2004, 1–9.

[264] Cheng Li, "Cooling Shanghai Fever: Macroeconomic Control and Its Geopolitical Implications," *China Leadership Monitor,* no. 12, Fall 2004, 1. A more detailed account is given by Barry Naughton, "Hunkering Down: The Wen Jiabao Administration and Macroeconomic Recontrol," *China Leadership Monitor,* no. 11, Summer 2004.

[265] Li, "Cooling Shanghai Fever: Macroeconomic Control and Its Geopolitical Implications," 1–12. Details of the overheating and the policy measures adopted are given in Chapter 4.

[266] Pamela Yatsko, *New Shanghai: The Rocky Rebirth of China's Legendary City* (New York: John Wiley & Sons, 2000), 26.

[267] James P. Sterba, "A Great Leap Where?" *Wall Street Journal,* December 10, 1993.

[268] Li, "Cooling Shanghai Fever: Macroeconomic Control and Its Geopolitical Implications."

[269] Ibid.

[270] Ibid., 5

[271] Ibid.

[272] Howard W. French, "Dream of High-Speed Rail May Prove Shanghai Politician's Final Nightmare," *The International Herald Tribune,* August 8, 2007.

[273] Ibid.

[274] Joseph Kahn, "China Crushes Peasant Protest, Turning 3 Friends into Enemies," *New York Times,* October 13, 2004.

[275] Rowan Callick, "Bitter Harvest for China's Rural Majority," *Australian,* March 13, 2006.

[276] French, "Dream of High-Speed Rail May Prove Shanghai Politician's Final Nightmare."

[277] Li, "Cooling Shanghai Fever: Macroeconomic Control and Its Geopolitical Implications," 9.

[278] Cheng Li, "Reshuffling Four Tiers of Local Leaders: Goals and Implications," *China Leadership Monitor*, no. 18, Spring 2006.

[279] Ibid.

[280] Joseph Fewsmith, "CCP Launches Campaign to Maintain the Advanced Nature of Party Members," *China Leadership Monitor*, no. 13, Winter 2005, 1–10.

[281] Ibid.

[282] Ibid., 2.

[283] *China Daily*, "Building Harmonious Society Important Task for Top of CPC: President," February 20, 2005.

[284] *China Daily*, "Concrete Steps for Harmonious Society," March 12, 2005.

[285] Cheng Li, "Think National, Blame Local: Central-Provincial Dynamics in the Hu Era," *China Leadership Monitor*, no. 17, Winter 2006.

[286] *China Daily*, "Township Governments Face Role Shift," April 1, 2005.

[287] John James Kennedy, "From the Tax-for-Fee Reform to the Abolition of Agricultural Taxes: The Impact on Township Governments in North-west China," *China Quarterly* 189 (2007): 43–59.

[288] They yielded a bare 24.2 billion yuan in 2004, which was less than 1 percent of the total tax revenues. This was in sharp contrast to the early days of the People's Republic, when the agricultural tax had accounted for 39 percent of the government's revenues. See *China Statistical Yearbook 2005*, table 8.12. See also Elaine Wu, "Central Government Scraps Tax on Farmers," *South China Morning Post*, December 20, 2005.

[289] Chow Chung-Yan, "Textile Factory Sees Migrant Labour Returning to the Land," *South China Morning Post*, September 23, 2005. See also "Labour Shortage Threatening Industrial Growth," *South China Morning Post*, May 26, 2005. But the official claim of declining unrest has been questioned by some scholars and journalists: see Mark Magnier, "China Says It's Calmed Down: Government Statistics Show a 22% Decline in Incidents of Unrest This Year," *Los Angeles Times*, November 8, 2006.

[290] Kennedy, "From the Tax-for-Fee Reform to the Abolition of Agricultural Taxes."

[291] Ibid. It took the first step in this direction even earlier. Since 2001 it has required the county governments to pay the fees of primary school teachers.

292 Richard McGregor, "China Aims to Cut Wealth Gap with 'New Deal' for Farmers," *Financial Times*, February 23, 2006.

293 Chua Chin Hon, "China Tries to Spend Its Way Out of Urban-Rural Problem," *Straits Times* (Singapore), March 7, 2006. Wen Jiabao honored his commitment. In 2007 the transfers rose to 392 billion yuan, an increase of 15 percent (*Economist* Intelligence Unit, "Poverty Lies Behind China's Rural Unrest," March 15, 2007).

294 Adam Wolfe, "China's Priorities on Display at the National People's Congress," Power and Interest News Report, March 21, 2007. See also Tracy Quek, "China Unveils Landmark Law to Protect Private Property," *Straits Times* (Singapore), March 9, 2007.

295 *Tasmanian Country*, March 10, 2006

296 Joseph Kahn and David Barboza, "As Unrest Rises, China Broadens Workers' Rights," *New York Times*, June 30, 2007.

297 FT Intelligence Wire, "Trade Unions to See 8m More Rural Migrant Workers Join In," Business Daily Update of the Financial Times Information Service Asia, October 16, 2006.

298 Quek, "China Unveils Landmark Law to Protect Private Property."

299 A large part, in some cases up to 90 percent, is retained by the village administration to cover a variety of expenses incurred during the transaction.

300 FT Intelligence Wire, "Trade Unions to See 8m More Rural Migrant Workers Join In."

301 Clifford Coonan, "Worried Chinese President Promises to 'Purify the Internet,'" *Irish Times*, January 26, 2007.

302 The above incidents were culled from newspaper reports by Thomas Lum, *Social Unrest in China*, US Congressional Research Service report to Congress, Order Code RL33416, May 8, 2006.

303 Jane Macartney, "Student Rampage Unnerves Leaders," *Times* (London), October 26, 2006.

304 Joseph Kahn, "Harsh Birth Control Steps Fuel Violence in China," *New York Times*, May 22, 2007.

305 Minnie Chan, "Third Riot in a Month Erupts in Chongqing," *South China Morning Post*, July 6, 2007.

306 Edward Cody, "In Chinese Uprisings, Peasants Find New Allies; Protesters Gain Help of Veteran Activists," *Washington Post*, November 26, 2005. See also Jonathan Watts, "Mob Attacks Key Chinese Democrat:

Activist Left for Dead Near Village at Centre of Fresh Wave of Unrest," *Guardian*, October 10, 2005.

[307] Cody later writes that there were 584 signatures in total, before people began to fall out.

[308] Jonathan Watts, "The Big Steal," *Guardian*, May 27, 2006.

[309] Li Fan, "China's Unquiet Countryside," *Time*, October 16, 2005. At the time of writing, Li Fan was a research fellow at the World and China Institute, a private think tank in Beijing.

[310] Baum, *Burying Mao*, Chapter 10, 237.

[311] Zhao is reported to have said this to a friend while still under house arrest in 2004. Reported in *Ming Pao*, January 30, 2005; quoted by Minchin Pei in *China's Trapped Transition*, 8.

[312] Wang Hui, *China's New Order: Society, Politics, and Economy in Transition*, ed. and trans. Theodore Huters, trans. Rebecca E. Karl (Cambridge, MA: Harvard University Press, 2003), 62.

[313] Wang Hui's description of the confrontation is confirmed by the detailed analysis of its causes made by scholars like Richard Baum, *Burying Mao: Chinese Politics in the Age of Deng Xiaoping*.

[314] Hui, *China's New Order: Society, Politics, and Economy in Transition*.

[315] Joseph Fewsmith, "Promotion of Qiu He Raises Questions About Direction of Reform," *China Leadership Monitor*, no. 17, Winter 2006.

[316] Cheng Li, "Hu's Policy Shift and the Tuanpai's Coming-of-Age," *China Leadership Monitor*, no. 15, Summer 2005.

[317] Cheng Li, "Reshuffling Four Tiers of Local Leaders: Goals and Implications," *China Leadership Monitor*, no. 18, Spring 2006.

[318] Prime Minister Tony Blair said China had developed an "unstoppable momentum" toward democracy. He could not have been more wrong. See Watts, "Mob Attacks Key Chinese Democrat: Activist Left for Dead Near Village at Centre of Fresh Wave of Unrest."

[319] Joseph Kahn, "Chinese Official Warns Against Independence of Courts," *New York Times*, February 3, 2007.

[320] Murray Scott Tanner, "Can China Contain Unrest?: Six Questions Seeking One Answer, *Brookings Northeast Asia Commentary*, no. 7, March 2007.

[321] Andrew G. Walder, "Social Stability and Popular Protest in China: How Serious is the Threat?" (paper presented at the International Conference on Contemporary China, University of Hong Kong, January 5–6, 2007).

[322] Perry, "Challenging the Mandate of Heaven."

[323] John King Fairbank, *The United States and China* (Cambridge, MA: Harvard University Press, 1983), 53–54.

[324] Ibid.

[325] Perry, "Challenging the Mandate of Heaven," 163.

[326] Chen Guidi and Wu Chuntao, "Chapter 5. An Ancient and Burdensome Subject," *Chinese Economy* 38, no. 1 (2005): 14–59.

[327] Carsten A. Holz and Tian Zhu, "Assessment of the Current State of China's Economic Reforms," *Chinese Economy* 35, no. 3 (2002): 71–109.

[328] Perry, "Challenging the Mandate of Heaven," 164.

[329] Ibid.

[330] Qinlian, *China: The Pitfalls of Modernization.* The contents were so explosive that even this did not get it published on the mainland. It was published in Hong Kong, however, and had a huge impact upon the intelligentsia in China.

[331] The *Blue Book of Chinese Society*, issued by the Chinese Academy of Social Sciences, and cited earlier, is an example of state-sponsored criticism. But as was pointed out in the previous chapter, and as several of the remarks made by Hu and Wen show, many appraisals carried out within the party are even more critical. In fact, when the leaders decide to release some of the findings of these inquiries, they are invariably in a highly sanitized form, when compared to the originals.

[332] Baum, *Burying Mao.*

[333] 97,260 party members were convicted of various crimes in 2006. Four-fifths were convicted for having taken bribes; they included seven persons of the rank of cabinet minister or provincial governor. See Tracy Quek, "China Punished 97,000 Party Members for Graft Last Year," *Straits Times* (Singapore), February 14, 2007.

[334] *China Daily*, "Officials Sacked for Corruption in Recent Months," October 24, 2006.

[335] Reuters, "Beijing Defends Execution of Corrupt Officials," *International Herald Tribune*, August 2, 2007.

[336] Baum, *Burying Mao*, 200–202.

[337] Ibid., 203.

[338] Ibid., 250.

[339] Ibid., 251.

[340] Ibid., 250.

341 Ibid., 276.

342 Ibid., 275.

343 Andrew G. Walder and Gong Xiaoxia, "Workers in the Tiananmen Protests: The Politics of the Beijing Workers' Autonomous Federation," *Australian Journal of Chinese Affairs*, no. 29, January 1993, 1–30.

344 Baum, *Burying Mao*, 287. Some of them, however, were fired upon after they left the square, and one batch, which encountered a tank column as it made its way to the square, had eleven of its members crushed under the treads of a tank that plowed straight into them. The lone student casualty in the square was one who had refused to leave the tents that had been set up by the students. He was killed when the tanks rolled in after the students had left, and began to bulldoze the now empty tents (292).

345 Ibid., 276.

346 Ibid., 292.

347 Ibid., 283

348 Ibid., 289–291.

349 Ibid., 316.

350 Ibid., 298–299.

351 Ibid., 317. Deng's anti-corruption drive netted 325,000 offenders in its first eighteen months. By October 1992, three-quarters of a million party members had been disciplined, of whom 154,289 had been expelled from the party.

352 Although the party suddenly rediscovered, and reinstated, Confucius in the first years of the new century, it did so to mobilize deep-seated Chinese values in favor of an unquestioning obedience to the state. This so-called revival was actually a reflection of how far its hold on the Chinese people had already slipped. See Ching Ching Ni, "She Makes Confucius Cool Again," *Los Angeles Times*, May 7, 2007. Fewsmith makes a similar observation but says that the revival of "superior elements of China's culture began in the nineties under Jiang Zemin"; see "CCP Launches Campaign to Maintain the Advanced Nature of Party Members."

353 It did the former mainly through the tax reforms of 1994, 1998, and 2002, and the banking reforms of 1997–'98.

354 John L. Thornton, "China's Leadership Gap," *Foreign Affairs* 86, no. 6 (2006): 133.

355 Moving eastwards from Maharashtra in the west, these are Andhra Pradesh, Chhattisgarh, Jharkhand, Orissa, and West Bengal.

[356] Government of India, *Economic Survey 2007–2008*, statistical table 1.11.

[357] Ibid., table 1.20.

[358] Ibid., table 1.10.

[359] Praveen Jha and Mario Negre, *Indian Economy in the Era of Contemporary Globalisation: Some Core Elements of the Balance Sheet*, MacroScan, May 17, 2007.

[360] P. Sainath, "When Farmers Die," *India Together*, June 2004, http://www.indiatogether.org/2004/jun/psa-farmdie.htm. Accessed December 16, 2008.

[361] P. Sainath, "Sinking Wells, Rising Debt," *India Together*, June 2004, http://www.indiatogether.org/2004/jun/psa-sinkbore.htm. Accessed December 18, 2008.

[362] **Table: Import Tariffs and Bound Tariffs for Various Agricultural Products**

Crop	1995–'96	1999–2000	2000–'01	2001–'02	2002–'03	Bound tariff
Non-basmati rice	0	0	92	77	70–80	70–80
Wheat	0	50	108	100	50	100
Crop	1995–'96	1999–2000	2000–'01	2001–'02	2002–'03	Bound tariff
Maize	0	0	60	50	50	70
Pulses	10	5	5	5	10	104
Oilseeds	50	35	35	35		100
Soybean oil	30	18	45	38	45	45
Ground-nut oil	30	18	35	35	75	300
Cotton	50	40	25	35	5	90*
Sugar	0	40	100	60	60	150

Source: Ramesh Chand, based on official statistics. Cited by Jayati Ghosh, "The Political Economy of Farmers' Suicides in India," Freedom from Hunger lecture series, Indian International Centre, New Delhi, December 9, 2005.

[363] Planning Commission of India, Task Force on Employment Opportunities, chaired by M. S. Ahluwalia, New Delhi, 2001.

[364] Amy Waldman, "India's Poor Bet Precious Sums on Private Schools," *New York Times,* November 15, 2003.

[365] Leela Visaria, "The Continuing Fertility Transition," in Tim Dyson, Robert Cassen, and Leela Visaria, *Twenty-First Century India: Population, Economy, Human Development, and the Environment* (New Delhi: Oxford University Press, 2004), 69.

[366] Planning Commission of India, *Approach Paper to the 11th Plan,* citing the results of the sixty-first round of the National Sample Survey, November 2006.

[367] Jha and Negre, *Indian Economy in the Era of Contemporary Globalisation.*

[368] Planning Commission of India, *Approach Paper to the 11th Plan.*

[369] Election Commission of India, *Statistical Report on General Elections, 1999, to the Thirteenth Lok Sabha,* vol. 1.

[370] Till 1967, elections to the Parliament and the state assemblies were held simultaneously. Since voters tended to vote for the same party in both elections, it reinforced the power of the leaders of the Congress, as the party that brought independence to India, to control the state assemblies. But the economic crisis of the mid-sixties, the 57 percent devaluation of the rupee in 1966, and the first sharp fall in the Congress' share of the vote in 1967 revived doubts in the party over the virtues of socialism and led to a split in the party in 1969. This forced Indira Gandhi to rule with a minority, supported by the Communist party of India from the outside, and to call for a fresh election a year ahead of schedule, in 1971. This early election separated the parliamentary from the state assembly elections, which were held a year later.

[371] L. K. Advani, Deputy Prime Minister of India under Atal Bihari Vajpayee, described this in 2002 as being in a permanent "election mode."

[372] M. Suchitra, "The High Cost of 'Easy' Foreign Exchange," *India Together,* January 10, 2007, http://www.indiatogether.org/2006/mar/eco-freezones.htm.

[373] By September 2006 they had notified 267 SEZs, of an average size of about 2,000 hectares each.

[374] *Hindu,* "Government Clarifies Land Acquisition for SEZs," September 27, 2006.

[375] This was true even in Communist-ruled West Bengal. When Tatas selected 1,000 acres of agricultural land for their small car project at Singur in West Bengal, the state government tried to make them accept an alternate

site on poorer land. But Tatas threatened to move the project to Uttaranchal Pradesh, in the Himalayan foothills, if their choice was not respected.

[376] Indiabulls, corporate announcement.

[377] Phase 1 of the project is to coincide with the completion of the Delhi-Mumbai Freight Corridor in 2012. Six investment regions of more than 200 square kilometers each and six industrial areas of about 100 square kilometers each have been identified, one in each state through which the DFC will pass.

[378] Maureen Fan, "Cashing In on Communism," *Washington Post*, February 18, 2007. What Deng really said was "Rang Yi Bu Fen Ren Xian Fu Qi Lai" (Let Some People Get Rich First).

[379] Planning Commission, Government of India, *11ᵗʰ Plan Approach Paper*, July 2006.

[380] Prem Shankar Jha, *Jobless Growth: The Political Causes of Economic Crisis* (New Delhi: Rupa Books, 2002). In 2001, when the media finally took up the cudgels against starvation deaths, the output of foodgrains had actually fallen by 6.3 percent, but the procurement of foodgrains had gone up by 16 percent from 30.8 million tons to 35.5 million tons. In the very next year, the state governments of the wheat producing states cornered 96 percent of all the wheat brought to the market; as a result the procurement of wheat rose by 27 percent over the previous year. The foodgrains then remained in the government's depots because the off take from the ration shops in the food deficit states was in free fall. In the previous year (2000), for instance, it had fallen to 12.1 million tons from 17.1 million tons in 1999. The starvation deaths and all-pervasive malnutrition in the poorer states of the country were therefore a man-made tragedy.

[381] The budget for 2008–'9 allocated Rs. 120 billion ($3 billion) for subsidies on locally made fertilizer, and Rs. 72.4 billion for subsidies on imported fertilizers. Only the latter portion can be considered a subsidy to the farmer (Government of India, *Union Budget 2008–2009*, explanatory memorandum on government expenditure, vol. 1, 12).

[382] Prem Shankar Jha, "The Price of Cowardice," *Deccan Herald*, November 28, 2005. The data were taken from a study by the National Council for Applied Economic Research, and quoted by the *Indian Express* in November 2005. Reliance's turnover was 27 billion dollars.

[383] These are Articles 310 and 311. They were lifted from the British drafted constitution that was drawn up under the Government of India

Act of 1935, and had been originally inserted to protect British officials from legal harassment by the Indian National Congress. None of the constitution makers of 1948–'49 noticed the insertion or understood the uses to which it would be put.

[384] Guidi and Chuntao, "An Ancient and Burdensome Subject," 53.

[385] Information on this nexus was collected by the author in the Rafiabad constituency (upper range), which is located in the mountains above the town of Baramula, through interviewing nine timber smugglers from three villages on June 9–11, 2008. According to a party worker for the Jammu and Kashmir People's Democratic Party who belongs to the region, there are about 6,000 unemployed persons in the constituency of whom 1,000 to 1,200 are engaged in timber smuggling. They are paid 20 percent of the local market value of the timber they bring down and are left, after they pay their "dues," with about 10 percent. The contractors to whom they sell the timber pay their dues in turn to people higher up the political-bureaucratic chain.

[386] Prafulla Das, "Kalinga Nagar Tribals Take Vow Not to Vacate Land for Industries," *Hindu*, January 11, 2006.

[387] Angad Chowdhry, "What Happened in Nandigram," posted on SacredMediaCow, March 25, 2007, http://sacredmediacow.com. According to the website, "SacredMediaCow is an independent postgraduate collective on Indian media research and production at the School of Oriental and African Studies (SOAS) at the University of London."

[388] The report was prepared by a highly regarded economist-administrator in the central government, Ajit Majumdar.

[389] Indian School of Women's Studies Development, *Monitoring and Evaluation Of National Rural Employment Guarantee Scheme with Special Focus on Gender Issues*, first report, based on field visits in June–August 2006, October 2006.

[390] For the full NREGP status report, see http://nrega.nic.in/states/nregampr.asp.

[391] Parshuram Rai, *Rural Job Scam: Survey Report on Implementation of NREGA in Orissa*, Centre for Environment and Food Security New Delhi, 2007.

[392] A strong indication is a huge rise in the number of mobile telephone connections. In the closing months of 2007, this had risen to eight million new connections a month. A very large proportion, possibly more than

half, of these connections are being taken by workers in the organized sector. Anecdotal evidence, based upon talks with many workers, suggests that ready availability on the phone has sharply increased the number of jobs they are able to do in a day or week. They therefore regard the mobile phone as an investment, which yields very high returns.

[393] The above data and observations are taken from two reports of the Planning Commission, Government of India: These are *Report of Task Force on Employment Opportunities*, July 2001, and *Towards Faster and More Inclusive Growth: An Approach to the 11th Five Year Plan*, November 2006.

[394] As a result, 35 percent of all the underweight and physically underdeveloped children in the world are to be found in India.

[395] R. K. A. Subrahmanya, "Welfare Funds: An Indian Model for Workers in the Unorganised Sector," in *The Unorganised Sector: Work Security and Social Protection*, ed. Renana Jhabvala and R. K. A. Subrahmanya (Thousand Oaks, CA: SAGE Publications, 2000), 62–72.

[396] It was presented to Dr. Montek Singh Ahluwalia, Deputy Chairman of the Planning Commission, by the author in June 2007, and rejected by his senor adviser, and later chief economic adviser to the government of India, Arvind Vimani, a month later.

[397] South Asia Terrorism Portal (SATPORG), *South Asia Intelligence Review* 6, no. 12 (2007).

[398] N. N. Sachitanand, "Is POSCO Getting into Orissa Quicksand?" *Hindu*, July 11, 2005.

[399] Lyla Bavadam, "Flood of Fears," *Frontline*, August 13, 2004.

[400] According to the central Ministry of Home Affairs, between January and November 2007 there were a total of 1,385 incidents in Maoist-affected states, as opposed to 1,398 in the whole of 2006.

[401] *Times of India*, "Chhattisgarh and Jharkhand Account for 68 Per Cent of Maoist Violence," January 13, 2008.

[402] South Asia Terrorism Portal (SATPORG), *South Asia Intelligence Review* 6, no. 17 (2007).

[403] Interview given to Karan Thapar, on the CNBC-TV18 channel in Delhi. It was a telling example of the disarray that prevails in the UPA government.

[404] China and India provide additional proof of the incompleteness of classical Marxist analysis as a framework for understanding the evolution of capitalism. For the motive force behind their social and economic

evolution has not been the much-overworked conflict between capital and labor, but one between two strata (or controllers) of capital. It therefore suggests the need for a more complex explicatory model than the one provided by Marx's theory of social classes.

[405] Joseph Fewsmith. See En. 410 below, and associated text, for more details.

[406] Mainland Affairs Council: Background Information, "The Frequent Occurrence of Mass Incidents in China Pushes It into Becoming a 'Risky Society.'" http://www.mac.gov.tw/english/english/macpolicy/risk961228.htm

[407] The judgment was in *S. R. Bommai vs. the Union of India* (1994).

[408] This is done by two articles of the Constitution of India, Articles 310 and 311.

[409] Central Vigilance Commission of India, Annual Report for 2006, 19, 72–75.

[410] Joseph Fewsmith, "An Upsurge in Political Reform? Maybe," *China Leadership Monitor* 24. Extract from the "Full Text of Report Delivered by Hu Jintao at 17th Party Congress," CCTV, 15 October 2007, trans. Open Source Center, CPP20071015035002.

[411] Ibid. Zhou Tianyong, Wang Changjiang, and Wang Anling, eds., *15 nian gongjian: 2006–2020 nian Zhongguo Zhengzhi tizhi gaige yanjiu baogao* [*The 15-year assault: A research report on China's political reform, 2006–2020*] (Beijing: Zhongyang dangxiao chubanshe, 2007). Zhou Tianyong is the deputy head of research at the Party School, Wang Changjiang is head of the party-building section at the Central Party School, and Wang Anling is director of research in Wuxi government.

[412] Ibid.

[413] Ibid.

[414] Its constitution has expressly provided for the creation of a National Development Council and an Inter-State Council to debate and evolve a consensus on important national issues.

[415] This would require an amendment to the constitution which could run somewhat as follows: "If a state government falls in less than the five years of its normal life, it shall come under president's rule for the period that remains. If the central government falls in less than five years, all state governments will also hold fresh elections at the same time as the new election to Parliament."

At first sight, these provisions seem draconian, even unfair. Is a long period of president's rule not a denial of the peoples' right to be ruled by their own representatives? And isn't it doubly unfair to force a new election on a stable state government simply because the central government coalition has broken down? A closer look at the effect that such a reform will have on the political system shows, however, that like Article 16 of the constitution of the Fifth Republic in France, the very enactment of such a provision will make its invocation unnecessary, for it will eliminate instability not only at the center but also in the states.

[416] James Cogan, "Chinese Manufacturing in Free Fall as Export Markets Collapse," World Socialist Website, November 7, 2008, http://www.wsws.org/articles/2008/nov2008/chin-n07.shtml.

[417] David Barboza, "Chinese Builders Hit the Brakes," *International Herald Tribune,* November 26, 2008.

[418] Gao Jiahai, a researcher at the Chinese Academy of Social Sciences, in an interview to the *Boston Globe,* cited by John Chan, "China's Huge Stimulus Package: Another Sign of Economic Crisis," World Socialist Website, November 11, 2008, http://www.wsws.org/articles/2008/nov2008/chin-n11.shtml. See also James Reynolds, "China Fears Grow over Job Losses," *BBC News,* November 20, 2008.

[419] John Chan, "Global Recession Threatens Mass Layoffs in China," World Socialist Website October 28, 2008.

[420] Ibid.

[421] Joseph Fewsmith, "Social Order in the Wake of Economic Crisis," *China Leadership Monitor,* no. 28, Spring 2009.

[422] Barry Naughton: Understanding the Chinese Stimulus Package. *China Leadership Monitor,* no. 28, Spring 2009.

[423] Only that can explain how Chen Liangyu, the former mayor of Shanghai, was able to commission a magnetic levitation project whose estimated payback period was 167 years. See Chapter 11.

[424] (Society of China: Analysis and Forecast, brought out annually by the Social system analysis and forecast group of the Chinese Academy of Social Sciences)

[425] Andrea Mitchell and Libby Leist, "State Report Takes Tough Tone on China." NBC News, February 25, 2009, http://firstread.msnbc.msn.com/archive/2009/02/25/1809242.aspxhttp://firstread.msnbc.msn.com/archive/2009/02/25/1809242.aspx. See also *Amnesty International Report*

2009: The State of the World's Human Rights. 107.

[426] Andrew Jacobs, "China Demands Filters on All New Computers," *International Herald Tribune,* June 9, 2009.

[427] Official statistics, reproduced by the Centre for the Monitoring of the Indian Economy. *Monthly Review of the Indian Economy,* June 2009, 62. The actual figure is minus 0.03 percent.

[428] Ibid. 101.

[429] The Impact of Global Recession on India, Merinews, February 7, 2009, http://www.merinews.com/catFull.jsp?articleID=15709750.

[430] *Business Standard, New Delhi's* , headline proclaimed, "Inflation Falls Into Negative Territory after Three Decades," but hastened to explain in a subheading that "deflation marked by a fall in demand is taken seriously, but in India's case it is principally due to the high 'base effect' because crude oil prices were nearing their peak this time last year." June 19, 2009, 1.

[431] A press release by the Ministry of Finance on June 18, 2009 claimed that "The de-seasonalised month to month inflation rate turned positive in March, 2009, and remains so in April and May. On an annualised basis, the (de-seasonalised) WPI inflation rate was 3.2% in March. Based on provisional data it declined, to 0.8%, in April and then shot up to double digit in May, 2009. Inflation is, therefore, very likely to turn positive before the end of the year and be positive for the year as a whole (average for 2009-10.)" http://www.pib.nic.in/release/rel_print_page1.asp?relid=49247.

[432] Naughton, "Understanding the Chinese Stimulus Packages": "The National Development and Reform Commission (NDRC) held an emergency (*jinji*) meeting to allocate the 100 billion fourth quarter increased investment. After, on the day of the meeting, 10 November, the quarter was already almost half over. The NDRC said that for all government agencies currently 'the absolutely most important economic work is to urgently implement the center's increased investment and other measures to increase domestic demand.' Agencies must 'make every second count.'"

[433] Reuters, "Indian economy -- on the road to recovery?" May 6, 2009.

[434] The most unequivocal sign that the recession was continuing to deepen was a sharp drop in the volume of new lending by the commercial banks. Net bank credit had actually fallen in absolute terms by Rs. 370 billion ($7 billion) in the six weeks between April 10, and May 22. The main cause is a drastic slow down in the growth of bank lending since November 2008. As a result, in the previous full year (May 23, 2008

to May 22, 2009) credit extended by the commercial banks had expanded by only 15.7 percent against 25.3 percent in the corresponding period of 2006–'07. Analysts concluded that the main cause was a postponement of borrowing by the corporate sector due to its high cost. Most investors had decided to wait for a possible decline in interest rates.

[435] For a detailed analysis, see the authors article: "The Pie in Smaller Slices. Tehelka (New Delhi), June 13, 2009, 22–23. http://www.tehelka.com/story_main42.asp?filename=Op130609the_pie.asp.

[436] P. Sainath, "Price of Rice, Price of Power," *Hindu,* June 10, 2009, http://www.hindu.com/2009/06/10/stories/2009061059450800.htm.